MATERIAL CONSTITUTION

On the Plurality of worlds

MATERIAL CONSTITUTION

A Reader

Edited by
MICHAEL C. REA

ROWMAN & LITTLEFIELD PUBLISHERS, INC.
Lanham • Boulder • New York • Oxford

ROWMAN & LITTLEFIELD PUBLISHERS, INC.

Published in the United States of America
by Rowman & Littlefield Publishers, Inc.
4720 Boston Way, Lanham, Maryland 20706

12 Hid's Copse Road
Cummor Hill, Oxford OX2 9JJ, England

British Library Cataloguing in Publication Information Available

Library of Congress Cataloging-in-Publication Data

Material constitution / edited by Michael C. Rea
p. cm.
Includes bibliographical references and index.
ISBN 0–8476–8383–4 (cloth : alk. paper). — ISBN 0–8476–8384–2 (pbk. : alk. paper)
1. Matter—Constitution. 2. Object (Philosophy) 3. Identity. 4. Space and time. I. Rea, Michael C. (Michael Cannon), 1968–
BD646.M27 1997
110—dc21 96-37532
CIP

ISBN 0–8476–8383–4 (cloth : alk. paper)
ISBN 0–8476–8384–2 (pbk. : alk. paper)

Printed in the United States of America

The paper used in this publication meets the minimum requirements of American National Standard for Information Sciences—Permanence of Paper for Printed Library Materials, ANSI Z39.48–1984.

For my Parents
Robert and Georgiana Rea

Contents

Foreword

Philosophers—at any rate, analytical philosophers—respect three things above all others: logic, common sense, and science. But few philosophers believe that logic, common sense, and science always speak with one voice. That common sense and science can be in conflict is very nearly a philosophical truism. (And such is the prestige of science that those who believe that common sense and science can be in conflict invariably say, "So much the worse for common sense.") That logic can be in conflict with either common sense or science, however, is very far from being a truism; most philosophers would probably say that logic provides a framework that can comprehend both common sense and science. Nevertheless, there are those who believe that logic—"orthodox" logic, textbook logic—and science can be in conflict. For example, those who believe that, whatever the logic textbooks may say, quantum mechanics demands a logic in which conjunction does not distribute over disjunction. (And such is the prestige of science that those who believe this say, "So much the worse for orthodox logic.") But what about logic and common sense?

Very few analytical philosophers have been willing to suppose that our commonsense beliefs could be refuted by logic alone. Those who deny that our commonsense beliefs are subject to refutation by logic alone are fond of cautionary tales: Zeno and motion; Spinoza and alternative possibilities; McTaggart and time; Bradley and numerical diversity. The deliverances of common sense—that things really move, that matters might really have been otherwise, that time is real, that there really does exist a plurality of things—come to us with such authority (the argument goes) that only the immense authority of science has any hope of contending with it. It is not (the argument continues) that common sense can "refute" logic. It is not that when logic and common sense come into conflict, common sense must prevail. It is rather that logic and common sense cannot come into conflict. If someone claims to be able to show that the deliverances of common sense are self-contradictory—as did Zeno, Spinoza, McTaggart, and Bradley—the only reasonable conclusion is that the alleged demonstrations of this contradiction contain some logical error. Sometimes we may be able to identify this error. (Zeno thought that an infinite number of non-overlapping spatial intervals laid end to end could not, as a matter of logic, compose a finite interval. He was wrong. Even if the modern analysis of the real line does not correctly describe the structure of spatial intervals in the physical world—that's as may be—the very fact that this modern analysis is internally consistent shows that *logic* does not endorse the thesis that an infinite number of non-overlapping spatial intervals laid end to end cannot compose a finite interval.) But even if we cannot identify the error, we may be confident that there is one, for it is absurd to suppose that the deliverances of common sense are self-contradictory, and it is not absurd to suppose that a philosopher sitting in an armchair and spinning out deductions has made a mistake. Or so many would say. So, perhaps, the majority of analytical philosophers would say. (And among those who would not say this, there are those who would say that if orthodox logic and common sense are in conflict, it is orthodox logic that must be rejected.) But a growing number of analytical philosophers are willing to follow the argument where it leads—even when it leads to the conclusion that our commonsense beliefs must be rejected because they are logically incoherent.

The essays in this collection concern a recent tendency of some philosophers to think that there is an at least *prima facie* conflict between logic and common sense, a conflict that involves material objects and their parts and their identity across time. Common sense (whatever exactly common sense may be) seems to tell us that the world contains lots of "material objects," that the resources of human thought and language are up to the task of identifying vast numbers of them, that these material objects endure through time (and that our everyday statements concerning the identity of material objects across time are in the main true), that most of these objects have parts that are themselves material objects (and that we are frequently able to identify many of these parts and are frequently able to determine which things they are parts *of*), that objects can sometimes gain or lose parts, and that no two material objects can occupy the same space at the same time. Common sense, I say, seems to tell us all these things. Can they all be true? If they cannot, can this impossibility be demonstrated? Can it in fact be shown that these propositions are mutually inconsistent?

To see why someone might think that these propositions were indeed mutually inconsistent, consider the puzzle of Tibbles the cat and Tib the cat-part. (The puzzle of Tibbles and Tib is due to David Wiggins and may be found on pp. 6–7 of the present collection. It is a simplified version of Peter Geach's "puzzle of Tibbles and the 1001 cats." Geach [pp. 309–310 below] claims to have "developed" the puzzle from a *sophisma* of William of Sherwood. A version of the puzzle was known to the Stoic Chrysippus [died *c.* 206 B.C.]). Can reflection on this puzzle lead us to any important metaphysical conclusions? In his essay "Temporal Parts of Four-Dimensional Objects" [Chapter 17], Mark Heller argues that reflection on the puzzle should lead us to conclude that material objects are not three-dimensional things that endure through time but are rather four-dimensional things, extended in time as well as in space. Heller identifies "five unpleasant alternatives" that, he argues, confront any philosopher who regards material objects as three-dimensional. (Heller's remarks are addressed to a different but equivalent version of the puzzle; I have adapted his formulation of the "unpleasant alternatives" so that they apply to Wiggins's version.) They are as follows:

(a) There is no such material object as Tibbles (i.e., either Tibbles does not exist or he is not a material object).
(b) There was (before Tibbles's tail was cut off) no material object in the space that was exactly occupied by all of Tibbles but his tail.
(c) No material object can undergo a loss of parts.
(d) There can be distinct material objects in the same space at the same time.
(e) Identity is not transitive.

If we assume that the denials of (a)–(d) are endorsed by common sense, and if we also assume that common sense tells us that cats and their parts are not four-dimensional objects, then (if Heller is right) a commonsense view of cats and their parts is inconsistent with the transitivity of identity (and is therefore inconsistent with Leibniz's Law, or the principle of the indiscernibility of identicals, of which the transitivity of identity is a logical consequence). And this result can be fairly described in the words "Logic is in conflict with common sense."

It is to problems like the problem of Tibbles and Tib that the essays in this collection are directed. These problems are of the first importance for metaphysics. To discover how to deal with them would be to achieve a metaphysical understanding of material objects. But the problems are deep and difficult, and it is by no means easy to discover how to deal with them. Many philosophers have hoped that they could find ways to eliminate all reference to various "problematic" entities from their metaphysical theories: qualities, propositions, regions of empty space, surfaces, pains. One of the lessons of the essays in this collection is that material objects may well be as problematic as propositions and pains.

Nothing I could say in this brief foreword would do justice to the philosophical richness of this volume, to the range of fascinating metaphysical problems and arguments that the authors are able to uncover simply by philosophical reflection on cats, statues, and piles of trash. I can, however, do justice to the quality of the essays. Leaving aside my own essay (whose quality I am not in a position to make an objective judgment about), these essays are the products of first-rate philosophical minds working at a very high level. (I look forward with real pleasure to teaching a course in which *Material Constitution: A Reader* is the central text.) The collection is both unique and timely—timely because it is about a set of problems that many very good philosophers are thinking about right now. My hope is that it will serve to introduce the next generation of philosophers to a very rewarding area of philosophical reflection.

Peter van Inwagen
University of Notre Dame

Acknowledgments

This work was supported in part by grants from the Department of Philosophy at the University of Notre Dame and from the Department of Philosophy and the College of Arts and Science at the University of Delaware. Special thanks are due to Trenton Merricks, Dean Zimmerman, and especially Alvin Plantinga, Ernest Sosa and Peter van Inwagen for their assistance in finding a publisher for this volume. Without their help, advice, and encouragement this project would not have come to fruition. I would also like to thank Michael Bergmann, Fred Haan, Jeff Jordan, Michael Loux, Trenton Merricks, Alvin Plantinga, Juliane Rea, and Dean Zimmerman for helpful comments on the introductory essay.

Portions of the introduction and appendix to this volume appeared in my article, "The Problem of Material Constitution," *The Philosophical Review* 104 (1995), pp. 525–552. That material is reprinted here by permission of the publisher. Copyright © 1995 by Cornell University.

"On Being in the Same Place at the Same Time" by David Wiggins appeared in *The Philosophical Review* 77 (1968), pp. 90–95. Reprinted by permission of the author. The Postscript to this article appears here for the first time.

"Spatially Coinciding Objects" by Frederick Doepke appeared in *Ratio* 24 (1982), pp. 45–60. Reprinted by permission of Blackwell Publishers Ltd. Copyright © 1982 by Blackwell Publishers Ltd.

"Parthood and Identity Across Time" by Judith Jarvis Thomson appeared in *The Journal of Philosophy* 80 (1983), pp. 201–220. Reprinted by permission of the author and *The Journal of Philosophy*. Copyright © 1983 by *The Journal of Philosophy*, Inc.

"Constitution Is Not Identity" by Mark Johnston appeared in *Mind* 101 (1992), pp. 89–105. Reprinted by permission of Oxford University Press. Copyright © 1992 by Oxford University Press.

"Subjects Among Other Things" by Ernest Sosa appeared in *Philosophical Perspectives, 1, Metaphysics, 1987* edited by James E. Tomberlin (copyright © by Ridgeview Publishing Co., Atascadero, CA). Reprinted by permission of Ridgeview Publishing Company.

"Contingent Identity" by Allan Gibbard appeared in *Journal of Philosophical Logic* 4 (1975), pp. 187–221. Copyright © 1975 by D. Reidel Publishing Company, Dordrecht, Holland. Reprinted by permission of Kluwer Academic Publishers.

"Counterparts or Double Lives? (Selections)" by David Lewis is excerpted from chapter 4 of his book, *On the Plurality of Worlds* (New York: Basil Blackwell, 1986). Reprinted by permission of the author and Blackwell Publishers. Copyright © 1986 by David Lewis.

"Identity and Time" by George Myro appeared in *The Philosophical Grounds of Rationality*, edited by Richard E. Grandy and Richard Warner (New York: Clarendon Press, 1986). Copyright © 1986 by Oxford University Press. Reprinted by permission of Oxford University Press.

"I Do Not Exist" by Peter Unger appeared in *Perception and Identity*, edited by G. F. MacDonald (London: The MacMillan Press, 1979). Reprinted by permission of the author and MacMillan Press Ltd. Copyright © 1979 by Peter Unger.

"The Doctrine of Arbitrary Undetached Parts" by Peter van Inwagen appeared in *Pacific Philosophical Quarterly* 62 (1981), pp. 123–37. Reprinted by permission of Blackwell Publishers Ltd. Copyright © 1981 by University of Southern California.

"Identity Through Time" by Roderick Chisholm appeared as chapter 3 of his book, *Person and Object* (La Salle, Ill.: Open Court Publishing Company, 1979.) Reprinted by permission of Open Court Publishing Company, La Salle, Illinois. Copyright © 1976 by Roderick M. Chisholm.

"Preserving the Principle of One Object to a Place: A Novel Account of the Relations Among Objects, Sorts, Sortals, and Persistence Conditions" by Michael B. Burke appeared in *Philosophy and Phenomenological Research* 54 (1994), pp. 591–624. Reprinted by permission of the publisher. Copyright © 1994 by The International Phenomenological Society.

"Entities Without Identity" by Terence Parsons appeared in *Philosophical Perspectives, 1, Metaphysics, 1987,* edited by James E. Tomberlin (copyright © by Ridgeview Publishing Co., Atascadero, CA). Reprinted by permission of Ridgeview Publishing Company.

"*De Re* Modality Entails *De Re* Vagueness" by Frances Howard-Snyder appeared in *Pacific Philosophical Quarterly* 72 (1991), pp. 101–112. Reprinted by permission of Blackwell Publishers Ltd. Copyright © 1981 by University of Southern California.

"Reference and Generality (Selections)" by Peter T. Geach is excerpted from his book, *Reference and Generality: An Examination of Some Medieval and Modern Theories*, 3rd edition (Ithaca: Cornell University Press, 1980). Copyright © 1980 by Cornell University Press. Used by permission of the publisher.

"Constitutivity and Identity" by Hugh S. Chandler appeared in *Noûs* 5 (1971), pp. 313–19. Reprinted by permission of the author and editor. Copyright © 1971 Wayne State University Press.

"Temporal Parts of Four-Dimensional Objects" by Mark Heller appeared in *Philosophical Studies* 46 (1984), pp. 323–34. Copyright © 1984 by D. Reidel Publishing Company. Reprinted by permission of Kluwer Academic Publishers.

Introduction

Imagine calling on a friend to collect a debt and receiving, instead of your money, the following philosophical argument:

> As we all know, a human being is just a collection of particles. But, as we also know, if you add particles to or subtract particles from a collection of particles, you get a new collection. Now, this debt was contracted several weeks ago, and many of the particles that composed the person who contracted the debt have long since passed into the environment. So I am a different collection of particles from the one that contracted the debt. Thus, since a human being is just a collection of particles, I am a different human being from the one who contracted the debt. Therefore, I do not owe you any money!

Obviously this line of reasoning is flawed. It can't be *that* easy to escape a debt. But how is it flawed? What false assumption or illegitimate inference is the debtor making? The answer is not immediately clear.

What the debtor has raised is a puzzle about material constitution. Material constitution occurs whenever an object *a* and an object *b* (in this case, the debtor and the collection of particles that constitutes her) share all of the same parts at the same time.[1] The phenomenon is puzzling because it is not at all clear what the relationship is between the relevant *a* and *b*. The debtor assumes that she is identical with the collection of particles that constitutes her and concludes that she is not the same person as the one who contracted an earlier debt. We, on the other hand, might be inclined to deny her assumption; but if we do, then it appears we are committed to the conclusion that there are two distinct objects (the debtor and the collection) located in exactly the same place at the same time. But, as one philosopher has aptly put it, those who embrace that conclusion seem to "manifest a bad case of double vision."[2] Surely there are not *two* objects located where the debtor is standing but one—namely, the debtor. The problem, then, is that we seem to have no good alternatives. It appears that we must either accept the debtor's conclusion or else embrace the possibility of there being two (or more) distinct objects in exactly the same place at the same time.

Puzzles like this are among the oldest, most widely discussed puzzles in the history of philosophy. They have appeared in the writings of Epicharmus, Aristotle, Chrysippus, Abelard, Locke, Leibniz, Hume, and

Hobbes, to name just a few; and they continue to be widely discussed even today, with an impressive and growing variety of solutions being offered for each of them. Over the past three decades in particular, a great deal of attention has been paid to such puzzles. And this is not surprising. In the latter half of this century, there has been an explosion of interest in the problems of traditional metaphysics. Since the late 1960s, questions about identity over time, the essential properties of objects and events, the nature of persons, the relations between material objects and their parts, the necessary and sufficient conditions for kind-membership, and other such ontological issues have loomed large in the philosophical literature. Puzzles about material constitution (or, better, their solutions) have ramifications for our views on all of these topics and many others.

There are many different kinds of puzzles about material constitution. Some involve artifacts; others involve organisms. Some show that growth, diminution, or part replacement is paradoxical; others show that even shape change is paradoxical. Some show that actual changes are paradoxical; others show that the mere *possibility* of change is paradoxical. But all of them present us with scenarios in which it appears that an object *a* and an object *b* share all of the same parts but are essentially related to their parts in different ways. This is what qualifies them as "puzzles about material constitution." The fundamental problem that they all raise is what I call "the problem of material constitution."

Each of the essays included in this anthology defends a view that will solve at least some of the puzzles that raise the problem of material constitution.[3] Moreover, many of them present views that will solve *every* puzzle that raises the problem. In what follows, I will explain in detail what the problem of material constitution is, and I will provide an exhaustive taxonomy of its possible solutions. Views that can be classified within this taxonomy are complete solutions: they will solve every puzzle that raises the problem. Views that cannot be so classified are partial solutions and will solve only some of the puzzles. In the course of presenting my taxonomy of solutions, I will briefly summarize the essays that follow.

1. The Puzzles

I have already said that there are various puzzles about material constitution. Thus, it seems most reasonable to begin our discussion by looking at a few examples. We have already seen one: the Debtor's Paradox. This puzzle is also known as the Paradox of Increase or the Growing Argument since, if the debtor's argument is sound, it follows that growth—which involves the *addition* of particles to an organism—is impossible. Below, I will discuss three other puzzles: the Ship of Theseus, the Body-minus Puzzle, and Allan Gibbard's Lumpl/Goliath Puzzle. These are not the only puzzles that will be encountered in the essays that follow, but they are the main ones. I will begin by presenting the puzzles; I will then provide some brief historical information about them; and, finally, I will explain why I classify all of them as puzzles about material constitution.

The Ship of Theseus: Consider a ship—the Ship of Theseus. At the beginning of its career, the ship is made entirely of wooden planks. The ship sails the same route for many decades and is "preserved" in the following way: whenever one of the wooden planks wears out, it is discarded and replaced by an aluminum one. Eventually the time comes when all of the wooden planks have been replaced by aluminum ones. One day, however, an historian decides to gather all of the discarded planks and rebuild them in their original form. She sells her ship to the local museum, and the curator then boasts that he has on display the Ship of Theseus. The crew of the aluminum ship, however, is outraged: "*We* are sailing the Ship of Theseus and have been for many years. The Ship of Theseus is here on the water, not there in your museum!" Who is right? Which ship is the Ship of Theseus?

Body-minus: Suppose that Tibbles is, at a certain time, a well-formed, properly functioning cat. At some later time, however, an unfortunate accident befalls her, resulting in the annihilation of her tail. Tibbles is understandably distressed. But we should be also. To see why, let us use the name 'Body-minus' to refer to that part of Tibbles that includes all of her except for her tail. Prior to the accident, it seems that both Tibbles and Body-minus exist, but they are distinct from one another. After the accident, however, it seems that Tibbles is identical with Body-minus. But how could this be? How could two distinct objects become the same object? It seems that they could not, and so we have a problem.

Lumpl and Goliath: A sculptor sets out to create a statue of the infant Goliath, but he does so in the following way: he sculpts Goliath's upper body from one piece of clay, his lower body from another, and then finishes the statue by sticking the two pieces of clay together. In joining the two pieces of clay he simultaneously brings into existence a *new* piece of clay and a completed statue of the infant Goliath. He allows the clay to harden, but then a day later (perhaps dissatisfied with his work) he smashes the statue, thereby terminating the careers of both the statue and the piece of clay. The question is whether the statue in this story (Goliath) is identical with the piece of clay (Lumpl). The trouble is, there seems to be no good answer to this question. An affirmative answer is implausible since Lumpl and Goliath seem to have different essential properties.[4] For example, (supposing the clay is still wet) Lumpl would survive if the piece of clay were reshaped in the form of a vase, whereas Goliath would not. And Goliath would survive if its left finger were annihilated, whereas Lumpl would not. But a negative answer is also implausible, at least initially, since such an answer appears to commit us to the conclusion that two distinct objects (a lump and a statue) can fully occupy the same region of spacetime.

All of these puzzles have roots in antiquity. The Debtor's Paradox is the oldest, first appearing in the writings of the comic playwright Epicharmus in the fifth century B.C. Of course, Epicharmus did not give the puzzle any sort of sophisticated philosophical treatment. In the scene in which it appears, the debtor's friend apparently decides that the best way to respond to the argument is simply to strike the debtor. The debtor becomes enraged, at which point the friend points out that, by the debtor's own reasoning, he cannot be held responsible for delivering the blow.[5] By the third century B.C., however, the debtor's argument was being taken a bit more seriously. The Skeptics at Plato's Academy took up the debtor's line of reasoning in defense of the conclusion that growth is impossible. Their opponents, the Stoics, sought to rebut that line of reasoning in order to establish the contrary conclusion.[6]

It was in connection with this debate that the Ship of Theseus and Body-minus Puzzles first appeared. Theseus's ship was a familiar vessel to the philosophers in Athens. It had (famously) sailed the same route for decades, and, according to Plutarch, it had been preserved in roughly the way described above.[7] Thus, the ship presented itself as a convenient and familiar example of part replacement. But, of course, the reasons given in the Growing Argument for thinking that growth is impossible are easily adapted to show that part replacement is impossible as well. Hence, it is easy to see why Theseus's ship came to be discussed in connection with that debate. Initially, however, the main question that arose with respect to the ship was simply whether or not it *survived* its many repairs.[8] It was not until the seventeenth century, when Thomas Hobbes reformulated the puzzle, that the central question became whether the continuously repaired ship (in our example, the aluminum ship) or a ship rebuilt from the original wooden planks would have greater claim to being identical with the original.

It is a bit less clear why the Body-minus Puzzle came to be discussed in connection with the Growing Argument. The puzzle is presented in a Stoic treatise on the Growing Argument, but since that treatise does not survive, we can only speculate that the puzzle was initially intended to serve as some kind of response to that argument.[9] The Stoic version of the puzzle involved a person (Dion) and that part of him (Theon) that includes all of him except for one of his feet. The present version, involving Tibbles the cat and her missing tail, was introduced by David Wiggins (Chapter 1), who in turn, attributes it to Peter Geach.[10] Peter van Inwagen, Frances Howard-Snyder, and Mark Heller (in Chapters 10, 14, and 17, respectively) present versions of the puzzle that most closely resemble the Stoic version.

The Lumpl/Goliath Puzzle is the newest of the four. It first appeared in Allan Gibbard's essay, "Contingent Identity."[11] Of course, it is far from being the first puzzle to ask us to consider the relation between a thing and its constitutive lump of matter; and so, in this sense, it has roots in antiquity just like the other three. But Gibbard's puzzle is different from its predecessors in that it is especially crafted so that the relevant object and lump share all of the same spatial parts *throughout their respective careers.* This is important for reasons that will become clear later when we talk about the doctrine of temporal parts.[12]

So much for historical remarks. Now, I would like to take a few paragraphs to explain why I classify all four of these puzzles as puzzles about material constitution. Earlier, I defined a puzzle about material constitution as one that presents us with an object *a* and an object *b* that share all of the same parts but are essentially related to those parts in different ways. It is easy to see how the Debtor's Paradox and the Lumpl/Goliath Puzzle do this; but what of the other two? What, exactly, are the relevant *a* and *b*?

Let us start with the Body-minus Puzzle. In my version of the story, the only objects mentioned are Tibbles and Body-minus, so they are the relevant *a* and *b*. At one point in the story, Tibbles and Body-minus share all of the same parts; but whereas Body-minus is essentially lacking a tail, Tibbles is not (as the story shows), and whereas Tibbles is essentially a cat, Body-minus is not (since at one point it is merely part of a cat). Thus, the story also provides us with reason to think that Tibbles and Body-minus are essentially related to their parts in different ways.

The Ship of Theseus Puzzle is a bit more complicated. Initially, it seems that the puzzle presents us not with two objects but *three*: the original ship, the continuously repaired ship, and the "plank-hoarder's" ship (that is, the ship that has been rebuilt from the original planks). Moreover, at the end of the story it is not at all clear which (if any) of these objects can reasonably be said to constitute one another. Obviously at the end of the story the plank-hoarder's ship and the continuously repaired ship do not constitute one another. One is made entirely of wood, the other of aluminum. But does either constitute the original ship? That question seems to be just another way of asking the question already under dispute. For if the aluminum ship is the Ship of Theseus, then it constitutes the original, and likewise for the plank-hoarder's ship. Moreover, since it is obvious that whichever of these ships constitutes the original will do so only because it is *identical* with the original, it is hard to see how this puzzle presents us with an object *a* and an object *b* that share all of the same parts but appear for some reason to be *distinct* from one another.

But suppose we focus our attention not on the end of the story but on the beginning. In particular, let us focus on the question: At the beginning of the story, what kind of thing do the original planks compose? Obviously, they compose a ship. But what kind of ship? We start with the intuition that they compose a ship that can survive complete part replacement, and this is what tempts us to identify the continuously repaired ship with the original. But during the story, another of our intuitions is uncovered. It turns out that we are also inclined to think that, at the beginning of the story, the planks compose a ship that *cannot* survive complete part replacement—a ship that either passes out of existence entirely or else comes to exist in a disassembled state once some proportion of its original parts have been removed. It is this intuition that tempts us to identify the plank-hoarder's ship with the original. But now we have our two ships after all. Let Ship A be the one that can survive complete part replacement; let Ship B be the one that cannot. At the beginning of the story, Ship A and Ship B share all of the same parts; but, because they have different persistence conditions—that is, because one can survive changes that the other cannot—they are essentially related to their parts in different ways. Of course, as in the Debtor's Paradox and the Lumpl/Goliath Puzzle, we are tempted to say that Ship A and Ship B are identical (after all, there seems to be only *one* Ship of Theseus). But to say this, it seems we must assign *either* the persistence conditions of Ship A or the persistence conditions of Ship B to the original ship. The fact that we cannot choose between the plank-hoarder's ship and the continuously repaired ship at the end of the story testifies to the difficulty of making this assignment. And so many philosophers have been tempted to deny that Ship A and Ship B are identical, thus embracing the conclusion that there are really two ships at the beginning of the story that share all of the same parts without being identical. And, as in the other puzzles about constitution, to make a decision about the relation between the relevant *a* and *b* is to solve the puzzle.

It should now be clear why each of the four puzzles presented in this section qualifies as a puzzle about material constitution. In the next section, I will provide a very general statement of the problem that underlies these puzzles.

2. The Problem Stated

Each of the puzzles discussed above presents us with a challenge. Earlier, I suggested that the challenge is to determine what the relationship is between the relevant objects *a* and *b*. This is true, but it is not the whole story. Underlying each of the puzzles discussed above are five assumptions. Individually, all of these assumptions are very plausible; but together they lead to contradiction, implying that the relevant *a* and *b* both are and are not identical with one another. The problem of material constitution is just the fact that these assumptions are individually plausible and jointly incompatible. Thus, the real challenge that these puzzles present us with is to decide which of the five assumptions ought to be rejected. In what follows, I will present these assumptions informally, explain why they are jointly incompatible, and show how they underlie each of the puzzles discussed above.[13]

To simplify our discussion a bit, let me begin by introducing some terminology. Let us use the term 'the *ps*' as a plural variable—a term of collective reference that refers neither to the *set* containing the *ps* nor to any *object* whose parts are the *ps*. For example, 'the present citizens of the United States' refers collectively to everyone who is presently a citizen of the United States. It does not refer to the set that contains all of the present citizens of the United States (just as 'the teacher of Plato' refers to Socrates and not to the set containing Socrates), nor does it refer to any object that is composed of them. 'The *ps*', in the expression 'the *ps* compose *x*', will thus refer collectively to all of the *ps*, whatever they are, that together compose the object *x*. Furthermore, let us say that 'the *ps* compose *x*' is an abbreviation for 'the *ps* are all parts of *x* and no two of the *ps* overlap and every part of *x* overlaps at least one of the *ps*'.[14] If the *ps* compose *x* and the *ps* compose *y* at the same time, then *x* and *y* constitute one another. Finally, let the letter 'F' stand in for kind-terms, or *sortals*, such as 'human being', 'ship', 'cat', 'statue', and so on (we will call such terms "substitution instances for F"); and let the letter 'R' stand in for relations such as 'is at all times composed by', 'is at all times composed by some proportion of', and so on (we will call such relations "substitution instances for R").[15]

Now for the assumptions. Recall that the problem of material constitution arises whenever it appears that we have an object *a* and an object *b* that share all of the same parts and yet are essentially related to those parts in different ways. In every puzzle that raises the problem, the following three assumptions together are responsible for this appearance:

Existence Assumption: Each of the puzzles assumes the existence of at least one object of a certain kind (e.g., ship, statue, cat, etc.), and each assumes that the object in question has parts. Of course, the relevant kind of object differs from puzzle to puzzle, so strictly speaking each puzzle has a different Existence Assumption. But each puzzle's Existence Assumption can be generated simply by taking different substitution instances for F in the following schema: There is an F, and there are *ps* that compose it.

Essentialist Assumption: Every puzzle also assumes that there is some relation such that wherever we have an object of the kind mentioned in the Existence Assumption, we have something that essentially bears that relation to its parts. The Debtor's Paradox, for example, assumes that where we have a human being, we have a collection of particles; and it also assumes that collections of particles cannot gain or lose parts. So, in other words, the Debtor's Paradox assumes that wherever we have a human being, we have something (namely, a collection of particles) that cannot gain or lose parts. This, roughly, is the Essentialist Assumption for that puzzle. We could put it a bit more precisely as follows:

(EA_D) For any *ps*, if the *ps* compose a human being, then the *ps* compose something such that, necessarily, if certain parts compose it at a particular time, they compose it at every time at which it exists.

As with the Existence Assumption, different puzzles make different Essentialist Assumptions. Moreover, for most puzzles it is a bit misleading to speak of *the* Essentialist Assumption. Few puzzles (if any) have a *unique* Essentialist Assumption. More often than not it turns out that what a puzzle presupposes about the objects it mentions is sufficient to generate *several* Essentialist Assumptions. Still, it only takes one to raise a problem, and each can be generated by taking different substitution instances for F and R in the following schema: For any *ps*, if the *ps* compose an F, then they compose an object such that, necessarily, it bears relation R to its parts. (In the present example, the relevant substitution instance for R can be defined as follows: An object bears R_D to its parts just in case it is composed of those parts at every time at which it exists.)

The Principle of Alternative Compositional Possibilities: This assumption complements the Essentialist Assumption. Whereas the Essentialist Assumption states that the parts of an F compose something that essentially bears a certain relation to its parts, the Principle of Alternative Compositional Possibilities (or PACP) states that the parts of an F compose something that does *not* essentially bear that relation to its parts. It asserts the existence of an object for which there are "alternative compositional possibilities": though it has certain parts, it might not have; though its parts are arranged in a certain way, it might have had parts arranged in a different way; and so on. For example, in the Debtor's Paradox, the paradox arises because of a tension between our intuitions that (i) the parts of a human being compose something (i.e., a collection of particles) that cannot gain or lose parts, and (ii) the parts of a human being compose something (i.e., a human being) that *can* gain or lose parts. The Essentialist Assumption expresses the first intuition; the PACP expresses the second. More precisely, the PACP for this puzzle states:

($PACP_D$) For any *ps*, if the *ps* compose a human being, then the *ps* compose something such that, possibly, certain parts compose it at a particular time and they do not compose it at every time at which it exists.

Like the Essentialist Assumption, few puzzles will have a unique PACP. But each of the different PACPs can be generated by taking different substitution instances for F and R in the following schema: For any *ps*, if the *ps* compose an F, then they compose an object such that, possibly, it exists and does *not* bear R to its parts.

So far, then, we have the following: The Existence Assumption tells us that there exists a composite object of a particular kind, F. So, consider an arbitrary object of that kind. Call the parts of that object "the *ps*." According to the Essentialist Assumption, the parts of *any* F compose something that is essentially such that it bears a certain relation R to its parts. Thus, the *ps* compose something that essentially bears R to its parts. Call that thing 'α'. Now, the PACP tells us that the parts of any F compose something that can exist and fail to bear R to its parts. Thus, the *ps* compose something that can fail to exist and bear R to its parts. Call that thing 'β'. We now have objects α and β that share all of the same parts and yet are essentially related to their parts in different ways. Given this, the remaining two assumptions lead us to a contradiction. They are the following:

The Identity Assumption: For any objects *x* and *y*, if *x* and *y* share all of the same parts at the same time, then *x* is identical with *y*.[16]

The Necessity Assumption: For any objects *x* and *y*, if *x* is identical with *y*, then it is necessary that *x* is identical with *y*.

Since the *ps* compose both α and β at the same time, the Identity Assumption entails that α is identical with β. And, given this, the Necessity Assumption entails that it is not possible for α to be distinct from β. But since α essentially bears R to its parts whereas β can exist and fail to bear R to its parts, it follows that it *is* possible for α to be distinct from β. Thus, we have reached a contradiction.

Denying any one of the above assumptions will solve any puzzle that raises the problem of material constitution. For example, to deny the Existence Assumption for a particular puzzle is to solve it by denying the existence of the very objects that the puzzle is about. Denying either the Essentialist Assumption or the PACP for a particular puzzle will be tantamount to denying that the relevant *a* exists, denying that the relevant *b* exists, or denying that *a* and *b* are essentially related to their parts in different ways. Thus, we can solve the problem of material constitution generally by denying the *conjunction* of these three assumptions for every substitution instance for F and R. We can also solve the problem generally by denying either the Identity Assumption or the Necessity Assumption. If we suppose (contrary to the Identity Assumption) that distinct objects *can* share all of the same parts at the same time, then there is nothing troubling about a scenario in which we have an object *a* and an object *b* that share all of the same parts and yet are essentially related to their parts in different ways. In such a case, we can simply concede that *a* and *b* are distinct. Similarly, if the Necessity Assumption is false—if there could be objects *x* and *y* that *are* identical but might not have been—then this kind of scenario again turns out to be unproblematic. We can simply say that, though *a* and *b* are in fact identical, in those possible cases where *b* fails to bear R to its parts, *a* and *b* are not identical.

We have now stated the problem of material constitution, and we have seen how denying any of the above five assumptions will solve it. The remainder of this section will be devoted to the task of showing how these assumptions underlie each of the puzzles presented earlier.

That each of the puzzles makes an Existence Assumption is obvious. The Debtor's Paradox assumes that there is at least one human being; the Ship of Theseus Puzzle assumes that there is at least one ship; the Body-minus Puzzle assumes that there is at least one cat; the Lumpl/Goliath Puzzle assumes that there is at least one statue; and all assume that the objects in question have parts.

The Essentialist Assumption and the PACP complement one another, so it will be convenient to discuss them together. To avoid complicating matters unnecessarily, I will pretend that each puzzle has a unique Essentialist Assumption and a unique PACP. But the reader should keep in mind that in most (if not all) cases this pretense is false. For each of these puzzles it may well be the case that the information given in the puzzle is sufficient to generate several Essentialist Assumptions and several PACPs in addition to the ones I identify here.

We have already discussed the Essentialist Assumption and PACP for the Debtor's Paradox, so I shall not repeat that discussion here. Let us begin with the Ship of Theseus Puzzle. In Section 1 we saw that the Ship of Theseus story is puzzling because it presupposes the following two intuitively plausible theses:

(1) The parts of a ship compose something that cannot undergo complete part replacement.
(2) The parts of a ship compose something that can undergo complete part replacement.

Obviously it is a short step from these to our Essentialist Assumption and PACP. Let us say that an object bears relation R_S to its parts just in case it is *always composed of some proportion of* those parts (i.e., it is composed of some proportion of those parts at all times at which it exists). Then (1) tells us that the parts of a ship compose something that necessarily bears R_S to its parts, and (2) tells us that the parts of a ship compose something that does not necessarily bear R_S to its parts. Thus, we may identify the following as the Essentialist Assumption and PACP for this puzzle:

(EA_S) For any *p*s, if the *p*s compose a ship, then the *p*s compose something such that, necessarily, if certain parts compose it at a particular time, then it is always composed of some proportion of those parts.

(PACP$_S$) For any *ps*, if the *ps* compose a ship, then the *ps* compose something such that, possibly, certain parts compose it at a particular time, but it is not always composed of some proportion of those parts.

In the Body-minus Puzzle, the crucial presuppositions seem to be the following:

(1) The parts of a cat compose a cat.
(2) Every cat is necessarily such that its parts are arranged catwise.
(3) The parts of a cat compose something that might fail to be a cat by being a proper part of a cat.[17]

Thus, if we say that an object bears relation R_B to its parts just in case those parts are arranged catwise, it turns out that (2) tells us that the parts of a cat compose something that necessarily bears R_B to its parts, and (3) tells us that the parts of a cat compose something that does not necessarily bear R_B to its parts. And so I am inclined to identify the following as the puzzle's Essentialist Assumption and PACP:

(EA$_B$) The parts of a cat compose something such that, necessarily, its parts (whatever they may be) are arranged catwise.

(PACP$_B$) The parts of a cat compose something such that, possibly, its parts (whatever they may be) are not arranged catwise.

Finally, the Lumpl/Goliath Puzzle presupposes that

(1) The parts of a statue compose a statue.
(2) Every statue is necessarily such that its parts are arranged statuewise.
(3) The parts of a statue compose a lump.
(4) Every lump is such that its parts might fail to be arranged statuewise.

So, let us say that an object bears R_L to its parts just in case those parts are arranged statuewise. Then, according to (1) and (2) the parts of a statue compose something that necessarily bears R_L to its parts, whereas according to (3) and (4) the parts of a statue compose something that does not necessarily bear R_L to its parts. Thus, we can identify the following as our Essentialist Assumption and PACP:

(EA$_L$) For any *ps*, if the *ps* compose a statue, then the *ps* compose something such that, necessarily, its parts (whatever they may be) compose a statue.

($PACP_L$) For any *ps*, if the *ps* compose a statue, then the *ps* compose something such that, possibly, its parts (whatever they may be) do not compose a statue.

We have now identified an Existence Assumption, an Essentialist Assumption, and a PACP in every puzzle. As I have said, these assumptions are what give us our objects *a* and *b* in every puzzle. The remaining assumptions (the Identity Assumption and the Necessity Assumption) typically remain tacit; but, as we have seen, the fact that we naturally make these assumptions is what explains why cases of material constitution are so puzzling. Without either of them, we no longer have a problem.

This concludes our discussion of the assumptions underlying the various puzzles. But before we move on to a full discussion of solutions to the problem of material constitution, one loose end remains to be tied. In the course of this discussion I have explained briefly with respect to each of the assumptions how rejecting it would enable us to solve puzzles about material constitution. But, though what I have said here may be sufficient to help us understand how most of the puzzles can be solved by rejecting one of these assumptions, there is one puzzle that we may yet have questions about: the Ship of Theseus. Most puzzles simply raise questions about the relation between *a* and *b*. Those questions receive obvious answers once we reject one of the above assumptions. The Ship of Theseus, however, raises a further question. It asks us to determine which of the two *resultant* ships is identical with the original. I want to close this section by showing how rejecting any one of the above assumptions will help us answer that question.

To reject the Existence Assumption is to deny either that there are ships or that ships are composite objects. In either case, the question is unanswerable. The puzzle needs to be restated in terms that do not presuppose the existence of ships that have proper parts.

If we reject the Essentialist Assumption (as defined above), then we effectively identify the Ship of Theseus with Ship A—the ship that can undergo complete part replacement. For in granting the PACP, we concede that the *ps* that compose a ship compose something that can undergo complete part replacement; and in denying the Essentialist Assumption, we deny that the *ps* that compose a ship compose anything that cannot undergo complete part replacement. But if the Ship of Theseus *can* undergo complete part replacement, then presumably it does in the case described; therefore, we should say that the continuously repaired ship is identical with the original.

On the other hand, if we reject the PACP, then (for reasons similar to those just described) we effectively identify the Ship of Theseus with Ship B—the ship that cannot undergo complete part replacement. In that case, it is natural to say that the plank-hoarder's ship is identical with the original. It is natural, but we should pause here to note that various "background" assumptions might lead us to a different solution. For example, if one thinks that no ship can survive disassembly, and that anything once destroyed cannot come back into existence, then if we reject the PACP, we should conclude that *neither* of the resultant ships is identical with the original. Rejecting the PACP rules out the continuously repaired ship; but rejecting the possibility of disassembly and intermittent existence rules out the plank-hoarder's ship as well. This is not the only place where background assumptions influence our solution to this puzzle, but I mention these here because questions about disassembly and intermittent existence are particularly controversial.[18]

To reject the Identity Assumption is to admit that at the beginning of the story there might have been two (or more) colocated ships, one of which came to be dismantled and rebuilt, the other (or *an*other) of which survived the replacement of all of its parts. If this were the case, then neither ship at the end of the story would be the Ship of Theseus, for there would be no such thing as *the* ship that was composed of the original planks. Hence, the question is simply defective.

Finally, to reject the Necessity Assumption (and no other) is, in the present context, to embrace temporary identity (the thesis that, possibly, there is an object *a* and an object *b* such that *a* is identical with *b* at one time and distinct from *b* at another). Why *temporary* identity? Because rejecting the Necessity Assumption solves a puzzle about material constitution by allowing us to identify the relevant *a* and *b*. Thus, if we solve this puzzle by rejecting the Necessity Assumption, we are saying that Ship A and Ship B at the beginning of the story are identical with one another. But clearly they are not identical at the end of the story (presumably one has undergone complete part replacement whereas the other has not); thus, they must have been only *temporarily* identical. Which one, then, is to be identified with the original? I say the continuously repaired ship. In presenting the puzzle, we start with the intuition that the original ship can undergo complete part replacement. Later, of course, we are led to question this intuition, but only because we are confronted with something (i.e., the plank-hoarder's ship) that apparently *was* identical with the original ship and has not undergone complete part replacement. Since it was identical with the original, we assume it must be now; thus, we are led to doubt that the original can undergo complete part replacement. Once we embrace temporary identity, however, the pressure to doubt that the original ship can undergo complete part replacement is relieved. And, I take it, if there is no intuitive pressure to doubt a view that we are otherwise inclined to hold, then we ought to continue holding it. Thus, if we embrace temporary identity, it seems we ought to continue to believe that the Ship of Theseus can undergo complete part replacement and, therefore, we ought to conclude that the continuously repaired ship is identical with the original Ship of Theseus.[19]

3. Solutions

We have now seen that one problem underlies each of the four puzzles described in Section 1. The problem is that for any composite object *a* we can (generally) identify an object *b* that constitutes it and is essentially related to its parts in a way that *a* is not. The Identity Assumption tells us that *a* is identical with *b*; the Necessity Assumption tells us that *a* and *b* could not have been distinct; hence, *a* and *b are not* essentially related to their parts in different ways. Thus we have a contradiction. To solve the problem, we must (i) reject the Identity Assumption, (ii) reject the Necessity Assumption, or (iii) reject some feature of every story that introduces the problem. If we choose (iii), then for any particular story that raises the problem, we must either claim that *a* does not exist, claim that *b* does not exist, or claim that one or the other is not related to its parts in the way we think it is.[20] As we have seen, to do this is just to reject the Existence Assumption, the Essentialist Assumption, or the PACP for whatever F and R are presupposed in the case at hand. Or, in other words, it is to reject the *conjunction* of those assumptions for *every* substitution instance for F and R. The puzzles we have considered in this essay differ only insofar as they supply different substitution instances for F and R and different stories to engage our intuitions about the five conflicting assumptions. Those who choose one of the above three alternatives provide *complete* solutions to the problem. That is, they provide solutions that solve every puzzle that raises the problem. To do less is to provide, at best, a *partial* solution to the problem.

We are now in a position to categorize the solutions to the problem of material constitution. One natural way to do it would be to identify three categories corresponding to (i), (ii), and (iii) above, and, for any given puzzle, three different ways for a solution to fall into the third category. However, since one may reject a proposition either by claiming that it is false or by claiming that it is *neither* true nor false, it seems appropriate to identify a fourth category as well: a category of "indeterminacy solutions." Thus, in the first three categories I include only solutions that *deny* the relevant assumption. Solutions that maintain that one of the five assumptions is neither true nor false are relegated to the fourth category. In what follows, I will discuss examples of the various kinds of complete solutions. I will also discuss examples of two of the most popular partial solutions.

3.1 Coincident Entities

Let us begin with solutions that deny the Identity Assumption. As I have already noted, the Identity Assumption corresponds (roughly) to the view that is sometimes expressed by the claim "Constitution is identity."[21] To deny it, one must hold that sometimes distinct objects have all of the same parts at the same time. For convenience, I call these "coincident entities" solutions, although we should be careful to note that to believe in the possibility of coincident entities is not necessarily to believe that there can be two distinct material objects in the same place at the same time. The contributors to this volume who defend this sort of solution are David Wiggins, Frederick Doepke, Judith Thomson, Mark Johnston, and Ernest Sosa.[22]

David Wiggins is perhaps the most well-known contemporary defender of this sort of solution. In Chapter 1, he presents a puzzle about material constitution, points out that the fact that the relevant *a* and *b* (a tree and the aggregate of cellulose molecules that constitutes it) have different essential properties seems to preclude their being identical, and concludes that the tree and the aggregate are distinct but colocated. Thus, he believes it is possible for there to be two things in the same place at the same time, but he emphasizes that it is *not* possible for there to be two things *of the same kind* in the same place at the same time. Wiggins gives several reasons for thinking that this is true, but I would like here to point out one interesting reason for thinking that it is *false*. (I mention it because it is discussed in several other essays that appear in this volume. See in particular Chapters 5 and 14.) Suppose two distinct objects share all of their parts in common. Presumably, then, any qualitative property that one of the objects has will be had by the other.[23] But then how could one be, say, a statue and the other not? It is hard to see how. Thus, one might be inclined to think not that it is impossible to have objects of the same kind colocated with one another but that it is impossible to have objects of *different* kinds colocated with one another. This raises a general problem for the colocationist, since the very puzzles that supposedly motivate the colocationist view always involve objects of different kinds.

In Chapter 2, Frederick Doepke defends colocation by providing arguments against four different ways of solving puzzles about material constitution. He takes as his initial examples of material constitution familiar substances and the various aggregates that can be seen as constituting them. He then argues against the following solutions to the puzzles that arise with respect to such objects: (i) deny that there are any such things as aggregates, (ii) embrace "relative identity" or "temporary identity," (iii) deny that the objects in question actually constitute one another, and (iv) deny that the relevant substances exist. The first solution is an obvious nonstarter as a general solution to the problem of material constitution: as Doepke points out, there are examples of constitution such that neither of the objects in question are aggregates. Alternatives (ii) and (iv) are discussed later in this essay, so I will not comment on them here. That leaves only (iii) in need of further discussion.

The third solution is what Doepke refers to as the "Dichronic View." According to the Dichronic View, when we talk about, say, the gold in a gold ring, we are not talking about an object that exists now; rather, we are talking about an object that *would* exist if the ring were smashed. So, I take it, if the ring is never smashed, 'the gold' refers to nothing, and if the ring does come to be smashed, 'the gold' refers to the product of the smashing. Thus, on the Dichronic View constitution never really occurs. Doepke's argument against this view is that this construes change as mere replacement of one thing by another: the gold pops into existence and the ring pops out of existence at the time of the smashing, but there is nothing that underlies the change. According to Doepke, it is much more plausible to believe that there *is* something that persists through the change—namely, the gold—and that is why we need to believe that 'the gold' refers to something that exists *before* the smashing as well as after. But if we do this, and if we do not avail ourselves of alternatives (ii) or (iv) above, then (according to Doepke) we ought to embrace colocation.

Judith Jarvis Thomson, in Chapter 3, defends colocation as an alternative to the doctrine of temporal parts. According to the doctrine of temporal parts, just as I am only partially present at every subregion of the total region of *space* that I occupy, so too I am only partially present at every subregion of the total region of *time* that I occupy (and likewise for every other material object). In other words, I have parts at the various times at which I exist instead of being wholly present at them, and I am "spread out" in time in much the same way that I am spread out in space (and, again, likewise for every other material object). If an object fills one of the subregions of space that I occupy at a particular time, then it is a *spatial* part of me; if it fills the sum of *all* of the subregions of space that I occupy at a given time or throughout a given period of time, then it is a *temporal* part of me.[24] How the doctrine of temporal parts solves certain puzzles about material constitution is a matter to be discussed below. Suffice it to say now that the doctrine does solve some of the puzzles, and Thomson's main concern in her article is to show that it is an inferior solution.

Thomson raises two main objections against the doctrine of temporal parts. First, it seems to commit its adherents to the bizarre conclusion that, for example, the legs, seat, and back of a chair are not parts of the chair unless they all come into and pass out of existence at the same time as the chair. Roughly, the reason is this. Temporal parts theorists hold that every object is a temporal part of itself.[25] Moreover, a temporal part of an object is, by definition, something that has no parts that exist before or after the stretch of time during which it exists. But these two claims together yield the conclusion that no *object* has parts that exist before or after the stretch of time during which it exists. Therefore, a chair cannot have parts that exist before or after the stretch of time during which it exists. Therefore, a chair cannot have parts that exist before or after the stretch of time during which it exists. So, unless the legs, seat, and back of a chair come into and pass out of existence at the same time as the chair, they cannot be parts of the chair. Second, the doctrine seems to commit its adherents to the bizarre conclusion that, for example, as I hold a bit of chalk in my hand, "new stuff, new chalk keeps constantly coming into existence *ex nihilo*" (p. 36, this volume). Why? Because a temporal part of a piece of chalk by definition exists only during a *part* of the total duration of time through which the total piece of chalk exists. At different periods in that duration, we have different temporal parts. But, Thomson points out, a temporal part of a piece of chalk is itself a piece of chalk; thus, at different periods in the duration of time through which the total piece of chalk exists, we have *many different pieces of chalk*. And this is just to say that, as I hold a piece of chalk in my hand, new pieces are continually coming into and passing out of existence. On the basis of these objections, Thomson rejects the doctrine of temporal parts. She then goes on to recommend colocation as an alternative solution.

In Chapter 4, Mark Johnston defends colocation by arguing that (in the Lumpl/Goliath Puzzle) there is no good reason to believe that Lumpl is identical with Goliath. As he sees it, there are only two arguments to be had for that conclusion. One is based on the mereological axiom of extensionality:[26]

(M) x is identical with y if and only if, for all z, z is a part of x if and only if z is a part of y.

The argument is straightforward: Lumpl and Goliath share all of the same parts; therefore, by (M), Lumpl is identical with Goliath. But the problem with this, according to Johnston, is that it is not entirely clear what *kinds* of parts (M) is supposed to be talking about. Lumpl and Goliath share all of the same *material* parts, but perhaps they have other parts that they do not share. And, according to Johnston, (M) cannot plausibly be construed as licensing claims to identity simply on the basis of shared material parts. Suppose a clay pot is smashed and reshaped as a bust of Napoleon. The pot and the bust share all of the same material parts, but presumably one cannot infer from this together with (M) that the pot and the bust are identical. Thus, Johnston says, what is needed to drive the argument from (M) is a suitable definition of 'part'; but, he argues, none is forthcoming. It is worth noting that the Identity Assumption is just a temporally qualified version of (M), and as such it does not suffer from the same deficiencies that Johnston thinks (M) suffers from. There is no problem with supposing (as I have) that 'part' in the Identity Assumption means 'material part', since the assumption only affirms the identity of objects that share all of the same parts *at the same time*. But, Johnston claims, to simply affirm something like the Identity Assumption is to beg the question in favor of the conclusion that Lumpl is identical with Goliath; anyone who doubts that Lumpl is identical with Goliath will doubt the Identity Assumption.

The other argument for the conclusion that Lumpl is identical with Goliath is based on the following principle:

(P) If y is a paradigm F and x is intrinsically exactly like y, then x is an F.

If (P) is true, then (assuming Goliath is a paradigm statue and Lumpl is intrinsically exactly like Goliath) it follows that Lumpl is a statue. Thus, Lumpl has the essential properties of a statue, contrary to one of the hypotheses of the puzzle. The problem with this argument, however, is that it seems that if (P) is true, then something like the following claim should also be true:

(P*) If y is a paradigm F and x differs in any respect relevant to being an F only very minutely from y, then x is an F.

But if we admit (P*), we encounter the notorious "problem of the many": for any macroscopic composite object (such as a statue), there are countless objects that overlap it and differ from it only very minutely.[27] For example, overlapping Lumpl there is an object composed of all of Goliath's parts except for a certain atom A_1, an object composed of all of Goliath's parts except for a certain other atom A_2, and so on. By (P*), all of these objects must be statues, and none is identical with Goliath. We could, of course, reject the offending (P*); but then it seems we ought also to reject (P), in which case our argument for the identity of Lumpl and Goliath is lost. There are various responses to the problem of the many. Johnston's own is to concede that there are countless statue-shaped objects overlapping Goliath and to deny that any *one* of them definitely constitutes Goliath or is a statue. Thus, constitution is a vague relation. But now it turns out that, instead of an argument *against* colocation, we have a further reason for believing in it: Constitution cannot be (or entail) identity because constitution is vague and identity is not. Therefore, objects are distinct from the lumps of matter that constitute them.

Ernest Sosa (Chapter 5) arrives at a colocationist solution by a somewhat different route. Sosa's essay is primarily concerned with the question of whether human beings could plausibly be considered to be immaterial souls (i.e., immaterial *substances*). He approaches this question by considering whether the problems attending belief in immaterial substances generally are greater than the problems attending belief in material substances generally. He notes that those who believe in immaterial substance face difficult questions about how such substances are individuated and about how their essential properties might be seen as being grounded in their intrinsic qualitative nature. Believers in material substance can overcome these problems; however, it turns out that they are confronted with a different but perhaps no less disconcerting set of worries. For our purposes, the most interesting of these worries is that, given a broadly Aristotelian view of what it is to be a material object, it turns out that "none of us can so much as wiggle a finger without destroying, and creating, infinitely many things" (p. 83, this volume).

What is this "broadly Aristotelian" view that Sosa lays out? Roughly, it is the view that a material object supervenes on, or is ontologically dependent on, the having of a certain property by its constituent matter. For example, the existence of a snowball supervenes on the having of the property of roundness by its constituent lump of snow. When the lump of snow loses that property, the snowball ceases to exist. On this view, objects, such as snowballs, are ontologically dependent on *events*, such as *this lump of snow's being round*.[28] This view is Aristotelian in the sense that it takes objects to be "matter-form compounds." In the snowball example, the lump of snow plays the role of matter, and roundness plays the role of form.

So on this view familiar macroscopic objects supervene on events. But they are not to be identified with the events on which they depend because, for example, any particular snowball could have existed either in the absence of the lump of snow that constitutes it (if, say, it had been constituted by a different lump of snow) or in the absence of the particular shape that the lump has. Thus, unless there is some restriction on what kinds of properties can count as "forms," this view obviously commits its adherents to the conclusion that there can be a great multiplicity of objects in the same place at the same time. And Sosa does not seem to think that there is any such restriction. For example, he says that, on this view, colocated with every snowball is what he calls a "snowdiscall": an object that exists just in case some lump of snow has any shape between being round and disc shaped. And, similarly, it will turn out that, colocated with every person whose arm happens to be raised is an object that exists just in case some particles are arranged in the shape of a human being with its arm raised, as well as another object that exists just in case some particles are arranged in the shape of a human being with its hand in any position between being raised and being unraised, as well as another object *ad infinitum*.[29] Sosa is uncomfortable with this consequence (and so it would probably be unwise to characterize him unqualifiedly as a *defender* of colocation), but he expresses even greater discomfort with some familiar suggestions for avoiding it.

So it turns out that, given this Aristotelian view of material objects, belief in material substance commits us to the conclusion that colocated with every composite material object are many other objects, each with a different set of persistence conditions. And, as I have indicated, Sosa points out several other problems with belief in material substance besides this one. These problems are ultimately not obstacles to belief in material substance, but he notes that they might be considered a mark in favor of belief in immaterial souls. Perhaps we cannot avoid the problems associated with belief in material substance altogether, but we *can* avoid them as far as persons are concerned.

Some might protest that Sosa's "Aristotelian" ontology is saddled with colocation only because he departs from the "true spirit" of Aristotle. According to Aristotle, these objectors will argue, the only "forms" that are truly object constituting are the forms of living organisms. Moreover, form on Aristotle's view is more than just shape; it is functional organization. So, though a human being's parts are arranged in many different shapes throughout its life, those parts exemplify only one (Aristotelian) form; hence, there is only one material object that they compose. However, it is not clear that the view Sosa sketches is really so far from the true spirit of Aristotle as these objectors might think. For, though Aristotle denies that anything other than living organisms exists in the *primary sense* of that word, he grants that a great many things other than living organisms exist in various secondary and tertiary senses. Artifacts, for example, exist in such a non-primary sense; but if, as Aristotle believes, statues and thresholds exist, why not snowballs? Moreover, on his view there are (in some sense) such things as "seated-Socrates"—things that exist when and only when a particular substance (e.g., Socrates) exemplifies a particular property (e.g., the property of being seated). But if there is such a thing as seated-Socrates, then presumably there is also such a thing as Socrates-with-his-arm-raised, as well as the various other kinds of objects Sosa was worried about. And if we simply stipulate that the term "object" is to apply to anything that exists in *any* (Aristotelian) sense whatsoever, then we arrive at a view very much like the one sketched by Sosa after all.[30]

3.2 Contingent Identity and Counterpart Theory

Next, we turn to solutions that deny the Necessity Assumption. These solutions hold that there are cases where '$a = b$' is true and it is possible that a exists or b exists and '$a = b$' is false. The contributors to this volume who endorse this sort of view are Allan Gibbard, David Lewis, and George Myro. I refer to all three generally as contingent identity theorists, though it should be noted that Lewis is explicitly wary of that label. Still, as we shall see, his counterpart theory bears strong resemblance to the view defended by Gibbard. It can also be extended to solve problems for the more radical "temporary identity" thesis that Myro defends.

Contingent identity theorists face at least two challenges, one linguistic and the other metaphysical. The linguistic challenge arises as a result of the widely held view that proper names are *rigid designators*. Roughly speaking (and a rough characterization will suffice for our purposes here), a name is a rigid designator just in case it always refers to the same thing, even in modal contexts.[31] A modal context is any context expressing possibility or necessity.[32] So, for example, the name 'Socrates' refers to Socrates in each of the following sentences:

(1) Socrates is snub-nosed.
(2) Possibly: Socrates is named 'Fred'.

(Note that (2) expresses the same proposition as the more colloquial sentence 'Socrates might have been named Fred.' The points in this section are more clearly made, however, if we avoid such colloquial expressions and if we understand (2) and other modal statements along the lines described in note 32.) Since 'Socrates' *always* refers to Socrates, regardless of what kind of sentence it occurs in, it is a rigid designator. Contrast this with a designator like 'the teacher of Plato'. This designator sometimes refers to Socrates and sometimes does not. Consider, for example, the following two sentences:

(3) The teacher of Plato was snub-nosed.
(4) Possibly: the teacher of Plato is someone other than Socrates.

On the most natural reading of these sentences, 'the teacher of Plato' refers to Socrates in (3) but not in (4) since (4) is true despite the fact that Socrates could not have been someone other than Socrates. Thus, 'the teacher of Plato' is not a rigid designator.[33]

The problem this theory of proper names raises for contingent identity theorists is the following. Consider the statue Goliath and its constitutive piece of clay, Lumpl. The names 'Lumpl' and 'Goliath' are proper names and therefore rigid designators. So whatever they refer to in non-modal contexts, they also refer to in modal contexts. But they are coreferential in non-modal contexts; therefore, it follows that they must be coreferential in modal contexts as well. This means that if

(5) Necessarily: If Goliath exists then Goliath is identical with Goliath.

expresses a true proposition, then so must

(6) Necessarily: If Lumpl exists then Lumpl is identical with Goliath.

and vice versa. But (5) is obviously true (and even the contingent identity theorists admit as much), whereas (6) is precisely what the contingent identity theorists want to deny.

So that is the linguistic problem. The metaphysical problem is that the claim that identity is contingent appears to be in violation of a venerable and fairly obvious principle of identity: Leibniz's Law. According to Leibniz's Law,

(LL) For all *x* and *y*, *x* is identical with *y* only if, for any property *P*, *x* has *P* just in case *y* does.

But, for any *x*, one property that *x* most certainly seems to have is the property of being necessarily identical with *x*. And so it turns out that, for any *x* and *y*, *y* is identical with *x* if and only if *y* has the property of being necessarily identical with *x* and *x* has the property of being necessarily identical with *y*. Thus, contingent identity is ruled out.

Allan Gibbard (Chapter 6) solves the linguistic problem by claiming that it makes no sense to ask whether an object in some possible world is identical with some actual object. For example, consider Goliath, and consider a possible world W in which the clay that constitutes Goliath is shaped in the form of a ball. Is the ball in W the same thing as Goliath? According to Gibbard, this question is meaningless. Goliath is the same *lump* as the ball but not the same *statue*; and so it makes no sense to ask whether Goliath is simply identical with, or the same *thing* as, the ball. How is this relevant to the linguistic problem? In short, it implies that there are no rigid designators in the sense described above. Consider again the following sentence:

(2) Possibly: Socrates is named 'Fred'.

If 'Socrates' is a rigid designator, this sentence asserts the existence of a possible world in which there is a person named Fred who is identical with Socrates. In other words, it asserts that some actual object (Socrates) is identical with an object in some other possible world (the person named Fred). But if Gibbard is right, such an assertion makes no sense. And since similar remarks will apply with respect to any name in any modal context, it follows that if proper names are rigid designators in the sense described above, then sentences expressing claims about possibility and necessity are simply not meaningful.

Is there an alternative account of rigid designation available? Gibbard's proposal is to take proper names as being rigid *relative to a sortal.* For example, 'Socrates' is a person-rigid designator: it refers to the same *person* in modal contexts as it does in non-modal contexts. Thus, (2) asserts that there is a possible world that contains someone named Fred who is the *same person* as Socrates. And this is unproblematic since, on Gibbard's view, there is no problem with sortal-relative assertions of identity between actual objects and objects in other possible worlds. Similarly, then, 'Goliath' is a "statue-rigid" designator, and 'Lumpl' is a "lump-rigid" designator. But it will not follow from the fact that a statue-rigid designator and a lump-rigid designator are coreferential in non-modal contexts that they will be coreferential in modal contexts, for (according to the contingent identity theorists, anyway) there might be worlds in which, for example, the same lump exists but the same statue does not. Thus,

(5) Necessarily: If Goliath exists then Goliath is identical with Goliath.

comes out true since it asserts that in every world that contains something that is the same statue as Goliath, that statue is identical with itself. But it is still open to the contingent identity theorist to say that

(6) Necessarily: If Lumpl exists then Lumpl is identical with Goliath.

is false since, on their view, it is certainly *not* the case that in every world that contains the same lump as Lumpl, that object is identical with something that is the same statue as Goliath. Some worlds that contain the same lump as Lumpl contain *nothing* that is the same statue as Goliath.

Gibbard's solution to the metaphysical problem is to deny that objects have modal properties. That is, he denies that objects have properties like *being possibly such and so* or *being necessarily such and so*. One implication of this is that for any *x*, there is no such property as *being necessarily identical with x*. Therefore, there is no longer any trouble with Leibniz's Law. But, as Gibbard himself notes, this solution comes at a heavy price. We tend to think, for example, that Socrates could not have been a rock or an egg. And it seems that the best way to express this intuition is to say that Socrates has essential properties that preclude his being a rock or an egg. Socrates is essentially a non-rock and essentially a non-egg. But if Gibbard is right, there are no essential properties. Therefore, it is not clear how we are to accommodate our intuitions about how things could and could not have been.

Gibbard attempts to solve this problem by adopting a nonstandard account of the way predicates and variables behave in modal contexts. According to Gibbard, names in modal contexts refer to "individual concepts" instead of to objects, and variables in modal contexts range over individual concepts instead of objects. An individual concept, according to Gibbard, is "a function whose domain is a set of possible worlds, and which assigns to each world W in its domain an individual that exists in W" (p. 108, this volume). So, for example, in the sentence

(7) Possibly: Lumpl exists and Goliath is not identical with Lumpl.

the name 'Goliath' refers to a statue-concept instead of a statue, and the name 'Lumpl' refers to a lump-concept instead of a lump. And the sentence is to be understood as saying, roughly, that there is some possible world W such that (i) Lumpl is the concept of an individual in W and (ii) Lumpl and Goliath are not concepts of the same individual.[34] Similarly, a sentence like

(8) It is not possible that Socrates is an egg.

is *not* to be understood as a claim about an *object* (i.e., Socrates). Rather, it is to be understood as a claim about the *concept* 'Socrates'. And that claim, roughly, is that there is no world W such that the individual assigned to W by the concept 'Socrates' is an egg. In this way, Gibbard enables us to preserve most of our talk about essential properties (e.g., we can still make sense of the claim that Socrates could not have been an egg), albeit at the price of making it mean something other than what we normally think it means.

David Lewis (Chapter 7) handles the two problems in a way quite similar to the way in which Gibbard handles them. The key to his solution is *counterpart theory*. Counterpart theory is Lewis's way of understanding what it is for objects to have modal properties. To say that Socrates could not have been an egg, for example, is (according to Lewis) to say that there is no possible world in which Socrates has a counterpart that is an egg. To say that David Letterman could have made his first television appearance wearing Bermuda shorts is to say that there are possible worlds that have Letterman-counterparts who make their first television appearances wearing Bermuda shorts. A counterpart of an object is just what you might expect from the label: it is an object sufficiently similar to the original to serve as a stand-in, or representative for it in its absence. Thus, on Lewis's view, we do not exist in other worlds. Rather, we are represented in them by our counterparts. In his terminology, we exist *according to* other worlds. An object exists according to a world just in case it has a counterpart in that world; and it has a property P according to a world just in case it has a counterpart in that world that has P. So, in general, an object has the property of *being possibly P* just in case there is a world according to which it has P, and it has the property of *being necessarily P* just in case it has P according to every world.

Given this understanding of what it is for objects to have modal properties, it is relatively easy to dispatch both of the problems described above. Consider first the linguistic problem. Like Gibbard, Lewis would deny that the names 'Lumpl' and 'Goliath' are both rigid designators in the normal sense of that term. According to Lewis, a proper name for *x* refers to *x* in non-modal contexts and to counterparts of *x* in modal contexts. Thus, it is *quasi-rigid*, or rigid with respect to a particular counterpart relation. And, as with Gibbard, which counterparts are referred to by a name depends on the connotations associated with that name. Different names evoke different counterpart relations.[35] Lewis does not explicitly consider the Lumpl/Goliath case, but I take it that on his view the name 'Lumpl' would refer to lump-counterparts and 'Goliath' would refer to statue-counterparts. And this suffices to explain the disparity in truth value between (5) and (6). To affirm (5) is just to affirm the trivial truth that in every possible world that contains a statue-counterpart of Goliath, that object is identical with itself. (6), on the other hand, implies that there is no possible world in which there is a lump-counterpart of Lumpl/Goliath that is not also a statue-counterpart. Denying this does not contradict (5) and, in fact, denying (6) now seems much more reasonable; for it seems to make perfect sense to think that Lumpl/Goliath could have statue-counterparts that are not lump-counterparts and vice versa.

What about the metaphysical problem? Leibniz's Law poses no threat here. Consider a property like *being necessarily identical with Goliath*. In terms of counterpart theory, this comes out as equivalent to something like *being such that all of one's own counterparts are statue-counterparts of the object picked out by 'Goliath' when that name occurs in non-modal contexts*. But not even Goliath has *this* property,[36] for (as the puzzle is intended to show) the object picked out by 'Goliath' when that name occurs in non-modal contexts has lump-counterparts that are not among its statue-counterparts. Thus, the argument from Leibniz's Law is blocked.

Notice that Lewis's strategy here is substantially the same as Gibbard's. Both deny that proper names are rigid designators in the normal sense, and both maintain that names are quasi-rigid—relative either to a kind-term or a counterpart relation, which in the end comes to about the same thing in both cases. Furthermore, both give similar accounts of the meaning of modal claims. Gibbard says that names and variables in modal contexts refer to individual concepts: functions that assign individuals that exist in worlds to the worlds in which they exist. But we could just as easily think of those individuals that get assigned to worlds by individual concepts as *counterparts* of actual individuals. And that is in fact how they function. To say that Socrates could not have been an egg is, according to Gibbard, to say that there is no world W where the individual assigned to W by the concept 'Socrates' is an egg. But we could just stipulate that the individuals assigned to various worlds by the concept 'Socrates' are to be called counterparts of Socrates. And, if we do, then Gibbard's analysis comes out substantially the same as Lewis's: to say that Socrates could not have been an egg is to say that there is no world that contains a counterpart of Socrates that is an egg. More exactly, it is to say that no world contains a counterpart of Socrates *under the concept 'Socrates'* (or, in Lewis's terminology, *under the counterpart relation evoked by 'Socrates'*) that is an egg. As I see it, the key difference between Lewis's theory and Gibbard's is just that Lewis takes his theory to be a realist theory of *de re* modality whereas Gibbard does not.[37]

George Myro's essay (Chapter 8) defends a more radical thesis than Lewis's or Gibbard's. Lewis and Gibbard want to say that there are cases where *a* is identical with *b* but might not have been. Still, on their view, if *a* is ever identical with *b*, then *a* is always identical with *b*. Not so for Myro, however. According to Myro, identity is sometimes *temporary*.

If we think of times as analogous to possible worlds, however, it turns out that the strategies at Myro's disposal for solving the linguistic and metaphysical problems are roughly the same as the strategies available to Lewis and Gibbard. Effectively, Lewis and Gibbard solve the metaphysical problem by claiming that what *a* and *b* are like in one possible world is not relevant to whether *a* and *b* are identical in another.[38] Similarly, Myro solves the metaphysical problem by claiming that what a and b are like at one time is not relevant to whether *a* and *b* are identical at another time. One difference, however, is that whereas Lewis and Gibbard either deny the existence of or reconceive the nature of modal properties, Myro simply imposes a restriction on Leibniz's Law. Thus, he does not deny, for example, that an object *O* may be such that it will be on a mantelpiece tomorrow; he simply denies that this is the sort of property that an object identical with *O* must have for Leibniz's Law to be satisfied.

Myro does not explicitly address the linguistic problem, but it seems that he could solve it in a way similar to the way in which Lewis solves his linguistic problem. Just as Lewis says that an object exists according to a world if and only if it has a counterpart in that world, so too Myro could say that an object exists according to a time if and only if it has a "counterpart" at that time. Then it would be open to Myro to say (again, in parallel with Lewis) that proper names in *temporal* contexts refer to counterparts of the objects they refer to in non-temporal contexts. Thus,

(8) Lumpl will not exist and be distinct from Lumpl.

would come out as equivalent to

(8a) There is no time at which the lump-counterpart of the object referred to by 'Lumpl' is distinct from itself.

And

(9) Lumpl will be distinct from Goliath.

would come out as equivalent to

(9a) There is a time at which there exists a lump-counterpart of the object referred to by 'Lumpl' that is not also a statue-counterpart of that object.

I do not mean to attribute any of this to Myro (though it does seem one can find traces of this view in his essay); perhaps he would have been quite displeased with it. Still, it is worth noting that since his view entails the weaker contingent identity thesis, Myro is saddled with all of the same modal problems that Lewis and Gibbard are saddled with. Thus, unless some alternative view is available, he will need to accept something like a counterpart theory of modality anyway; so why not extend it to the temporal case as well?[39]

3.3 Eliminativism and Dominant Kinds

In this category I list the views of philosophers who *accept* the other two assumptions and thus solve every puzzle that raises the problem of material constitution by rejecting some feature or other of the stories that raise it. Most philosophers whose views fall into this category do not solve every puzzle the same way. They deny the conjunction of the three schematic assumptions for every substitution instance for F and R, but they deny different conjuncts for different instances. The contributors to this volume who defend this sort of solution are Peter Unger, Peter van Inwagen, Roderick Chisholm, and Michael Burke. The first three defend "eliminativist" solutions: they deny the existence of at least one of the objects mentioned in every puzzle. Burke defends a "dominant kinds" solution: he holds that one of the kinds mentioned in every puzzle (e.g., statue, lump, etc.) dominates the other, so that something could be a member of *both* kinds but have only the essential properties associated with one of them.

In Chapter 9, Peter Unger denies that there are Fs for all substitution instances of F except those where Fs are simple.[40] Thus, Unger denies the Existence Assumption for everything except simples. It should be noted, however, that Unger's reasons for denying the existence of everything except simples in fact have nothing to do with the problem of material constitution. Instead, he makes these denials in the face of the *sorites* paradox, which is explained in clear detail in his essay. It should also be noted that Unger has since abandoned this radical view. (See, for example, Unger 1990.)

Peter van Inwagen (Chapter 10) effectively denies the Essentialist Assumption for cases where it implies that the parts of a human being compose something that cannot survive changes in its parts, and the PACP for cases where it implies that the parts of a human being compose something that could be a proper part of a human being.[41] Van Inwagen's stated aim is to show that what he calls the "Doctrine of Arbitrary Undetached Parts" (or DAUP) is false. DAUP is (roughly) the doctrine that in every occupiable subregion of the region of space occupied by an object *O* at a certain time *t*, there is an object that exists at *t* and is a part of *O*. Briefly, van Inwagen's argument is that if DAUP is true, then no material object can survive changes in its parts; but human beings are material objects, and they can survive changes in their parts; therefore, DAUP is false. The Body-minus Puzzle is integral in this argument. Consider a human being—Descartes, say. If DAUP is true, then there is such a thing as Descartes-minus, the object that includes all of Descartes except for his left leg. Now, if it is possible for Descartes to survive the loss of his leg, then it is possible for Descartes to become identical with Descartes-minus. But Descartes cannot become identical with Descartes-minus, since it is impossible for *two* things to become *one*. Therefore, either Descartes cannot survive the loss of his left leg, or there is no such thing as Descartes-minus. Van Inwagen opts for the latter alternative, and since the existence of Descartes-minus is entailed by DAUP, he concludes that DAUP is false. Since the existence of something like Descartes-minus is also entailed by

(EA_V) If the *p*s compose a human being, they compose something that could be a proper part of a human being.

van Inwagen effectively denies the PACP for cases where it implies that (EA_V) is true. And since he obviously thinks that human beings *can* survive changes in their parts, and since he denies the possibility of colocation and (in other work) contingent identity, he is furthermore committed to the conclusion that the Essentialist Assumption is false for cases where it implies that the parts of a human being compose something that cannot survive changes in its parts.

In Chapter 11, Roderick Chisholm effectively denies the PACP for all substitution instances of R that imply that objects do not have their parts essentially. On Chisholm's view, for any objects x and y, if x is a part of y, then, necessarily, y exists only if x is a part of it. This view is known as "mereological essentialism." Mereological essentialism solves some of the puzzles that raise the problem of material constitution. For example, it solves the Ship of Theseus Puzzle by denying that the *p*s that compose a ship compose anything that can undergo part replacement. If mereological essentialism is correct, then presumably the plank-hoarder's ship is identical with the original, since that is the ship composed of all of the original parts. (Though one might also think that to disassemble a ship is to destroy it and that a ship once destroyed cannot be brought back into existence, in which case no ship is identical with the original.) But there are also puzzles that it will not solve.[42] For example, Lumpl can survive being squeezed into a ball, whereas Goliath cannot; thus, there is pressure to identify Lumpl and Goliath and also pressure to say that they are distinct, and none of this comes from the presupposition that either can gain or lose material parts. Clearly, then, mereological essentialism by itself is not a complete solution to the problem.[43] Still, I have included it in this category rather than the "Partial Solutions" category because I take it that it is unlikely that one will both endorse mereological essentialism and reject the Identity Assumption or the Necessity Assumption. Thus, like van Inwagen's rejection of DAUP and unlike the other partial solutions, mereological essentialism seems most likely to be part of a total solution that will ultimately belong in the present category.

Perhaps the most pressing concern for mereological essentialism is that it does not seem to accord with our ordinary intuitions about certain objects—for example, ships, statues, and stars—that they *do* persist through changes in their parts. This is the concern that Chisholm mainly tries to address in Chapter 12. According to Chisholm, there are at least two different senses of the "is" of identity: a "loose and popular" sense and a "strict and philosophical sense." Suppose you have a ship that is composed of certain parts, and suppose one of those parts is annihilated. On Chisholm's view, strictly speaking the resulting ship is distinct from the original; but since it is inconvenient to pay attention to minor differences like that, in ordinary parlance we treat the two ships *as if* they were identical. We refer to them by the same name (e.g., the Ship of Theseus); and we say things like "This ship is getting run down; look at how its planks have been chipped." But strictly speaking, the Ship of Theseus (and every other putatively persisting object) is a logical fiction, and all of our statements about such things must be recognized as really being about the various objects that "stand in" for them, or represent them, at various times.[44] So, for example, "The Ship of Theseus had *p* as a part yesterday but does not today" is true in the loose and popular sense only if "The object that stood in for the ship of Theseus yesterday had *p* as a part and the object that stands in for it today does not have *p* as a part" is true in the strict and philosophical sense.

One might be tempted to interpret this view as implying that there really are no such things as tables, chairs, ships, and so on. And in one sense this interpretation would be correct. We ordinarily assume that a ship, table, or chair is the sort of thing that can survive changes in its parts. Thus, given our understanding of what it is to be a ship, table, or chair, Chisholm denies that there are any such things. But another way to take Chisholm's view is as a *revision* of our understanding of what it is to be a ship, table, or chair. We think that they are the sorts of things that can survive changes in their parts; Chisholm disagrees. It's not that he thinks that there are no tables, chairs, or ships; it's just that where we see *one* ship lasting over time, Chisholm sees many, coming into and passing out of existence.

Finally, in Chapter 12, Michael Burke effectively rejects the conjunction of the Essentialist Assumption and PACP for every substitution instance for F and R. On Burke's view, puzzles about material constitution arise whenever we have objects *a* and *b* that appear to be of different kinds (i.e., objects that appear to be of kinds that have different persistence conditions associated with them).[45] So, for example, the Lumpl/Goliath Puzzle arises because we appear to have a *statue* and a *piece of clay* sharing all of the same parts and because the persistence conditions associated with the term 'statue' differ from those associated with the term 'piece of clay'. But, according to Burke, this appearance poses a problem only if we suppose that *every* statue has the persistence conditions associated with the term 'statue' and *every* piece of clay has the persistence conditions associated with the term 'piece of clay'. If we reject that supposition, the problem goes away. The way is clear for us to say that Lumpl is identical with Goliath; for we can say that Lumpl/Goliath is *both* a statue and a piece of clay, but it has just one set of persistence conditions—presumably those associated with the term 'statue'. In general, then, Burke's solution is to grant that the same object can satisfy more than one sortal, to deny that every object that satisfies a given sortal has the persistence conditions associated with that sortal, and to claim that every object has the persistence conditions associated with just *one* of the sortals it satisfies. Thus, it turns out on Burke's view that we can never have a case where there are *p*s that compose an object *a* that has one set of persistence conditions and an object *b* that has another, different set of persistence conditions. In other words, we can never have a case where there are *p*s that compose an object *a* that essentially bears a certain relation R to its parts and an object *b* that does not essentially bear R to its parts. But if that is true, then there can be no instances of R and F for which the Essentialist Assumption and PACP are both satisfied.

3.4 Indeterminacy Solutions

These will be any solutions that attempt to solve the problem by saying that the Identity Assumption, the Necessity Assumption, or the conjunction of the other three is neither true nor false. The only indeterminacy solutions that I am aware of that have been discussed in any detail as such are solutions (such as Parsons's) that maintain that the Identity Assumption is indeterminate because it is sometimes indeterminate whether '$x = y$' is true. But, as we shall see, Frances Howard-Snyder at least opens the door for other indeterminacy solutions to be considered as well.

In Chapter 13, Terence Parsons defends the conclusion that identity is sometimes indeterminate. Parsons's view is motivated in part by puzzles about material constitution, but also by a variety of other cases where our intuitions about identity claims seem to be clouded. On his view, the reason we sometimes cannot tell whether an object *a* and an object *b* are identical is that sometimes there simply is no fact of the matter whether *a* is identical with *b*. It's not just that we can't discern the facts, or that our language is too imprecise to express the facts; rather, on his view, in some cases there really *is* no fact about whether or not a given identity claim is true.

Of course, this claim is not without its problems, and Parsons's essay is aimed specifically at addressing some of them. Suppose, for example, that there are objects x and y such that it is indeterminate whether x is identical with y. Clearly, it is not indeterminate that x is identical with x; thus, it seems, there is something true of x—namely, that x is definitely identical with x—but not true of y. Thus, it seems x must be distinct from y, contrary to the initial hypothesis. Moreover, it seems that the set $\{x, x\}$ will be distinct from the set $\{x, y\}$ since, again, it is definitely true that the members of the first set are identical, whereas it is indefinitely true that the members of the second set are identical. But if $\{x, x\}$ and $\{x, y\}$ are distinct, that could only be because they have different members; thus, it seems to follow that x and y are distinct, again, contrary to the initial hypothesis. Finally, it seems that x has a property that y lacks: namely, the property of being indeterminately identical with y. But then, by Leibniz's Law, it follows that x and y are distinct, again contrary to the initial hypothesis.

These might appear to be just different formulations of the same objection, but in fact they rely on different principles. The first objection relies on this principle:

(P1) If it is true of x that P and it is not true of y that P, then $x \neq$ y.

The second relies on this:

(P2) If it is indeterminate whether sets A and B have the same members, then A ≠ B.

The third relies on a version of the principle of *property abstraction*. Roughly, the principle of property abstraction allows us to convert *predicates* into *properties*: it allows us to infer from the fact that, say, Sam *is human* that there is a property *being human* that Sam has. More exactly (and more generally), the principle says:

(P3) There is some class C of predicates such that, for any φ in C, if 'φx' is true then (i) there exists the property of being a y such that φy and (ii) x has that property.[46]

The principle comes in different versions depending upon what kinds of predicates are taken to be members of C.

Parsons replies to the first two objections by arguing that the principles they rely on are false, at least where indeterminacy is concerned. Regarding the third, he shows that the argument employed by that objection can be employed to rule out *any* claim of indeterminacy, not just claims of indeterminate identity. Thus, if one believes that there is indeterminacy in the world, one might just conclude from this that property abstraction is invalid for predicates involving indeterminacy. And this is the conclusion that Parsons recommends. He points out that various well-known paradoxes show that there are some predicates for which (P3) is obviously invalid;[47] some, therefore, will need to be excluded from C. Thus, he concludes that what the argument shows is just that predicates involving indeterminacy are among those that need to be excluded; and since this restriction is not peculiar to indeterminate *identity*, he concludes that the third objection fails to show that indeterminate identity is any more problematic than indeterminacy in general.

Closely related to the view that sometimes identity is indeterminate is the view that sometimes *existence* is indeterminate. This latter view is the view that Frances Howard-Snyder sets out to defend in Chapter 14. In particular, she argues that if we accept the view that objects have essential properties, then we are committed to the view that sometimes existence itself is vague. In other words, we are committed to the view that there "are" borderline objects—things that neither exist nor fail to exist. I should note that in one sense Howard-Snyder's essay does not belong in the present section. Her favored solution to the Body-minus Puzzle is to reject outright the claim that Body-minus exists (and with it the Essentialist Assumption, DAUP, and the stronger doctrine that every filled region of space contains an object). But I have included her essay in this section because it ultimately defends a view that opens the door to a variety of other indeterminacy solutions. If there really is indeterminacy in the world (and not just in our language about the world), then the door is open for one to solve any particular puzzle about material constitution by denying that it is definitely true that *a* exists or that *b* exists or that *a* and *b* are essentially related to their parts in different ways. In other words, one might appeal to indeterminacy to deny the Existence Assumption, the Essentialist Assumption, or the PACP.[48]

In brief outline, Howard-Snyder's argument is that if we reject the doctrine of temporal parts, then we must solve the Body-minus Puzzle by rejecting the view that Body-minus exists; but if we do that, then we must reject the view that, for any filled region of space, there is an object that fills that region; and if we do that, then we are committed to the conclusion that *composition* is vague; and if composition is vague, it follows that existence is vague. There are many places along the way where one might resist her argument, but I will discuss only one here. I point it out merely because to pursue it would be to chase a red herring.

One might try to resist her argument by defending the doctrine of temporal parts. But, as we shall see below, even if the doctrine of temporal parts is true, there are still puzzles about material constitution that the doctrine of temporal parts alone cannot solve. In particular, the doctrine cannot solve puzzles about objects that in fact share all of their parts throughout their whole lives but might not have. Consider the collection of all the objects that ever were and ever will be parts of me. According to the temporal parts theorist, that collection (as opposed to the collection of all the objects that are parts of me *at the present time*) constitutes me. But it might not have. I might have had an additional molecule as a part at every moment throughout my entire life. But, in that case, the collection of molecules that in fact constitutes me would have been just a *part* of me—a very large, temporally extended part, no doubt; but still just a part of me. Thus, we face a puzzle just like the Body-minus Puzzle: Something that in fact constitutes me (call it Body-minus) could have failed to constitute me by being only a part of me. The doctrine of temporal parts does not solve this puzzle, but denying (as Howard-Snyder does) the claim that there is such a thing as Body-minus *does* solve the puzzle. Thus, defending the doctrine of temporal parts is no way to escape Howard-Snyder's argument.

3.5 Partial Solutions: Relative Identity and the Doctrine of Temporal Parts

We have now completed our taxonomy of complete solutions to the problem of material constitution. What remains is to discuss two of the most popular partial solutions to the problem.

One way to solve many of the puzzles that raise the problem of material constitution is to maintain that it is possible to have an object *a* and an object *b* that are the same F but not the same G (where F and G are sortal terms), even if *a* is a G and *b* is a G. So, for example, one might think that Tibbles and Body-minus are the same cat but not the same lump of feline tissue, or that the debtor-today and the debtor-several-weeks-ago are the same human being but not the same collection of particles. On this view, it does not follow from the fact that *a* is the same F as *b* that *a* is *identical* (absolutely and unqualifiedly) with *b*. Hence the attractiveness of this solution: in puzzles about material constitution, we don't want to say that the relevant *a* and *b* are identical, but we do generally want to say that they are the same *something*. This sort of solution enables us to say both of these things. To adopt it is to adopt a "relative identity" solution, for, on this view, identity is seen as being relative to a sortal.[49]

As far as I know, the view that identity is sortal relative has its origin in the work of Peter Geach. Chapter 15 contains three selections from the third edition of his book, *Reference and Generality*. In the first selection, Geach briefly states his view that identity is sortal relative. According to Geach, it simply makes no sense to affirm a claim of the form '$x = y$'

unless that is taken to be shorthand for a claim of the form '*x* is the same F as *y*'. Thus, for Geach, there is no such thing as absolute, unqualified identity. The second selection provides background information on Geach's distinction between a name *for* something and a name *of* something, which is crucial for understanding the discussion that follows in the third selection. In the third selection Geach presents the following version of the "problem of the many" (see above, p. xxxiii): Consider Tibbles the cat, and consider that part of Tibbles that includes all of her except for one hair. Now, if Tibbles were to lose a hair, that part would be a cat. But, of course, destroying a hair doesn't bring a cat into existence; therefore, that part must already be a cat even before Tibbles loses the hair. But that means that for every hair that Tibbles has, there is a cat that shares all of its parts with Tibbles except for that hair. Thus, there are countless cats in the region occupied by Tibbles. Obviously this puzzle bears strong resemblance to the Body-minus Puzzle, but strictly speaking it raises a different problem. The problem raised by this puzzle is that it seems certain proper parts of, say, cats have all of the relevant qualities to themselves count as cats, but we do not ordinarily count them as such; therefore, it is not clear whether we should admit that there are countless *more* cats, ships, and people than we think there are or whether we should simply refuse to count *anything* as a cat, ship, or person. Geach chooses neither of these alternatives. His solution, in short, is to say that all of these "cats" are the *same* cat but different lumps of feline tissue.

In Chapter 16, Hugh Chandler recommends what is essentially a relative identity solution to a puzzle that is very much like the Ship of Theseus Puzzle. Chandler does not describe his own view as a relative identity solution, and he says nothing about whether he thinks that there are any true unqualified (or absolute) identity claims. Nevertheless, it seems clear that this is the sort of solution he means to endorse. Consider the Ship of Theseus. (Since Chandler's puzzle is substantially the same as the Ship of Theseus Puzzle, I will for the sake of convenience discuss his solution in terms of the latter puzzle rather than in terms of his own.) The problem is that we seem to have equally good reason to identify the continuously repaired ship with the original and to identify the plank-hoarder's ship with the original. But, given our ordinary notion of identity, we can't have it both ways. Chandler, however, offers the following solution: We grant that it is possible for an object to have the property of being such that, when it is traced according to one set of rules of re-identification it is traceable to one object, and when it is traced according to another set of rules of re-identification, it is traceable to another object. Thus, if we trace the original ship according to the rules of re-identification for ships, we might trace it to the continuously repaired ship; but if we trace it according to the rules for collections of planks (or historical relics), we will trace it to the plank-hoarder's ship. Why does this count as a relative identity solution? Suppose we define '*x* is the same F as *y*' as follows:

> *x* is the same F as $y =_{DF}$ if *x* is traced according to the rules for re-identifying Fs, *x* is traceable to *y*.

Given this definition, it turns out that Chandler's proposal is equivalent to the claim that something might be the same F as *y* but not the same G, and that the original Ship of Theseus in particular is the same ship as the continuously repaired ship, but not the same collection of planks, despite the fact that the original ship and the continuously repaired ship are both ships and collections of planks.

There is a vast literature discussing the merits and demerits of the view that identity is sortal relative, and it is beyond the scope of this essay to take those up here. However, what I do want to point out is that even if relative identity is viable, it does not really qualify as a complete solution to the problem of material constitution. Relative identity theorists fall into a variety of different camps, but I take it that what they would all agree on is that all expressions of the form '$x = y$' in the assumptions listed in Section 1 should be replaced by claims of the form '*x* is the same F as *y*'. But this alone will not suffice to solve the problem of material constitution. To see why, consider the Lumpl/Goliath Puzzle from the point of view of a relative identity theorist. If what I have said so far is right, the relative identity theorist will reject the Identity Assumption and Necessity Assumption as they stand, but she could endorse appropriately modified versions of those assumptions. So, for example, she could endorse:

> Identity Assumption$_R$: For all *x*, *y*, *ps* , and *t*: If the *ps* compose *x* at *t* and the *ps* compose *y* at *t* then, for some F, *x* is the same F as *y*.

> Necessity Assumption$_R$: For all *x* and *y*: If *x* is the same F as *y* then, necessarily, *x* is the same F as *y*.

These assumptions are no less reasonable than the original versions. But once we have these in place, the problem of material constitution arises again with a vengeance. For suppose Lumpl and Goliath come into and pass out of existence in the way described in the original puzzle, and suppose they have the essential properties assigned to them in the original puzzle. Then, by the Identity Assumption$_R$, for some F, Lumpl is the same F as Goliath; by the Necessity Assumption$_R$, if Lumpl *is* the same F as Goliath, then Lumpl could not have failed to be the same F as Goliath; but for any sortal you pick as the value of F (such that Lumpl could plausibly be construed as in fact the same F as Goliath), you could tell a story to show that

Lumpl could have failed to be the same F as Goliath. Clearly Lumpl could have failed to be the same statue as Goliath (the original story shows that); Lumpl could also have failed to be the same lump as Goliath (if, say, Goliath's finger had been annihilated). Thus, to solve this puzzle the relative identity theorist must reject the new version of the Identity Assumption, reject the new version of the Necessity Assumption, or reject the conjunction of the other three. But that is just to say that she must still solve the problem of material constitution like everyone else. Appeal to relative identity alone is not sufficient.

The second partial solution is the doctrine of temporal parts. We have already discussed this view briefly above (pp. xxx and xlvi), but now it is time to fill in some missing details. The doctrine of temporal parts is a theory about how objects persist over time. Some say that objects persist over time by being wholly present at every moment at which they exist; others say that objects persist by being only partially present at those moments. The latter view is the doctrine of temporal parts. On that view, as we have already seen, objects are "spread out" in time in much the same way they are spread out in space. The object that exactly fills the region of spacetime occupied by my body from 1 p.m. today until 2 p.m. is not *me*; rather, it is just a part of me. What *I* am, strictly speaking, is an object that fills the region of spacetime occupied by my body from the beginning of my life to its end. Everything in that region is either a spatial part of me or a temporal part.[50]

Mark Heller's main goal in Chapter 17 is to provide a clear statement of the doctrine of temporal parts. He also responds to what he takes to be Thomson's main objection to the doctrine—that the doctrine seems to imply that new things are continually coming into existence *ex nihilo*. (See Chapter 3 and the above discussion of it for details.) What I want to focus on, however, is simply how the doctrine is supposed to solve the Body-minus Puzzle. Consider again Tibbles and Body-minus. According to the doctrine of temporal parts, Tibbles and Body-minus are both four-dimensional objects, spread out in time just as they are spread out in space. In other words, what Tibbles is, strictly speaking, is that thing that fills the region of spacetime occupied by her body *throughout her entire life*; and similarly for Body-minus. But now the pressure to identify Tibbles and Body-minus is relieved. Clearly Tibbles does not share all of her spatial parts with Body-minus throughout her entire life; thus, she does not share all of her temporal parts with Body-minus. For example, consider the *temporal* part of Tibbles that includes all of her life up to the annihilation of her tail. That object is not a temporal part of Body-minus. It is too big: it includes the whole career of a tail, whereas no temporal part of Body-minus includes any such thing. But if Tibbles and Body-minus do not share all of their temporal parts, then they do not share all of their parts;

thus, the Identity Assumption gives us no reason to identify Tibbles and Body-minus.

One might object here that the Identity Assumption *does* give us reason to identify Tibbles and Body-minus. It says that if the *p*s compose *x* at *t* and the *p*s compose *y* at *t*, then *x* is identical with *y*; but, though Tibbles and Body-minus don't share all of the same spatial parts throughout their entire lives, there is nonetheless *a time* at which they share all of their spatial parts. And at that time, it seems the Identity Assumption forces us to identify Tibbles with Body-minus. But here we need to distinguish between two ways of reading the Identity Assumption:

(IA1) For all *x*, *y*, *p*s, and *t*: If the *p*s compose *x*-at-*t* and the *p*s compose *y*-at-*t*, then *x* is identical with *y*.

(IA2) For all *x*, *y*, *p*s, and *t*: If, at *t*, the *p*s compose *x* and, at *t*, the *p*s compose *y*, then *x* is identical with *y*.

Normally, these two claims are equivalent. But within the context of the doctrine of temporal parts, they are not. In that context, (IA1) is obviously false. Tibbles-today is a temporal part of Tibbles, just as Body-minus-today is a temporal part of Body-minus. But, of course, it does not follow from the fact that Tibbles-today and Body-minus-today share all of the same parts that Tibbles herself and Body-minus herself are identical. To say that would be as absurd as saying that if my arm and myself share a part in common (e.g., my forearm), then my arm and myself are identical. Thus, (IA2) is what we want; but there is no pressure from (IA2) to identify Tibbles with Body-minus. The *p*s that today compose Tibbles (i.e., the *p*s that are such that today it is true that they compose *all* of Tibbles and not just one of her temporal parts) compose a four-dimensional object; and if they compose her today, then they composed her yesterday and in fact every day of her life. And similarly for Body-minus. Thus, properly understood, the Identity Assumption gives no reason to identify Tibbles with Body-minus.

Again, there are various objections one might raise to the doctrine of temporal parts, but my main goal here is simply to point out why it does not count as a complete solution to the problem of material constitution. In short, the doctrine of temporal parts solves the puzzles it solves only because it turns out that, within the context of that doctrine, the objects mentioned in the puzzles do not constitute one another. Thus, those puzzles do not present the temporal parts theorist with an object *a* and an object *b* that share all of the same parts and yet are essentially related to those parts in different ways. But other puzzles do. In particular, any puzzle that presents us with an object *a* and an object *b* that share all of their spatial parts throughout their entire lives and yet are essentially related to those parts in different ways will raise the problem of material constitution for a temporal parts theorist. Hence the importance of the Lumpl/Goliath Puzzle, which was crafted specifically to be a problem for temporal parts theorists.

Notes

1. For purposes of this introduction, constitution is to be understood as symmetric. That is, for any *x* and *y*, *x* constitutes *y* if and only if *y* constitutes *x*. This is nonstandard. Often people are inclined to say, for example, that a lump constitutes a statue but not vice versa. (See, e.g., the contributions by Doepke and Chandler.) However, it will simplify my presentation to take constitution as symmetric, and nothing substantial hangs on this decision.

2. Noonan 1988, 222.

3. Though in fact Peter Unger (Chapter 9) and Peter Geach (Chapter 15) do not defend their views as solutions to puzzles about material constitution. Unger defends his view as a response to the *sorites* paradox; Geach defends his as a solution to what is now referred to as "the problem of the many." For discussion of the sorites paradox, see Unger's essay in this volume. For discussion of the problem of the many, see below pp. xxxii and xlviii and Chapter 4, as well as Unger 1980 and van Inwagen 1990.

4. A property P is *essential* to an object *x* just in case *x* could not exist and fail to have P.

5. My information about Epicharmus's play comes from Sedley 1982, 255-56.

6. For details see Sedley 1982.

7. See Plato, *Phaedo* 58a and Plutarch, *Life of Theseus* 23.

8. According to Plutarch,

> The ship on which he [Theseus] sailed with the youths and was kept safe [coming] back, the thirty-oared vessel, the Athenians preserved until the time of Demetrius of Phalerus, removing the old pieces of wood and putting in strong ones, and putting them together so that the ship was a model for the philosophers with respect to the disputed argument about growing, some of them saying it remained the same, some of them saying it did not remain the same. (*Life of Theseus* 23, my translation)

9. See Sedley 1982 for details.

10. Geach, in turn, developed the puzzle from a *sophisma* of William of Sherwood. (See pp. 60–61. of Sherwood 1968.) Sherwood's puzzle closely resembles the Stoic version of the puzzle. A similar puzzle involving Tibbles the cat appears in Geach's third edition of *Reference and Generality* (the selection is reprinted here in Chapter 15). It is not clear to me whether Geach takes that puzzle to be a version of the Body-minus Puzzle; but, as it is formulated there, it seems to raise issues other than those raised by the Body-minus Puzzle. (For more on this, see my discussion of Geach's article on pp. xlvii–xlviii below.)

11. Chapter 6 of this volume.

12. See below, Section 3.5.

13. I have tried to keep the discussion in this section as informal and non-technical as possible. The appendix at the end of this volume contains a formal presentation of the five assumptions, as well as a formal argument showing how they are incompatible with one another. See also Rea 1995a.

14. It will be convenient to think of the relevant *ps* in the puzzles discussed in this essay as particles (the one exception being the Ship of Theseus Puzzle, where it is more convenient to think of the relevant *ps* as planks of wood).

15. F and R are thus schematic letters rather than variables.

16. This thesis is similar to the mereological axiom of extensionality. (See Simons 1987, 28 as well as pp. xxxi and 48 below.) Mereology is the logic of the part/whole relation. Mereological extensionality corresponds to the set-theoretic axiom of extensionality, according to which a set A is identical with a set B just in case A and B share all of their members in common. According to mereological extensionality, if *x* and *y* share all of the same parts, *x* is identical with *y*. The only difference between the two theses is that the Identity Assumption requires that *x* and *y* share all of the same parts *at the same time*, whereas mereological extensionality does not.

17. One might doubt that this is a presupposition of the puzzle. After all, one might very reasonably think that the point of the puzzle is just to show that the parts of cats *like post-accident Tibbles* compose something that might fail to be a cat by being a proper part of a cat. Thus, one might think, we should take the Existence Assumption of the puzzle as asserting the existence of cats just like post-accident Tibbles—call them "stubbies"—and we should take the crucial assumptions of the puzzle as being assumptions about stubbies rather than about cats. This is indeed a reasonable approach to the puzzle, but it is one I reject. The reason, in short, is that we can construct versions of the Body-minus Puzzle that do not involve stubbies. For example, any story about a cat that *gains* a part (no matter how small) will present us with a version of the Body-minus Puzzle. And I take it that it is more plausible to construe all of these different versions as simply supplying different examples to motivate (3) rather than as providing us with a wide variety of Existence Assumptions about strange kinds of cats.

18. See, for example, Burke 1980.

19. One might object that the point of the puzzle is to show that our intuition that the original can't undergo complete part replacement is just as strong as our intuition that it can. And, indeed, some of what I said earlier might be taken to suggest as much. The point is well taken, and I suppose that if this is really true, then rejecting the Necessity Assumption will not suffice to tell us which ship is identical with the original. We will need, in addition, further investigation into the essential properties of ships. Or, to put it another way, we will need to know whether the essential properties for ships are those associated with Ship A or with Ship B. Once we have answered that question, we can simply identify the Ship of Theseus with whichever of the two has the essential properties of a ship. (Obviously it can't be the case that both have the correct set of essential properties, for their essential properties are incompatible with one another.) This same difficulty will beset *any* puzzle about material constitution where the relevant *a* and *b* do not belong to well-defined kinds, or where it is not reasonably clear what are the essential properties associated with the kinds to which *a* and *b* belong.

20. If, in a particular story, it turns out that *a* and *b* exist but do not constitute one another, then we simply do not have a story that raises the problem. Thus "deny that *a* and *b* constitute one another" will not count as a general strategy for solving the problem.

21. We would have a more precise correspondence if the assumption contained a biconditional.

22. Others include Peter Simons 1985 and 1987, and E. J. Lowe 1989.

23. A *qualitative* property is one that can be had by more than one object. So, for example, such properties as *being six feet tall*, *being blue all over*, and *weighing 500 pounds* are qualitative. Properties such as *being identical with Socrates* are not.

24. This is the most common way of describing the distinction; but obviously it ignores the fact that, according to some scientific theories, space and time are so intertwined that there is no objective distinction between spatial and temporal regions. It also ignores the fact that I might have parts that are neither spatial parts nor temporal parts according to these definitions. For example, my-hand-from-now-until-two-o'-clock seems to be some kind of part of me in the temporal parts theorist's universe, but, given the above definitions, it is neither a spatial part of me nor a temporal part of me. Thus, temporal parts theorists might do better to cease talking of temporal parts altogether and to talk instead of *spatiotemporal* parts. For present purposes, however, I will continue to use the usual terminology.

25. This just follows from the above definition of 'temporal part' and the obvious fact that every object fills the sum of all of the regions of space that it occupies throughout its entire career.

26. See note 16.

27. Strictly speaking, we need a further assumption to get from P* to the problem of the many: the assumption that for any occupiable subregion R of the region of space occupied by a particular object O, there is another object (a part of O) that occupies R. Some philosophers, such as Peter van Inwagen (Chapter 10) deny this assumption; and without it, we have no reason to think that the "countless overlapping objects" are really objects at all.

28. Though, Sosa notes, the reverse is true as well. For example, *this lump of snow's being round* is an event that is ontologically dependent on an object—namely, this lump of snow.

29. Sosa explicitly denies that *basic* entities can be colocated (where a basic entity is one that depends on nothing but the coexistence of its proper parts). But, on this view, familiar macrophysical objects will not count as basic entities in that sense.

30. In fact, I think that Aristotle's own view was very much like the one sketched by Sosa, with the following exception: Aristotle did not believe that two objects could be in the same place at the same time. Rather, he believed (so I think) that in cases of material constitution such as those described throughout this essay, the relevant *a* and *b* are distinct but nevertheless *one thing*. In other words, he believed that *numerical* sameness does not entail identity. For more on this view, see Matthews 1982 and 1992, and Rea 1995b.

31. It is more common to say that a rigid designator is a name that refers to the same thing in every possible world in which that thing exists and to nothing in worlds in which that thing does not exist (where a "possible world" is just a complete way things might have been). However, there are a variety of problems with this for-

mulation, and it would take us too far afield to try to discuss them here. (But see Plantinga 1974, 77-81 and 1985, 76-87.) The formulation I have chosen expresses what I take to be the intent of the more common formulation but (I hope) avoids some of the problems.

32. On the usual understanding of modal statements, (i) 'Possibly P' is equivalent to 'There is a possible world in which P', (ii) 'Necessarily P' is equivalent to 'P is the case in every possible world', (iii) '*x* is possibly F' is equivalent to 'There is a possible world in which *x* is F', and (iv) '*x* is necessarily (or essentially) F' is equivalent to '*x* is F in every possible world in which *x* exists'. A possible world is just a (complete) way things might have been, and an object *x* exists in a world W just in case *x* would have existed had W been actual.

33. Notice that the name 'the teacher of Plato' *can* be used to refer to Socrates in modal contexts. For example, a sentence like 'Possibly: The teacher of Plato is not snub-nosed' could be taken to mean that *Socrates* might not have been snub-nosed rather than that Plato might have had a different, non-snub-nosed teacher. Thus, one might say that a name for *x* is *used rigidly* whenever it is used to refer to *x* in modal contexts, and one might then go on to say that though any name *can* be used rigidly, only proper names are *always* used rigidly, and hence only proper names really deserve to be called *rigid designators*.

34. I take it that this is intended to be a refinement or an explanation rather than a contradiction of the earlier claim that, for example, the name 'Lumpl' refers to the same *lump* in modal contexts as it does in non-modal contexts. The idea, as I see it, is that the earlier claim is *appropriate*, though, strictly speaking, it is not true. According to the above theory, what 'Lumpl' really refers to in modal contexts is an individual concept; and, of course, a *concept* is not the same lump as anything. Thus, the earlier claim is false. Still, sentences like (7) express propositions that are ultimately about lumps in other possible worlds, and those lumps (Gibbard thinks) *are* the same lump as Lumpl. So it is appropriate to say that 'Lumpl' refers in (7) to the same lump as it does in non-modal contexts, but we must keep in mind that it is not strictly correct to say this.

35. Presumably names such as 'α' evoke no counterpart relations.

36. And this despite the fact that 'Necessarily, Goliath = Goliath' is true.

37. I do not at all mean to suggest that this is the *only* difference, nor do I mean to suggest that the differences are merely terminological. Lewis 1986 section 4.2 shows clearly and thoroughly how his counterpart theory resembles and differs from Gibbard's (but see also p. 123, n. 3 of this volume). Plantinga 1987 takes up the question whether Lewis's theory really should be considered a realist (rather than a reductionist) theory about what it is for objects to have modal properties.

38. Recall that the actual world is itself a possible world.

39. One might think that by extending counterpart theory in the way that I have suggested, we effectively deny that anything exists at more than one time. But if we believe that there is such a thing as the *sum* of an object's temporal counterparts—that is, if we believe that an object's temporal counterparts compose some further object—we are not committed to this conclusion. For we can say that the sum of an object's temporal counterparts exists at more than one time just in case it has parts at more than one time, which, presumably, it does. This view is essentially equivalent to the doctrine of temporal parts described in Section 3.5.

40. Something is simple just in case it lacks proper parts—that is, just in case it lacks any parts other than itself.

41. This alone, of course, does not constitute a complete solution to the problem of material constitution. But in fact he has one. In his 1990 essay, van Inwagen makes it clear that (i) he would deny the Existence Assumption for all substitution instances of F except those where F is a living organism, (ii) he would deny the Essentialist Assumption in all cases where it implies that the *p*s that compose a living organism compose something that cannot survive complete part replacement, and (iii) he would deny the PACP in all cases where it implies that the *p*s that compose an F (where F is a natural-kind term) compose something that could become a non-F.

42. Unless the properties of a thing are considered to be among its parts.

43. Elsewhere, however, Chisholm completes his solution. The solution rests on a distinction between *substances* and *modes*. A substance is any object that has all of its parts essentially; a mode is a non-substance that exists just in case a particular substance exemplifies a certain property. Everything that we would normally be inclined to call an object is either a substance or a mode. So, for example, the collection of particles that constitutes Goliath at a certain time might be a substance, whereas both Goliath and Lumpl might simply be modes of that substance (since Lumpl exists just in case the collection exemplifies the property of being lumpish, and Goliath exists just in case the collection exemplifies the property of being Goliath-shaped). Modes, on his view, are not objects in the fullest sense of the term—they are more like events. Thus (assuming the Identity Assumption talks about objects) it is no violation of the Identity Assumption to suppose that modes can share all of their parts with substances or with one another. Chisholm's solution, then, is to say that in every case where it appears that an object *a* and an object *b* constitute one another and yet are essentially related to their parts in different ways, either *a* is a mode of *b*, *b* is a mode of *a*, or *a* and *b* are both modes of some further substance.

44. One might notice a resemblance between Chisholm's view and those of our contingent identity theorists. In particular, Chisholm's view bears strong resemblance to the sort of counterpart theory I suggested on behalf of Myro, according to which an object (such as the Ship of Theseus) does not *itself* exist at many different times; rather, it exists according to many different times by having counterparts—or representatives—at those times.

45. I take it that, for Burke, persistence conditions include at least some essential properties that have nothing to do with persistence. For example, I take it that on Burke's view an object that could have originated from an unfertilized egg and an object that couldn't have originated from an unfertilized egg differ in their persistence conditions, despite the fact that persistence does not seem to be what is at issue in this case.

46. Still more formally, this principle states that from φx we can infer $\lambda y(\varphi y)(x)$, where 'φx' is any formula in which x is a free variable, and '$\lambda y(\varphi y)(x)$' is to be taken as an abbreviation for 'x has the property of being a y such that φy'.

47. For example, Grelling's paradox: Consider the predicate 'is heterological'. 'Heterological' means 'is not true of itself'; so, for example, the word 'unspeakable' is heterological (since it can be spoken), 'long' is heterological (since it is relatively

short), and so on. But if 'unspeakable' is heterological, then, by the principle of property abstraction, we can infer that there exists the property of *being a* y *such that* y *is heterological.* And, by the law of excluded middle, it follows that 'heterological' either has that property or does not. But if 'heterological' has the property of being heterological, then it is not true of itself, in which case it is not heterological. On the other hand, if it lacks the property of being heterological, then it is true of itself, in which case it is heterological. So it turns out that 'heterological' is heterological if and only if 'heterological' is not heterological. Thus, we might conclude that property abstraction is invalid for this predicate. For discussion of other, similar paradoxes, see Haack 1978, Chapter 8.

48. The only kind of indeterminacy solution I have not yet considered is one that would hold that the Necessity Assumption is neither true nor false. The reason I have not considered it is that I cannot imagine any reason for endorsing such a solution. The view that identity is sometimes indeterminate constitutes no reason to think that the Necessity Assumption is neither true nor false, for that assumption simply says that *if* a particular identity claim is true—that is, definitely true—then it is necessarily true. So if it turns out that a particular identity claim is neither true nor false, the Necessity Assumption still holds; it just does not follow from that assumption that the claim in question is necessarily true.

49. Some contributors to this volume (e.g., Doepke and Burke) classify this sort of solution together with the sort offered by George Myro. Their reason for doing so is that in this sort of solution, identity is seen as relative to a *sortal*, whereas in Myro's identity is seen as relative to a *time*. I do not follow them in this, however, because typically those who think that identity is relative to a sortal think that expressions of the form '$x = y$' are simply ill-formed. Thus, as we shall see shortly, they do not just reject the Necessity Assumption as it is stated; they reject several others as well. Not so with Myro, however. On Myro's view, '$x = y$' is well-formed, but may only be temporarily true.

50. Or, as we saw in note 24, a *spatiotemporal* part.

PART I

Coincident Entities

1

On Being in the Same Place at the Same Time

(With One Remark About Categories and Materialism)

David Wiggins

It is a truism frequently called in evidence and confidently relied upon in philosophy that two things cannot be in the same place at the same time. Plainly this principle, which I shall call *S*, ought really to say that two things cannot *completely* occupy exactly the same place or exactly the same volume (or exactly the same subvolumes within exactly the same volume) for exactly the same period of time. No man is the same as his forearm. But there is a volume such that a man can wholly occupy it and such that both man and forearm are in it at exactly the same time. But this does not count.

More interestingly, think of a sponge and the water that makes it a wet sponge. That does not count against principle *S* either. Here we can press into service the chemical theory of molecules to distinguish subvolumes or sub-subvolumes of the total volume occupied by the sponge from those occupied by the water. But it is difficult to believe that this determination of ours to allow nothing to count against *S* gets us to the bottom of the matter. At very least, it would help to know what was the a priori or metaphysical compulsion to think in our present way about these questions. What if in defiance of fact and the actual laws of chemistry and physics the water and the sponge were so utterly mixed up that spatial distinction seemed impossible, not only at the molecular level but also at the atomic and at the subatomic? And what if you had only to squeeze to get water and sponge apart again? Surely they would be the same sponge and the same (consignment of) water afterward? And would they not have been in exactly the same place at the same time? I think I know how to resolve one, but only one, of the difficult questions which arise out of all this. For one part of the a priori basis for principle *S* is not too difficult to uncover. But *S* is still not correctly formulated.

A certain tree *T* stands (leafless, suppose) at a certain spot at time t_1 and occupies a certain volume v_1 at this time t_1. All and only v_1 is also occupied by the aggregate *W* of the cellulose molecules which compose the tree. Indeed it is their occupation of v_1 which precisely determines that the volume which the tree occupies is volume v_1. The tree *T* and the cellulose molecules *W* are thus in exactly the same place at exactly the same time. Are they identical? Now $T = W$ only if whatever is true of *T* is true of *W* (Leibniz' Law). It follows, I think, that $T = W$ only if *T* and *W* have exactly the same conditions of persistence and survival through change. But self-evidently they do not.

Suppose *T* is chopped down and then dismembered and cut up in such a way that no cellulose molecule is damaged. It seems that *W* then survives. And there is just as much wood in the world as there was before. But *T*, the tree, cannot survive such treatment. Conversely, suppose the tree is pruned and the clippings are burned, or that it undergoes an organic change which destroys some of the original wood cells. Then the tree *T* survives but *W*, the aggregate defined as the aggregate of such and such particular cellulose molecules, does not survive. Of course, you could define another notion of aggregate and give detailed conditions for suitable co-option and expulsion of members of such an aggregate. Perhaps you could get these conditions for gradual organic variation of membership exactly right and produce an entity W' with exactly the same criterion of individuation as *T*. But that would be a boring trick. You would have defined a *tree*—and not wholly in terms of molecules or wood cells. You would only have contrived an identity connection between something in the category of stuff and something in the category of substance by introducing the concept of something organized and substance-like—that is, something foreign to the category—into the category of stuff.[1]

None of this is to say that *T* is something *over and above* *W*. It precisely is not. The "is" of material constitution is not the "is" of identity. The tree is *made of* (or *constituted of* or *consists of*) *W*, but it is not identical with *W*. And "*A* is something over and above *B*" denies "*A* is (wholly composed of) *B*" or "*A* is merely (or merely consists of) *B*." If *A* is something over and above *B*, then of course $A \neq B$, but the proper point of saying "over and above" is to make the further denial that *B* fully *exhausts* the matter of *A*. But *W* does fully exhaust *T* and so *T* is not something over and above *W*.

If it is a materialistic thesis that $T = W$, then my denial that $T = W$ is a form of denial of materialism. It is interesting how very uninteresting an obstacle these Leibnizian difficulties—real though they are—put in the way of the reduction of botany and all its primitive terms to organic chemistry or to physics. (If it does not follow from $T \neq W$ that trees are something over and above their matter, how much the less can it follow that they are immanent or transcendent or supervenient or immaterial beings. This is obviously absurd for trees. A Leibnizian disproof of strict identity could never be enough to show something so intriguing or obscure.) I should expect there to be equally valid, and from the point of view of ontology almost equally unexciting, difficulties in the reduction of persons to flesh and bones,[2] in psychophysical event-materialism, and in the materialisms which one might formulate in other categories (such as the Aristotelian categories *property* and *state* or the categories *situation* and *fact*). *Over and above* is one question, *identity* is another. But of course the only stuff there is is stuff.

I shall say no more about *T* and *W* here, except to remark that what I have tried to show by this simple example is not wholly different from a philosophical thesis which it has become a commonplace of philosophy to defend in terms of different *logical types* to which such things as trees and the aggregates they "are" (= consist of) belong. I prefer to put the matter my way because it makes a smaller claim, because it leaves room for a clear statement in the object language of a perfectly intelligible connection between trees and cellulose molecules, and because of the high degree of intelligibility enjoyed by this Leibnizian principle for predicative (as opposed to constitutive) "is": If and only if *A* is an *f* (or is ϕ) then *A* is identical with an *f* (or with one of the ϕ things); and if and only if *A* is one of the *f*'s (or ϕ things) then it must share all its properties with that *f* (or ϕ thing).[3] This does not exhaust the content of standard doctrines of ranges of significance (that is, those which derive from Russell's simple or ramified Theory of Types[4]). They say much more than this about what you can and cannot say about *A*. But my own opinion is that the residue remains obscure. Let me now, however, revert to our principle *S*.

The tree and its molecules and wood cells do not disprove what was originally intended by principle *S*. What has been shown is only that we must reformulate *S* to read:

> S*: No two things *of the same kind* (that is, no two things which satisfy the same sortal or substance concept) can occupy exactly the same volume at exactly the same time.

This, I think, *is* a sort of necessary truth. It has at least three sources of support.

(*i*) Space can be mapped only by reference to its occupants, and spatial facts are conceptually dependent on the existence of facts about particulars and the identities of particulars. If space is to be mapped by reference to persisting particulars, then the nonidentity of particulars *A* and B, both of kind f, must be sufficient to establish that the place of A at $t_1 \neq$ the place of B at t_1.

(*ii*) A criterion of identity for material objects will have to be something like this:

> I_m: A is identical with B if there is some substance concept f such that A *coincides* with B under f (where f is a substance concept under which an object can be traced, individuated and distinguished from other f's, and where *coincides under f* satisfactorily defines an equivalence relation all of whose members $\langle x, y \rangle$ also satisfy the Leibnizian schema $Fx \equiv Fy$).[5]

Now I_m logically implies S^*. So if I_m is an a priori truth, then so is S^*. Finding that A and B coincide under f *settles* the question whether $A = B$. There is nothing more to decide.

(*iii*) There is a conceptual basis for an even stronger truth than S^*, namely:

> S^{**}: A and a proper part or constituent B of a third thing C, where $A \neq C$ and $A \neq B$, and where no part or constituent of A is any part or constituent of B or of C, cannot completely occupy exactly the same volume at exactly the same time.

The basis for this truth elucidates its import. Suppose A and B were distinct and in the same place at the same time. Then they could not have been distinguished by place. But then they would have had to be distinguished by their properties. But no volume or area of space can be qualified simultaneously by distinct predicates in any range (color, shape, texture, and so forth).

I think (*i*), (*ii*), and (*iii*) may come near to accounting for most of the conceptual basis for the truth that material things have to *compete for room* in the world, and that they must tend to *displace* one another, although I should not claim that they clear up all the questions which can arise about the water and the sponge, or about scientifically more realistic examples concerning chemical compounds and alloys.

A final test for the soundness of S^* or, if you wish, for Leibniz' Law, is provided by a puzzle contrived by Geach out of a discussion in William of Sherwood. A cat called Tibbles loses his tail at time t_2. But before t_2 somebody had picked out, identified, and distinguished from Tibbles a different and rather peculiar animate entity—namely, Tibbles *minus* Tibbles' tail. Let us suppose that he decided to call this entity "Tib." Suppose Tibbles was on the mat at time t_1. Then both Tib and Tibbles were on the mat at t_1. This does not violate S^* or S^{**}. But consider the position from t_3 onward when, something the worse for wear, the cat is sitting on the mat without a tail. Is there one cat or are there two cats there? Tib is certainly sitting there. In a way nothing happened to *him* at all. But so is Tibbles. For Tibbles lost his tail, survived this experience, and then at t_3 was sitting on the mat. And we agreed that Tib ≠ Tibbles. We can uphold the transitivity of identity, it seems, only if we stick by that decision at t_3 and allow that at t_3 there are two cats on the mat in exactly the same place at exactly the same time. But my adherence to S^* obliges me to reject this. So, I am obliged to find something independently wrong with the way in which the puzzle was set up. It was set up in such a way that before t_2 Tibbles had a tail as a part and Tib allegedly did *not* have a tail as a part. If one dislikes this feature (as I do), then one has to ask, "Can one identify and name a part of a cat, insist one is naming just that, and insist that what one is naming is a *cat*"? This is my argument against the supposition that one can: Does Tib have a tail or not? I mean the question in the ordinary sense of "have," not in any peculiar sense "have as a part." For in a way it is precisely the propriety of some other concept of *having as a part* which is in question. Surely Tib adjoins and is connected to a tail in the standard way in which cats who have tails are connected with their tails. There is no peculiarity in this case. Otherwise Tibbles himself might not have a tail. Surely any animal which has a tail loses a member or part of itself if its tail is cut off. But then there was no such cat as the cat who at t_1 has no tail as a part of himself. Certainly there was a cat-part which anybody could call "Tib" if they wished. But one cannot define into existence a *cat* called Tib who had no tail as part of himself at t_1 if there was no such cat at t_1. If someone thought he could, then one might ask him (before the cutting at t_2), "Is this Tib of yours the same cat as Tibbles or is he a different cat?"[6] If you cut just a little of Tibbles tail off so that Tib still still existed plus a little tail and drained Tibbles of all his blood, it does not explain why Tibs also dies: does it? Maybe.

Postscript

In this article, I urge that there are three possible bases, namely, (i) (ii) (iii) for S*. I am less happy than I must once have been with each of (i) (ii) (iii).

(i) is inconclusive—as can be seen by the possibility of adding to my last sentence the following words ".... unless, of course, there is some other way or some group of other ways of establishing that these places are different."

As regards (ii), I doubt now that I_m non-question beggingly implies S*. In order that I_m should be serviceable to our individuative practice, do we have to suppose that A's and B's coinciding *precludes* the possibility of whatever we find in the place where A is and B is separating into two separate things? Even if we do have to suppose that this is precluded, does that make it *true* to suppose it?

Meanwhile (iii) seems inconclusive too. Perhaps A and B, distinct things but supposedly co-occupying at a time *t* one and the same place, could be distinguished in respect of properties or attributes and distinguished so without any volume of space taking on inconsistent properties. It is true that if A and B were things of the same kind, then all the predicates of each of them would have to be identified within a common range. But here there is still the doubt expressed under (ii) above.

The matter is more difficult then than I supposed thirty years ago. But now let me try to make a move on an adjoining square of the board.

Insofar as we continue to take material substances of this or that particular kind seriously, and insofar as this seriousness of ours engages with an interest in the casual explanation of the interactions of bodies in the physical world, the substance concepts that we cherish will be concepts of things that *compete* for space in the world, things that do not slide into one another and out of another again and that exclude one another from a given place. These are concepts of things that oppose one another and *interact*, dependably. (For some connected and further thoughts here, see my "Substance" in Anthony Grayling (ed), *Philosophy: A Guide through the Subject* (Oxford University Press 1995).) What then is the status of S*? Is it perhaps a candidate to be an *a posteriori* necessary truth, but one founded in the expectations we have to have of sound concepts of substances? (Nb. The plural. Concepts I mean of this, that or the other kind of substance, e.g., man, bear, oak-tree, etc.)

Notes

1. There is much more to be said both about identity and about mereological treatments of the notion of aggregate. I have tried to say a little of it in *Identity and Spatio-Temporal Continuity* (Oxford, 1967), pp. 11–13, 67–68, 72.

The argument seems to apply equally to artifacts. Mrs. Jones at t_2 unpicks her husband's old sweater and winds the wool into a ball. Equating matter and object, we shall have to say the wool is the sweater. But suppose she then at t_3 crochets a pair of bed-socks with the wool. Then by transitivity the sweater is the pair of bed-socks. But the bed-socks were crocheted at t_3 out of a ball of wool which was before t_2 a sweater, and the sweater was not at t_3 crocheted out of a ball of wool which was before t_2 a sweater. We must refuse to equate matter and object, and refuse to think of this as a paradoxical refusal. It is not. Crocheting, like knitting or weaving, is a way of *making* bed-socks. The material must pre-exist the making, and survive it. But *what* is made cannot pre-exist its fabrication.

2. See *Identity*, p. 57.

3. See *ibid.*, pp. 10–11, 61.

4. See Russell's *Lectures on Logical Atomism*, VII (reprinted in *Logic and Knowledge*, ed. by R. Marsh [London, 1956], pp. 254 ff.), and G. Ryle, "Categories," *Proceedings of the Aristotelian Society* (1937–1938).

5. See "Individuation of Places and Things" (symposium with M. J. Woods),

Aristotelian Society supp. vol. XXXVII (1963), where a certain difficulty of circularity is discussed. Also *Identity*, pp. 34–36, 72.

Leibniz' Law is only a criterion of difference, and in any case it can be used to show $A \neq B$ only where we already know that A is not ϕ for some ϕ which we independently know B is.

6. Professor Geach kindly permitted me to allude to his formulation of this puzzle, but he has no responsibility for the purpose to which it is put here; and I understand that he originally devised it for the different purpose of posing a challenge to Leibniz' Law.

2

Spatially Coinciding Objects

Frederick C. Doepke

David Wiggins has argued that two or more things can occupy the same place at the same time.[1] He maintains that you and your body are not the same thing, even though they have the same head, trunk and limbs. A gold statue and the gold of the statue he would count as two things, despite the fact that they are in the same place, weigh the same, feel the same and look the same. I believe that he is correct and that our discomfort in allowing these consequences can be eliminated with an account of how such objects are related when they occupy the same place at the same time. The major project of the following is to provide such an account. The account is used to explain an age-old reductivist tendency to favor metaphysically certain material objects, like fundamental constituents, over others, like artifacts and organisms which are composed of these and whose existence is implied in our ordinary talk and thought. Finally, an anti-reductivist argument is offered in favor of these objects of ordinary talk and thought.

Wiggins emphasizes (rightly, I believe) that Leibniz's Law expresses a necessary condition of numerical identity, i.e., that $a = b$ only if (Fa if and only if Fb). Conversely, if a and b differ in any way, they are two things—not one. Consider a man and his body. Suppose the man dies and his body remains under a tree. Then, his body has the property of being under the tree then, but the man does not, since he no longer exists. Also, if the brain of the man were transferred fully functioning to a new body six feet tall and his previous body were destroyed, the man would then be six feet tall. The first body with which the man previously coincided in space, however, would not have the property of being six feet tall then, since that body would not exist then. Therefore, the man and his body are two things—not one. Similar arguments can be easily constructed for other pairs, like Theseus' ship and a collection of boards, a stone monument and a stone, a gold statue and the gold of the statue.

Within the framework of accepting the existence of persisting material particulars in general, there are four ways of attempting to block Wiggins' conclusion which I find especially appealing. For future reference, let us name these as follows:

1. The One-Many View,
2. The Relative Identity View (two versions: temporal and sortal relativity),
3. The Dichronic View,
4. The Reductivist View.

Two of these are alike in *not* allowing both of the purported examples spatially to *coincide*. The One-Many View recognizes only one of the pair as a *single* object in the place in question. The Dichronic View[2] denies that the objects exist at the same *time*. The remaining views *allow* both objects spatially to coincide. Both versions of the Relative Identity View attempt to modify Leibniz's Law. The Reductivist View challenges, as the others do not, the metaphysics of ordinary talk and thought, by construing the existence of one as merely a phase in the existence of the other.

The rest of this paper is divided into four sections, each of which is ostensibly a refutation of one of these views. In the course of these refutations, however, there will emerge an account of how spatially coinciding objects are related which *is* compatible with Wiggins' conclusion. This account addresses itself first to the question of how distinct, spatially coinciding objects are *similar*, then, to how they are *different*, and finally, to why we should accept this alternative.

1. The One-Many View

Consider the case of Theseus' ship—which is made of wooden boards—and the collection of those boards. The One-Many View disallows this as a case of two spatial cooccupants by maintaining that 'the collection of those boards' does not denote one material object. It might be allowed to denote a set which has members, each of which occupies space, but which does not itself occupy space. Or, this expression might be deemed singular only in grammatical, but not logical form, as Russell considered 'matter' a 'collective name' logically equivalent to the grammatical plural, 'material objects.' On this reading, 'the collection of those boards' would be logically equivalent to 'those boards,' denoting more than one object, so that Theseus' ship and the collection of boards would not be two spatial cooccupants, but would stand to each other in a one-many relation. And of the one and the many, only the one would be in the place in question. Perhaps terms like 'the gold of the gold statue' can also be interpreted as collective names, so that even the gold statue and the gold of the statue do not count as spatial cooccupants.

Although most of Wiggins' examples would be eliminated by the One-Many View, there are some for which this interpretation is plainly impossible, e.g., people and their bodies, a stone and a stone monument, a phonograph record and its plastic disc, and Hume's example of a church and a building.[3] Although it may not be obvious that in all these examples there is more than one object, it is certain that if there are more than one there are two—not one and a plurality. We shall consider in more depth the grounds for counting them distinct when discussing the Reductivist View.

Invoking the One-Many View may be attractive when considering terms like 'the collection of boards' or even 'the gold of the statue.' Since it does not deal with all cases, however, let us in this paper leave it an open question whether it deals with any cases. Thus, we will be forced to be sufficiently general to include collections and the like and keep our account independent of the issue of whether any is really one or many things.

2. The Relative Identity View

(a) The Temporal Version

When speaking of a person and that person's body, or a gold statue and the gold of the statue, the following interpretive idea is very attractive. There is really only one thing being referred to, but it has various properties, and depending upon *which* of these properties one is interested in its having, certain expressions are appropriate for referring to it and others are not. For example, when we speak of something *as* a person we are interested in it *as* something with a will, something which is accordingly free, etc. We speak of that *same* thing as a human body, however, when interested in it as a biological system. Similarly, when we speak of a gold *statue*, as such, we are primarily interested in its *shape*. If it were a poor work of art, a pawn broker would likely disregard its shape, take interest in its property of being composed of gold, and think of it as some *gold*.

Wiggins' argument is allegedly a *formal* disproof of such interpretations, given only such mundane facts as that you can replace parts of objects and that bodies of people persist even after these people die. Since Leibniz's Law is generally held to be at least partially *definitive* of numerical identity. Wiggins would question the *coherence* of the above interpretations in light of such mundane facts. Paul Grice and George Myro have challenged the claim that this is a formal disproof.[4] They point out that all the properties alluded to by Wiggins to show that objects *a* and *b*, spatially coinciding at one time, are not identical are properties which these objects have at some *other* time. But, they ask, why cannot *a* and *b* be one thing *when* spatially coinciding and *two* things at other times when they are not? They challenge an assumption (uncovered by Grice) that things which can differ at *any* time are *never* identical. Most of their work has been devoted to show that identity is a *time*-variant notion, so that *a* and *b* can be one thing at one time and two things at another time. But what of Leibniz's Law? For the time-variant notion of identity, Grice and Myro modify Leibniz's Law, the Indiscernibility of Identicals, so that the indiscernibility in question pertains as well only to the times of identity. Objects *a* and *b* are held to be identical at time *t* only if (*Fa at t* if and only if *Fb at t*), where *F* is any property, the instantiation of which at *t* does not entail the instantiation of any property at any other time. For example, you and the body you now have are *now* one and the same thing only if in the same place, of the same shape, color and weight. The fact that your body, but not you, could be under a tree at some *other* time, as would be the case if you expired under the tree, is held to be irrevelant in deciding whether you are *now* the same thing.

Although Grice and Myro are mainly concerned to show the consistency of this notion with the mundane facts we ordinarily accept, three philosophical arguments for favoring this alternative are offered by them. Since I know of no appealing arguments other than these, we shall consider just theirs in weighing this alternative.

A. It has intuitive appeal, e.g., it is natural to say that a person *is* his or her body, or that the gold of the statue *is* the statue—reading these with the 'is' of identity.
B. It is favored by Occam's Razor.
C. It solves the following problem. If, for example, you are now 5′8″, weigh 150 pounds, have a certain tint to the color of your skin and have a certain shape, then your body has all of these properties—but not, one would think, by sheer coincidence. An explanation is called for, and is provided by the account offered, since there is no mystery in a thing's being of the same size, weight, color and shape as *itself*. If, however, one opts for *any* theory which would count these as *two* objects (spatially coinciding), then the problem arises of explaining why they are similar in all these respects. It certainly does not follow straightforwardly from the fact that you and your body are now in the same *place* that the two of you should be of the same weight, color, etc.

We shall critically discuss these arguments in the order just presented.

(A) Why respect *any* appeal to intuition on the applicability of a term? Like all animals, our survival depends largely on our ability to recognize similarities. The fact that an object *appears* to all or most of us to be similar to certain others is consequently very good evidence that it *is*. We can, therefore, respect appeals to intuition on the applicability of words like 'red' and 'cow,' which are applied on a similarity basis. Some words, however, are not applied on a similarity basis. We are not, I submit, inclined to apply the expression, 'is the same thing as' (and related expressions), to objects *a* and *b* by *recognizing* that they are similar to other identicals. Rather, we are inclined to think that objects *a* and *b* are identical whenever, while comparing them, we do not think that they are different. Now, it may be either that *a* and *b* are not, in fact, different in any way, or we may simply be failing to notice certain differences. If you and your body are distinct objects by virtue of differences which appear *only* at times *other* than now, it is easy to see why we are inclined to think of these as the same thing. We merely restrict our attention to how they are *now*. Moreover, *this* way of narrowing attention has for us a certain appeal. The tendency to become absorbed in the present is part of our animal heritage.

(B) Still, one may contend, why not identify the objects at a time if we can? (Occam's Razor) My chief objection to the defense of the Temporal Identity View is that it purports to offer a notion of identity which does not really involve satisfaction of Leibniz's Law. We recall that Leibniz's Law was allegedly *modified* in such a way as to restrict the range of properties which one is entitled to transfer from one to another object, temporally 'identified', to only those properties which do not entail the instantiation of any property at any other time. But when Leibniz's Law is *changed* in this way, by what right is this called a *modification*, implying thereby that we have the *same* principle, which, I take it, must in any formulation serve to define numerical identity? For *any* two objects which are similar in *any* way there are *some* predicates which transfer from one to the other. A material object and its surface, for example, are similar in respect of 'surface' properties like color and shape. Suppose we suggested that Leibniz's Law could be modified in such a way as to restrict the range of properties which one was entitled to transfer to only 'surface' properties. Could we invoke this 'modified version of Leibniz's Law' to support the claim that a material object and its surface were the same thing? The absurdity of this suggestion brings to light the fact that what is really distinctive of Leibniz's Law is that it demands that *no* restrictions be imposed on which predicates transfer in a true case of numerical identity. 'Temporally relative identity' appears to be merely a misnomer for a certain form of *resemblance*.

(We shall consider argument (C) shortly.)

(b) The Sortal Version

According to the Sortal Version of the Relative Identity View, it is possible for *a* to be the same *F* as *b* even though not the same *G* as *b*, since identity, at least sometimes, is not an absolute relation, but must, like goodness, be related to a *kind* of thing. Recalling our example of the man who died under a tree, it would be said that the man was the same body as the corpse under the tree, though not, of course, the same person.

It is this thesis which has been Wiggins' principal target, and his main point of attack is that it violates Leibniz's Law. He argues that since *b* is the same *G* as *b*, then if *a* and *b* are the same thing, *a must* be the same *G* as *b*. By far the fullest attempt to rebut Wiggins' argument is Nicholas Griffin's recent book, *Relative Identity*.[5] Like Grice and Myro, Griffin defends his view by claiming that Leibniz's Law can be *modified* in such a way as to restrict the range of properties one is entitled to transfer in a case of relative identity. For *sortal* relative identity, he says,

> The formal solution is simple, what it amounts to is more difficult. For each general noun 'A' there is a class Δ_A of predicates such that A-identity implies indiscernibility with respect to the predicates in Δ_A, or Δ_A-indiscernibility.[6]

In light of this defense, Wiggins allows that 'the final test of a theory of relative identity is not its internal coherence, but how it subverses a total theory of the individuation and existence of particulars.'[7] This seems to me to concede far too much. Exactly the same objection we raised to Grice's and Myro's supposed 'modification' of Leibniz's Law applies to Griffin's so-called 'restricted' version. Any objects which are *similar* in any way are 'indiscernible' in *some* respects. So, *any* resemblance could be dignified by calling it a 'restricted form of indiscernibility'. In contrast with all forms of restricted, or relative, indiscernibility, identity is unrestricted, or absolute, indiscernibility. Unless Griffin can explain why 'relative identity' is not merely a misnomer for a certain kind of resemblance, I'm afraid at least much of his book falls like a house of cards.

(C) Let us now recall a problem introduced by Myro and attempt to solve it in a way which allows that distinct objects *can* spatially coincide. Why, just because *a* and *b* are in the same place (at time *t*), should they *also* be of the same weight, smell and taste? Let us take note of the following facts: the place, shape and (spatial) size of an object are determined by the places of its outermost parts; the weight of an object is a function of the weights of its parts; its taste is determined by how certain of its parts affect our gustatory senses; the color and smell of an object are determined by the qualities and interrelations of certain of its outermost parts. Therefore, if objects have exactly the *same parts* at the same time, they will be in the same *place* and of the same *shape*, (spatial) *size, weight* and *color* and will have the same *taste* and *smell*. Since it is logically possible for two things to share the same parts at the same time, we *can* explain why objects are alike in all these ways *otherwise* than by identifying them.

Do *all* pairs of spatially coinciding objects have exactly the same parts? There are relatively boring exceptions. Consider Wiggins' example of a wet sponge.[8] The sponge and the water which makes the sponge wet have *no* parts in common; they are in the same place, and so, of the same shape, but need not be of the same weight, color, taste or smell. Wiggins endorses Locke's formulation of the Principle of the Impenetrability of Matter: that no two things *of the same kind* can simultaneously occupy the same place. Given this example, however, it is easy to construct a similar example in which the principle, so formulated, is violated. Imagine two tables, coming to occupy the same place by the thorough intermingling of tiny parts, like atoms. Pairs like these seem *merely* to coincide in space. There are other pairs, however, which are alike in all the ways exhibited by objects which share the same parts, but which do not share *all* the same parts.

Consider you and the collection of atoms of which you are now composed. Appealing to intuition, I suggest that your heart is a part of you but not a part of this collection of atoms. Similarly, Theseus' ship, but not the wood of the ship, is composed of boards. Though every part of the collection of atoms is a part of you and every part of the wood is a part of the ship, you and the ship have 'additional' parts not shared by the collection of atoms and the wood. It is clear, however, that you and the collection of atoms, like the ship and the wood, are similar in all those respects exhibited by objects with exactly the same parts. For, unlike the results of adding a chunk of some material, these 'additional' parts result only because certain parts of the collection of atoms (and of the wood) are *accidentally* interrelated in ways *essential* to the existence of the 'additional' parts. For example, those of your atoms which are parts of your heart *happen* to be interrelated in a certain complex pattern, the presence of which is *needed* for there to be a heart there and then. However, whether some interrelation among certain constituent parts is essential or not is irrevelant in determining the place, shape, weight, color, taste and smell of an object. For, any property which can be ascribed to an object *solely* on the basis of its *having* certain parts which *are* interrelated in certain ways will belong to it regardless of whether it *must* have *those* parts or *must* have parts interrelated in those *ways*. Since it was on precisely this 'modal-neutral' basis that we argued for indiscernibility of place, (spatial) size, shape, etc., in the case of objects with the *same* parts, objects like you and the collection of atoms, and Theseus' ship and the wood, though not having *all* the same parts, will share this same variety of properties we saw exhibited by objects which *do* have the same parts.

With the following recursive definition we state succinctly what all such very similar pairs fundamentally have in common. (Our variables, '*x*' and '*y*,' can range over pluralities to accommodate the One-Many View.)[9]

y is completely-composed of *x* at time *t* $\text{iff}_{(\text{def.})}$

at time *t*, *x* has parts &

every part of *x* is a part of *y* &
any part of *y* which is not a part of *x*
is completely-composed of parts of *x*.

I submit that in all cases of spatially coinciding objects which share the whole variety of properties we have discussed, the reason they are so alike is the fact that one object is completely-composed of the other. (Notice that objects like you and your body, and a rock and itself, which have exactly the same parts, are completely-composed of each other; the last conjunct of the definition is vacuously satisfied. Please note that this is a *stipulated* definition of the technical term, 'completely-composed'; the fact that it may sound counterintuitive to say that you are completely-composed of your body is, therefore, irrelevant.)

In discussing the Temporal Identity View we intuitively recognized what appears to be a whole class of exceptions to its claim that ('interesting') pairs of spatially coinciding objects are all indiscernible *at* the time(s) of coincidence. A tree, but not the collection of molecules of which the tree is composed, is composed of wood cells. Nothing *follows* from this about how the tree is at any other time. It is, after all, conceivable that the tree should have been brought suddenly into existence composed of these cells and instantly destroyed. In our discussion of the Dichronic View we shall attempt to find the ground for such intuitively recognizable differences in composition.

3. The Dichronic View

The Dichronic View stems from a certain theory of the nature of substantial change (i.e., creation and destruction, in general). According to the Dichronic View, the gold of a gold ring is *not* something which occupies the place of the ring *at the same time*. Rather, it is something which *would begin* to exist were the ring to be destroyed in a change, like the smashing of the ring, in which the result was some gold not in the shape of the ring. Similarly, talk of your body (if not just a specialized way of talking of you as a physical object) is talk of your corpse of the future. This interpretation of phrases like 'the gold of' and 'the body of' is clearly suggested by the theory of substantial change which denies that in creation and destruction there is a particular thing which *persists* throughout the change—a 'substratum' which change*s*—and sees instead a *replacement* of one object by another into which it 'turns'.[10] According to the Dichronic View, smashing the ring would 'turn it into' some gold; this would *not* be an alteration in shape undergone by some gold which began in spatial coincidence with the ring and continued to exist after the ring was destroyed.

Which view of substantial change is theoretically preferable? I shall now argue that there is a clear advantage to allowing that the gold of the ring *does* begin in spatial coincidence with the ring, so that it does not come into existence with the ring's destruction, but persists throughout as the 'substratum' of the destruction, i.e., that which changes. Consider the fact that when the ring is smashed, although there is a change in shape, there are many kinds of properties in which there is (or, at least, may not have been) no change, e.g., place, weight, material composition, and color. *If* all we say is that as the ring ceases to be, the gold comes to be, it becomes a mystery why the gold is similar in all these respects with the ring. However, the supposition that the gold *began* the change with all these properties *explains* this fact in the attenuated sense that it obviates the need for an explanation. It is change, not lack of change, which calls for explanation. Why is the gold still yellow, still composed of gold, still half an ounce, still in the same place it was? There is no need to explain these facts. But whenever something comes *into* existence, its possession of *all* of its properties calls for explanation. Denying that the gold does come into existence obviates the need to explain any of its properties *except* its new shape. We may note that in a *genuine* case of creation, by allowing that that which begins the change, like the gold *from* which the ring was made, persists throughout the change, so that it ends up in spatial coincidence with the created object, we can explain at least a vast array of the created object's properties on the assumption that it comes into existence completely-composed of the persisting object, which ends up with such-and-such properties. E.g., if the ring is made from some gold, *and* the gold persists throughout, so that the ring, when it comes into existence, is completely-composed of this previously existing gold, then, as we saw in Section 2, there are many properties of the gold, like its shape, place, weight, smell and color which we can immediately transfer to the ring. In both kinds of substantial change, identifying a substratum of the change at beginning and end helps to render the change intelligible by avoiding gratuitous mysteries. This amounts to rejecting the Dichronic View.

The notion of composition, as we have seen, serves to pick out a spatial cooccupant. Given that a cup is composed of glass, we can speak of *the* glass of which the cup is composed. In criticizing many accounts of truth, Michael Dummett observed that a satisfactory account of any concept must go beyond a mere description of the circumstances in which we apply the relevant word, to give an account of the (or a) *point* of the concept, explaining how the classification in question serves some interest we have.[11] I submit that one reason for having the notion of composition is to pick out, in relation to a certain perishable object, a spatial cooccupant which could be a substratum of that object's destruction. This classification thereby serves the purpose of making intelligible the perishability of an object. How could the glass cup perish? One way we would find intelligible is for the glass to lose the shape of a cup and assume that of a pancake.

We recognized an intuition not to allow that all spatial coccupants were composed of the same things. The tree, but not the collection of molecules of the tree, was composed of wood cells. In illustrating the notion of material cause, Aristotle was aware of the fact that the notion of composition can be successively applied to produce a *series* of objects, e.g., a wooden basket, the (earthen) wood of the basket, the (firey) earth of the wood, the fire of the earth.[12] But composition is not the only notion which can pick out a material cause for Aristotle, since the body of an organism was also held to be a material cause of the organism. Yet it would be strange (and unilluminating) to say that an organism was 'composed' of its body.

With Aristotle's notion in mind, let us define 'constitution' as follows: x constitutes y at time t if and only if x could be a substratum of y's destruction. 'Constitution,' like 'material cause,' is thus wider in extension than 'composition,' and is defined in a way which explicitly indicates what *purpose* the concept serves. I submit that in every one of the cases we have seen of distinct, spatially coinciding objects which were similar in the variety of respects we were concerned to explain in the second section, one of the objects constituted the other. We shall explicate this relation.

A satisfactory account of any relation must account for its *formal* properties. Identity, for example, is *symmetrical* in that $x = y$ only if $y = x$, and *transitive* in that $x = y$ and $y = z$ only if $x = z$. These formal properties follow obviously from Leibniz's Law. Composition (at time t), though also transitive, is *asymmetrical* in that x is composed of y (at time t) only if it is *not* the case that y is composed of x (at time t). Composition (at time t) has these formal properties just because it generates a series. A series, like that of the whole numbers from 1 to 5, can be non-arbitrarily generated from a set, like the one consisting of 3, 5, 2, 4 and 1, just in case there is an asymmetrical, transitive relation, like being greater than, which obtains between every two members of the set. Constitution (at time t), I submit, is also asymmetrical and transitive, as we shall try to see. Let us begin by considering why constitution (at time t) is asymmetrical.

If x constitutes y at time t, then the fact that y could perish at time t is explainable by describing a certain change, beginning at time t, in which x would be the substratum. A man is perishable because his body could undergo a change in which the neural structures responsible for consciousness would be lost. (Compare: a plastic phonograph record is perishable because the plastic disc could undergo a change in which the grooves would be lost.) Since the description of this change explains how y might perish, the description of *x* in the *initial* condition of the change, *at* time *t*, provides one explanation of why *y exists* (at time *t*). A man exists at time *t* because his body (at *t*) has certain neural structures at that time. Since *x can* undergo this change, its being in the initial condition is merely *accidental* for *x*. (A body with the neural structures in question has those neural structures 'accidentally' in the sense that it can exist without them.) Since the fact that *x* is in that condition at time *t* explains the fact that *y* exists at time *t*, if *x* continued to be in exactly that condition for some period after *t*, then this would explain the fact that *y* continued to exist throughout that period. Throughout any such period, *y*'s continued existence would depend on the fact that *x* happened to remain in a condition it need not be in order to exist—a condition which is therefore irrelevant in accounting for the existence of *x* throughout this time. We cannot, therefore, explain why *x* continues to exist throughout any such period by describing a condition of *y* throughout this time, since the continued existence of *y* will always be irrelevant in accounting for *x*'s existence. The continued existence of your body depends on such things as whether the organization of organs of certain kinds, or of atoms of certain kinds, is preserved. Whether or not it happens to continue to have certain neural structures which are accidental to it is irrevelant to whether it continues to exist. Consequently, whether or not you continue to exist is irrevelant to whether your body does. Thus, you do *not* constitute your body.

In the destruction of some object it may happen that something it constitutes continues to exist. Theseus' ship would survive the destruction of its boards in the event they were slowly crushed in place so that the wood of the ship remained throughout in the shape of a ship. If this happened, it would be possible to contrive a description of the ship from which the destruction of the boards could be inferred, e.g., the ship is composed of wood which undergoes such and such changes. Clearly, though, the reference to the ship is irrevelant, since the continued existence of the ship is merely incidental to the destruction of the boards.

It is easy to see why constitution (at time *t*) is transitive. Suppose that, at time *t*, *z* exists because *y* is *F* and *y* exists because *x* is *G*. In order to explain why *z* exists with a description of *x*, all we have to do is enrich our description of *x* so that it follows not only that *y exists*, but exists *with* property *G*. For example, if some sub-atomic particles happen to have the property of being entirely divided into sub-groups, each of which forms a gold atom, then these particles constitute some gold; if, further, they are spatially related in such a way that the gold is ring-shaped, then these particles are like the gold in constituting a gold ring.

Following Wiggins' suggestion, we can admit that a person *is* his or her body and that a table *is* a collection of particles, provided that we read these with the 'is' of constitution. The preceding explications of complete-composition and of the point and formal properties of constitution can then be accepted as comprising an account of this sense of 'is.'

From this account can be derived explanations of a certain age-old metaphysical bias. Aristotle observed that in response to the question of *what* something *is* some people (like Democritus) favor the *material* cause. To the question of what is a house, they will say, 'bricks and boards,' or 'atoms.' Why is that? In the remainder of this section I offer two explanations. A third motivation is discussed in the next section.

Let us assume (reasonably, I think) that at any time a perishable object exists its perishability can be explained by describing something which constitutes it and that this other thing completely-composes at that time the perishable object in question. It will follow, as we have seen, that there will be a vast array of properties they share, i.e., all those which follow from the fact that each is completely-composed of the constituting object. Consequently, in order to ascribe any of these properties to something at that time and place we have the *choice* of *disregarding* the perishable object in question and referring, instead, to an object which constitut*es* it. Take, for example, a ring's properties of being ring-shaped, of being on your finger, of having gold throughout, of weighing half an ounce, of having a dark yellow color and a faint, metallic odor. Since the *gold* of the ring has all of these properties, we need not ascribe any of these to the ring in order to ascribe it to a bearer. There is, by contrast, no need for an object to constitute anything at any time. Whenever an object does not constitute something, we do *not* have a choice of disregarding it and ascribing properties of it to something it constitut*es*. In light of these facts, we can understand one reason for favoring metaphysically constitut*ing* objects (or material causes), which is that they are generally less dispensible for thought than objects constitut*ed*.

There is a related difference which also contributes to the idea that constituting objects are somehow more real. Whenever something is created or destroyed there is some time during the change in which the existence of the object created or destroyed is indeterminate. During the melting of the gold of a gold ring there would come a point when there would be no way of saying whether the gold was still sufficiently well in the shape of a ring for there to be a ring there and then. The 'problem' of trying to refer to the ring at this time, however, would be eliminable by referring instead to the gold, whose existence would be relatively determinate.

4. The Reductivist View

The realization that references to objects constituted can *often* be replaced by references to objects which constitute them naturally raises the question of whether they can *always* be so replaced. If x constitutes y, then y exists because *x* accidentally has a certain property. But are we ever *justified* in making this inference to the existence of *y*? According to the Reductivist View, we are not.

The Reductivist View has been found attractive by metaphysicians throughout the ages, from Democritus, with his atoms, to Quine, who presses for the adequacy of an ontology of particle-stages and their sets. In order to illustrate a typical metaphysical problem (i.e., one for the study of being *qua* being), Aristotle chose the question of whether Socrates is Socrates-seated.[13] We think so. Why, then, not say the same thing of you and the collection of particles of which you are now composed and *deny* that you survive replacement of these particles? Why not maintain, instead, that each time after this material replacement occurs each new reference to 'you' is really a reference to a *different* collection of particles causally related to the previous one in such a way as to be endowed with a certain complex of humanoid properties?

A very tempting reply is that there are truths to the effect that certain properties are instantiated and that these are properties which cannot be instantiated by other than the objects constitut*ed*. For example, it may be maintained (à la Descartes) that it is true that consciousness is instantiated in the world and therefore people exist as separate substances, since they are the only ones which can be conscious. It may be pointed out that, unlike having a certain weight or shape or color, *some* properties entail that an object satisfies certain *persistence* conditions other than those satisfied by collections of particles. For example, your now having a memory of first hearing of John Kennedy's death is not a property which *could* be instantiated by a collection of particles. The collection of particles persists just as long as the particles do, in whatever array or disarray. But this is a true *memory* only if it is a state of something whose career can be traced back in time in accordance with certain criteria of identity so that this state of remembering is assignable to the *same* thing which had the experience of hearing of the assassination. Nothing can *begin* to exist with a memory, yet this collection of particles may now be in a humanoid form for the first time. Does it not follow that *you* exist as a separate substance?

The ardent reductivist, however, will remain undaunted; so much the worse, he will say, for these properties and alleged truths. What makes all interesting metaphysical reductions to a special category of objects interesting is that for every such apparent truth and property eliminated, the reductivist can offer a corresponding truth, concerning only the favored objects, which appears to capture all the facts, and it thus becomes challenging to see how one can justify talk of the objects rejected. What more is there to the fact that you heard something, carried a memory of it and later recalled it than that a certain collection of particles was slightly rearranged into a certain pattern as a result of commerce with sound waves and that this pattern was preserved from one collection of particles to another, so that now another collection, partly as a result of receiving this pattern, undergoes a certain internal motion? Since, it seems, we *can* capture all the facts without mention of objects constitu*ed*, like people, is there really a philosophically respectable reason for allowing their existence? Should we *think* with the vulgar?

Let us regard the so-called hearing of the assassination, the preservation in memory of this experience and its conscious recollection as phases of one event, *E*. And let us go so far as to allow that, in some intuitive sense, all that happens in the occurrence of *E can* be captured by referring only to collections of particles. Why admit something constituted, like you, as a separate substance persisting as the substratum of *E?*

Let us bear in mind that you differ essentially from a collection of particles in that you can literally gain and loose particles. Throughout the development of *E* you undoubtedly would, and certainly could, suffer changes in particle composition. And only because you do continue to be present throughout these changes in the development of *E can* we explain, at each stage of the development, how that stage came about as the result of some one thing (you) having advanced through the various, earlier stages, in accordance with certain laws. You remain present through these changes in particle composition only because you are *accidentally* composed of certain particles. When we describe the development of *E* as involving only collections of particles as substrata, however, we can*not* explain how each stage resulted from the fact that some one collection of particles has advanced through the various, earlier stages in accordance with certain laws, since every time you gain and lose particles a *different* collection of particles becomes involved in the development of *E*. Consequently, after any loss or gain of particles, in order to explain how the collection of particles involved came to have the relevant properties (e.g., of having memory traces), we would have to explain how it *became* involved in a history which previously involved *other* collections of particles. And to do this, we would have to take account either of the fact that some of its particles, which had been randomly scattered, have joined the others in a single, humanoid configuration (when you *gain* particles), or of the fact that the particles of the previous collection have separated, leaving only a subportion—those of the present collection—in a humanoid form (when you *lose* particles). In contrast with collections of particles, an advantage which you offer as a substratum, because you are accidentally composed of certain particles, is that when describing you thoughout *E* we can *ignore* these comings and goings of particles. When restricted to collections of particles, however, we are *forced* to take into consideration these phenomena. Since, in order to explain how *E* occurred, it is pointless to take account of these phenomena, we ought not to do so. But this requires acknowledging the existence of an object constitut*ed*, like you. And this amounts to rejecting the Reductivist View.

It is worth emphasizing that the Reductivist View is rejected because we sometimes have a certain *kind* of explanatory purpose which is best served by acknowledging constituted objects. There is *another* explanatory aim which has been found interesting to metaphysicians throughout the ages and which has undoubtedly often given rise to the Reductivist View. This is the philosophically laudable aim of displaying the greatest generalities discernible among material objects. If, for example, one wants to show what the occurrence of *E* has in common with non-living processes, then one will choose only laws which apply to non-living things, like the particles of physics. But I can see no reason to regard the objects needed for this latter purpose as being in any absolute way metaphysically sacrosanct.

Notes

1. David Wiggins, 'On Being is the Same Place at the Same Time'. [chapter 1 of this volume.] *Identity and Spatio-temporal Continuity*, Basil Blackwell, Oxford 1967, and *Sameness and Substance*, Harvard University Press, Cambridge, Massachusetts, 1980. I am indebted to him and to Paul Grice, Charles Jarrett, George Myro and Stephen Schiffer for many helpful suggestions.

2. 'Dichronic' is a neologism I distinguish from 'diachronic'. The former is intended to allude to *two* times; the latter pertains to phenomena *through* time.

3. David Hume, *A Treatise of Human Nature*, Oxford, Clarendon Press, 1978, ed, L. A. Selby-Bigge, Bk. I, Part IV, p. 258.

4. In seminars, conversation and in George Myro's *Change and Identity* (currently in manuscript form). [The main ideas of that manuscript appear in chapter 8 of this volume.—Ed.]

5. Nicholas Griffin, *Relative Identity*, Oxford at the Clarendon Press, 1977.

6. *Ibid.*, p. 140.

7. *Sameness and Substance, op. cit.*, p. 23.

8. David Wiggins, 'On Being in the Same Place at the Same Time.'

9. Of course, if *x* and *y* are *both* pluralities, they stand to each other in a *many*-many relation.

10. This theory is argued for by Barrington Jones in 'Aristotle's Introduction of Matter,' *J. Phil.*, 1976, and is at least allowed for by W. Charlton, *Aristotle's Physics, I, II*, Appendix, 'Did Aristotle Believe in Prime Matter?' Clarendon Aristotle Series, Oxford at the Clarendon Press, 1970. Although it does appear to be Aristotle's view in *On Generation and Corruption*, I would argue that it is a view he abandoned in his more mature treatment of the issue in the *Physics*.

11. Michael Dummett, 'Truth', *Proceedings of the Aristotelian Society*, 1958–1959, Vol. LIX.

12. Aristotle, Metaphysics, Θ7.

13. Aristotle, Metaphysics, Γ2.

(1) Does this mean that we should admit that they are in fact real or just that we should regard them as real for the purpose of explanation?

3

Parthood and Identity Across Time

Judith Jarvis Thomson

Temporal parts have come in handy in a number of areas in philosophy.[1] Let us take a close look at one use to which some may be inclined to want to put them.

I

Suppose I own some Tinkertoys. I make a house out of them, finishing the task at 1:00. I put the house, which I shall call "*H*," on an otherwise empty shelf. Since *H* is the only Tinkertoy house now on the shelf, and since also the time now is 1:15, we may truly say

(1) H = the Tinkertoy house on the shelf at 1:15

A Tinkertoy house is made of Tinkertoys. And surely a Tinkertoy house is made only of Tinkertoys: surely it has no additional ingredients, over and above the Tinkertoys it is made of. (Perhaps there is such an entity as "house-shape." Even if there is, it certainly is not literally part of any Tinkertoy house.)

It is an attractive idea that the logic of parthood is the Leonard-Goodman Calculus of Individuals,[2] which takes "x D y" (read: x is discrete from y) as primitive, defines '$x < y$' (read: x is part of y) and 'x O y' (read: x overlaps y) as follows:

$$x < y =_{\text{df}} (z)(z \text{ D } y \supset z \text{ D } x)$$
$$x \text{ O } y =_{\text{df}} (\exists z)(z < x \;\&\; z \text{ D} < y)$$

and contains the following distinctive axioms:

(CI_1)	$(x = y) \equiv (x < y \;\&\; y < x)$	identity axiom
(CI_2)	$(x \text{ O } y) \equiv -(x \text{ D } y)$	overlap axiom
(CI_3)	$(\exists x)(x \in S) \supset (\exists y)(y \text{ Fu } S)$	fusion axiom

where 'x Fu S' (read: x fuses S, or the Ss, or the members of S) is defined as follows:

$$x \text{ Fu } S =_{df} (y)[y \text{ D } x \equiv (z)(z \in S \supset y \text{ D } z)]$$

(Another way in which we might have defined 'x fu S' is this: x fuses S just in case a thing y is part of x if and only if every part of y overlaps a member of S.)

It is worth stressing that the fusion axiom says only that, if anything is a member of S, then there is a thing that fuses the Ss. What I shall call *the fusion principle*[3] says that if anything is a member of S, then there is a unique thing that fuses the Ss:

$$(\exists x)(x \in S) \supset (E!y)(y \text{ Fu } S) \qquad \text{fusion principle}$$

Or, as we may put it: if anything is a member of S, then there is such a thing as *the fusion of* the Ss. The fusion principle is provable in the Calculus of Individuals.

I said it is an attractive idea that the logic of parthood is the Leonard-Goodman Calculus of Individuals. If the axioms are true under their intended interpretation, then so is the fusion principle. There are Tinkertoys on the shelf at 1:15; so the fusion principle tells us that there is such a thing as the fusion of the Tinkertoys on the shelf at 1:15. I shall call it "*W*"; so we can say

(2) W = the fusion of the Tinkertoys on the shelf at 1:15

Surely a Tinkertoy house is made only of Tinkertoys. The Tinkertoys H is made of are the Tinkertoys on the shelf at 1:15. So it very naturally suggests itself that we should say

(3) $H = W$

So far so good; no problem yet.

II

But we should take note of the fact that that fusion axiom makes some people feel nervous. Few, I think, feel nervous about the definitions or about the identity and overlap axioms, but many object to the idea that there is something that fuses (as it might be) the set whose members are all giraffes and all apples. They think the fusion axiom grossly overstrong.

But why? The fusion axiom does commit us to the existence of some pretty odd things, but, so far as I can see, their oddity is no objection to them.

Never mind: the problem I want to set before you arises even if we reject the fusion axiom.

For suppose you have some bits of wood in your hand now; doesn't it follow that there is such a thing as *the wood* in your hand now?

There are some Tinkertoys on the shelf at 1:15, and, since Tinkertoys are bits of wood, it seems right to say there therefore is such a thing as the wood on the shelf at 1:15. Let us call it "*W′*"; so we can say

(2′) *W′* = the wood on the shelf at 1:15

Surely a Tinkertoy house is made only of Tinkertoys. The Tinkertoys *H* is made of are the Tinkertoys on the shelf at 1:15. The Tinkertoys on the shelf at 1:15 are themselves bits of wood. So it very naturally suggests itself that we should say

(3′) H = *W′*

If the fusion principle is true, then there is such a thing as the fusion of the Tinkertoys on the shelf at 1:15. I gave that thing the name '*W*'. If there is such a thing as *W*, it seems plausible to suppose that *W′* is identical with it; i.e., it seems plausible to suppose that the wood on the shelf at 1:15 *is* the fusion of the Tinkertoys on the shelf at 1:15.

Even if the fusion principle is not true—in that the fusion axiom is overstrong—it seems plausible to suppose that there is such a thing as *W* and that *W′* is identical with it; i.e., even if the fusion principle is not (in general) true, it seems plausible to suppose that there is such a thing as the fusion of the Tinkertoys on the shelf at 1:15 and that the wood on the shelf at 1:15 is identical with it.

But whether or not there is such a thing as *W*, it really does seem plausible to suppose that there is such a thing as *W′*, the wood on the shelf at 1:15. *And* that the Tinkertoy house *H* is identical with it. That will suffice for generating the problem I want to set before you.

III

For let us give the name 'alpha' to one of the sticks that help attach the roof of the house to its front wall. At 1:30, I remove alpha; I then replace alpha with a new stick, beta, and I throw alpha on the floor. Shortly thereafter, the time is 1:45. Is *H* still on the shelf at 1:45? That is, can we truly say

(4) *H* is on the shelf at 1:45 ?

Most of us are, I think, inclined to think we can; most of us are inclined to think that *H* survives replacement of alpha by beta and is still on the shelf at 1:45.

Now there is trouble. For the conjunction of (3′) and (4) entails

(5′) *W′* is on the shelf at 1:45

which is not true, for *W′* is only partly on the shelf at 1:45—the wood on the shelf at 1:15 is partly on the floor at 1:45, since alpha is on the floor at 1:45.

So also of course the conjunction of (3) and (4) entails

(5) *W* is on the shelf at 1:45

which is also not true, even if there is such a thing as *W*. For *W* is only partly on the shelf at 1:45—the fusion of the Tinkertoys on the shelf at 1:15 is partly on the floor at 1:45, since alpha is on the floor at 1:45.

What to do? Something has to give.

Well, we really must retain (4). Surely that *is H* on the shelf at 1:45. (This *is* the typewriter I bought five years ago, though I had a key replaced.)

So it is the identity sentences (3) and (3′) which have to go. But it seemed intuitively right to say that a Tinkertoy house is made only of Tinkertoys. It was that intuition which led us to identify *H* first with *W* and then, anyway, with *W′*. There has got to be something right in that intuition; but what is the something right in it, if (3) and (3′) are not true? How *is H* related to *W′*—and to *W*, if there is such a thing as *W*?

David Wiggins,[4] I think, would say that *W*, or anyway *W′*, *constitutes H* at 1:15, and that that is the most that can be retained of the intuition that a Tinkertoy house is made only of Tinkertoys. He may be right. But we cannot tell until we are made clearer than Wiggins makes us about just what it is for a thing *x* to constitute a thing *y* at a time *t*.

Richard Cartwright (*op. cit.*) draws attention to a solution that appeals to temporal parts. By hypothesis, *H* came into existence at 1:00, and alpha was removed from *H* at 1:30. *H* was in existence throughout that time; and suppose we allow ourselves to say that *H* therefore had a temporal part that came into existence at 1:00 and went out of existence at 1:30. If you like the fusion principle, you will think there is such a thing as *W*. It too was in existence throughout that time; and suppose we allow ourselves to conclude that it too had a temporal part that came into existence at 1:00

and went out of existence at 1:30. Let us call these entities, respectively, "*H*-from-1:00-to-1:30" and "*W*-from-1:00-to-1:30". Friends of temporal parts take it that the temporal parts of a thing are, literally, parts of it; so we should say

$$H\text{-from-1:00-to-1:30 is part of } H$$

and

$$W\text{-from-1:00-to-1:30 is part of } W$$

A Tinkertoy house is made only of Tinkertoys. Throughout 1:00 to 1:30, *H* was made of the Tinkertoys that *W* fuses; so shouldn't we say

$$H\text{-from-1:00-to-1:30} = W\text{-from-1:00-to-1:30}$$

and thus that *H* and *W* share a part—that they literally overlap? Tinkertoy houses may be made of different Tinkertoys at different times, however; so don't we preserve as much as anyone could want of the spirit of "A Tinkertoy house is made only of Tinkertoys" if we say, quite generally, that, for every temporal part *x* of a Tinkertoy house, there is a Tinkertoy fusion *y* such that *x* is identical with, or at least overlaps, some temporal part of *y*?

Of course you may not think there is any such thing as *W*. Then you are cordially invited to rewrite the preceding paragraph, replacing '*W*' by '*W'*', and making the necessary changes elsewhere in it.

But what exactly *are* these putative entities *H*-from-1:00-to-1:30 and *W*-from-1:00-to-1:30? Friends of "temporal parts" do seem to be just a bit casual about the manner in which they explain their use of that term; and a number of people have, rightly, complained that we are owed something more careful in the way of an account of them than we are commonly given.

IV

There are a number of different ways of defining the expression 'temporal part'. I shall try to define it in such a way as to lend the greatest possible plausibility to the metaphysical theses commonly asserted by use of it.

What we are interested in here is physical objects and their parts. Could I have said, more briefly, that what we are interested in here is physical objects? That is, is *not* every part of a physical object itself a physical object? I should think so. But let us not assume this. (I shall come back to it below.) Let us take the variables '*x*', '*y*', etc. to range over physical objects and their parts. Then the first of the metaphysical theses that must be accommodated is this:

$$(M_1) \quad \text{If } x \text{ is a temporal part of } y, \text{ then } x \text{ is part of } y.$$

As I said, friends of temporal parts take it that the temporal parts of a thing are *literally* part of it.

Or at least I think they do. For all I know there may be those who think that the temporal parts of a thing are not parts of it, but only parts of something else, perhaps of the thing's history. I shall ignore that idea. (In any case, it is not clear exactly how appeal to temporal parts is to help anyone see how H is related to W and W' if their temporal parts are not among their parts.)

I should think that M_1 rules out taking the temporal parts of a physical object to be sets. Thus the temporal parts of my chair, for example, cannot be identified (as it might be) with the sets whose members are the chair and a time-point or time-stretch at or through which the chair exists, for I should think that no set is literally part of my chair.

What I suggest we do is attend to places as well as times. We have the idea that no two things can occupy the same place at the same time. Well, I hope that on reflection we shall conclude that that idea is false. But if two things occupy the same place at the same time, then don't they at least overlap? Don't they literally share a part? That at any rate is the root idea that generates the definitions I shall give.

It will be simplest if we can make a certain assumption, viz., that every physical object, and every part of every physical object, exactly occupies exactly one place at every time-point at which it exists. I mean to include among "places," of course, discontinuous places, since there are physical objects that occupy such places now—for example, my suit now occupies a discontinuous place, the jacket being on one hanger and the skirt on another.

On one way of construing 'places', that is a strong, and presumably false, assumption. Suppose we take places to have "sharp boundaries." (Because they are sets of space-points? Because they are fusions of sets of space-points? No matter.) Common or garden physical objects presumably do not have sharp spatial boundaries. (What *exactly* are the spatial boundaries of my chair now?) But let us simply ignore the questions raised here. Let us take places to have sharp boundaries, and ignore the fact that making the assumption therefore involves spatial idealizing.

We are letting 'x', 'y', etc. range over physical objects and their parts. Let 'P' range over places. Let t range over time-points, and 'T' over times. I include time-stretches among the times. I also include time-points among the times, since many (most? all?) friends of temporal parts take it that physical objects have temporal parts that exist only at a time-point—i.e., that physical objects have temporal "slices" as well as temporal "chunks." (So the range of 't' is included in the range of 'T'.)

We go in two steps. Let us say, first,

x is a cross-sectional temporal part of $y =_{df}$
$(\exists T)$ [y and x exist through T & no part of x exists outside T & (t) (t is in $T \supset (P)$ (y exactly occupies P at $t \supset x$ exactly occupies P at t))].

Consider again the Tinkertoy house *H*. It existed through the time-stretch 1:00 to 1:30. If there is an x such that x exists through that time-stretch and such that no part of x exists outside that time-stretch and such that, for all time-points in that time-stretch, if *H* exactly occupies a place, then x exactly occupies it too—*if* there is such an x, then this definition tells us that x is a cross-sectional temporal part of *H*. The definition does not tell us that there is such an x. The friends of temporal parts, of course, think there is; but telling us there is is the job, not of any definition, but of a second metaphysical thesis, viz.,

(M_2) (T) [y exists through $T \supset (\exists x)$ (x exists through T & no part of x exists outside T & (t) (t is in $T \supset$ (P) (y exactly occupies P at $t \supset x$ exactly occupies P at t))].

Consider again alpha, the stick that was in *H* until I removed it at 1:30. M_2 tells us that alpha had a cross-sectional temporal part that existed only from 1:00 to 1:30. Shouldn't all cross-sectional temporal parts of alpha which existed only during that time be temporal parts not merely of alpha, but also of *H* itself? Presumably they should; so let us say

x is a temporal part of $y =_{df}$
$(\exists T)$ [y and x exist through T & no part of x exists outside T & (t) (t is in $T \supset (P)$ (y exactly occupies P at t $\supset x$ exactly occupies P, or a place in P, at t))].

This definition tells us that cross-sectional temporal parts of alpha which exist only during 1:00 to 1:30 are temporal parts of alpha—and of *H*.

Nothing so far said ensures uniqueness. For example, nothing so far said ensures that, if *H* exists through 1:00 to 1:30, then there is *exactly one* x such that x exists through that time-stretch and such that no part of x exists outside that time-stretch and such that, for all time-points in that time-stretch, if *H* exactly occupies a place, then x exactly occupies it too. But shouldn't uniqueness be ensured? I think that friends of temporal parts would like it ensured; indeed, I think they accept a third metaphysical thesis, viz.,

(M_3) If x is part of y and y is part of x, then x is identical with y.[5]

Between them, M_1 and M_3 ensure the desired uniqueness. For suppose, for example, that x and x' both have that rather complicated relation to H which I just drew attention to. Then x and x' have it to each other. Then x and x' are cross-sectional temporal parts of each other and, hence, temporal parts of each other and, hence, by M_1, parts of each other. It follows, by M_3, that x is identical with x'.

M_3 is obviously a consequence of the identity axiom

$$(x = y) \equiv (x < y) \,\&\, (y < x)$$

of the Calculus of Individuals under its intended interpretation. Friends of temporal parts need not assent to all the axioms of that Calculus: for all I know, some of them reject the fusion axiom as too strong. (So far as I can see, there is nothing in the metaphysic of temporal parts which commits its adherents to the existence of a thing that fuses the set whose members are all giraffes and all apples.) But I think they are all of them happy to assent to the identity axiom.

M_2 tells us that there is an x that is a cross-sectional temporal part of alpha lasting only from 1:00 to 1:05 and that there is a y that is a cross-sectional temporal part of H lasting only from 1:10 to 1:15; and the definition of 'temporal part' tells us that both x and y are temporal parts of H. Does it follow that there is an entity that fuses x and y? I think that even those friends of temporal parts who think that the fusion axiom is not (in general) true would assent to

If x is a temporal part of z and y is a temporal part of z, then there is a z' that fuses the set whose members are x and y

If this is true, then (in light of what precedes) they can say that there is exactly one such z' and that it is, itself, a temporal part of z. But I do not give this further metaphysical thesis a name, since I suppose it is just barely possible that some friend of temporal parts thinks that even *this* "fusion thesis" is too strong.

I have obviously been so using the expression 'is part of' to stand for a reflexive relation: I have been throughout using it in such a way as to make it true to say that everything is part of itself. I think all friends of temporal parts use the expression 'is a temporal part of' in that way too—i.e., in such a way as to make their fourth and final metaphysical thesis

$$(M_4) \qquad x \text{ is a temporal part of } x$$

true.

That looks at first glance like an uninteresting metaphysical thesis; so it pays us to take note of the fact that it is very strong indeed.

In the first place, with M_4 in hand we can now easily deduce that every physical object, and every part of every physical object, is the fusion of its temporal parts. But after all, that consequence is presumably just as it should be—the friends of temporal parts would welcome it.

In the second place, we should ask: do "times" have "sharp boundaries"? If so, something that is presumably false now follows. Consider a common or garden physical object—my chair, for example. M_4 tells us it is a temporal part of itself. The definition of 'temporal part' tells us that this means there is a time *T* such that my chair exists through *T* and such that no part of my chair exists outside *T* and so, in particular, such that my chair itself does not exist outside *T*. But is there? Is there a time-point *t* such that my chair was in existence at *t* and at no time before *t*? Or a time-point *t* such that my chair was not in existence at or before *t*, but was in existence at times as close after *t* as you like? I should think not: I should think there is no such thing as the *exact* temporal boundary of a chair.

Well, temporal idealizing is presumably no worse than spatial idealizing, and those who are still reading are already engaging in the latter activity—see p. 30 above.

The third consequence is far more serious. M_4 tells us that my chair is a temporal part of itself, and this means there is a time *T* such that my chair exists through *T* and such that no part of my chair exists outside *T* and so, in particular, such that my chair exists through and only through *T* and no part of it exists before *T*. Now my chair was made out of wood: four wooden legs, a wooden seat, and a wooden back were screwed together to make that chair. So the legs, seat, and back existed before the chair existed; so neither the legs, seat, nor back of the chair are parts of the chair. What an absurd result to have arrived at!

"No doubt it sounds odd," says the friend of temporal parts with a sigh. "But it can be lived with. For keep this in mind: if the legs, seat, and back of the chair are not themselves parts of the chair, they do at all events overlap the chair—since they have temporal parts that are temporal parts of the chair."

And perhaps the friend of temporal parts doesn't even sigh. A Tinkertoy house is made only of Tinkertoys; and isn't a chair made only of bits of wood, metal, cloth, etc.? And how is this intuition to be more tidily accommodated than by saying that every temporal part of a chair overlaps a temporal part of one or other of the bits of wood, metal, cloth, etc., of which it is made—and that the chair itself just is the fusion of its temporal parts?

More precisely: by saying that every temporal part of a chair overlaps a temporal part of one or other of the bits of wood, etc., of which the chair is at some time or other made. A Tinkertoy house is made only of Tinkertoys, but it may be made of different Tinkertoys at different times—remember the replacement of beta for alpha in *H*. Similarly, a chair may be made of different bits of wood, etc., at different times. How better to capture what goes on when a chair or house is made or when a bit of stuff is replaced in a chair or house, than by adoption of the metaphysic of temporal parts?

V

It seems to me a crazy metaphysic—obviously false. But it seems to me also that there is no such thing as a *proof* that it is false.[6]

Some people have the idea that it follows from this metaphysic that the world is static, that nothing changes, and that, that being false, the metaphysic must be false. But why should we think that this does follow? A thing changes if and only if it has a feature at an earlier time which it lacks at a later time. And a friend of temporal parts says that changes take place all the time, but that a thing does have a feature at an earlier time which it lacks at a later time if and only if earlier cross-sectional temporal parts of the thing have it and later cross-sectional temporal parts of the thing lack it.

Again, some people object to the fact that this metaphysic yields that more than one thing can occupy a given place at a given time—e.g., the cross-sectional temporal part of *H* which exists only from 1:00 to 1:30 occupies the very same place at 1:15 as *H* itself occupies at 1:15. But should we take this seriously? On reflection, it does not appear to be a conclusive objection. For after all, the metaphysic also yields that those two things, though not identical, are not discrete—it yields that the former is part of the latter.

I have deliberately refrained from including among the metaphysical theses anything that says that the temporal parts of a thing are ontologically or epistemologically "prior" to it. These are dark notions; but I think we have *some* grip on what they are, enough perhaps to be able to construct a (more or less messy) argument to the effect that the temporal parts of a physical object are not ontologically or epistemologically prior to it. No matter. What concerns me now is not their priority, but their very existence.

Why should we accept this metaphysic? I am inclined to think that the friends of temporal parts are largely motivated by two things: one, the fact that so many problems in philosophy having to do with identity across time can be so tidily solved by appeal to them, and, two, what might be called "the spatial analogy." I shall come back to the first later; let us attend now to the second.

Suppose I have a piece of chalk in my hands now, one end in my right hand, the other in my left. It is a plausible idea that there is such a thing as the "right-hand half" of the bit of chalk. (No part of it is in my left hand.) If there is such a thing, we might as well call it "Alfred."

Friends of temporal parts say that, analogously, there is such a thing as the "later half" of the bit of chalk. (No part of it existed when the chalk first came into existence.) If there is such a thing, we might as well call it "Bert."

I think it is not merely plausible to think that there is such a thing as Alfred, but that we are under considerable pressure to say that there is. For I can break the bit of chalk in half. (Actually, it isn't easy to break a bit of chalk *exactly* in half, but I might be lucky.) If I do, I will have something in my right hand which is white, roughly cylindrical in shape, dusty, etc.; and it could hardly be said that that thing will come into existence at breaking-time—surely the thing does exist before I break it (note that "it") off. And surely the thing does exist now, even if I never break it off.

There is no analogous pressure to say that there is such a thing as Bert, (Homework: try breaking a bit of chalk into its two temporal halves.)

Friends of temporal parts are quite unmoved by this difference. They say: No doubt there are differences, but why shouldn't we take lasting through time to be analogous with extending through space? Why shouldn't we say that, just as there is Alfred, so also there is Bert?

Let us look at the consequences for Bert of the idea that Bert is to be Alfred's temporal analogue.

Is Alfred a physical object? It would presumably be wrong to say that Alfred is a bit or piece or chunk of chalk. If I break Alfred off, Alfred will become a bit of chalk; but I have not in fact broken Alfred off. It is an interesting and not easily answerable question why Alfred is not now a bit of chalk. The point isn't that Alfred isn't independently movable, for you can glue two bits of wood together, which are then two bits of wood that are not independently movable. (Of course you could break off one of the bits of wood; but so could you break Alfred off.) And I think the point isn't that Alfred is continuous with more chalk; for if Alfred had been broken off and were now being held carefully in place again, it is arguable that Alfred would have been a bit of chalk continuous with another bit of chalk. No matter: as things stand, Alfred is not a bit or piece or chunk of chalk.

Something similar should presumably be said of Bert, viz., that it too is not a bit or piece or chunk of chalk. (For temporal parts come and go during a time in which I have only one bit of chalk in my hand.)

Now perhaps it may be thought that a thing is not a physical object unless it is a bit or piece or chunk of stuff of some kind. It would be no surprise if one who took this view thought that neither Alfred nor Bert is a physical object. It was to allow for the possibility that someone might take this view that I said we should take '*x*', '*y*', etc. to range not merely over physical objects, but also over anything that is part of a physical object.

What are Alfred and Bert then? Well, perhaps it will be said that they are quantities[7] of chalk. Or portions[8] of chalk. Which leaves it open for them to be perfectly respectable entities, with any number of ordinary physical properties. Thus Alfred presumably is white, roughly cylindrical in shape, and dusty; if the bit of chalk now weighs three ounces, then Alfred presumably now weighs an ounce and a half; and so on. And shouldn't we say, analogously, that Bert is white, roughly cylindrical in shape, and dusty? Perhaps by the time Bert comes into existence, the bit of chalk will weigh less than three ounces; but surely Bert will have some weight or other at every time at which it exists—just as Alfred does. If Alfred and Bert are not bits of chalk, and therefore not physical objects, they are anyway, both of them, surely *chalk*.

If Bert has not got these properties, then it is very obscure what Bert is, and hard to see why drawing our attention to Alfred should incline us to think there is such a thing as Bert.

I said this seems to me a crazy metaphysic. It seems to me that its full craziness comes out only when we take the spatial analogy seriously. The metaphysic yields that if I have had exactly one bit of chalk in my hand for the last hour, then there is something in my hand which is white, roughly cylindrical in shape, and dusty, something which also has a weight, something which is chalk, which was not in my hand three minutes ago, and indeed, such that no part of it was in my hand three minutes ago. As I hold the bit of chalk in my hand, new stuff, new chalk keeps constantly coming into existence *ex nihilo*. That strikes me as obviously false.

At a minimum, we ought to see whether there isn't some less extravagant way of solving the problem with which we began.

VI

What exactly is the problem? Whether or not there is such a thing as *W* (the fusion of the Tinkertoys on the shelf at 1:15), there is such a thing as *W′* (the wood on the shelf at 1:15). A Tinkertoy house is made only of Tinkertoys; that is an intuition we should like to preserve. Tinkertoys are bits of wood. So it seems right to say that the Tinkertoy house *H* is identical with *W′*. But at 1:30, I remove alpha from *H*, and then replace it with beta. *H* is on the shelf at 1:45, but *W′* is not then on the shelf, for alpha is on the floor at 1:45. So how *is H* related to *W′*?

I spoke earlier of alpha's having been "in *H*" until 1:30, when I removed it from *H* and replaced it with beta. I have been trying throughout (not without difficulty) to avoid speaking as common sense speaks. Common sense says: alpha was part of *H*, and then ceased to be; beta was not part of *H*, but became part of *H*.

It really is the most obvious common sense that a physical object can acquire and lose parts. Parthood surely is a three-place relation, among a pair of objects and a time. If you want to construe parthood as a two-place relation, you really will have to indulge in temporal parts to accommodate what common sense calls acquisition and loss of parts. But why should anyone want to?

If parthood is a three-place relation, then it is not possible to read the expression '$x < y$' of the Calculus of Individuals as: x is part of y. And it cannot be said that the logic of parthood is the Calculus of Individuals.

But we can easily construct a Cross-temporal Calculus of Individuals, by emending the Leonard-Goodman definitions and axioms. I think it pays us to do so.

Let us take as primitive 'x D y @ t', and read it as: x is discrete from y at t.[9]

But we cannot move on just yet. For the intended interpretation of 'x D y @ t' to be fixed, it has to be fixed for all threesomes of a pair of objects and a time-point which make 'x D y @ t' true and which make it false. There is no difficulty if both objects exist at the time-point: your nose is now discrete from my nose, your nose is not now discrete from your face, and so on. But what if one or more of the objects does not exist at the time-point? Is Caesar's nose now discrete from your nose?

Looking ahead, we know that the intended interpretation of 'x D y @ t' is to be such as to link it with parthood-at-a-time. For example, the threesome containing *A*, *B*, and 9 P.M. should make 'x D y @ t' true if and only if *A* and *B* have no part in common at 9 P.M. More precisely: if and only if there is no z such that z is part of *A* at 9 P.M. and z is part of *B* at 9 P.M. Well, is there a z such that z is *now* part of Caesar's nose? After all, Caesar's nose does not exist now. I think it will seem right to say: if x does not exist at t, then there is no z such that z is part of x at t. (If my car goes out of existence at midnight tonight, nothing will be part of it tomorrow.) If we do adopt this view, we are committed to saying that there is no z that is now part of Caesar's nose and, therefore, no z that is now part of both Caesar's nose and your nose and, thus, that Caesar's nose is now discrete from your nose. More generally, adopting this view is adopting an existence principle expressible as follows:

$$x \text{ does not exist at } t \supset (y)(x \text{ D } y \text{ @ } t) \qquad \text{first existence principle}$$

I think it really does seem right to say these things—until it strikes us that it follows that not even Caesar's nose is now part of Caesar's nose and that Caesar's nose is now discrete even from itself. There is no entirely happy alternative in the offing here. We might weaken the first existence principle; e.g., we might choose to say, instead,

$$x \text{ does not exist at } t \supset (y)(x \text{ D } y \text{ @ } t \equiv y \neq x)$$

But this has its own unhappy consequence, viz., that a thing is atomic at all times at which it does not exist; and choosing it would impose complications elsewhere. So I suggest we accept the unhappy consequences of what

I called the "first existence principle," and take it to control the intended interpretation of 'x D y @ t'.

We should surely say also that, if everything is now discrete from a thing, then that thing does not now exist—more generally, that

$$(y)\ (x \text{ D } y \text{ @ } t) \supset x \text{ does not exist at } t \qquad \text{second existence principle}$$

The conjunction of the first and second existence principles is

$$x \text{ does not exist at } t \equiv (y)(x \text{ D } y \text{ @ } t)$$

or, alternatively,

$$x \text{ exists at } t \equiv \sim (y)(x \text{ D } y \text{ @ } t)$$

So we may introduce 'x E@ t' (read: x exists at t) by definition as follows:

$$x \text{ E@ } t =_{\text{df}} \sim(y)(x \text{ D } y \text{ @ } t)$$

'$x < y$ @ t' (read: x is part of y at t) and 'x O y @ t' (read: x overlaps y at t) are now definable as follows:

$$x < y \text{ @ } t =_{\text{df}} x \text{ E @ } t \ \&\ y \text{ E @ } t \ \&\ (z)(z \text{ D } y \text{ @ } t \supset z \text{ D } x \text{ @ } t)$$
$$x \text{ O } y \text{ @ } t =_{\text{df}} (\exists z)(z < x \text{ @ } t \ \&\ z < y \text{ @ } t)$$

The old overlap axiom is easy enough to emend: what we want is

$$(\text{CCI}_2) \quad (x \text{ O } y \text{ @ } t) \equiv \sim(x \text{ D } y \text{ @ } t) \qquad \text{new overlap axiom}$$

The old identity axiom is not so easily emended, however. That is, we obviously cannot replace it with

$$(x = y) \equiv (x < y \text{ @ } t \ \&\ y < x \text{ @ } t)$$

for this tells us that, whatever time you choose, x is identical with y only if x is part of y at that time and y is part of x at that time and, thus (by the definition of '$x < y$ @ t'), only if x and y exist at that time. That is far too restrictive. Caesar's nose is surely identical with Caesar's nose, even if it does not exist now.

What we want is instead this: x is identical with y if and only if for all times t such that one or the other of them exists at t, x is part of y at t, and y is part of x at t—i.e.,

$$(\text{CCI}_1) \quad (x = y) \equiv (t)[(x \text{ E@ } t \vee y \text{ E@ } t) \supset (x < y \text{ @ } t \ \&\ y < x \text{ @ } t)]$$

new identity axiom

A great many analogues of theorems of the Calculus of Individuals are now provable in the Cross-temporal Calculus of Individuals. It is perhaps just worth drawing attention to the fact that, although '$x < x$' is provable in the Calculus of Individuals, '$x < x @ t$' is not provable in the Cross-temporal Calculus of Individuals. But it plainly ought not be; for what it tells us is that, whatever time you choose, x is part of itself at that time and thus (by the definition of '$x < y @ t$') that everything exists all the time. What is provable in the Cross-temporal Calculus of Individuals is, instead, this:

$$x \text{ E@} t \equiv x < x @ t$$

which says only that, whatever time you choose, x is part of itself at that time if and only if it exists at that time.

The old fusion axiom presents a different kind of problem. If things can have different parts at different times, then a thing can fuse one set at one time and a different set at a different time. Indeed, fusing has to be regarded as relativized to times, and I suggest we redefine it as follows:

$$x \text{ Fu } S @ t =_{\text{df}}$$
$$x \text{ E@} t \;\&\; (y)\big[y \text{ D } x @ t \equiv (z)\big[(z \in S \;\&\; z \text{ E@} t) \supset t \text{ D } z @ t\big]\big]$$

One possible analogue of the old fusion axiom is, then, this:

$$(\text{CCI}_3) \quad (\exists x)(x \in S \;\&\; x \text{ E@} t) \supset (\exists y)(y \text{ Fu } S @ t)$$

But that is only one of the possibilities. It is, after all, rather weak. It allows us to say, for example, that there is something that fuses Caesar's nose in 44 B.C. and that there is something that fuses Nixon's nose in 1979; but it does not allow us to conclude that there is something that both fuses Caesar's nose in 44 B.C. and fuses Nixon's nose in 1979. Admirers of the Calculus of Individuals will surely want that there be such a thing and will, therefore, regard the axiom I set out as too weak to be regarded as the appropriate analogue of the old fusion axiom.

There are a number of available middle grounds, but I suspect that the truly devoted friends of fusions will want to go the whole distance. The simplest way of expressing their view is to take them to say that there is not one fusion axiom in the Cross-temporal Calculus of Individuals, but indefinitely many, the procedure for generating them being this. Take any set of n sets $S_1 \ldots Sn$. For $n = 1$, write what I earlier called (CCI_3). For $n = 2$, write

$$\big[t_1 \neq t_2 \;\&\; (\exists x)(x \in S_1 \;\&\; x \text{ E@} t_1) \;\&\; (\exists y)(y \in S_2 \;\&\; y \text{ E@} t_2)\big]$$
$$\supset (\exists z)(z \text{ Fu } S_1 @ t_1 \;\&\; z \text{ Fu } S_2 @ t_2)$$

and so on. For my own part, I have no objection—it seems to me that one has only to live with fusions for a while to come to love them. But I shall not argue for all or even any of these fusion axioms. I do not know what an argument for them would look like. By the same token, however, I do not know what an argument against them would look like, "What an odd entity!" not seeming to me to count as an argument. So I shall leave it open which fusion axiom or axioms should be regarded as replacing the old fusion axiom.

More precisely, I shall leave it open which fusion axiom or axioms should be regarded as replacing the old fusion axiom, so long as the axiom or axioms chosen do not guarantee the uniqueness of fusions. For we do not want an analogue of what I earlier called "the fusion principle" to be provable in the Cross-temporal Calculus of Individuals. The fusion principle, it will be remembered, says that, if anything is a member of *S*, then there is a unique thing that fuses the *S*s. We do not want to have it provable that if anything is a member of *S* and exists at *t*, then there is a unique entity that fuses the *S*s at *t*: we want, precisely, to leave open that there may be more than one. My reason for saying that issues from the use to which I would like to be able to put these notions. Consider again the Tinkertoy house *H*. A Tinkertoy house is made only of Tinkertoys; and *H* is, at 1:15, made only of the Tinkertoys on the shelf at 1:15. I would like, therefore, to be able to say that *H* fuses, at 1:15, the Tinkertoys on the shelf at 1:15. And what about *W′*, the wood on the shelf at 1:15? I would like to be able to say that that too fuses the Tinkertoys on the shelf at 1:15. But nothing can be true if it licenses our concluding from this that *H* is identical with *W′*.

With fusions now relativized to times, we cannot single out a thing to call "*W*" as I did in section I above:

(2) *W* = the fusion of the Tinkertoys on the shelf at 1:15

now lacks a sense, for there now is no fusing *simpliciter*, there is only fusing-at-a-time. And, without an analogue of the fusion principle, we cannot even single out a thing to call "W" by drawing attention to the fact that there is something that fuses, at 1:15, the Tinkertoys on the shelf at 1:15: i.e., we cannot replace (2) with

W = the unique thing that fuses, at 1:15, the Tinkertoys on the shelf at 1:15

for there may be more than one thing that does this. Indeed, I suggest we agree that there are at least two things which do this, viz., H and W′.

Perhaps you have no taste for fusions, and regard the new fusion axioms (like the old one) as grossly overstrong. All the same, the difficulty we began with can be eliminated, and without appeal to temporal parts, if we say that parthood is a three-place relation[10] and that the new identity axiom (interpreted as I indicated) is true. How is H related to W'? We can say, quite simply, that

$$H < W' @ t \& W' < H @ t$$

is true for all times t between 1:00 and 1:30 (which was when alpha was removed from H); but that it is not true for any other times t. Since H and W' exist at times at which it is not true, H is not identical with W'.[11]

More generally, a Tinkertoy house is made only of Tinkertoys and Tinkertoys are bits of wood; so, at every time throughout its life, a Tinkertoy house is part of, and contains as part, the wood it is made of at that time.

VII

There is a difficulty analogous to the one we began with, which I suggest we look at briefly.

Let us supply the Tinkertoy house H with a different history. Suppose H came into existence on a shelf at 1:00 and that all the Tinkertoys it was then made of, indeed, all the bits of wood, indeed, all of the stuff it was then made of, came into existence at 1:00 along with H. Suppose that the whole thing rested quietly on the shelf until 5:00, and then everything—house, bits of wood, stuff—all went out of existence together. Let W' be, as before, the wood on the shelf at 1:15. Now we can say more than that W' is part of H from 1:00 to 1:30, and H part of W' from 1:00 to 1:30: we can say that, for all times t such that either of them exists at t, W' and H are parts of each other at t. It follows, by the new identity axiom, that H is identical with W'.

Is that an acceptable conclusion? I am sure that there are those who will say it is not. For isn't it true of W', and false of H, that W' could have failed to have the form of a house? Can't wood come into existence in ship shape as well as in house shape? But houses can't.

But is that a possible history? Normally, a house that *is* made of Tinkertoys *was* made of Tinkertoys; i.e., normally, the Tinkertoys existed before the house did, and the house was then built out of them. Could a house, and the Tinkertoys it is made of, come into existence together?

Again, could some wood have come into existence *ex nihilo*? (Compare the temporal parts of the bit of chalk.)

Well, I was being unfair to those who think there is a problem in the offing here. Let us suppose I make a house, not out of Tinkertoys, but out of ice. I do so, not by fitting bits of ice together, but by pouring water into a house-shaped ice-tray, and freezing it. Four hours later, I melt the whole thing down, and throw out the water. Worries about temporal idealizing apart, we can say that the house and the ice it was made of came into existence (and went out of existence) together. And the ice didn't come into existence *ex nihilo*—it came into existence *ex aqua*. But surely (it will be said) the house is not identical with the ice. For the ice, but not the house, could have failed to have the form of a house. I could have poured that very same water into a ship-shaped ice-tray instead.

I don't myself find it obvious that a piece of house-shaped ice could have been a piece of ship-shaped ice; but my informants tell me it could have been. If they are right, we must give up the Cross-temporal Calculus of Individuals, because we must give up the new identity axiom.[12]

Suppose they are right. Then we must take the logic of parthood to be a modal logic, which might be called the Modal Cross-temporal Calculus of Individuals.

I shall not construct such a logic, since I think it does not pay to rehearse the alternative possible replacements for the fusion axiom or axioms. What matters for present purposes, in any case, is really only what should be said about identity. It seems to me, however that that is plain enough: we should replace CCI_1 with:

$$(MCCI_1)(x = y) \equiv \Box(t)\left[(x\,E@t \vee y\,E@t) \supset (x < y\,@t\ \&\ y < x\,@t)\right]$$

That eliminates the difficulty. Let 'House' be the name of the house, and 'Ice' be the name of the ice it is made of. Then (if my informants are right) there is a world, and a time *t* in that world, such that

Ice E@*t*

is true, and (since House does not exist in that world)

Ice < House @ *t* & House < Ice @ *t*

is false. That being so, $MCCI_1$ tells us that House is not identical with Ice.

But this is of interest only if my informants are right about this case, or would be right about a better case.

Notes

I am grateful to George Boolos, Paul Horwich, Fred Katz, and Sydney Shoemaker for comments on an earlier draft.

1. It is familiar enough that they have been used by those interested in the metaphysics of matter. But so also have they been used by those interested in philosophy of mind [cf., for example, David Lewis, "Survival and Identity," reprinted in A. O. Rorty, ed., *The Identities of Persons* (Berkeley: Univ of California Press, 1976)],

and even by moral philosophers [cf., for example, Alan Gibbard, "Natural Property Rights," *Noûs*, x, 1 (March 1976): 77–88, and the views of Jonathan Edwards on moral responsibility, described by Roderick Chisholm in Appendix A of his *Person and Object* (London: Allen & Unwin, 1976)].

2. Henry S. Leonard and Nelson Goodman, "The Calculus of Individuals and Its Uses," *Journal of Symbolic Logic*, v. 2 (June 1940). For perspicuousness in the discussion to come, I have strengthened their identity axiom.

3. Following Richard Cartwright, in "Scattered Objects," in Keith Lehrer, ed., *Analysis and Metaphysics* (Dordrecht, Holland; Boston, Mass.: Reidel, 1975).

4. *Sameness and Substance* (Cambridge, Mass.: Harvard, 1980), p. 30ff.

5. But see section VII, n. 12 in particular.

6. But see section VII, n. 12 in particular.

7. In the sense singled out by Helen Morris Cartwright, in "Quantities," *The Philosophical Review*, LXXIX, 1 (January 1970): 25–42.

8. Following Allan Gibbard, in "Contingent Identity." [chapter 6 of this volume]

9. The variables of the Calculus of Individuals range only over existing entities. In the same spirit, the variables '*x*', '*y*', etc. of the Cross-temporal Calculus of Individuals are to range only over entities that exist at some time or other.

10. Unlike physical objects, events really do have temporal parts (though the term must be defined differently for events); hence there is no need to use tenses in ascribing parthood relations to events. We can take events to be a model of the Cross-temporal Calculus of Individuals (reading x E@ t as: x is occurring at t). But the event-identities so obtained would be the same as those I obtained [in *Acts and Other Events* (Ithaca, N.Y.: Cornell)] by taking events to be a model of the simpler Calculus of Individuals.

11. David Wiggins would say that *W′ constitutes H* at 1:15—see p. 28 above. I said: fine, but what is it for a thing x to constitute a thing y at a time t? I have no great confidence in the likelihood of his accepting the gift, but I offer him the following

$$x \text{ constitutes } y \text{ at } t =_{df} x < y \; @ \; t \; \& \; y < x \; @ \; t$$

On this account of the matter, *H* constitutes *W′* at 1:15 if *W′* constitutes *H* at 1:15, but that strikes me as harmless.

12. If my informants are right, then the friends of temporal parts must give up metaphysical thesis M_3 and, therefore, the old identity axiom and, therefore, the Calculus of Individuals. They can still construe parthood as a two-place relation: but they must take identity to be governed, instead, by

$$(x = y) \equiv \Box[(x < y) \; \& \; (y < x)]$$

4

Constitution Is Not Identity

Mark Johnston

I

Suppose that a statue of Goliath is made by fusing together two appropriately shaped pieces of clay and that after a few minutes, the artisan, frustrated with his work, dissolves the statue in a solvent which destroys clay and statue alike. Then a natural thing to say is that the careers of the statue and the lump or piece of clay which made it up are entirely coincident. The statue and the piece of clay came into being at the same time and ceased to be at the same time. Throughout their respective careers, the piece of clay constituted the statue.

Had the artisan despaired only of the arms and calves of Goliath and dissolved only them, replacing them with new pieces of appropriately molded clay, then we should say that distinct but not wholly distinct pieces of clay constituted the statue of Goliath over its lifetime.

In this second case we naturally conclude that the statue is not absolutely identical with the whole piece of clay which originally constituted it, since the piece arguably did not survive the dissolving of significant parts of it, while the statue clearly did survive the dissolving; as is evidenced by the fact that the statue had *new* arms and calves attached to *it.*

So also, it seems natural to conclude that even in the first case in which the original piece of clay constituted the statue throughout its entire career, the statue is not absolutely identical with the clay, since the statue could have survived certain changes which the piece of clay would not have survived, e.g. the changes described in the second case.

Philosophers have gone to some lengths to resist this last conclusion. Thus David Lewis, Allan Gibbard, Anil Gupta and Denis Robinson all allege that something special about modal predication invalidates the argument to non-identity in the case of complete coincidence.[1] Concentrating on Lewis's way of putting the point, since it fits neatly into a familiar systematic way of thinking of modality, the situation is supposed to be as follows.[2] If the term "Lumpl" names the piece of clay which makes up the statue *Goliath*, the aim is to defend

(1) In the case of complete coincidence, Lumpl = Goliath

while allowing

(2) Lumpl could not have survived the loss of those of its parts which made up the arms and calves of Goliath. Goliath could have.

How then are we to avoid the following contradiction, got by substituting in (2) on the basis of (1)?

(3) Lumpl could not have survived the loss of those of its parts which made up the arms and calves of Goliath. Lumpl could have.

Lewis's answer is essentially this: The position held by "Goliath" in (2), even if *de re*, i.e. outside of the scope of the modal "could have", is not referentially transparent, i.e. does not support the substitution of codesignative names *salva veritate*. This is because "Goliath" as a name of a statue is performing more than a referential function in (2). "Goliath" not only picks out the statue but it also, perhaps with the cooperation of context, indicates a particular counterpart relation or set of necessary and sufficient qualitative conditions for tracing Goliath across the worlds—if you like, the "statue" counterpart relation.[3] This relation determines for Goliath a set of otherworldly, relevantly similar individuals, or *counterparts*, which represent the possibilities for Goliath. We have a different set of counterparts determined if we employ the "lump of matter" counterpart relation indicated by the name "Lumpl". Since, on the view in question, what could have happened to a thing is what happens to at least one of its counterparts, the truth values of the modal predication in (2) are sensitive to which counterpart relation or principle of cross-world tracing is invoked by the names used (perhaps in conjunction with context). That is why we have (2) true and (3) false. The substitution of codesignative names alters the tracing principles in terms of which the relevant modal predications are to be evaluated.

It is instructive to investigate those analogous moves which in the case of temporal predication could be employed to defend

(1′) In the case of only partial coincidence, Lumpl = Goliath. The obvious problem with (1′) is

(2′) Lumpl will not survive the loss of those of its parts which make up the arms and calves of Goliath. Goliath will.

In conjunction with (1′), this seems to imply a contradiction, namely

> (3′) Lumpl will not survive the loss of those of its parts which make up the arms and calves of Goliath. Lumpl will.

There are three slightly different ways of understanding temporal predication so as to make (1′) and (2′) true but avoid the inference to the contradiction apparent in (3′). The first way takes "Goliath" and "Lumpl" to be names of continuants, and claims that (2′) is true because it is properly read as

> (2*) Lumpl will not survive-qua-Lumpl the loss of those of its parts which make up the arms and calves of Goliath. Goliath will survive-qua-Goliath.

where something survives-qua-Lumpl some event just in case Lumpl is around before and after the event, and something survives-qua-Goliath some event if Goliath is around before and after the event. From (1′) and (2*) we derive

> (3*) Lumpl will not survive-qua-Lumpl the loss of those of its parts which make up the arms and calves of Goliath. Lumpl will survive-qua-Goliath.

(3*) is true on the intended construal of "*x* survives-qua-*y*". However, the unattractive artificiality of this suggestion is immediately obvious. Surviving some event is plausibly taken to consist in being around before and after the event, but "Goliath survives-qua-Lumpl" (or "Goliath-qua-lump survives") just means that Lumpl survives, and "Lumpl survives-qua-Goliath" (or "Lumpl-qua-statue survives") just means that Goliath survives. Better then to avoid this kind of "qua" talk, since it only serves to mask paradox if *a*'s surviving-qua-*b* has nothing essentially to do with *a*'s continuing to be around. The real force of (2′) is not captured by this first proposal.

Matters are not much different on the second proposal, which takes "Goliath" and "Lumpl" to be names of continuants now explicitly understood as four-dimensional sums of temporal stages united by appropriate gen-identity criteria, i.e., criteria for aggregating the short-lived stages into longer-lived continuants. Then it is said that for the continuant *x* to survive-qua-Lumpl or to survive-qua-lump some event *e* is for there to exist, after *e*, lump of clay stages which stand in the relation of being stages of the same lump of clay to stages of *x* existing before *e*. Mutatis mutandis for the continuant *x* to survive-qua-Goliath (or to survive-qua-statue or qua-statue to survive). Now we construe (2′) as saying that (2*) and replace (3′) by (3*). The inference from (1′) and (2′) to (3*) is unproblematic.

But once again we have a quite artificial sense of "survival" at work: *x*'s surviving-qua-*y* some event *e* has nothing essentially to do with *x* being around after the event *e*. To say that *x* exists in world *w* is to say no more than that the abstract representation of the way the world might have been that is *w* represents a possibility for *x*. This leaves it open just how this possibility is represented by *w*, e.g., by having *x* do the representing or by having *x*'s counterparts do it. But to say that *x* actually survives *e* is to say something that requires *x* to exist after *e*. Mere descendants of *x* won't do.[4]

The third theory of temporal predication is the closest analogue of Lewis's multiple counterpart theory and has it that "Lumpl" and "Goliath" each denote a *stage*, and in fact the same stage, a stage existing at the period during which (1′)–(3′) are uttered. But the theory has it that these names do more semantically than merely denote. They carry with them, perhaps via the associated nominal "piece of clay" and count noun "statue", distinct gen-identity criteria, i.e. criteria for aggregating momentary or short-lived stages into longer-lived continuants. Necessary and sufficient conditions for being a stage of the same persisting *piece of clay* as Lumpl is a stage of are somehow associated with the name "Lumpl", and necessary and sufficient conditions for being a stage of the same persisting *statue* that Goliath is a stage of are somehow associated with the name "Goliath". Since a stage will survive some change only if it is gen-identical with a stage which exists after the change, the question as to whether the stage referred to twice over in (1′) will survive some specific change is sensitive to which name is used in putting that question. Hence, although (1′) and (2′) are true while (3′) is false, (3′) does not follow from (1′) and (2′).

This theory of temporal predication also breaks down. For it to begin to work we must once again think of continuants as four-dimensional aggregates of stages. Then it is natural to say that *continuants* undergo or *survive* changes like coming to be constituted by different matter, while their *stages succeed* each other through such changes. The change in question is the replacement of the arms and legs of Goliath and hence of much of the matter of Lumpl. On the theory in question "Lumpl" and "Goliath" are supposed to denote a pre-replacement stage shared by the statue and the piece of clay. But then it follows that Goliath (the pre-replacement stage) does not survive the change described in (2′) and (3′) any more than Lumpl does. The continuant statue that includes Goliath literally survives but, on the third theory, this continuant is *not* Goliath. On that theory, "Goliath" names a short-lived stage. So the third theory of temporal predication is just like the first two theories in failing to capture the force of (2′).

Despite the similarities between the cases of complete and partial coincidence, there is little to be said for defending (1′) by understanding de re temporal predication as introducing referential opacity. Yet in ordinary language the use of modal and temporal predication seems strikingly similar.

(They shade into each other when the topic is which possibility is likely to occur next.) So we should inquire into the claim which motivates the construal of de re modal predication as introducing referential opacity. This is the claim that (1) is true, more generally the claim that a material object is identical with the matter which constitutes it over its lifetime.

II

I know of only two arguments for (1) with any prima facie plausibility. The first is an argument from mereology, allegedly the logic of the part/whole relation. Mereology employs the primitive predicate "$O(x,y)$" where the intended construal of this predicate is that x and y "overlap in content" in the broadest "logical" or topic neutral sense of these terms. (As we shall see, it is an important question just what this sense is.) Given this notion of overlap, the logical or topic neutral notion of one thing being a part of another may be defined thus

(4) $P(x,y) \leftrightarrow \forall z(O(z,x) \rightarrow O(z,y))$

Mereology is interesting for our purposes because, depending on the details of its formulation, mereology contains as an axiom or a theorem

(5) $x = y \leftrightarrow \forall z(P(z,x) \leftrightarrow P(z,y))$

Now we seem to have a powerful tool for arguing to identities. Exhaustively enumerate the "parts" (in the broadest topic neutral sense) of x and of y. If they have just the same parts "they" are identical.[5] So the mereologist might argue in favor of (1) as follows: clearly in the case where Lumpl and Goliath are coincident throughout their entire careers they have just the same parts—there is nothing that is a part of Lumpl that is not a part of Goliath nor vice versa. After all, isn't this what we are saying when we say that throughout their careers all of Lumpl constitutes Goliath and Goliath is constituted only by Lumpl. But then, using (5), we must conclude that Goliath = Lumpl.

So long as we think of continuants as four-dimensional sums of stages, the argument does not generalize to encompass (1′) understood as a claim about continuants. In the case of partial coincidence the four-dimensional statue Goliath will have different material parts from the four-dimensional piece of clay Lumpl. After the change of head and calves there will be parts of Goliath which are not parts of Lumpl.

Does the argument for (1) stand up to scrutiny? I think not. Indeed, I believe it simply equivocates on the term "part". Throughout their entire careers Goliath is wholly constituted by Lumpl. One thing wholly consti-

① Referential opacity: a modal predicate depends on not only depends on the referent of the object alone but also relies on the context
② Modal predication introduces referential opacity.
③ King denies that modal predicates and temporal predicates are that similar.

tutes another iff every *material* part of the first stands in the ancestral of *being a material part of* to some material part of the second.[6] At most, then, constitution implies sameness of material parts. But we cannot plausibly construe (5) as licensing claims of identity simply on the basis of sameness of material parts. For suppose we have a plasticene pot. We squash the plasticene, thereby destroying the pot. We then use the plasticene—all of it—to make a bust of Napoleon. Clearly the pot is not identical with the bust, even though they have the same material parts. Someone might say that the trouble here is that the pot and the plasticene, although made of the same matter, were made of it at different times, so that we get identity just when we have x and y made of the same matter over just the same range of times. But this condition for identity is too close a claim to the claim that (1), i.e., that in the case of complete coincidence, Goliath = Lumpl, to provide an argument for (1). Anyone who has doubts about (1) will doubt the condition. Nor will it help to cast the condition in the language of material temporal parts, where a material temporal part is the content of a matter-occupied region of space-time, and material continuants are thought of as sums of such temporal parts. For then the argument for (1) which goes by way of

$$(5) \quad x = y \leftrightarrow \forall z\big(P(z,x) \leftrightarrow P(z,y)\big)$$

interpreting "$P(z,x)$" as z is a temporal part of x, and understanding Goliath and Lumpl as sums of temporal parts, will simply beg the question against someone who has doubts about (1). Such a person will reject the motivating metaphysical model of Goliath and Lumpl as four-dimensional sums of temporal parts.

If there is to be a non-question begging argument for (1) from (5), the mereologist owes us an account of a topic neutral or logical notion of a part for which (5) is true. Only then can he be said to be motivating (1) by means of (5), rather than appealing to a metaphysical view of continuants which is plausible only if particular claims like (1) are true. But what is this logical or topic neutral notion of a part, supposedly available prior to conversion to metaphysical views about continuants? Unfortunately, mereologists are far from unanimous on this point.

Thus, for example, in their original paper "The Calculus of Individuals and Its Uses" H.S. Leonard and Nelson Goodman write

> in our interpretation [of mereology] parts and common parts need not necessarily be spatial parts. Thus in our applications of the calculus to philosophical problems, two concrete entities to be taken as [non-over-lapping or] discrete not only have to be spatially discrete, but also temporally discrete, *discrete in color, etc. etc.* (1940, pp. 46–7; my emphasis)

The idea of objects being mereological sums of property parts with the explicit condition that properties are in the first instance particular and not universal was a leading motive in the eminently clear-headed metaphysics of D.C. Williams.[7] David Lewis, also working within a mereological framework, opts for a more restrictive notion of a property part when he writes

> It is quite easy to believe that a point particle divides into a few non-spatiotemporal parts in such a way that one of them gives the particle its charge, another gives it its mass and so on. But it is just absurd to think that a thing has (recurring or non-recurring) non-spatiotemporal parts for *all* its countless abundant properties. (1986, pp. 66–7)

Elsewhere, an even narrower construal of the notion of part relevant to mereology has set in. Thus Judith Jarvis Thomson, discussing a prima facie argument for the doctrine of temporal parts—an argument which involves applying mereology to a scattered sum of parts which was temporarily unscattered and shaped in the form of a house—writes

> Even if there is [such an entity as house-shape] it certainly is not literally part of any house. [this volume, p. 25]

Evidently there is much dispute about the metaphysical parts of objects and hence much dispute about the detailed metaphysical interpretation of the crucial mereological predicate "$O(x,y)$".

Adjudicating the dispute is not to the point here. For we are not interested in implementing a metaphysics but only in evaluating a mereological argument for the conclusion that an object is identical with the matter which invariably constitutes it. In evaluating that argument we should not rely upon any substantive metaphysical conception of the parts or ingredients of entities. Rather our question is whether there is any metaphysically neutral or *logical* conception of a part which could be used in conjunction with ordinary judgements about constitution and material parts to motivate claims such as (1).

For those who are comfortable with thinking of second order logic as the logic of properties the following may provide a way of thinking about the question. This principle of second order logic

(6) $$x = y \leftrightarrow \forall F(Fx \leftrightarrow Fy)$$

has a good claim to define the logical notion which is identity. From left to right we have Leibniz's Law, surely an a priori principle if anything is. From right to left we have a triviality secured by instantiation; among the properties which x and y are asserted to have in common by the right hand side

Max Black might deny this

"50,51,52 could be deleted," says King.

are identity with y and identity with x. Moreover, from (6) we can prove the familiar features of identity, *viz.*, that it is reflexive, symmetric and transitive. So the second order definition of identity has a good claim to be *the* definition of identity.

Now in standard mereology the following is the definition of identity:

(7) $x = y \leftrightarrow \forall z(O(z,x) \leftrightarrow O(z,y))$

So it seems that if we want to give "$O(x,y)$" its proper *logical* interpretation, and by means of

(4) $P(x,y) \leftrightarrow \forall z(O(z,x) \rightarrow O(z,y))$

fix the logical interpretation of "$P(x,y)$", and thereby find out what a *logical* part is, we should consider this question: How then must we understand the mereological primitive "$O(x,y)$" so that the second order characterization of identity is logically equivalent to the mereological characterization of identity?

This quite determinate question is the question to face if we are to take mereology as a "generalization of the logic of identity" i.e. a set of principles, including a characterization of identity, which purport to have as much claim on us as

(6) $x = y \leftrightarrow \forall F(Fx \leftrightarrow Fy)$

Our problem then is to find an appropriate pure logical construal of the mereological primitive "$O(x,y)$".

Clearly, if we interpret the mereological primitive "$O(x,y)$" as saying that x is identical with y, then (7) and (6) will be logically equivalent. For then $\forall z(O(z,x) \leftrightarrow O(z,y))$ is logically equivalent to $x = y$.

If we interpret the mereological primitive "$O(x,y)$" as saying that x is not identical with y, then (7) and (6) will be logically equivalent. For then $\forall z(O(z,x) \leftrightarrow O(z,y))$ is logically equivalent to $x = y$.

In order to make (7) come out logically equivalent to (6) it will not do to understand "$O(x,y)$" as meaning that x and y stand in some relation R that neither guarantees identity nor guarantees distinctness. For then there will be no logical guarantee that $x = y$ just in case for every z, z stands in R to x if and only if z stands in R to y.

The simple but important observation is this: if we accept (6), the second order characterization of identity, and we ask ourselves how we should understand the mereological primitive "$O(x,y)$" so that the mereological definition

(7) $x = y \leftrightarrow \forall z(O(z,x) \leftrightarrow O(z,y))$ –

has the same status as (6), the answer is that we should take "$O(x,y)$" either to guarantee that x is identical with y or to guarantee that x is not identical with y. Given this conclusion and

$$(4) \quad P(x,y) \leftrightarrow \forall z(O(z,x) \rightarrow O(z,y))$$

it follows that whichever of these two ways we construe "$O(x,y)$", "$P(x,y)$" will mean that x is identical with y! The exercise has shown what most of us probably suspected all along: there is available no non-trivial notion of a *logical* part. x is a *logical part* of y just in case x is y. Pure logic can offer no interesting interpretation of the predicate "$P(x,y)$".

Of course, the mereologist may accept this and yet still urge (7) on us as an extension of what we learned in the logic class. (He may not be very interested in securing the honorific "logic" for a principle in which he has complete confidence.) However, what should embarrass the mereologist is that we do have a perfectly good *logical* characterization of identity, *viz.* the second order characterization, whose status no mereological characterization can either impeach or approach.

That status is importantly different from the status of the metaphysical views about objects which would guarantee the equivalence of (6) and (7). These two characterizations of identity would be equivalent on the assumption that objects are sums of their properties, and hence have their properties as "parts". Then (7) would have it that x is identical with y just in case every sum of properties which overlaps with x overlaps with y and vice versa. But the picture of objects as sums of properties is neither forced on us by logic nor capable of being the upshot of any empirical discovery. In that sense it is sheer metaphysics. Moreover, in order to use (7) so interpreted in a defence of the claim that

(1) In the case of complete coincidence, Lumpl = Goliath

we would have to accept the further metaphysical principle that sameness of material or spatiotemporal parts is sufficient for sameness of property parts.

Obviously, all this is substantial metaphysics, not formal logic. There is no metaphysically neutral, *logical* conception of a part which could be used in conjunction with ordinary judgements about material parts so as to motivate claims such as (1). If that is so, then in *motivating* a metaphysics, as opposed to merely implementing one, mereology is about as useful as ① Mariology.

The metaphysically neutral guide to identity is just (6)

$$(6) \quad x = y \leftrightarrow \forall F(Fx \leftrightarrow Fy)$$

① Part of Christian theology dealing w/ the "virgin" Mary.

and in our original case of complete coincidence we have good reason to think that there is a property that holds of Goliath but not of Lumpl: it is the property of being able to survive the loss of those of its material parts which make up the arms and calves of Goliath. Alternatively, supposing Lumpl to be squashable, we have good reason to think that there is a property that holds of Lumpl but not of Goliath: it is the property of being able to survive being squashed. Appeals to (7) or (5) on behalf of (1) notwithstanding, there is good reason to think that (1) is false since (6), unlike (7) and (5), is uncontroversially a logical principle.

Even so, some are unsatisfied by this use of (6) against (1) precisely because it depends upon exploiting modal or dispositional differences as between things with just the same categorical intrinsic properties. The second argument for (1) develops the worry that sameness of categorical intrinsics is sufficient for identity.

III

This second argument for (1), though not explicitly employed in the literature, is one that seems to me especially worthy of respect. Sometimes in discussion it is said on behalf of (1) "How can you distinguish between Goliath and Lumpl on the basis of mere modal or counterfactual or dispositional differences; after all, Goliath and Lumpl are intrinsically exactly alike, how could they fail to be identical?"[8] As it stands, this goes too far, for there is no reliable road to identity from qualitative similarity. After all

(6) $x = y \leftrightarrow \forall F(Fx \leftrightarrow Fy)$

is a theorem of second order logic only because the second order quantifier ranges over non-qualitative properties like identity with x. A fortiori, there is no utterly reliable road to identity from *intrinsic* qualitative similarity. But there is a powerful point in favor of (1) to be made by exploiting the fact that Goliath and Lumpl seem to be intrinsically exactly alike, i.e. both are made up of exactly the same sort of clay, have exactly the same shape and texture, weigh exactly the same and so on.

Take any sort of thing F, then this principle will be plausible:

(8) If y is a paradigm F and x is intrinsically exactly like y then x is an F.[9]

Now suppose for *reductio ad absurdum* that Goliath and Lumpl are distinct. Goliath is a paradigm statue of Goliath and Lumpl is intrinsically exactly like Goliath. By (8), Lumpl is a statue of Goliath. Two bizarre consequences follow. First, an intolerable type of co-occupancy: in the case in which Lumpl and Goliath are completely coincident, we have at least two *statues of Goliath* in the same place throughout their entire careers. At *least* two because we can invent a name for the piece of matter which constitutes Lumpl, say "Lumpl*", and argue first that Lumpl* is distinct from the statues Lumpl and Goliath, and then argue by (8) that it is a statue. So we have an endless multiplication of statues.

Secondly, as this last elaboration also shows, concerning something which we originally assumed not to have the modal properties of a statue, we have shown that it is a statue, and so *does* have the modal properties of a statue. We started out, as in (2) above, by saying that Lumpl could not survive the loss of those of its parts which make up the arms and calves of Goliath. The grounds were that, unlike Goliath, Lumpl is a piece of clay and not a statue. But by using (8) we have undermined those grounds and in proving that Lumpl is a statue we have thereby established that it could survive the loss of those parts.

Surely, if (8) is true, then this is a reductio of the claim that Goliath is not identical with Lumpl.[10] So Lumpl = Goliath.

IV

(1) If (8) is true, then certain related similarity principles ought also be true. In particular, it ought to be true that

> (9) If *y* is a paradigm *F* and *x* is an entity that differs from *y* in any respect relevant to being an *F* only very minutely then *x* is an *F*.

For how can such very minute differences make for the difference between a paradigm *F* and something not an *F* at all? This principle can be given strong theoretical support in those cases in which "*F*" is a sortal that can be taught by ostending paradigms. In such cases, (9) seems to state the grounds for counting as *F*s things other than the ostended paradigm *F*s. (Imagine that the minute differences do not add up to a perceptible difference, and that we can recognize *F*s by perception.)

That (9) is very surprisingly *not* true I take to be the upshot of Peter Unger's (1981) nice "problem of the many". The problem begins with the observation that

> (10) In the closest vicinity of any paradigm middle sized material *F* there are usually very many entities that differ only very minutely from the paradigm in any respect.

This is a familiar consequence of material atomism. Unger illustrates the point by means of the example of a cloud. Whenever there is a cloud or dense cluster of water droplets, there is in its closest vicinity a relatively

(1) the switch is obvious here.

large number of cloud-shaped, equally dense clusters of water droplets. All of these clusters are highly coincident, many differing in composition from the others and from the original cloud only in respect of a single droplet. Hence in the closest vicinity of any paradigm cloud there are very many entities—cloud-shaped clusters of water droplets—that differ only very minutely from the paradigm cloud. So, by (9), in the closest vicinity of any paradigm cloud there are very many clouds, in fact an enormous number. They are highly coincident, almost completely overlapping, differing only minutely in constitution. Moreover, clouds are here functioning only as a vivid example. The same holds for tables, chairs, trees and animals—anything that is materially complex. ✓

Rather than conclude that there are enormously many more tables, chairs, trees, etc. than we would ever have dreamt of, Unger himself prefers to say that there are no tables, chairs, trees, etc.—no materially complex *F*s for any sort *F*. So far as I can reconstruct the reasoning. Unger's thought is that since terms like "table", "chair", etc. are supposed to both function as count nouns, and give rise to reasonable counts of the numbers of these things, *and* be governed by principles like (9), they turn out to be not coherently usable, thanks to the truth of (10).✓

I think that we can do better than Unger's Eliminative Nihilism. We can explain why (9), though plausible, is nonetheless false. The explanation will similarly redound to the discredit of (8), thereby undermining the main argument for taking invariant constitution to be identity. Indeed, doing better on Unger's problem will involve us in supposing that constitution is *never* identity.

No! only taken & the same space!

First we must locate the role played by the phenomenon of vagueness in the problem of the many, lest some think that the problem is simply and completely a problem of vagueness and will disappear once one or other of the more or less adequate treatments of vagueness is applied. It is true that we were adopting a pretense of precision when we supposed that there would be a particular and definite dense cluster of water droplets constituting any paradigm cloud, a definite cluster of which we could say that many other, almost exactly overlapping, cloud-shaped clusters differed from it only minutely in constitution, e.g. by not including one water droplet included in the paradigm cloud. However, the pretense was harmless for the purposes of generating the problem of the many. The problem of the many still looms if we admit that our paradigm cloud has no privileged cluster of water droplets as *the* cluster which exactly constitutes it, the truth being instead that with respect to various sharpenings, or legitimate ways of drawing the boundaries of the cloud, slightly different such clusters will constitute the cloud. For after all, on any sharpening, or way of fixing on a sharply defined cluster to constitute our paradigm cloud, we will have the cloud c, the precise cluster k_0 and a very large number of precise clusters

k_1, k_2 differing from k_0 only very minutely and hence differing from c only very minutely. Now (9), if true, is definitely true; i.e. it ought to hold on any legitimate sharpening. But then on any legitimate sharpening, such as the one just described, we will have our paradigm cloud c and, by (9), a very large number of almost exactly similar clouds k_1, k_2 . . . So the problem of the many arises on each legitimate sharpening.

What then is the way out? Sticking to the harmless fantasy of precision, consider the cloud c and the clusters k_0, k_1, k_2 . . . On any ordinary way of talking, clusters like k_0, k_1, k_2, etc. are not themselves clouds but may constitute clouds. On ordinary ways of talking, when counting the number of clouds we do *not* contemplate a count of all the distinct, precise, cloud-shaped clusters of water droplets in the nearest vicinity of any cloud. These do not count as clouds. Despite their being quantities of matter which constitute clouds, we do not count them *as* clouds. That is, our ordinary use of a count noun like 'cloud' does not strictly conform to (9) but rather to

(9′) If y is a paradigm F and x is an entity that differs from y in any respect relevant to being an F only very minutely *and x is of the right category, i.e. is not a mere quantity or piece of matter*, then x is an F.

Hence Unger's insistent and ironic question "But *which* of k_0, k_1, k_2 . . . is our paradigm cloud c?" has as its proper answer "None". None of these count as clouds because they are mere quantities of matter and hence mere constitutors of clouds. The problem of the many simply shows that constitution is a vague relation. Our cloud c is not only not identical with any one of k_0, k_1, k_2 but also it is not definitely constituted by any one of k_0, k_1, k_2 . . . Rather, on one legitimate sharpening it is constituted by one of the ks, on another, another of the ks, and so on. What is important for our purposes is that on no legitimate sharpening is c identical with any one of the ks. For if that were so there would be a precise cluster k_1 which on one legitimate sharpening was a paradigm cloud and there would be entities of the same category as k_1—all the other precise clusters—which deserve the name of a cloud if k_1 does. We would be back with the problem of the many.

So we see that recognizing that constitution is not ever identity, which involves recognizing a distinction of category between a material object and the matter which constitutes it, is crucial in dealing with the problem of the many.[11] So also, the alleged reductio of §3 only serves to show that instead of (8) we need (8′).

(8′) If y is a paradigm F and x is intrinsically exactly like y and x is of the right category, i.e. x is not a mere quantity or piece of matter, then x is an F.

(8′) reflects the fact that in counting *F*s we never dream of counting as still more *F*s the enormous number of *F*-shaped bundles of matter which (on some or other legitimate sharpening) constitute *F*s. Now perhaps someone with a feel for the problem of the many will admit this as a descriptive claim, but will insist "By what right do we not count such *F*-shaped bundles of matter as *F*s? By what right do we ignore the striking intrinsic similarities between *F*s and their constituting matter, counting *F*s only on one side of this so-called distinction of category? What is there to the distinction anyway once we admit that there is nothing more to an *F* than its constituting matter? Isn't this just a distinction without a difference?"

V

What gives these questions force is their appeal to a particular conception of what is required to justify certain systematic patterns and demarcations in our judgements of identity, difference and sortal-relative number. The insistence on no distinction between an *F* and its *F*-shaped constituting matter without a difference to justify the distinction is uncontroversial on its face. It is a certain seductive conception of what a justifying difference must consist in which ought to be controversial. The conception has it that the justifying difference has to be substantial and characterizable independently of our practice of making judgements which exhibit certain patterns and demarcations. So on this substantial conception it is not enough *first* to say that the difference between an *F* and its *F*-shaped constituting matter is just the difference we mark when for example we standardly don't count *F*-shaped constituting matter as an *F*, and *then* having said that go on to give an internal and pragmatic justification of this in terms of how a practice which marks this distinction serves our purposes. In contrast with such a minimal and practice-dependent justification, *practice-dependent* because it only has recourse to our practices and their internal rationales, the substantial and independent justification would resort to some metaphysical model of the relation between an *F* and its *F*-shaped constituting matter. The practice-*in*dependent justification of the distinction will then be that there is some metaphysical *extra* which an *F* includes and an *F*-shaped bundle of matter does not.

The catalogue of proposed extra ingredients is none too impressive. Among the entities proposed as ingredients in *F*s along with their matter, we have had bare, that is non-qualitative, but somehow essentially *F*-ish particulars, *F*-ish substrata which hold together the proper features of *F*s as if those features were like pins in a pin cushion, and haecceities or particular identity properties, such as *being Mt. Fujiama*. Not that all of these ideas are just silly. Most of them have their origins in reasonable thoughts about material objects which then become perverted by the demand for a metaphysical model of a material object which discerns extra ingredients besides the object's constituting matter. So, for example, the idea of non-qualitative bare particulars or haecceities as ingredients is a mistaken hypostasizing of a rather good idea, which has of late been called (along with many other different ideas of varying merit) haecceitism,[12] the idea that there is no purely qualitative criterion for the identity of objects. So too the idea that each *F* includes as an ingredient besides its constituting matter a substantial form, which unlike the *F*'s constituting matter is essentially *F*-ish, is a mistaken hypostasis of the rather good idea that if we have objects classified into substance sorts or relatively natural kinds and *F* is one such sort or kind then we will not countenance as possible a situation in which something that is actually an *F* exists without being in that situation *F*-ish in important ways. Just as we can have haecceitism without bare particulars or haeccieties as extra ingredients, we can have essentialism without having substantial forms or essences as extra ingredients.

Alternative conclusions can be drawn from surveying at once both the catalogue of proposed metaphysical extras and the problem of the many. The first conclusion is that there is no credible metaphysical extra and *therefore* no justifiable distinction to be made between an *F* and its constituting matter. Then the problem of the many is a straight proof to the effect that our practice of using count nouns or sortals is incoherent. The better conclusion is that our practice and the distinction it embodies is acceptable as it stands and what is bogus is the conception of justifying our practice which requires that, for the distinction to be justified, the difference between an *F* and its constituting matter must be a deep metaphysical difference secured by an extra ingredient of the *F*.

It is the Minimalist who characteristically draws the second conclusion. Here, as elsewhere, he aims for ontology without metaphysics, which is to say general talk about reality without the postulation of extra ingredients which it is the peculiar privilege of philosophy to discover. The Minimalist accuses both the Eliminativist like Unger and the Hyperrealist, who believes in extra ingredients, of making the same error, the error of supposing that our practice of distinguishing *F*s and their constituting matter and counting accordingly could only be justified if the distinction is secured by the independent metaphysics of the matter.[13]

What then does justify our practice of employing the distinction and counting accordingly? Probably only this: in representing the world as made up of material objects of various sorts, persisting through all but substantial changes in respects crucial to their sort, we provide for ourselves certain explanatory strategies. We are able to explain sortal relative continuities in terms of the persistence of objects of the relevant sorts, and to explain change and discontinuity in terms of the natures and interactions of persisting objects of various sorts. But since the middle-sized persisting objects of our experience are materially complex and constantly undergo material change which falls short of being substantial change in respects important to objects of their sort, we cannot take them to be identical with the parcels or bundles of matter which make them up at various times. For often, as with the case of Goliath and Lumpl, such material changes are substantial changes in respects important to the persistence of bundles or quantities of matter in question. Goliath is thus typical in being able to survive changes which the piece of matter which originally constituted it cannot survive. Hence within our scheme of persisting objects and their constituent pieces or quantities of matter there are systematic reasons to distinguish objects from the matter which constitutes them. The crucial distinction is a consequence of representing the world as a world of both objects and pieces of matter surviving material change, but surviving different kinds and degrees of material change.

The explanatory strategies which this style of representation makes possible are sometimes contrasted with an explanatory strategy which accounts for change and continuity in terms of the laws governing the propagation of material property instances over space-time. This last style of explanation has been extraordinarily successful in serving the purposes of modern science. But there is an enormous gulf, so far unabridged by argument, falling between properly respecting that style of explanation and accepting scientism, which in this context amounts to the view that there are only patterns of distribution of material property instances, so that persisting objects, if they are to exist at all, must be identical with some such patterns.

In the absence of a defense of scientism, we can rest content with our scheme of persisting objects distinct from their constituting matter. After all, the scheme has served us very well in making intelligible a world of change and continuity. Russell said that we can properly do without the metaphysics of the stone age. Just so, but we can also properly do without the scientistic metaphysics of our own age. The ontology of the stone age is however another matter. It, fortunately, is still with us and well deserves its place.[14]

Notes

1. See Lewis (1971), Gibbard (1975) [Chapter 6 of this volume], Gupta (1980) and Robinson (1982a and 1982b).

2. The remarks that follow are adapted from Lewis (1971).

3. For counterpart theory see Lewis (1968). Lewis discusses multiple counterpart relations in Lewis (1986), §4.5 [Chapter 7 of this volume.]

4. Some will say that I have illegitimately supposed that we can always pick out a continuant x, whereas in this context one can only pick out x-qua-statue and x-qua-clay. I find this very implausible. To see its implausibility, imagine that we view the history of the statue and the clay from a later date. Why can't we *then* introduce the name "Goliath" to denote the continuant with the more inclusive history—i.e., the

history of the statue, which continued on after the change of parts—and introduce the name "Lumpl" to denote the continuant with the less inclusive history—the history which came to an end with the change of parts. The claim that qua-prediction is irreducible may look plausible when contemplating future occurrences but its plausibility vanishes when we contemplate histories from the perspective of the remembrance of things past.

5. For examples of such uses of mereology see Thomson (1983) [Chapter 3 of this volume].

6. The slightly roundabout wording is to accommodate those who might wish to worry whether for example the subatomic parts of the clay are really material parts of the statue—maybe the statue's material parts are only parts like the clay, the legs, the torso, the arms, and the head.

7. Williams (1966) and (1986).

8. Here, and in what follows, those who think of modal properties and dispositions as intrinsic should understand "intrinsic" to mean categorical and intrinsic. I particularly remember Denis Robinson urging the argument just quoted.

9. To make such a principle ultimately defensible certain restrictions not pertinent to the argument of the main body of the paper have to be added. Thus if things intrinsically just like human beings grew on trees or sprang from the teeth of a certain dragon many would think that a case could be made for denying them the name of human beings since they do not have the characteristic *origins* of human beings. *Mutatis mutandis* for statues; a statue of Mt. Fujiama that was full size and made of the same sort of matter as the real Mt. Fujiama might be intrinsically exactly like Mt. Fujiama. But it would be wrong to say that Mt. Fujiama is a statue. (This example is due to Giden Rosen.) For something to be a statue it has to be shaped or constituted with the intention of generating an art object. But just because it could be said of Lumpl that it was originally shaped or constituted (by putting together two pieces of clay) with the intention of generating an art object, the required restriction on (8) would affect the argument to follow.

In a similar vein, some *F*s are subject to a requirement of "maximality" so that nothing that is a proper part of an *F* can count as another *F*. The status of such a principle and the required qualifications for such principle are delicate matters. Two tables can make up a third table, and the Pope's crown consists of three crowns.

10. Some might object that the paradigm statue used to argue that Lumpl is a statue is none other than Goliath, the very statue which Lumpl constitutes. But of course a duplicate of Goliath made from the same mold using the same material would have done as well.

11. In understanding the issue as whether constitution is ever identity I have in mind the temporal part theorist who admits that in the second case where the head and calves of Goliath are replaced, Goliath is not identical with Lumpl. Rather Goliath and Lumpl, understood as four dimensional continuants, overlap. Constitution is the overlap of the temporal parts of persisting quantities of matter and of persisting material objects. Identity is just the case of complete overlap. For a development of this view see Robinson (1982a) and (1982b). Someone who construes identity as the limiting case of this kind of overlap will not be able to justify any distinction of ontic type between a material object and its constituting matter. For on this view it will sometimes be true that a material object's constituting matter is identical with that material

object. Since constituting matter is all of the same category and if $x = y$ then y is of the same category as x, it follows that some material objects are of the same category as pieces of constituting matter. So the problem of the many looms.

The version of the problem of the many which holds most directly against the view that identity is the limiting case of overlap of temporal parts is the four-dimensional version. Think of a four-dimensional sum of cloud stages that is supposed to be a paradigm persisting cloud. In the paradigm's nearest spatiotemporal vicinity there are very many sums of cloud stages which differ only very minutely from the paradigm. The problem of the many is underway if on a legitimate sharpening the persisting cloud is identical with one of the sums, so that one of these sums deserves the name of a persisting cloud. Why don't the others? ✓

What of the idea (suggested by David Lewis) that they do, but that this is harmless since, because of massive overlap, the many are almost one? Well, I do not think that this gives a general solution. Michael's house has an extension almost as large as his original house, which in fact was a near duplicate of the next door neighbour's house. While some have houses consisting of two houses (a hacienda often consists of the main house and the servants' gatehouse) Michael doesn't. His house is a single suburban dwelling made larger than it originally was by an extension. Yet (8) implies that Michael has (at least) two houses—the large house with the extension, and the proper subpart of that house which made up the original house and is intrinsically just like the next door neighbour's house. The point is that these two houses do not massively overlap, they are not almost one. Michael's extension is almost as large as his original house. I conclude that the "many but almost one" solution does not work here. (8) needs restricting anyway, and when the right restriction is made the original problem of the many is blocked along with the problem of Michael's house.

12. For various versions of haecceitism see Kaplan (1975), Adams (1979) and Lewis (1986, §4.4.).

13. For more on the advantages of Minimalism see Johnston (1987). Unger seems to have become more sympathetic to Minimalism in his (1990) in which Minimalist themes are deployed against Derek Parfit's attempt to derive revisionary consequences in ethics from the observation that we are not "seperately existing entities distinct from our brains and bodies".

14. I wish to thank Ned Hall, Saul Kripke, David Lewis, Denis Robinson, Gideon Rosen, Sarah Stroud, Jamie Tappeneden and Peter Unger for useful discussions on these topics.

References

Adams, R. M. 1979: "Primitive Thisness and Primitive Identity". *Journal of Philosophy*, 76, pp. 5–26.

Gibbard, A. 1975: "Contingent Identity". *Journal of Philosophical Logic*, 4, pp. 187–221.

Gupta, A. 1980: *The Logic of Common Nouns*. New Haven, CT: Yale University Press.

Johnston, M. 1987: "Is There a Problem About Persistence?" *Proceedings of the Aristotelian Society*. Supp. 61, pp. 107–135.

Kaplan, D. 1976: "How to Russell a Frege-Church". *Journal of Philosophy*, 72, pp. 716–729.

Leonard, H. S. and Goodman, N. 1940: "The Calculus of Individuals and Its Uses". *The Journal of Symbolic Logic*, 5, pp 46–7.

Lewis, D. K. 1968: "Counterpart Theory and Quantified Modal Logic", *Journal of Philosophy*, 65, pp. 113–126.

———1986: *On the Plurality of Worlds*. London: Basil Blackwell.

———1971: "Counterparts of Persons and Their Bodies". *Journal of Philosophy*, 68, pp. 203–211.

Robinson, D. 1982a: *The Metaphysics of Material Constitution*. Ph.D. Dissertation, Monash University.

———1982b: "Re-Identifying Matter". *Philosophical Review*, 81, pp. 317–342.

Thomson, J. J. 1983: "Parthood and Identity Across Time". *The Journal of Philosophy*, 80, pp. 201–219.

Unger, P. 1981: "The Problem of the Many" in *Midwest Studies in Philosophy*, Vol. VI, French, P. A., Uehling, Jr. T. E., and Wettstein, H. K., eds., University of Minnesota Press, Minneapolis.

———1990: *Identity, Consciousness and Value*. Oxford: Oxford University Press.

Williams, D. C. 1966: "The Elements of Being" in *Principles of Empirical Realism*, Ruja, A., ed., Springfield: Charles Thomas.

———1986: "Universals and Existents". *Australasian Journal of Philosophy*, 64, pp. 1–14.

5

Subjects Among Other Things

Ernest Sosa

Analytical Table of Contents

A. Body and Soul. Arguments by Hume and by Locke and Kant against substantial souls considered and resisted.

B. Against Souls. Further arguments against souls: 1. The argument from individuation. 2. The intrinsic nature problem. 3. The argument from causation.

C. Might Souls be Located in Space? This seems the most promising way to deal with the problems of B, but is not free of cost: for one thing, souls would then seem essentially spatial since spatial and fundamental, and further puzzles about the dynamics of souls would still call for the attribution to souls of special intrinsic properties or relations, though we have no clue as to the content of these.

D. Radical Materialism. This loses much appeal with the realization that nothing material could be ontologically fundamental. If we allow real status to the materially derivative, it seems arbitrary to rule out objects that though immaterial are no more derivative; all the more so if in each case the mode of derivation is equally well understood. So it seems ill-advised and unnecessary to strain against the immaterial, or at least against that which is sufficiently meta-material (metaphysical?) to be distinct from the chunk of material that constitutes it at that time.

E. On the Constitution of Ordinary Objects. A broadly Aristotelian conception of everyday reality is sketched. Ordinary objects are viewed as ontologically derivative from constitutive matter(s) and constitutive form.

F. Some Principles of Ontological Dependence. These explain how the existence, identity, and persistence of objects derive from their matter(s) and form.

G. Modal Properties of the Supervenient and Their Basis in Actuality. Problems in understanding what actual (non-modal) intrinsic character of an ontologically supervenient or dependent entity (like a smile, a snowball, or perhaps even a person) could possibly yield and explain its differential modal properties, its could-bes, might-have-beens, etc.

H. Further Problems of Constitution and Supervenience. 1. The explosion of reality. (And the anti-realist proposed solution.) 2. *Which* original sources are essential?

I. An Event or Process Ontology? Given the problems surveyed, should we not yield to the implicit pressure of the arguments by Hume, Locke, and Kant (sketched in section A) by accepting an ontology of events and processes, one that dispenses with concrete, contingent substances having any permanence? It is not obvious we should accede, when the plausible reducing events and processes themselves embed substantial things with apparent permanence (beyond an instant at least). What is more, the events and processes in a thing's actual career will not suffice for the reduction anyhow, since ordinary things generally might have had very different careers.

J. Persons Again. If we decide against substantial souls, against radical materialism, and against an event or process ontology, then a broadly Aristotelian view of persons has its attractions. But it will have the problems already presented in sections G and H. It must also deal with some further questions, six of which are highlighted in this section. And how would experiential and intentional states derive from properties of the live human being? The mystery here darkens when we consider that properties of the human being necessarily derive from properties and relations of its physical parts. No simple analogy between digestion and thought is likely to illuminate this darkness.

A. Body and Soul

One cannot be the very same thing as one's body. For one's body normally remains in existence when one passes away, and no one thing could concurrently pass away and remain in existence. And if one's death is so violent that one's body is utterly destroyed, even so one's body *might* have endured beyond the time of one's passing whereas one could not oneself have survived one's passing. So, again, one still cannot be the very same as one's body. What more then is there to a person beyond that person's body? According to a longstanding view important in religion and philosophy, a person essentially involves a soul, something so far different from any body as not to be extended in space at all. Souls are unextended subjects of thought or experience, subjects of consciousness. And a person is either just a soul and nothing more, or else it is somehow a combination or a team constituted essentially by a soul and a body. This view of the ghost in the machine is still widely prevalent in contemporary Western culture. Though retaining a great number of adherents, however, and not just the hosts of fundamentalism, it is now often dismissed as a relic no longer credible. Since reasons in support of that attitude are increasingly hard to elicit, let us consider for ourselves, if only briefly, just what is so wrong with the very notion of immaterial, unextended subjects of consciousness.

The history of philosophy yields two important arguments, one due to Hume, the other to Locke and Kant, which we begin by reviewing in brief.

According to Hume introspection reveals not one's very self but only experiences, feelings, thoughts, only ". . . some particular perception or other, of heat or cold, light or shade, love or hatred, pain or pleasure"; and he never can catch himself ". . . at any time without a perception, and never can observe any thing but the perception."[1] So he finds no empirical evidence for the existence of any substantial mind underlying such phenomena, and is willing to admit a mind at most as a construction that bundles them. A substantialist reply is found already in Descartes, however, who points out that in experiencing the qualities of a piece of wax we can feel more confident of the subject of such experiences than of their object. And as the object is experienced through its qualities experienced at that time, so the subject is experienced through its experiences experienced at that time. If a snowball can be experienced by experiencing its very whiteness, coldness, and roundness, might one not also experience thereby one's own self with even more assurance?[2]

Perhaps so, say Locke and Kant, but what can possibly assure us that as the subject of such experience one is a perduring soul?

> It ". . . must be allowed, that, if the same consciousness (which, as has been shown, is quite a different thing from the same numerical figure or motion in body) can be transferred from one thinking substance to another, it will be possible that two thinking substances may make but one person. For the same consciousness being preserved, whether in the same or different substances, the personal identity is preserved." (John Locke, *Essay Concerning Human Understanding*, chapter 27, section 13.)
>
> "An elastic ball which impinges on another similar ball in a straight line communicates to the latter its whole motion, and therefore its whole state (that is, if we take account only of the positions in space). If, then, in analogy with such bodies, we postulate substances such that the one communicates to the other representations together with the consciousness of them, we can conceive a whole series of substances of which the first transmits its state together with its consciousness to the second, the second its own state with that of the preceding substance to the third, and this in turn the states of all the preceding substances together with its own consciousness and with their consciousness to

another. The last substance would then be conscious of all the states of the previously changed substances, as being its own states, because they would have been transferred to it together with the consciousness of them. And yet it would not have been one and the same person in all these states." (Immanuel Kant, *Critique of Pure Reason*, trans. Norman Kemp Smith, note a to A363.)

Even granted one's experiences give one experiential access to oneself as subject and not just to the objects of such experiences, little follows about the ontological nature of the subject. What is more, even granted a soul whose experiencing at a given time constitutes one's experiencing at that time, even *that* does not yet entail that one is oneself a soul. What rules out one's being constituted by a long sequence of such souls each quickly yielding its position to the next in the way each moment a collection of water molecules gives way to a new one in the constitution of a river?

Though a mainstay of materialist refutations of dualism, such an argument is truly an attack on substance, whether the substance be material or mental. Even assuming the existence of a material substance whose roundness, whiteness, and coldness at a given time underlies the being round, white, and cold of a snowball at that time, even *that* does not yet entail that the snowball is itself that material substance. What rules out the possibility that the snowball is constituted by a long sequence of such material substances each quickly yielding its position to the next in the way a collection of water molecules gives way continuously to a new and different collection in the constitution of a river? "But this consequence supposed so unpalatable to the materialist," comes the reply, "is precisely what he accepts with regard to living beings, whose cellular constitution is supposed to change constantly with no effect on our view of them as just a special kind of material beings." Such a reply misses the full import of the Locke-Kant argument, however, which might press its doubt even at the points in material nature where we are happy to assume substantial permanence. For the point of the argument is that there is no way to tell when you have a sequence of items bundled by a successive relation (a causal one most likely) as opposed to a true permanence by a single persisting substance. And the doubt could of course be pressed until the member substances play their role in the relevant sequence as close to instantaneously as could be desired, which raises the question of why we should suppose it to be substances at all that constitute the sequence, as opposed to events, even instantaneous events.

What is more, our skeptical doubts would surely apply not only to the persistence of a single substance across time, but also to the coexemplification of various qualities by a single substance at a time. Perhaps it is not the snowball itself that more fundamentally has the roundness of the snowball, and again not the snowball that has its whiteness, and again not the snowball that has its coldness, so that we have really four different things here:

and perhaps it is only because the white thing, the cold thing, and the round thing are related appropriately that we have a single snowball (derivatively) bearing its own properties of whiteness, coldness, and roundness. Even at a single time, therefore, our skeptical train of thought shatters the world of substance into about as many fragment substances as there are corresponding states or events. So the pressure of the argument is really towards an event ontology that dispenses with substances at a fundamental level. The argument hence does not call into question only an ontology of minds or mental substances. It calls into question rather an ontology of substance, period. Hence to the extent that we are willing to resist the argument with an epistemology that allows room for substantial tables or at least for substantial atoms, to that extent should room also be allowed—at least so far as *this* argument is concerned—for substantial minds or souls.

Is there a better argument against substantial souls, one for example that will not apply with equal force against substantial bodies?

B. Against Souls

1. The Argument from Individuation.

Against souls as nonspatial particulars it might be argued that they are unacceptably deprived of a principle of individuation:

> Call a property qualitative if its exemplification does not entail with regard to any concrete particular that it specifically must exist. Two distinct spatial things can conceivably share all their qualitative properties, as shown by Max Black's universe populated only by two identical spheres. The distinctness of such spheres must hence be understood in terms of their differing spatial locations. Absent spatial location, as with souls, we lack any way to understand the distinctness of allegedly distinct but qualitatively identical souls.

Let's call this The Argument from Individuation.

Though not lacking in intuitive appeal, such an argument is open to doubt. Consider first the assumption that in Black's universe the two spheres share absolutely all their qualitative properties. Would there not be a direction such that one of the spheres would have a sphere a certain distance away from it in *that* direction, whereas the other sphere would have no sphere any distance away from it in that same direction (but would rather have a sphere that distance away from it in the *opposite* direction)? It might be replied that there are no such qualitative properties of direction but that seems just an assumption that is really not obviously true but needs defense. Even sticking to just one dimension, say the x axis (with a given orientation), it does seem as though there is a property of being one foot away *positiveward* which is distinct from the property of being one foot away *negativeward*. And these properties do not require for their exemplification the existence of any specific concrete particulars, or so it seems, which makes them qualitative properties.

Even granting qualitative properties of direction, however, the basic problem yet remains in an extension of the Black universe containing infinitely many equidistant and identical spheres whose centers all lie on a single straight line. Each sphere will hence have infinitely many spheres in the positive direction from it, and infinitely many in the negative direction. No qualitative difference at all hence distinguishes any two of them, not even any differences essentially involving direction.

The Argument from Individuation appeals to the spatial locations of qualitatively indiscernible entities as a way of individuating them and accounting for their diversity. But it is not clear how spatial location can help thus to solve the alleged problem of individuation for located entities. Entities at different places can be understood to be diverse via the principle that no one entity can be wholly present at two places at any one time and no two entities can exhaustively occupy a single place at any one time (or at least that is so for "basic" entities not dependent on any other entities but their proper parts). But does this not simply pass the buck from the located entities to the places they are said to occupy? And indeed what qualitative properties can account for the diversity of two dimensionally identical places? One might try to think of places themselves as properties. Unable as I am to find any difference in content between two dimensionally identical places, however, I cannot fathom how they could manage to constitute diverse properties. It might be replied that we need not be able to understand every property we have reason to postulate. But the case in question is particularly puzzling since we lack any inkling of what might conceivably make two such properties diverse. (And anyhow, is the problem, if there really is one here, really less troubling for places themselves than for the properties that supposedly correspond to them? The identity of such absolute places could perhaps be understood by relation to other, already given places, in the way all places in a dimensional system are determined by an origin and a set of dimensions. If the choice of origin is arbitrary and there is no intrinsic difference to found such choice, however, we again have no inkling of what might conceivably constitute the identity of any such place. But why do we need something to "constitute" the identity of a place? In any case, the problem does seem anyway rather more troubling for the properties than for the corresponding places. Why is that? Maybe it's because properties are supposed to be accessible, at least in principle, to the mind, and accessible intrinsically through the very content of the property, not just extrinsically through some contingent relation that it bears uniquely to something already grasped. Such differentiating intrinsic content is just what seems hopelessly lacking in the supposed properties proposed as correlates of places.)

Finally, it might be wondered about our Argument just what is meant by "understanding" the diversity of two distinct entities. With regard to ontologically dependent beings it should be possible for a powerful enough mind well enough stocked with information to provide some explanation of their diversity on the basis of the assumed diversity of some or all of the more basic items that make them up. But there is of course no way to do that with regard to fundamental entities, which are not made up by any more basic items. Why not reply therefore against the Argument that spirits are fundamental entities whose diversity is just a brute and fundamental fact that requires no explanation, and indeed allows none?

Those do seem to me serious doubts about the Argument from Individuation. And yet there still seems something important to be learned from the argument, something we have yet to pinpoint. Perhaps the lesson is simply that entities x and y *cannot possibly be related simply by diversity.* Otherwise you might have not just one right foot but indefinitely many of them, all related only by diversity! (The idea is made more precise in an appendix, which defines and employs a number of preliminary concepts.)

That lesson may now enable us to understand the Argument from Individuation in a way that would guard it from the doubts raised above. Assume the principle that two basic spatial entities could not exhaustively coincide in space, and the principle that a single spatial entity could not be wholly present at two distinct places. (Where a spatial entity is "basic" iff it ontologically depends on nothing but the coexistence of its proper parts.) It follows that any two basic spatial entities must be spatially apart (in some relevant sense). Hence no two basic spatial entities could ever be related *only* by diversity (and mere equivalence relations). Every two basic spatial entities will be spatially apart, and their distinctness may hence be understood as correlative with their spatial apartness. (Even a manifold of absolute space would not drive us to a mystery so utter as that of identical entities related only by diversity, since the absolute points would be related not only by diversity but also by spatial relations.)

The problem with supposed nonspatial particulars like souls is simply that no pure relation can be found to play the role for them that spatial apartness plays for spatial particulars. We have no inkling of any relation that can help us grasp the diversity of two souls alike in every qualitative respect. The universe with infinitely many identical spheres, all equidistantly arrayed on a straight line, still permits some further understanding of the distinctness between any two of the indiscernible spheres, for each and every one of them is spatially apart from every other sphere. Consider a world with infinitely many souls all indiscernible in every qualitative respect in respect of all their experiences, thoughts, desires, moods, et cetera. How are we to understand the diversity of all these identical souls? What irreflexive relation between them can we appeal to? Is there anything that can do for them what spatial apartness does for spatial entities?

It might be suggested that no soul x could directly experience the mental states of another soul y and that this provides us with the desired relation to accompany with necessity every case of diversity among souls. But this seems to me to put things backwards. For the (transitive) *experiencing* done by substances like souls is a causal matter which is a form of "causally registering a state of." And direct experiencing is then a form of (roughly) "causally registering a state of, without reliance on causally intermediary states." Now either *self*-registering states are allowed or they are not. If they are allowed, then the only states directly experienced would be those which are self-registering. And then it follows that one cannot directly experience states of anyone else. For to *register* a state X is to *have* a state Y with an appropriate causal relation to X. But if the only states directly registered by one are those states of one's own which are *self*-registering (as a limiting causal relation), then it follows trivially that one can only register directly states of one's own, and hence that these are the only states one can experience directly. But this follows only because of the way experiencing is understood as a form of registering and because of the way the *directness* of such registering is conceived.

If on the other hand *self*-registering states are *not* allowed, then it's hard to see why one can not *directly* experience the states of another soul, why God for example could not directly inspect our souls. What would be needed for that purpose is only a causal chain in which a certain mental state of the direct experiencER has as its immediate causal antecedent the directly experienced state. And it is not at all obvious why the experiencing state and the experienced state *must* both belong to the same soul. Again, why can't God be so in tune with the rest of us that certain of His mental states directly reflect our own, and enable Him thereby to directly experience our souls?

This whole discussion of direct experiencing is of course very rough, but it makes one skeptical that impossibility of direct experiencing could be the key to a relation that might necessarily accompany the diversity of souls.

2. The Intrinsic Nature Problem

The potentialities, powers, dispositions, etc., of a physical thing are grounded in the intrinsic physical nature of that thing. A basketball has its power of rolling down an inclined plane (in certain conditions) grounded in its roundness, in its intrinsic physical shape of being round, whereas a wheel has a similar power in virtue of its different physical shape of being cylindrical. The intrinsic primary qualities of a physical object generally determine its intrinsic nature, thus grounding its various powers, dispositions, et cetera.

What intrinsic monadic qualities of a soul could ground that soul's faculties, virtues, vices, and its powers and dispositions generally? (An intrinsic monadic quality is one not constituted by any relation—to any sort of entity, whether concrete or abstract. But compare definition PI in the appendix.)

Consider again a ball's disposition to roll down an inclined plane, or, somewhat more accurately, to roll down the plane if placed at its top in certain conditions. That disposition seems grounded in the roundness of the ball. But is it really? In what sense? After all, the ball's disposition is really to roll *if* placed at the top of the incline in the absence of obstacles, etc., *and* in a state of roundness. For it it were placed there disinflated, it would not roll. But then even an object that is *not* round surely has *that* disposition.

Call a disposition "differential with regard to category C" if it is possibly present in some objects of category C while absent from others. Thus a marble has a disposition to roll down an incline (in certain conditions) but a die does not have it, so the disposition to roll that way is a differential disposition with regard to the category of bodies. If we recognize that physical objects may have differential essential properties, as the marble may be said to have its roundness and the die its cubicity, then the marble and the die may be said to have *absolutely* differential dispositions absolutely grounded in their essential properties in the way the marble's disposition to roll down an incline is absolutely grounded in its essential roundness. One does not have to think of that disposition of the marble as the disposition to roll down an incline if placed at its top *while round*. Its roundness being essential to it, there is really no alternative to that marble's being round. If we think instead of the piece of material of which that marble is constituted, and we say that the roundness of that is accidental, then insofar as we recognize a differential disposition to roll down an incline on the part of that piece of material, not shared by the piece of plastic that makes up the die, that disposition will be not an absolutely differential disposition absolutely grounded in the piece of material's roundness, but only a differential disposition of the piece of material *relative* to its roundness held constant. If spatial objects have no essences, then all their differential dispositions will be relative. In the absence of any relativization to properties that objects happen to have at a time, all spatial objects will share all their dispositions. In any case, both relative and absolute differential dispositions derive from lawlike generalizations in the way a round thing's differential disposition to roll derives from the generalization that anything round placed atop an incline (in certain conditions) will roll down that incline. Take a lawlike physical generalization of the form: For all x, x is F and G only if x is H. In the absence of physical essences, physical objects will all share the corresponding disposition to be H when in the condition of being F and G. The differential disposition to be H when in the condition of being G will then be possessed by objects that are F *relative* to their being F. And so on.

The Intrinsic Nature problem for souls derives from the fact that souls seem to have differential dispositions. Virtues and vices, for example, are not uniformly distributed to all. Whether souls have essenses or not, whether dispositions of souls are absolutely differential or only relatively differential, it remains that we have no inkling of any intrinsic monadic properties of souls that can serve to ground, absolutely *or* relatively, any such dispositions. Perhaps the advocate of souls would reply that with souls it is not so much the intrinsic, monadic properties (if any) that matter, but rather the various intentional relations to properties, relations, and propositions—relations of desire, belief, etc. This would raise a further question: What intrinsic, monadic properties could possibly underlie in souls their differential intentional relations to such properties, relations, and propositions? But one could perhaps brush the question aside by alleging that such intentional relations are as brute and fundamental as the brute properties and relations that must be strewn differentially amongst the fundamental physical entities in a contingent physical universe. Spatial relations among bodies, for example, would not supervene upon any monadic, intrinsic properties of them. Bodies are differentially spatially related, yet their spatial relations do not supervene on their monadic, intrinsic qualities. Perhaps the intentional relations that relate subjects with properties, relations, and propositions are *in that respect* like the spatial relations that relate bodies with bodies.

In upshot the Intrinsic Nature problem does not seem so formidable as the Argument from Individuation against souls. It does I believe raise some interesting and puzzling questions, but it remains to be seen whether the similar questions for bodies end up admitting better answers; anyhow there is here no very compelling refutation of souls, nor even any argument as compelling as the Argument from Individuation when interpreted by appeal to the principle that, with regard to concrete particulars, Diversity Cannot Stand Alone.

3. The Argument from Causation

This has been detailed elsewhere[3] so here I only summarize. We make now *not* the strong assumption that causal relations are supervenient, and derive necessarily from the non-causal facts that constitute the world (so that no two worlds could be exactly alike in absolutely all non-causal respects while yet differing in some causal respects). Let us assume, more weakly, that in no one world could there be two pairs of entities relevantly quite alike non-causally but each differently interrelated causally. Given that assumption, it is a great mystery how souls could interact causally with bodies. Take two exactly identical twins facing each other in a symmetrical universe (like Black's), and assume their souls to be exactly identical in all respects of experience, thought, virtue, etc.: in all psychological respects. How could we possibly understand the notion that soul S1 interacts with body B1 yet not with body B2, while soul S2 interacts with body B2 yet not with body B1? Since S1 and S2 are alike in all qualitative respects, while B1 and B2 are also alike in all qualitative respects, there must be some relation present between S1 and B1 while absent between S1 and B2, et cetera. Since souls are not spatially located, however, the relation in question is not spatial, and in fact I for one have no clue as to what relation it might be.

C. Might Souls be Located in Space?

Notice the similarity in form between the Argument from Individuation and the Argument from Causation. In both cases the essential problem turns out to be our inability to find a relation involving souls needed for theoretical purposes: first, a relation that would relate souls with other souls and would help explain their diversity; second, a relation between souls and bodies that would help explain their causal interaction. It might be replied that we can solve both problems with one move by allowing souls to be spatially located (though not spatially extended, which would make them bodies or at least shadows or the like). Since souls are on the present view supposed to be fundamental entities (and not supervenient modes like smiles or shadows), therefore souls seem fundamentally located if located at all (unlike smiles, whose location would always derive from the location of the corresponding smiling face). And anything thus fundamentally located is presumably essentially located. This goes against the tradition that souls are just not spatial at all. (Heaven, for example, would have to be literally a place, a real physical place somewhere.)

Other questions and puzzles would soon follow: souls would move, and would have velocity and acceleration, yet no physical force or energy seems required. More, what would explain such motion by a soul? Would it be its intentional relations to properties, relations, and propositions? That seems unlikely. Must we not hence appeal once again to some special relations between souls and bodies or to intrinsic, monadic properties of souls? Unless we do so, how can we explain their differential dispositions and their differential spatial relations to other souls and to bodies, including their different velocities and accelerations? But if on the other hand we do appeal to special relations between souls and bodies or to intrinsic, monadic properties of souls, we are back to the mystery of what could possibly serve as such relations or properties of punctiform souls. Absent any promising lines of inquiry into such questions, it seems wise to explore some alternative philosophical framework that will commit us to no entities so elusive and mysterious. Of course, we philosophers soon learn to live with mystery, but unlike Agatha Christie we should also try to reduce it.

D. Radical Materialism

We might try returning to the radical materialism that a person is just a body in the state of being "personal," so that death represents a "mere" change on the part of a body from being personal to being not-personal. But of course the body itself exists in virtue of the physical coherence of its physical parts. And these, being material, will have constitutive parts of their own, and so on ad infinitum. There is hence nothing materially fundamental at all, there are no *fundamental* material entities, no material entities that do not depend ontologically on how it is with certain *other* entities (the parts)—on how it is in a broad sense that includes their *coexisting* as among the ways it is with them. And if we regard a person as a sort of fiction that represents just a body with certain properties, by parity we must regard the body as a sort of fiction that represents just certain other entities (parts) properties in certain ways or interrelated in certain ways. But each of these in turn must be regarded as equally a fiction representative of certain other entities yet. And so on, ad infinitum. If we say that there is really no person over and above its personal body, then by parity we must now say that there is really no human body over and above its parts propertied and interrelated; and we must then say in turn that there are really no parts over and above their subparts propertied and interrelated. And indeed for *anything* material that might be said to exist, we would have to say that there is really no such thing over and above its parts propertied and interrelated in certain ways, and that for the alleged thing to "cease to be" is just for its relevant parts to lose their relevant properties and interrelations. More, since the same thing is true at every level down the infinite hierarchy of parts, subparts, subsubparts, et cetera, there is then "really" *nothing* material at all over and above something *else.* No such conception of what there "really" is seems plausible, surely, which inclines me in the opposite direction of granting "real" existence to items at every level, and hence not only to human bodies but also to persons. Yet since persons are thus distinct from their bodies, it would then be only reasonable to wonder what distinguishes the two, a question that gains momentum when we notice the extent of similarity between a live human body at a certain time and the person it constitutes at that time. The two seem thoroughly alike at that time, down to occupying the very same place.

E. On the Constitution of Ordinary Objects

Let us focus for simplicity on a simple ordinary object: say, a snowball. Here again we have a distinction like that between a person and that person's body, now between the snowball and the piece of snow that makes it up. Since squashing the piece of snow into a flat layer destroys the snowball but not the piece of snow, these cannot be one and the same thing. In order to constitute a snowball, the piece of snow must be (roughly) round (and separate from other snow, or at least largely so). But once it does constitute a snowball, that piece of snow is then very hard to distinguish from the snowball it constitutes. The two do seem exactly alike in every physical respect, down to occupying the very same space. What can possibly distinguish them? Leaving aside how the two relate to minds, since a difference in such relations would seem to presuppose some other prior difference, the main differences that come to mind are temporal and modal. As we have seen, the piece of snow can outlast the snowball. Supposing it does, there is then a temporal difference between them. And even if it does not actually outlast the snowall, the piece of snow is squashable so as to form a flat layer while the snowball does not share that modal property.

Compare a cube made up of six square boards related so that each end of each board is joined to exactly one end of another board (so that they are, for short, "box-related"). Just as the snowball exists in virtue of the constitutive snow's roundness, just so the box exists in virtue of the six boards' being square and box-related. Let us say that the snowball "supervenes" on its matter's being round, where its matter is the lump of snow that constitutes it. And let us say that the box "supervenes" on its matters' (sic) being square and box-related. The form of a snowball is then the shape required in its constituent matter for that matter to constitute that snowball. And the form of the box is the relation that the six sides bear to one another by each being square and the six being box-related. For that is the relation the having of which by the six sides enables them to constitute that box.

So far we have considered briefly the matter and form of an object at a given time. But the matter and form of an object can change over time, and the limits of such possible change may surely themselves be included somehow in the fuller "form" for that object: fuller in that it is not just its form at a given instant, but rather its form over time. Before expanding on this, however, it will be useful to touch on the ontology of events, in a generic sense that includes states and processes as well as events proper.

The lighting of a match occurs at a certain time because the match's head catches fire (becomes aflame) at that time. The calm at sea occurs at a certain time or over a certain period because the relevant air and water are quite still at that time or over that period. The projection of Gone With the Wind occurs over a certain period because the first film frame is screened in the first time frame followed by the second film frame being screened in the second time frame followed by . . . followed by the last film frame being screened in the last time frame. An event proper, the lighting, requires change like that of the match's becoming aflame. A state requires persistence like the persistent stillness of the air and water. A process requires a sequence of changes. But in each case the generic event involved occurs because of the properties and interrelations among certain entities at a time or over a period of time. On the present view events (generically) hence seem ontologically derivative entities that supervene on various things (matches, portions of air or sea, film frames, etc.) when these behave in various pertinent ways (become aflame, remain still, are screened). But actually on our view the opposite appears equally true: the snowball supervenes on the event of the lump of snow's being round, the box supervenes on the event of the six boards' being square and box-related. Et cetera. This last indeed suggests the possibility of simply identifying a thing with its underlying event (and if there is a hierarchy of deeper and deeper underlying events, then identifying it with the topmost member of the hierarchy). Why not think of the snowball as simply the being round of the piece of snow, and of the box as simply the being square and box-related of the boards? Of course, the piece of snow will itself be identical with its own underlying event, and the boards with their several underlying events, which events may in turn have matters of their own to be identified in turn with *their* underlying events, and so on, perhaps ad infinitum, or until the hierarchy hits bottom with some fundamental atoms or fields ungrounded in any underlying events, or perhaps until it reaches bottom rather with some events that are pure and derive from no underlying matters. Since I do not see how to decide whether physical reality hits bottom with events or with atoms or fields, or indeed whether it hits bottom at all, and since that seems at best something for our most successful physical theory to settle, let us stay with the more accessible yet puzzling enough concepts by which we live each day, and consider whether it is possible to conceive of ourselves and the things around us as events, states or processes. But before turning to that (in section I below) we need to get a somewhat greater diversity of cases before us and to take stock of our position and resources. These two things occupy the remainder of this section and sections F, G, and H.

Consider first the career of a certain chain, represented as follows:

January	D	E	F	G	H	I	J	K	L	M	N	O	P
February	C	D	E	F	G	H	I	J	K	L	M	N	O
March	B	C	D	E	F	G	H	I	J	K	L	M	N
April	A	B	C	D	E	F	G	H	I	J	K	L	M

Assuming that there is no significant difference among the links in respect of either their monadic or their relational properties, it seems very plausible that such a chain does last as a single chain through the four months. More, if someone were to link together in April the discarded links (P, O, and N) with enough new links (Q, R, S, etc.) to make a chain, that chain would be no threatening competitor to the chain now assigned to the month of April for the title of successor to our chain of January, February, and March. The persistence of our chain through the four months of January through April derives from the fact that enough links remain linked together as we go from January on, together with the fact that the qualitative and substantial variation of links from month to month stays within the acceptable limits. Note the consequence that the constitution of an ordinary object at any time after its time of origin is not a constitution that it must have at that time, since presumably it might always have reached that stage via a different route. Thus think of our chain above and suppose it had lost links from the left and gained them from the right rather than the reverse. The variation then would surely have been equally within the allowable limits (since we have postulated the lack of significant differences amongst the links). Yet the constitutive links in April would have been different from what they are in fact in our story as it stands, though it would still have been the very same chain.

As a final example, consider the collision between two billiard balls b1 and b2. That very collision c occurs because b1 hits b2 when, where, and how it does so (more or less, within allowable limits). Thus the matters of that collision are b1 and b2 and let's take its form for simplicity to be just the relation of hitting. The event occurs because its matters are linked in a certain order by the relation that is its form.

In sum, then, about ordinary things and events, states, and processes like snowballs, boxes, chains, match lightings, collisions, we conclude that these are derivative entities each ontologically determined by the fact that its constitutive matter(s) has (have) its constitutive form. Here now is a summary tabulation of our examples (table 1).

Table 1

The Supervenient	Its Constituent Matters	Its Constituent Form
1. Snowball S	Lump of snow L	Roundness and separation from other snow
2. Box B	Boards b1, . . ., b6	Squareness of boards severally and joint interrelation among them
3. Chain C's persistence	Links l1, . . ., ln	Linkage among the n links at the original stage and variation from stage to stage within limits, with regard to number, membership, and arrangement of links
4. Match lighting 1	Match m	Becoming aflame
5. Collision c	billiard balls b1 and b2	The relation of one thing hitting another

F. Some Principles of Ontological Dependence

Such supervenient or ontologically dependent entities come with corresponding principles, among them the following.

1. *Weak Principle of Existence.* The superveniently existing at a time t exists at t because its constituent matters at t exemplify its constituent form (in the order in which they do so).

2. *Weak Principle of Persistence.* The superveniently persisting throughout a period π persists throughout π because for every time t within π, the constituent matters exemplify its constituent form (in the order in which they do so).

3. *Principle of Identity.* Supervenient things X and Y are identical at time t iff the matters of X at t are identical to the matters of Y at that time, and the constituent form of X at t is identical to the constituent form of Y at that time (and in the case of supervenient events, it must be required also that the matters of X exemplify that shared form in the same order as the matters of Y).

4. *Principle of Derivation.* For every property ϕ of a supervenient entity X, that X has ϕ must derive necessarily from certain properties of the matters of X or certain relations among them. (The existence and persistence of the supervenient may be considered special cases of this—see 1 and 2 above.)

The first two principles are called weak because they do not provide necessary and sufficient conditions, but only specify what it is that the existence or persistence of the supervenient does derive from. Note however that a supervenient entity might well have existed at a time t even though wholly different both with regard to its constituent matters at that time and also with regard to its constituent form at that time. For it might have begun with approximately the same origin, as it must needs do, and yet have developed gradually and well within the allowable bounds to reach a wholly different constitutional outcome by the time of t.

G. Modal Properties of the Supervenient and Their Basis in Actuality

We saw earlier that when a thing has a differential dispositional property—one that not every thing shares—there must be some actual property of that thing to explain why it has that dispositional property while things that lack that actual property do not have the dispositional property. For example, if a marble has the disposition to roll whereas a die does not, we can explain it by appeal to the roundness of the marble and the cubicity of the die. This explanatory requirement still seems quite reasonable and in fact extensible to differential modal properties generally. If a thing has a differential modal property, then there must be some actual property of that thing to explain why it has that modal property. Take the property of *not being squashable so as to form a flat layer*. Such unsquashability is a modal property of a snowball, and also a differential property: the piece of snow that constitutes the snowball does not share that modal property, since unlike the snowball, the piece of snow may surely be flattened into a layer. So what actual property of the snowball, not shared by the constituent piece of snow, accounts for its possession of that differential modal property of being unflattenable into a layer: i.e., of not being *itself* flattenable so that *it* emerges from the process still present but now in a state of being quite flat? (By an "actual property" here I mean a property with content restricted purely to the realm of the actual, to the actual world. Its analysis hence should not include any appeal to modality, to might-have-beens, have-to-bes, would-have-beens, et cetera. Primary qualities seem therefore prime examples of actual properties which, while entailing modal consequences, do not include in their very content, analysis, or definition any appeal to modality.)

Why is there a special problem here? What more exactly is its source and nature? This requires a brief digression on essentialism, three grades of which may be distinguished as follows.

1. *The lowest grade*: for x to have ϕ essentially is simply for x to have ϕ as a necessary consequence of some other (implicitly or explicitly) singled out property that it has (or kind to which it belongs). This is "relativistic" essentialism, which requires only a belief in de dicto necessity.

2. *An intermediate grade*: there is fundamental de re necessity; x can have ϕ essentially where that is not just a matter of ϕ following necessarily from some (implicitly or explicitly) singled out property that x is simply recognized to have. According to this grade, however, it is a necessary truth that any property ever had essentially is never had without being had essentially. Thus, necessarily if something is a body, then it is necessarily a body. This might be called "property based" essentialism. In a sense essentiality is here fundamentally a feature of properties. Some properties are essential (and, most would say, some are not).

3. *A higher grade*: there is essentiality of both grade 1 and grade 2, but there are also cases where x has ϕ essentially but ϕ is not necessarily had essentially whenever it is had at all. Thus the snowball is round and necessarily so, but the constituent piece of snow is round yet not necessarily so. This might be called "particularistic" essentialism.

Isn't there a sense now in which both grade 1 and grade 2 essentialism allow an explanation for the modal on the basis of the merely actual? This seems obvious for grade 1. As for grade 2, the idea is that whenever x has ϕ essentially, its having ϕ essentially follows necessarily from its simply having ϕ. So there seems a sense in which its non-modal possession of ϕ

"explains" its essential possession of ϕ. And it is just this "explanation" that is missing once we move to grade 3. For the piece of snow and the snowball could be exactly the same in all non-modal properties while yet one had modal properties that the other lacked.

Roundness is therefore "differentially" and "distinctively" essential. (A property is *differentially* essential iff it is possible that something have it essentially while something else does not. A property is *distinctively* essential iff it is possible that something have it essentially while something else has it also but *not* essentially.) Notably, some properties are "differentially" and "distinctively" essential, like roundness, while yet, unlike roundness, their possession *can* still be explained by the actual. Thus the number eight is essentially non-yellow whereas the pencil in my hand is also non-yellow but only accidentally so. But the number eight is essentially-non-yellow because it is essentially colorless, in the sense of having no color at all, and it is essentially colorless because it is essentially nonspatial. And here we do seem to have a property whose essential possession can be explained by its actual possession. (Similarly for being black or even, which my pencil has accidentally but the number eight has essentially.) Is it then Aristotelian supervenience specifically that yields our special difficulty of modal properties with no explanation in the actual—as in the case of the essential roundness of a snowball, which cannot be explained by the mere actual roundness of it, since the round piece of snow is also actually round without being essentially round. (This again is to be contrasted with properties like being even, or being a person, which nothing can possibly have without having them essentially, so that their essential possession can always be explained by their mere actual possession.) The apparent mystery is what can possibly distinguish the snowball and its constitutive piece of snow to account for why one is necessarily round and the other is just round without being necessarily round. What I at least am finding quite puzzling is how two things (the snowball and the piece of snow that constitutes it) could be absolutely the same in all their non-modal properties and relations, while yet differing in de re modal properties.

Now if among the actual properties of an ordinary object we allow its having the constitutional structure that it does have, we enable ourselves to explain its possession of differential essential properties by appeal to its actual properties. The essential roundness of a snowball for example could then be explained by noting two things: *first*, that the constitutional structure of that snowball must include at a certain level a certain piece of snow as matter and approximate roundness as form, so that the existence of the snowball derives from the being approximately round of the piece of snow; and, *second*, that no piece of snow can possibly constitute a snowball by being approximately round without that snowball being round as well.

Hence we can see that the conditions required for the existence of a particular snowball include the presence of a round piece of snow, not necessarily the one that in actuality constitutes that very snowball but at least one related appropriately to its actual matters at some level of its constitutional structure and at some state of its development. For example, perhaps in order for that snowball to exist in some other possible world W it need only be constituted by the molecular constitution and structure of the snowball in the actual world A, or perhaps it need only be constituted by a molecular constitution and structure that eventually would succeed, by an appropriate chain of succession, a certain molecular constitution and structure at the moment of its origin, one which is sufficiently like its original constitution and structure in the actual world A. We had seen how the differential modal properties of ordinary things derive sometimes from the monadic actual properties of such things—in the way the capacity to roll of a bowling ball derives in part from its roundness. We now see that a differential modal property of a thing can also derive from its ontological constitution, from the conditions required for it to exist at a time or from the conditions required for it to perdure through a period.

On reflection that does however seem something of a dodge. If we speak of the ontological conditions for a thing's existence at a time t, though modal vocabulary may not be explicit, is it not clearly implicit in the notion of an ontological condition for existence? What is such a condition if not a circumstance or situation that *must* obtain for the thing to exist. Consider now a snowball, a particular given snowball that we may suppose picked out for the sake of argument is it not now a differential modal property of that snowball that for it to exist there *must* exist a piece of snow to be its matter, one with the required form of being round. And if it is this we must invoke to explain why that very snowball cannot but be round, are we not explaining the differentially modal by appeal again to the differentially modal?

Can we do better in the case of events? A lighting is essentially a lighting, and this is a differential modal property of that lighting. Can't we now explain here that the ontological constitution of that lighting involves a match m and the property of becoming aflame, that the lighting simply is a structure composed ontologically of that match and that property, and that the structure in question exists if and only if its first member, the match m, has its second member, the property of becoming aflame? (We need also of course a further assumption: that necessarily when the match has the property of becoming aflame, the supervenient lighting has the property of being a lighting.)

That bit of reasoning seems sound, but just how does it explain the differential modal property of being essentially a lighting? In doing so must it not assume that the postulated identity between that lighting and the structure made up of the match and the property of becoming aflame is itself a necessary identity, as is all true identity? And if the relation of identity may be assumed necessary, may we not with comparable plausibility assume that the relation of ontological constitution is also necessary? For if we may assume this and if we may understand the ontological constitution of a lighting as the structure made up of its constituent match and the property of becoming aflame, then again we are able to explain the modal property of that lighting of being necessarily a lighting by appeal to its actual property of being ontologically constituted by a certain structure. And then we can extend this explanatory strategy to cover not only events but supervenient entities generally and their possession of differential modal properties, such as the essential properties distinguishing them.

In fact, however, it is "tree-constitution" not "node-constitution" that is necessary for such explanation. A thing could be correlated with a different node in another possible world, but it could not be correlated with another tree altogether. Different matters related by different properties might in a different world constitute at that same time the very thing under consideration. So it is not being actually constituted at t by matters m1, . . ., mn related by form F that explains why the thing T has E as an essential property. Nor is it sufficient to bring in the constitution of T throughout its career from an origin to the time of t, since it might have been otherwise constituted across time as well, at least so long as it retained the same constitution at an original stage. Nothing less than an entire tree of possibilities that ramifies from an actual origin, specifying all the possible careers of T will provide a sufficient explanation of T's having E essentially. But in appealing to such a tree, we appeal again to the differential modal!

H. Further Problems of Constitution and Supervenience

1. The Explosion of Reality

We are supposing a snowball to be constituted by a certain piece of snow as constituent matter and the shape of (approximate) roundness as constituent form. That particular snowball exists at that time because of the roundness of that piece of snow. More, if at that time that piece of snow were to lose its roundness, then at that time that snowball would go out of existence.

Compare now with our ordinary concept of a snowball, the concept of a snowdiscall which we may define as an entity constituted by a piece of snow as matter and as form any shape between being round and being disc-shaped. "Every snowball is hence a snowdiscall but not conversely," or so it may be thought. But actually that is false and in strict truth no snowball is a snowdiscall. More accurately, every piece of snow that constitutes a snowball must also at that time constitute a snowdiscall, but a piece of snow may of course constitute a snowdiscall without constituting a snowball. For every piece of snow that is round (and constitutes a snowball) also has a shape between being round and being disc-shaped (and hence constitutes a snowdiscall). But every disc-shaped piece of snow constitutes a snowdiscall without constituting a snowball.

Consider now a particular snowball β. It is constituted on our view by a particular piece of snow π, which must then also of course constitute a particular snowdiscall δ. Recall that β is distinct from π. Since β would not survive flattening, whereas π would. For the same reason, δ is distinct from π. And, what is more, δ is distinct from β; partial squashing of π so that it becomes disc-shaped would destroy β, but would not destroy δ, so β and δ cannot be the very same thing. The crucial point now is that there are infinitely many shapes σ1, . . ., σn, . . ., between roundness and flatness (of a piece of snow), and for each i, having a shape between roundness and σi would give the form of a distinctive kind of entity to be placed beside snowballs and snowdiscalls. It follows that whenever a piece of snow constitutes a snowball, it constitutes infinitely many distinct entities all sharing its place with it. It follows also that none of us can so much as wiggle a finger without destroying, and creating, infinitely many things.

The foregoing line of reasoning yields a persuasive argument for a kind of idealism or at least for a kind of conceptual relativism. We might perhaps resist the "explosion" of our ordinary world by refusing to countenance any sort of supervenient entity (constituted essentially by a required form) except as a sort of entity countenanced within a "conceptual scheme" that gives constitutive status to such a form. (Thus snowballs can exist relative to our American or Western or human conceptual scheme of 1986, and perhaps even relative to all human conceptual schemes ever, but not relative to every conceivable conceptual scheme, including extraterrestrial ones.) That is why we are not even willing to countenance the existence of snowdiscalls, much less the existence of the infinitely many entities coincident with any snowball in virtue of their relations to the various shapes in the sequence σ1, . . ., σn,. . . . The reason is simply that our conceptual scheme does not give any of those shapes the status required for it to be a proper constitutive form within our scheme (and that includes even the relatively simple one of being in shape between round and disc-shaped). This of course makes existence relative to conceptual scheme, and the question then arises whether we must conceive of the existence even of the conceptual scheme itself and of its framers and users as also relative to that conceptual scheme. That introduces a kind of ontological circularity, one that at least initially does appear vicious, since it apparently requires that one's intellectual activity of giving certain properties (those that constitute oneself, for example) the status of constitutive forms is ontologically required for the very existence of the conceptual scheme relative to which one manages to exist. The conceptual scheme seems to depend on one's existence and intellectual activity, and yet one's existence is itself only relative to that conceptual scheme. The whiff of vicious circularity is hard to ignore if we put the matter this way: the conceptual scheme exists and has the character it does only because of one's intellectual activity, and yet one manages oneself to exist only relative to that very conceptual scheme and because of the character it has. One might perhaps try to escape this result by viewing the relevant thinkers and their intellectual activity as transcendent to the scheme that they thus create and sustain. This way lies a transcendental idealism whose coherence with real inter-subjectivity would seem suspect.

2. WHICH Original Sources are Essential?

The problem here derives from the fact that at any given time, including the times of its original stages, an ordinary thing has more than one constitution level, and that the matters and format at any one such level differ respectively from those at any other. Thus a snowball at a given time exists because a certain piece of snow is round (level 1) but also because certain H2O molecules are related in certain ways (level 2). Now is the origin of that snowball the becoming round of that very piece of snow and essentially so? Or is it rather the becoming related in the relevant ways of the H2O molecules involved in its actual origin, and essentially so? What creates a difficulty in these questions is simply the fact that the piece of snow could have been there without those very molecules being there, and those very molecules could have been there, and indeed could have been there forming a round piece of snow, without that very piece of snow being there. The reason is of course that the routing from the origin of the piece of snow to the moment when it becomes round could have been quite different, so different that at that moment it might well have had a largely or perhaps even wholly different molecular constitution. What then is essential in the material basis of the snowball at its origin: its piece of snow constitution or its molecular constitution? As we have seen, these might after all diverge, so which is to be dominant in a case of divergence? Or shall we require coincidence of *all* original constitutions for the very same entity to appear in any other possible world? At this time I am unable to find any convincing reasoning to determine a choice: perhaps others will be able to help.

I. An Event or Process Ontology?

We are now finally in a position to attack the question whether ordinary things can be identified with their matters' having their form (in the right order). And the answer is in a word "No." At any given time an ordinary object will have certain constitutive matters and a constitutive form, and the existence of that object at that time will derive from its matters' having its constitutive form in a certain order. But the object at that time cannot be identified with its matters' having its form in the relevant order, for as we have seen already that very object could have had different constitutive matters *at that time* and a different constitutive form. For similar reasons we could not identify the object even with its career up to the time in question, for it might have had a different career, nor even with its entire career from the time it comes into being to when it passes away. At best we might try identifying a given ordinary object with its entire tree of possibilities which branches out from its origin in all the various different allowable ways determined by its allowable changes of substance and its allowable changes of instantaneous constituent form (where the limits of such allowable change define the objects' broader constituent form, the constituent form that takes in not just its existence at a time but its persistence throughout its career). Ordinary things could perhaps be conceived as such trees of possibilities, with corresponding changes elsewhere in our ordinary conceptual schemes: e.g., reinterpreting predications about ordinary things. That could perhaps be made to work smoothly. But I see little point in trying seriously to do so when the trees themselves would contain ordinary things as constituents, in the way the tree for a snowball would contain pieces of snow, and the tree for a cubical box would contain square boards, and the tree for a chain would contain links, and so on. It might be argued that these contained ordinary things would themselves be reduced each to its own tree. But since from our vantage it is hard to tell what the bottom of the induced hierarchy looks like or even whether there is a bottom at all, it seems better to leave open the question of reduction and to recognize instead a relation between things and their underlying events which though compatible with reduction or identity does not necessarily require reduction or identity.

(In fact, any supervenient object that has always been in existence cannot be identified even with the tree of possibilities that ramifies from its origin *since it has no origin*. We might try identifying such an object with an infinite sequence of trees ramifying from initial segments ("origins") that end earlier and earlier. But if there is a finite interval between the endings of the origins in our receding infinite sequence, then even that infinite sequence would be inadequate by *missing* possibilities for ramification emerging from *between* the endings.)

J. Persons Again

Returning finally to persons let's first distinguish six questions as follows:

Q1 What are the requirements for there to be a person at a given time?
Q2 Given a certain person P at a given time t, on what does P's existence supervene at t?

Q3 Given P at t, what is essential to (required for) there being the very person P at t?

Q4 What are the requirements for there to be a person who endures from t1 to t2?

Q5 Given a person P who endures from t1 to t2, from what does P's endurance from t1 to t2 derive?

Q6 Given P who endures from t1 to t2, what is essential (required) for that very person P to endure from t1 to t2?

Now if a person is just a fundamental, simple, and indivisible subject of consciousness, a soul, then the answers to our questions are all relatively straightforward. The requirement for there to be a person at a time is just that there be such a soul. A person's existence supervenes then just on that person's existence (allowing this therefore as a limiting case of supervenience). What is required for that very person to exist at t is just for that very person (that very simple, indivisible, fundamental soul) to exist at t, and what is essential to that person's being that very person at that time is just being that very person at that time. And similarly simple, straightforward answers are also then available for our last three questions as well the ones about persistence through a span of time.

If we decide against souls, however, and we hold firm against the simple identification of persons with their bodies, then we have the problems discussed in earlier sections above. More, we must then be prepared to face the many difficult controversies about the relation between mind and body and about the identity of a person through time. We cannot take up here the enormous structure of questions involved. I wish to consider only one specific question that arises on one specific approach.

Suppose we take a person to supervene on a live, functioning human body, so that at a given time that person exists because a certain live human body is then functioning (where what it is for a human body to function in this context requires only a certain physical and psychological minimum and not any very full thriving or flourishing). Recall now the principle of derivation according to which when a thing T supervenes on matters m1, . . ., mn, then every property of T should derive necessarily from properties of and interrelations among those matters m1, . . ., mn (Principle 4 of section F above). This principle is I think borne out by consideration of our examples of supervenient entities. I for one am unable to imagine any property of a snowball or a box or a chain or a collision that cannot be plausibly regarded as deriving necessarily from properties of the constitutent piece of snow, or from properties of or interrelations respectively among the square sides, or the links, or the billiard balls. More problematic however is the case of persons when we regard them as supervenient on their bodies or brains or the like. For example, what properties of or interrelations among the neurons of a certain brain may be thought to entail the thoughts and experiences of the person supervenient partly or wholly on that brain? Recall the box that supervenes on the six square sides. There we may very plausibly view the cubicity of the box as deriving necessity from a certain relation among the six sides, the box-relation, the relation among the six that holds iff each is square and joins each of its edges to exactly one edge of exactly one of the other six. Reflection enables us to see how cubicity will derive necessarily from such a relation among six sides. But at present reflection is impotent to reveal just how my present headache must derive necessarily from any properties of the neurons in my brain or any interrelations among them. And yet if I supervene on my neurons when these are organized appropriately, etc., in the way the box supervenes on the six sides when these are organized appropriately, then my headaching must derive necessarily from how it is with the neurons just as the cubicity of the box derives necessarily from how it is with the sides. And though we can see the derivation of cubicity from how it is with the sides, we haven't a glimmer of how to derive headaching necessarily from how it is with the neurons. We might of course expect to discover correlations between how it is with someone's brain at a given time and how it is with his experience at that time. Indeed, many such correlations have long been under scientific study, and some now seem nicely supported. But that is not yet enough to give us what we want. For in no such generalization is there the suggestion that the experiencing (e.g., the headaching) follows from the brain state with the kind of necessity that attends the connection between cubicity in a box and the relation among its sides.

Of course, necessity is sometimes thickly screened from us but still there. And I for one am not unwilling to grant that much necessity may be accessible to us only a posteriori, and even only posteriori to complex scientific theory. So I do not for a moment consider the argument about the necessary derivation of the mental from properties of the brain to be any sort of decisive refutation or even any refutation at all. Rather is it only a set of considerations worth pondering. What is required to relate one's mental properties with their body in the brain seems indeed to be just such necessary derivation and is found in the derivation of cubicity from the relation of the side. That anyway is how it should plausibly seem to anyone who accepts the supervenience of the person on the body. Anyone like that does therefore have reason to consider carefully the Derivation Principle and also the view that the physical necessity of the relevant scientific laws is just a necessity as plain as that which joins the relation of the sides of a cube to the cubicity of the whole, a posteriori though our access to it may have to be.[4]

Appendix

Let us try to make more precise the notion that x and y cannot possibly be related simply by diversity, and the principle that entities require a dimensional framework. First we need several preliminary concepts, as follows.

Par x is a contingent particular iff x exists contingently and x is neither a property (nor a relation) nor a state of affairs.

In the following five definitions (Dep, OD, OI, MD, MP, and BSubs), the range of the variables x, y and z is restricted to contingent particulars.

Dep x depends on y iff x ≠ y & Necessarily (x exists ⊃ y exists)

OD x ontologically derives at t from y [symbolically: ODt(x,y)] iff x ≠ y & (∃R)(∃z1, . . ., zn)[(x exists at t formally-because at t R(z1, . . ., zn)) & (∃i)(zi = y)]

OI x is at t ontologically independent of y [symbolically OIt(x,y)] iff x ≠ y & not-ODt(x,y) & not-ODt(y,x) [In alternative terminology, x is at t ontologically independent of y iff x and y are discrete at t.]

MD x mereologically derives at t from y [symbolically: MDt(x,y)] iff x ≠ y & (∃z1, . . ., zn)[(x exists at t formally-because z1 exists at t & ... & zn exists at t) & (∃i)(zi = y)]

MP y is at t a mereological part of x [symbolically MPt(y,x)] iff (∃z)[y ≠ z & OIt(y,z) & MDt(x,y) & MDt(x,z)]

[Compare an analogous definition:

AP y is at t an Aristotelian part of x [symbolically: APt(y,x)] iff (∃z)[y ≠ z & OIt(y,z) & ODt(x,y) & ODt(x,z)]

No formal use is made here of AP, but it may perhaps capture a legitimate sense of 'part'.]

Subs x is a substance iff x is a particular and x ontologically derives from no particular but its own mereological parts

Each of the following three definitions (C, PI, and PR) is to be understood as implicitly relative to a universe of discourse restricted to substances and to the properties and relations exemplified by them.

C A property F is contingent iff it is not necessarily exemplified.

PI A contingent property F is purely intrinsic iff the exemplification of F does not necessarily imply the existence of anything contingent and discrete from what exemplifies it, and the existence of F does not entail the existence of any contingent particular.

FR R is a fundamental relation iff R is a relation that does not supervene on purely intrinsic properties of its relata.

Consider finally the principle that diversity cannot stand alone, and the principle that entities require a dimensional framework.

DCSA No entities x and y can possibly be related only by diversity in such a way that the following three conditions are satisfied: first, x is numerically distinct from y; second, x is otherwise the same as y in every qualitative respect; and, third, x is related to y by no relation that is irreflexive, except only for the relation of diversity (and its deductive progeny).

ERDF If entities x and y belong to the same category, they must fall within a dimensional framework, which requires the presence of some ordering relation that relates the two.

Each of these principles is now qualified further as follows: (a) the universe of discourse of each is restricted to substances; and (b) the relations appealed to in each are restricted to fundamental relations.

Notes

1. David Hume, *A Treatise of Human Nature*, ed. Ernest C. Mossner (Middlesex, England and Baltimore, Maryland: Penguin Books, 1969), p. 300.

2. "And now what shall I say of the mind, that is to say, of myself? For so far I do not admit in myself anything other than the mind. Can it be that I, who seem to perceive this bit of wax so clearly and distinctly, do not know my own self, not only with much more truth and certainty, but also much more distinctly and evidently? For if I judge that the wax exists because I see it, certainly it follows much more evidently that I exist myself because I see it. For it might happen that what I see is not really wax; it might also happen that I do not even possess eyes to see anything; but it could not happen that, when I see, or what amounts to the same thing, when I think I see, I who think am not something. For a similar reason, if I judge that the wax exists because I touch it, the same conclusion follows once more, namely, that I am. And if I hold to this judgment because my imagination, or whatever other entity it might be, persuades me of it, I will still reach the same conclusion. And what I have said here about the wax can be applied to all other things which are external to me." (René Descartes, *Meditations on First Philosophy*, trans. Laurence J. Lafleur (Indianapolis: The Library of Liberal Arts, 1960), p. 32).

3. "Mind-Body Interaction and Supervenient Causation," *Midwest Studies in Philosophy IX* (1984).

4. Many thanks for discussion or written comments to Felicia (née Diana) Ackerman, Roderick Chisholm, Eli Hirsch, Jaegwon Kim, and James Van Cleve. Also to Vrinda Dalmiya, John Greco, David Martens, and David Sosa. Also to colloquium audiences at Brandeis and Rochester for helpful questioning. And especially to Gary Rosenkrantz, for his excellent commentary on the version delivered at the 1986 Greensboro Colloquium.

PART II

Contingent Identity and Counterpart Theory

6

Contingent Identity[1]

Allan Gibbard

This brief for contingent identity begins with an example. Under certain conditions, I shall argue, a clay statue is identical with the piece of clay of which it is made—or at least it is plausible to claim so. If indeed the statue and the piece of clay are identical, I shall show, then the identity is contingent: that is to say, where *s* is the statue and *c* the piece of clay.

$$s = c \;\&\; \Diamond(s \text{ exists } \;\&\; c \text{ exists} \;\&\; s \neq c). \qquad (1)$$

This claim of contingent identity, if true, has important ramifications. Later I shall develop theories of concrete things and proper names which are needed to fit the claim. These theories together form a coherent alternative to theories which hold that all true identities formed with proper names are necessary—a plausible alternative, I shall argue, with many advantages.

Most purported examples of such contingent identity fail: that much, I think, has been shown by Saul Kripke's recent work (1971, 1972). Kripke's work has transformed the subjects of necessity and reference, and the usual examples of contingent identity depend on accounts of those subjects which Kripke's attacks undermine. Take, for instance, one of Frege's examples of *a posteriori* identity, somewhat reworded (1892, p. 57).

If Hesperus exists, then Hesperus = Phosphorus. (2)

On the account of necessity which prevailed before Kripke, a truth is necessary only if it can be known *a priori*. Now as Frege pointed out, (2) is clearly *a posteriori*, since it reports a discovery which could only have been made by observation. On the old account, then, (2), although true, is not a necessary truth. Kripke's attacks undermine this account of necessary truth as *a priori* truth. Whether something is a necessary truth, he argues, is not a matter of how we can know it, but of whether it might have been false if the world had been different: a proposition is a necessary truth if it would have been true in any possible situation. The necessary-contingent distinction and the *a priori–a posteriori* distinction, then, are not drawn in the same way, and to prove a truth contingent, it is not enough simply to show that it is *a posteriori* (1971, p. 150; 1972, pp. 260–4).

Kripke's attacks also undermine accounts of reference which would make (2) a contingent truth. On both Russell's theory (1905) of descriptions and the later "cluster" theory, a name gets its reference in some way from the beliefs of the person who uses it. On Russell's view, the heavenly body Hesperus of which the ancients spoke would be the thing which fitted certain beliefs they had about Hesperus; on the cluster theory, it would be the thing which fitted a preponderance of their beliefs about it. Now the ancients' beliefs about Hesperus and their beliefs about Phosphorus were such that, in some possible worlds, one thing would fit the former and another the latter. On such an account of proper names, then, (2) would be false in some possible worlds, and is therefore contingent.

I shall not repeat Kripke's attacks on the description and cluster theories of proper names (1972, pp. 254–60, 284–308). My purpose here is to argue that even if these attacks are successful, there may well remain some contingent identities consisting of proper names. The identity of Hesperus and Phosphorus is not contingent, on the theories I shall develop, but I shall give an example which is. Kripke's attacks, if I am right, transform the subject of contingent identity, but they do not eliminate it.

I

In what sort of case might a statue *s* be identical with the piece of clay, *c*, of which it is made? Identity here is to be taken in a strict, timeless sense, not as mere identity during some period of time. For two things to be strictly identical, they must have all properties in common. That means, among other things, that they must start to exist at the same time and cease to exist at the same time. If we are to construct a case in which a statue is identical with a piece of clay, then, we shall need persistence criteria for statues and pieces of clay—criteria for when they start to exist and when they cease to exist.

Take first the piece of clay. Here I do not mean the portion of clay of which the piece consists, which may go on existing after the piece has been broken up or merged with other pieces. I shall call this clay of which the piece consists a *portion* of clay; a portion of clay, as I am using the term, can be scattered widely and continue to exist. Here I am asking about a *piece* or *lump* of clay.

A lump sticks together: its parts stick to each other, directly or through other parts, and no part of the lump sticks to any portion of clay which is not part of the lump. The exact nature of this sticking relation will not matter here; it is a familiar relation which holds between parts of a solid object, but not between parts of a liquid, powder, or heap of solid objects. We know, then, what it is for two portions of clay to be parts of the same lump of clay at a time *t*, and if they are, I shall say that they are *stuck to* each other *at t*.

For how long, then, does a piece of clay persist? As a first approximation, the criteria might be put as follows. A piece of clay consists of a portion *P* of clay. It comes into existence when all the parts of *P* come to be stuck to each other, and cease to be stuck to any clay which is not part of *P*. It ceases to exist when the parts of *P* cease to be stuck to each other or come to be stuck to clay which is not in *P*. Thus a piece of clay can be formed either by sticking smaller pieces of clay together or by breaking it off a larger piece of clay, and it can be destroyed either by breaking it apart or by sticking it to other pieces of clay.

This standard is probably too strict; we ought to allow for such things as wear and the adherence of clay dust to a wet piece of clay. Nothing will change, though, for my purposes, if we allow the portion of clay which composes a piece of clay to change slowly over time. In the actual world, then, a piece of clay might be characterized by a function **P** from instants to portions of clay. In order for it to characterize a piece of clay, the function **P** would have to satisfy the following conditions.

(a) The domain of **P** is an interval of time *T*.

(b) For any instant *t* in *T*, **P**(*t*) is a portion of clay the parts of which, at *t*, are both stuck to each other and not stuck to any clay particles which are not part of **P**(*t*).

(c) The portions of clay **P**(*t*) change with *t* only slowly, if at all. (I shall give no exact standard of slowness here, but one might be stipulated if anything hinged on it.)

(d) No function **P*** which satisfies (a), (b), and (c) *extends* **P**, in the sense that the domain of **P*** properly includes the domain of **P** and the function **P** is **P*** with its domain restricted.

Both on this standard, then, and on the earlier, stricter one, a piece of clay comes into existence when parts in it are stuck to each other and unstuck from all other clay, and goes out of existence when its parts cease to be stuck to each other or become stuck to other clay. That is what I shall need for what follows.

What, now, are the persistence criteria for clay statues? By a statue here, I do not mean a shape of which there could be more than one token, but a concrete particular thing: distinct clay statues, as I am using the term, may come out of the same mold. A clay statue consists of a piece of clay in a specific shape. It lasts, then, as long as the piece of clay lasts and keeps that shape. It comes into being when the piece of clay first exists and has that shape, and it goes out of existence as soon as the piece of clay ceases to exist or to have that shape.

These criteria too may be overly strict: again we may want to allow for slow changes of shape from wear, accretion, and slight bending. So let us say, a clay statue persists as long as the piece of clay it is made of persists and changes shape only slowly.

I do not claim that the criteria I have given are precisely set forth that way in our conceptual scheme. I do think that the criteria I have given fit at least roughly what we say about statues and pieces of clay. My argument will depend on no such claim, though, and for all I shall have to say, the criteria I have given might have been purely stipulative. I do need to make one claim for those criteria: I claim that as I have defined them, pieces of clay and clay statues are objects. That is to say, they can be designated with proper names, and the logic we ordinarily use will still apply. That is all, strictly speaking, that I need to claim for the criteria I have given.

Now we are in a better position to ask, are a clay statue and the piece of clay of which it is made identical? The persistence criteria I have given make it clear that often the two are distinct. In a typical case, a piece of clay is brought into existence by breaking it off from a bigger piece of clay. It then gets shaped, say, into the form of an elephant. With the finishing touches, a statue of an elephant comes into being. The statue and the piece of clay therefore have different properties: the times they start to exist are different, and whereas the statue has the property of being elephant-shaped as long as it exists, the piece of clay does not. Since one has properties the other lacks, the two are not identical (cf. Quine, 1950, Sec. 1).

Suppose, though, a clay statue starts to exist at the same time as the piece of clay of which it is made, and ceases to exist at the same time as the piece of clay ceases to exist. Will the statue then be identical with the piece of clay? It is indeed possible for a statue to endure for precisely the same period of time as its piece of clay, as the persistence criteria I have given make clear. Consider the following story.

I make a clay statue of the infant Goliath in two pieces, one the part above the waist and the other the part below the waist. Once I finish the two halves, I stick them together, thereby bringing into existence simultaneously a new piece of clay and a new statue. A day later I smash the statue, thereby bringing to an end both statue and piece of clay. The statue and the piece of clay persisted during exactly the same period of time.

Here, I am tempted to say, the statue and the piece of clay are identical. They began at the same time, and on any usual account, they had the same shape, location, color, and so forth at each instant in their history; everything that happened to one happened to the other; and the act that destroyed the one destroyed the other. If the statue is an entity over and above the piece of clay in that shape, then statues seem to take on a ghostly air. No doubt other explanations of what the statue is can be offered, but the hypothesis that the statue and piece of clay are identical seems well worth exploring.

If indeed the statue and piece of clay are the same thing, then their identity is contingent. It is contingent, that is to say in the sense of (1) at the beginning of this paper. (1) uses proper names, and so let me name the statue and the lump: the statue I shall call '*Goliath*'; the piece of clay, 'Lumpl'. Naming the piece of clay, to be sure, seems strange, but that, presumably, is because it is unusual to name pieces of clay, not because pieces of clay are unnamable. With these names, (1) becomes

$$\textit{Goliath} = \text{Lumpl} \;\&\; \Diamond (\textit{Goliath} \text{ exists } \& \text{ Lumpl exists } \& \; \textit{Goliath} \neq \text{Lumpl}). \tag{3}$$

It is in this sense that I want to claim that *Goliath* = Lumpl contingently.

Suppose, then, that *Goliath* = Lumpl. Then their identity is contingent in the sense of (3). For suppose I had brought Lumpl into existence as *Goliath*, just as I actually did, but before the clay had a chance to dry, I squeezed it into a ball. At that point, according to the persistence criteria I have given, the statue *Goliath* would have ceased to exist, but the piece of clay Lumpl would still exist in a new shape. Hence Lumpl would not be *Goliath*, even though both existed. We would have

$$\text{Lumpl exists } \& \; \textit{Goliath} \text{ exists } \& \; \textit{Goliath} \neq \text{Lumpl}.$$

If in fact, then, *Goliath* = Lumpl, then here is a case of contingent identity. In fact *Goliath* = Lumpl, but had I destroyed the statue *Goliath* by squeezing it, then it would have been the case that, although both existed, *Goliath* ≠ Lumpl. The identity is contingent, then, in the sense given in (3).

II

The claim that *Goliath* = Lumpl, then, has important consequences for the logic of identity. How can the claim be evaluated?

Initially, at least, the claim seems plausible. *Goliath* and Lumpl exist during precisely the same period of time, and at each instant during that period, they have, it would seem, the same shape, color, weight, location, and so forth: they share all their obvious properties.

The claim that *Goliath* = Lumpl, moreover, fits a systematic account of statues and pieces of clay. A clay statue ordinarily begins to exist only after its piece of clay does. In such cases, it seems reasonable to say, the statue is a temporal segment of the piece of clay—a segment which extends for the period of time during which the piece of clay keeps a particular, statuesque shape. Here, then, is a systematic account of the relation between a statue and its piece of clay. By that account, however, there will be cases in which a clay statue is identical with its piece of clay. For in some cases the very temporal segment of the piece of clay which constitutes the statue extends for the entire life of the piece of clay. In such a case, the segment is the piece of clay in its entire extent: the statue and the piece of clay are identical.[2]

That leads to my main reason for wanting to say that *Goliath* = Lumpl. Concrete things, like statues and pieces of clay, are a part of the physical world, and we ought, it seems to me, to have a systematic physical account of them. Concrete things, I want to maintain, are made up in some simple, canonical way from fundamental physical entities. Now what I have said of the relation between a statue and its piece of clay fits such a general view of concrete things. Suppose, for example, we take point-instants to be our fundamental physical entities, and let a concrete thing be a set of point-instants. In that case, *Goliath* = Lumpl simply because they are the same set of point-instants. Suppose instead we take particles to be our fundamental physical entities, and let a concrete thing be a changing set of particles—which might mean a function from instants in time to sets of particles. Then again, *Goliath* = Lumpl, because at each instant they consist of the same set of particles. Now particles and point-instants are the sorts of things we might expect to appear in a well-confirmed fundamental physics—in that part of an eventual physics which gives the fundamental laws of the universe. A system according to which *Goliath* = Lumpl, then, may well allow concrete things to be made up in a simple way from entities that appear in well-confirmed fundamental physics. Concrete things, then, can be given a place in a comprehensive view of the world.

In the rest of this paper, then, I shall work out a theory according to which *Goliath* = Lumpl. Concrete things, for all I shall say, may be either sets of point-instants or changing sets of particles; the appendix gives an account of concrete things as sets of point-instants. The sections which follow develop a theory of proper names and a theory of modal and dispositional properties for concrete things.

III

If, as I want to claim, *Goliath* = Lumpl, then how do proper names like '*Goliath*' and 'Lumpl' work? Kripke gives an account of proper names from which it follows that *Goliath* cannot be identical with Lumpl; thus if Kripke's were the only plausible account of proper names, then the claim that *Goliath* = Lumpl would have to be abandoned. In fact, though, accepting that *Goliath* = Lumpl leads to an alternative account of proper names, which, I shall argue, is fully coherent and at least as plausible as Kripke's.

Kripke's account of proper names is roughly this. We in the actual world use proper names both to talk about the actual world and to talk about ways the world might have been. According to Kripke, if a proper name denotes a thing in the actual world, then in talk of non-actual situations, the name, if it denotes at all, simply denotes that same thing. A proper name is a *rigid designator*: it refers to the same thing in talk of any possible world in which that thing exists, and in talk of any other possible world, it refers to nothing in that world (1972, pp. 269–70).

Now if all proper names are rigid designators, then *Goliath* cannot be identical with Lumpl as I have claimed. For suppose they are identical. Call the actual world W_0, and the world as it would be if I had squeezed the clay into a ball W'; then

(i) In W_0, *Goliath* = Lumpl,

but as I have shown,

(ii) In W', *Goliath* ≠ Lumpl.

Now if the names '*Goliath*' and 'Lumpl' are both rigid designators, then (i) and (ii) cannot both hold. For suppose (i) is true. Then the names '*Goliath*' and 'Lumpl' both denote the same thing in W_0. Hence if they are both rigid designators, they both denote that thing in every possible world in which it exists, and denote nothing otherwise. Since they each denote something in W', they must therefore both denote the same thing in W', and thus (ii) must be false.

The claim that *Goliath* = Lumpl, then, is incompatible with Kripke's account of proper names. Suppose, then, that *Goliath* is indeed identical with Lumpl; what view of proper names emerges? How, on that supposition, could we decide whether the name '*Goliath*' is a rigid designator? Consider the situation. In the actual world, '*Goliath*' refers to a thing which I made and then broke, which is both a statue and a piece of clay. Hence the name '*Goliath*' is a rigid designator if it refers to that same thing in any possible situation in which the thing exists, and refers to nothing otherwise.

What, though, would constitute "that same thing" if the statue and the piece of clay were different? Take the situation in W': suppose instead of breaking the statue, as I actually did, I had squeezed the clay into a ball. Would that single thing which in fact I made and then broke—which in fact was both a piece of clay and a statue—then be the statue *Goliath* which I squeezed out of existence, or the piece of clay Lumpl which went on existing after I squeezed it?

I can find no sense in the question. To ask meaningfully what that thing would be, we must designate it either as a statue or as a piece of clay. It makes sense to ask what the statue *Goliath* would be in that situation: it would be a statue; likewise, it makes sense to ask what the piece of clay Lumpl would be in that situation: it would be a piece of clay. What that thing would be, though, apart from the way it is designated, is a question without meaning.

A rough theory begins to emerge from all this. If *Goliath* and Lumpl are the same thing, asking what that thing would be in *W′* apart from the way the thing is designated, makes no sense. Meaningful cross-world identities of such things as statues, it begins to seem, must be identities *qua* something: *qua* statue or *qua* lump,[3] *qua Goliath* or *qua* Lumpl. It makes sense to talk of the "same statue" in different possible worlds, but no sense to talk of the "same thing".

Put more fully, what seems to be happening is this. Proper names like '*Goliath*' or 'Lumpl' refer to a thing as a thing of a certain kind: 'Goliath' refers to something as a statue; 'Lumpl', as a lump. For each such kind of thing, there is a set of persistence criteria, like the ones I gave for statues and for lumps.[4] In rare cases, at least, one thing will be of two different kinds, with different persistence criteria, and whereas one proper name refers to it as a thing of one kind, another proper name will refer to it as a thing of another kind. In such cases, the identity formed with those names is contingently true. It is true because the two names designate the same thing, which ceases to exist at the same time on both sets of criteria. It is contingent because if the world had gone differently after the thing came into existence, the thing might have ceased to exist at different times on the two sets of criteria: it would have been one thing on one set of persistence criteria, and another thing—perhaps a temporal segment of the first—on the second set of criteria.

If all that is so, it makes no sense to call a designator rigid or non-rigid by itself. A designator may be rigid with respect to a sortal: it may be statue-rigid, as '*Goliath*' is, or it may be lump-rigid, as 'Lumpl' is. A designator, for instance, is *statue-rigid* if it designates the same statue in every possible world in which that statue exists and designates nothing in any other possible world. What is special about proper names like '*Goliath*' and 'Lumpl' is not that they are rigid designators. It is rather that each is rigid with respect to the sortal it invokes. '*Goliath*' refers to its bearer as a statue and is statue-rigid; 'Lumpl' refers to its bearer as a lump and is lump-rigid.

In short, then, if we accept that *Goliath* = Lumpl and examine the situation, a rough theory of proper names emerges. A proper name like '*Goliath*' denotes a thing in the actual world, and invokes a sortal with certain persistence criteria. It then denotes the same thing-of-that-sort in every possible world in which it denotes at all. The name '*Goliath*' itself, for instance, denotes a lump of clay and invokes the sortal *statue*; hence it denotes the same statue in every possible world in which that statue exists.

That leaves two questions unanswered. First, how does a name like '*Goliath*' get its reference in the actual world? Second, what makes a thing in another possible world "the same statue" as the one which in fact I made and then broke? I shall tackle this second question first.

Once I made my statue, that statue existed, and nothing that happened from then on could change the fact that it had existed or the way it had come to exist. It would be that same statue whether I subsequently broke it, squeezed it, or sold it. Its origin, then, makes a statue the statue that it is, and if statues in different possible worlds have the same beginning, then they are the same statue.

The name '*Goliath*' picks out in W' the one statue which begins in W' like *Goliath* in W_0. Consider the case more fully. The world W' bears an important relation to W_0 and the statue *Goliath* in W_0: W' *branches* from W_0 after *Goliath* begins to exist; that is, until some time after *Goliath* begins to exist in W_0, the histories of W_0 and W' are exactly the same. In the branching world W', then, *Goliath* is the statue which has exactly the same history before the branching as *Goliath* in W_0. The name 'Lumpl' too picks out a thing in W' which begins exactly like the statue *Goliath* in W_0. 'Lumpl', though, picks out, not the unique statue in W' which begins that way, but the unique piece of clay in W' which begins that way. Since that piece of clay in W' is distinct from that statue in W', the two names pick out different things in W'—different things which both start out in the same way.

Here, then, is a theory of reference for the special case of branching possible worlds. Let proper name α denote a thing X in the actual world W_0; the theory will apply to any possible world W which branches from W_0 after X begins to exist in W_0. According to the theory, α not only denotes X in W_0, but also invokes a set C of persistence criteria which X satisfies in W_0. The reference of α in W, then, is the thing in W which has the same history before the branching as X has in W_0 and which satisfies the persistence criteria in set C.

According to the theory, then, the reference of a name in branching world W depends on two things: its reference in the actual world, and the persistence criteria it invokes. The reference of the name in the actual world determines how the thing it denotes in W begins; the persistence criteria it invokes determine which of the various things that begin that way in W the name denotes.

That leaves the problem of possible worlds which do not branch from the actual world, or which branch too early. How to handle reference to things in such obdurate worlds I do not know. Perhaps the best course is to deny that any such reference is possible. The clearest cases of reference by a speaker in one possible world to a thing in another are ones like the clay statue case, where a world branches from the actual one after the thing to which reference is made starts to exist. I am inclined, then, for the sake of clarity, to rule out any other sort of reference to concrete entities in other possible worlds. If, though, a clear criterion which allowed such reference were devised, that criterion could probably be adopted without much changing the system I am proposing.

There remains the question of how a name gets its reference in the actual world. Its reference in branching worlds, I have said, depends partly on its reference in the actual world. Until we say how a name gets its reference in the actual world, then, even the theory of reference for branching worlds is incomplete. Nothing I have said about the names '*Goliath*' and 'Lumpl' has any direct bearing on the question of reference in the actual world. The account Kripke gives (1972, pp. 298–9) seems plausible to me, and everything I have said in this paper is compatible with it.

On that account, a name gets its reference from a causal chain that connects the person who uses the name with the thing denoted. In my mouth and in the mouth of anyone else who uses the names '*Goliath*' and 'Lumpl', those names denote the actual thing they do because I applied those names to it directly and others got the names from me. Other people, then, are connected to that clay statue by a tradition through which the name was handed down; I am connected more directly, by having perceived the thing and named it.

Persistence criteria play a role in starting the tradition. I named the thing I did by pointing to it and invoking persistence criteria: "I name this statue '*Goliath*'," I said, "and this piece of clay 'Lumpl'." The name '*Goliath*', then, denoted the unique thing at which I was pointing which satisfied the persistence criteria for statues—that is, the unique statue at which I was pointing. Since the same thing satisfied both the criteria for statues and the criteria for pieces of clay, both names denoted the same thing, but if I had invoked different persistence criteria, I might have named a different thing. When I pointed at the statue, I pointed at a number of things of various durations. I pointed, for instance, at the portion of clay which made up the statue. I might have said, "I name the portion of clay which makes up this statue 'Portia'." If I had done so, I would have named a portion of clay which survived the breaking of the statue. Thus when the tradition is started which gives a name a concrete reference in the actual world, the persistence criteria invoked help determine what entity bears that name.

I have given a theory of proper names, and on that theory, it is clear why the identity '*Goliath* = Lumpl' is contingent. It is equally clear, on that theory, why the identity 'Hesperus = Phosphorus' is necessary, in the sense that it holds in any possible world in which Hesperus exists. At least it is clear if identity of concrete things across possible worlds is confined to branching cases in the way I have described. Both names, 'Hesperus' and 'Phosphorus', invoke the persistence criteria for heavenly bodies. Both refer to Venus. Hence in any possible world W which branches from the actual world after Venus begins to exist, they both refer to the heavenly body in W which starts out in W like Venus in W_0. Both, then, refer to the same thing in *W*. On the theory here, then, as on Kripke's theory, the identity 'Hesperus = Phosphorus', even though *a posteriori*, is a necessary truth: it would hold in any situation in which Hesperus or Phosphorus existed.

In short, then, if we accept that *Goliath* = Lumpl, the following theory of proper names for concrete objects emerges. The reference of a name in the actual world is fixed partly by invoking a set of persistence criteria which determine what thing it names. The name may then be passed on through a tradition, and the reference is fixed by the origin of that tradition. The name can also be used to refer to a thing in a possible world which branches from the actual world after the thing named in the actual world begins to exist. In that case the name refers to the unique thing in that possible world which both satisfies the persistence criteria the name invokes and starts out exactly like the bearer of the name in the actual world.

IV

Kripke's theory of proper names is incompatible with the theory I have developed, and Kripke gives a number of forceful arguments for his theory. Do any of those arguments tell against the theory here? Let me try to pick out arguments Kripke gives which are germane.

According to the theory here, it makes no sense to call a designator rigid and leave it at that, because it makes no strict sense to call things in different possible worlds identical and leave it at that: identity across possible worlds makes sense only with respect to a sortal. According to Kripke, qualms about identity across possible worlds are unfounded, and plain talk of rigid designators makes perfectly good sense. What Kripke says most directly on this point, however, shows no more than what I have already accepted: that it makes sense to call a designator rigid with respect to a sortal, like *statue, number*, or *man*. ". . . we can perfectly well talk about rigid and non-rigid designators. Moreover, we have a simple, intuitive test for them. We can say, for example, that the number of planets might have been a different number from the number it in fact is." The designator 'the number of planets', then, is non-rigid. "If we apply this intuitive test to proper names, such as for example 'Richard Nixon', they would seem intuitively to come out as rigid designators. . . . It seems that we cannot say 'Nixon might have been a different man from the man he in fact was,' unless, of course, we mean it metaphorically." (1971, pp. 148–9).

Does it make sense, then, to call a designator "rigid" independently of a sortal it invokes? Kripke's examples here prove no such thing. Nixon indeed could not have been a different *man* from the man he in fact is. That, however, shows only that the designator 'Nixon' is rigid with respect to the sortal *man*, not that it is rigid independently of any sortal. To show it rigid independently of any sortal, one would have to go beyond what Kripke says in the passage I have quoted, and show that Nixon could not have been a different *entity* from the one he in fact is.

For that purpose, the "simple, intuitive test" Kripke offers will not help. We speak and think of "the same person" but not of "the same entity". The point at issue is how everyday talk of "the same person" best fits into systematic talk of "entities". To this issue, everyday intuitions about entities, if we had them, would be irrelevant: the matter has to be settled by working out rival systems and comparing their implications.

Kripke attacks qualms about cross-world identity in another way: those qualms, he says, may just grow out of a confusion about what possible worlds are. Talk of "possible worlds" suggests that they are like distant planets to be explored. If that were what they were like, I might explore a possible world and discover someone who looked like Benjamin Franklin; I would then have to determine whether it actually was Franklin I had discovered, or just someone who looked like him (1972, p. 268).

Instead, according to Kripke, possible worlds are situations which we stipulate—'counterfactual situations' may be the best term. What thing is what in a counterfactual situation is not something I find out; it is part of what I stipulate: it is "given in the very description" of the stipulated situation. "And there seems to be no less objection to *stipulating* that we are speaking of certain *people* than there can be to stipulating that we are speaking of certain *qualities*" (1971, p. 148).

Is that so? The statue example seems to provide an objection—an objection, at least, to stipulating that we are speaking of certain *entities*. In that example, a possible situation was stipulated, just as Kripke demands. "For suppose I had brought Lumpl into existence as *Goliath*, just as I actually did, but before the clay had a chance to dry, I squeezed it into a ball." In this stipulated situation, I showed, there are two distinct things, a statue and a piece of clay. It might be tempting to ask which of the two is the one thing which, in the actual world, I made and then broke. To that question, though, there is no plain answer—or so I argued. Now the problem is not one of understipulation. It is not as if the thing I actually made could appear in two different possible situations in which I squeezed it: in one as a statue that ceased to exist when squeezed, and in another as a piece of clay which persisted after it was squeezed. After I made that thing, I held it in my hands and I could have squeezed it; if I suppose that I did squeeze it, I have stipulated as much about the identities of the things in that supposed situation as can be stipulated. A situation, then, can be fully stipulated even though questions of identity across possible worlds remain unsettled.

Kripke agrees to something like this. "Given certain counterfactual vicissitudes in the history of the molecules of a table, *T*, one may ask whether *T* would exist, in that situation, or whether a certain bunch of molecules, which in that situation would constitute a table, constitute the very same table *T*." Such a conception of 'transworld identification', he says, "differs considerably from the usual one"; for one thing, "the attempted notion deals with criteria of identity of particulars in terms of other particulars, not qualities"—in terms of particular molecules, that is to say (1972, pp. 271–2). This qualification, though, has no bearing on the point in question here. Take a possible world in which I squeeze Lumpl into a ball, and suppose all the molecules involved are clearly identified. There are still two distinct things in that world, the statue *Goliath* which I destroy by squeezing, and the piece of clay Lumpl which survives the squeezing. The question remains, then, which of those two distinct things in that possible world is the single thing which in fact I made and then broke. There is, in short, a genuine problem with cross-world identification—Kripke's arguments notwithstanding.

V

The most prominent objection to contingent identity remains to be tackled: the objection that it violates Leibniz' Law. If *Goliath* is contingently identical with Lumpl, then although

$$\Box(\text{Lumpl exists} \rightarrow \text{Lumpl} = \text{Lumpl}) \tag{4}$$

is true

$$\Box(\text{Lumpl exists} \rightarrow \textit{Goliath} = \text{Lumpl}) \tag{5}$$

is false. Yet (5) is derived from (4) and

$$\textit{Goliath} = \text{Lumpl} \tag{6}$$

by substitutivity of identicals. Thus, the objection goes, *Goliath* cannot be contingently identical with Lumpl.

The usual answer will serve my purpose here. Leibniz' Law settles very little by itself: put as a general law of substitutivity of identicals, it is just false; in its correct version, it is a law about properties and relations: *If x = y, then for any property, if x has it then y has it, and for any relation and any given things, if x stands in that relation to those things, then y stands in that relation to those things.* The law so stated yields substitutivity of identicals only for contexts that attribute properties and relations. (5) follows from (4) and (6) by Leibniz' Law, then, only if the context

$$\Box(\text{Lumpl exists} \rightarrow \underline{\quad\quad} = \text{Lumpl}) \tag{7}$$

attributes a property. We can block the inference to (5), then, simply by denying that the context (7) attributes a property.

It may seem arbitrary to deny that (7) attributes a property, but whether it does is the very point in question here. A property, if it is to be a property, must apply or not apply to a thing independently of the way the thing is designated. (7) gives a property, then, only if it gives something that is true of Lumpl or false of Lumpl independently of the way Lumpl is designated, and whether it does is the point in question.

The proponent of contingent identity, then, has a reasonable, consistent position open to him—a position that is familiar in the literature on the subject (cf. Quine, 1961, Sec. II). Expressions constructed with modal operators, he can say, simply do not give properties of *concrete things*, such as statues and pieces of clay. Modal expressions do not apply to concrete things independently of the way they are designated. Lumpl, for instance, is the same thing as *Goliath*: it is a clay statue of the infant *Goliath* which I put together and then broke. Necessary identity to Lumpl, though, is not a property which that thing has or lacks, for it makes no sense to ask whether that thing, as such, is necessarily identical with Lumpl. Modal contexts, then, do not attribute properties or relations to concrete things—so the proponent of contingent identity can respond to Leibniz' Law.

Now this response comes at a stiff price. Quantificational contexts must attribute properties or relations; they must be true or false of things independently of the way those things are designated. If modal contexts do not attribute properties or relations to concrete things, it follows that such contexts are not open to quantification with variables whose values are concrete things. A large number of formulas, then, must be ruled out as ill-formed.

Although, for instance, the sentence

$$\Diamond(\text{Lumpl exists} \ \& \ \textit{Goliath} \neq \text{Lumpl})$$

is well formed, the expression

$$\Diamond(\text{Lumpl exists} \ \& \ x \neq \text{Lumpl}) \qquad (8)$$

turns out to be ill-formed—at least, that is, if the variable *x* can take *Goliath* as a value. Now on the basis of what I have said, that seems reasonable. Take the expression (8), and consider the thing I made and then broke, which is both a statue and a lump. There is no apparent way of saying that (8) is true or false of that thing; it is true of it *qua* statue but not *qua* piece of clay. By that test, the free variable *x* does not belong in its context in (8) if it takes concrete things like statues and lumps among its values.

Here, then, may be a telling objection to contingent identity: if in order to maintain contingent identity we must restrict quantification so drastically, the objector can argue, we shall be unable to say many of the things we need to say, both in scientific talk and in daily life. Concrete things will have no modal properties: there will, that is, be no such thing as *de re* modality for concrete things. Indeed on some accounts, there will also be problems with dispositions—as I shall later show. Perhaps we can maintain contingent identity only at the cost of tying our tongues, and that, if it is true, might be a strong reason for rejecting contingent identity.

The remainder of my argument for the plausibility of the system I am advocating will concern this issue. I shall give devices which I think will enable us to say anything that we ought seriously to regard as meaningful, and say it in the system I am advocating. What I have to say will center around the system Carnap proposed in *Meaning and Necessity* for quantifying into modal contexts.[5] Carnap's system, I think, is the best one for handling quantified modal talk of concrete things. In what follows, I shall draw loosely both on Carnap's system and on Aldo Bressan's extension of it (1972) to give ways of saying what we need to say.

Carnap's system has many advantages. It fits my claim that *Goliath* = Lumpl, and it allows variables in any context in which a proper name can appear. Indeed on Carnap's account, variables in modal contexts act almost exactly as proper names do on the account in Section III of this paper. Carnap, in short, gives a clear, consistent theory which fits what I have been saying.

There is, to be sure, a price for all this: Carnap gives a non-standard account of the way predicates and variables behave in modal contexts. The account he gives, though, makes sense, and it departs from the standard account of quantifiers in much the same way as I departed in Section III from the standard account of proper names. It is non-standard, then, in ways that fit nicely the theory in this paper.

Carnap's treatment of variables is suggested by part of Frege's treatment of proper names. According to Frege (1892, p. 59), a proper name in a modal context refers *obliquely*: its reference there is its usual sense. Hence in

$$\Diamond(\text{Lumpl exists } \& \textit{ Goliath} \neq \text{Lumpl}), \tag{9}$$

the name '*Goliath*' refers, not to a statue, but to a statue-concept which is the normal sense of the name. Any other name with that same normal sense could be substituted for '*Goliath*' in (9) without changing its truth-value. This part of Frege's account fits what I have said of proper names, as I shall later illustrate.

Now just as, on Frege's account, proper names shift their reference in modal contexts, on Carnap's account, variables in modal contexts shift their range of values: they range over senses. In the formula

$$\Diamond(\text{Lumpl exists } \& \ x \neq \text{Lumpl}),$$

then, x ranges not over concrete things, like statues and pieces of clay, but over what Carnap calls "individual concepts"—including statue-concepts and lump-concepts. Call things of the kind the variables take as values in non-modal contexts *individuals*: an *individual concept* is a function whose domain is a set of possible worlds, and which assigns to each world W in its domain an individual that exists in W.

I spell out what is roughly Carnap's proposal in the appendix; here I give it by example. Let the individuals in the system be concrete things, like statues and lumps. Let 'E' in non-modal contexts be the predicate *exists*, and let 'H' in such contexts be the predicate *is humanoid*, by which I shall mean *is human-shaped throughout its early history*. Then in the formula

$$\Box(Ex \rightarrow Hx), \tag{10}$$

on Carnap's proposal, both the variable and the predicates make a shift. The variable x in (10) now ranges over individual concepts, and the predicates in (10) make compensating shifts as follows: 'E' now means not *exists*, but rather *is a concept of an individual that exists*. 'H' now means not *is humanoid*, but rather *is a concept of an individual that is humanoid*. For any possible world W and individual concept f, that is to say, 'H' in modal contexts is true of f in W if and only if the individual f assigns to W is humanoid in W.[6]

That gives (10) a clear interpretation: the open sentence (10) is true of any individual concept f such that for every world W, if f assigns an individual to W, then f assigns to W an individual that is humanoid in W. In particular, then, (10) is true of the *Goliath*-concept—the individual concept that assigns the statue *Goliath* to each possible world in which that statue exists, and assigns nothing to any other possible world. For *Goliath* in any possible world, according to the theory I have given, is humanoid: in any world in which it exists, it starts out in the shape of the actual *Goliath*, and changes shape only slowly. (10) is false of the Lumpl-concept correspondingly defined, since in possible worlds in which I squeeze Lumpl into a ball, Lumpl loses its human shape during its early history, and thus is not humanoid in the stipulated sense. To such a possible world, then, the Lumpl-concept does not assign an individual which is humanoid.

Variables on this proposal work very much like proper names on my account of them in Section III. Just as on that earlier account,

$$\Box(E\,\textit{Goliath} \rightarrow H\,\textit{Goliath}) \tag{11}$$

is true and

$$\Box(E\,\text{Lumpl} \rightarrow H\,\text{Lumpl}) \tag{12}$$

is false, so on the Carnapian account I am now giving, the open sentence $\Box(Ex \rightarrow Hx)$ is true of the *Goliath*-concept and false of the Lumpl-concept.

Indeed just as, on Carnap's account, variables in modal contexts range over individual concepts, so on the account in III, proper names in modal contexts can be construed as denoting individual concepts. Proper names work, in other words, roughly as Frege claims. Let the name '*Goliath*' in (11), for instance, denote the *Goliath*-concept, and suppose predicates shift in modal contexts as Carnap suggests. Then (11) attributes to the *Goliath*-concept the property

$$\Box\left(E\_\_\_\_ \rightarrow H\_\_\_\_\right),$$

that in every possible world *W*, if it assigns to *W* an existing individual, then it assigns to *W* an individual that is humanoid. The *Goliath*-concept has that property, and so (11) on this construal is true. The Lumpl-concept does not have that property, and so (12) on this construal is false. That is as it should be on the account in Section III. Modal properties can be construed as attributing properties and relations to individual concepts, much as Frege claims.

VI

What happens to identity on this account? Identity of individual concepts x and y is not now expressed as '$x = y$'; that, in modal contexts, means just that x and y are concepts of the same individual. The way to say that x and y are the same individual concept is

$$\Box\left[\left(Ex \vee Ey\right) \rightarrow x = y\right].$$

I shall abbreviate this '$x \equiv y$'.

It could now be objected that the thesis of contingent identity has collapsed. Identity in the system here, it seems, is given not by '=', but by '≡', and the relation '≡' is never contingent: if it holds between two individual concepts, then it holds between them in every possible world. No genuine relation of identity, then, is contingent; the illusion that there are contingent identities came from using the identity sign '=' to mean something other than true identity.

To this objection the following answer can be given. '=' indeed is the identity-sign for individuals in the system, and if I am right that a piece of clay is an individual in the Carnapian sense, then '=' is the identity sign for pieces of clay. For consider: in non-modal contexts, I stipulated, the variables range over individuals. Now '=' in such contexts holds only for identical individuals; it is the relation a piece of clay, for instance, bears to itself and only to itself. Moreover, applied to individuals, '=' satisfies Leibniz' Law:

individuals related by it have the same properties in the strict sense, and stand in the same relations in the strict sense. The contexts where '=' is not an identity-sign are modal contexts, but there the variables range not over individuals, but over individual concepts. '=' in the system, then, is the identity sign for individuals, and according to the system, '=' can hold contingently for individuals: A sentence of the form '$a = b$', then, asserts the identity of two individuals, and it may be contingent.

Quine would object to this answer. It depends on a "curious double interpretation of variables": outside modal contexts they are interpreted as ranging over individuals; inside modal contexts, over individual concepts. "This complicating device," Quine says, "has no essential bearing, and is better put aside" (1961, p. 153). "Since the duality in question is a peculiarity of a special metalinguistic idiom and not of the object-language itself, there is nothing to prevent our examining the object language from the old point of view and asking what the values of its variables are in the old-fashioned non-dual sense of the term" (letter in Carnap, 1947, p. 196). The values in the old-fashioned sense, Quine says, are individual concepts, for '$(\forall x)\, x \equiv x$' is a logical truth, and on "the old point of view", that means that entities between which the relation $\equiv$ fails are distinct entities. In all contexts, then, the values of the variables are individual concepts, and identity is given by '$\equiv$'.

All this can be accepted, however, and the point I have made stands: '=' in the system expresses identity of individuals. '$a = b$', on Quine's interpretation, says that a and b are concepts of the same individual. That amounts to saying that the individual of which a is the concept is identical with the individual of which b is the concept. Even on Quine's interpretation, then, '$a = b$' in effect asserts the identity of individuals, and does so in the most direct way the system allows.

On either Quine's interpretation or Carnap's, then, to assert

$$\textit{Goliath} = \text{Lumpl} \tag{13}$$

is in effect to assert the identity of an individual. For all Carnap's system says, (13) may be true, though *Goliath* might not have been identical with Lumpl. If (13) is true but contingent, then it seems reasonable to call it a contingent identity. The claim that there are contingent identities in a natural sense, then, is consistent with Carnap's modal system on either Carnap's or Quine's interpretation of values of variables.

VII

One further Quinean objection needs to be answered. I am embracing "essentialism" for individual concepts. Essentialism, if I understand Quine, is the view that necessity properly applies "to the fulfillment of conditions by objects . . . apart from special ways of specifying them" (1961, p. 151). Now what I have said, as I shall explain, requires me to reject essentialism for concrete things but accept it for individual concepts. That discriminatory treatment needs to be justified.

First, a more precise definition of essentialism: *Essentialism for* a class of entities *U*, I shall say, is the claim that for any entity *e* in *U* and any condition ϕ which *e* fulfills, the question of whether *e* necessarily fulfills ϕ has a definite answer apart from the way *e* is specified.[7]

Now according to what I have said, essentialism for the class of concrete things is false. In the clay statue example, I said, the same concrete thing fulfills the condition

$$E\_\_\_\_ \rightarrow H\_\_\_\_$$

necessarily under the specification '*Goliath*' and only contingently under the specification 'Lumpl'; whether that thing, apart from any special designation, necessarily fulfills that condition is a meaningless question.

Essentialism for the class of individual concepts, on the other hand, must be true if Carnap's system is to work. That is so because Carnap's system allows quantification into modal contexts without restriction. For let ϕ be a condition and *e* an individual concept which fulfills ϕ. Then $\Box\phi x$ is well formed and the variable '*x*' ranges over individual concepts, so that *e* is in the range of '*x*'. Thus *e* either definitely satisfies the formula $\Box\phi x$ or definitely fails to satisfy it. The question of whether *e* necessarily fulfills ϕ must have a definite answer even apart from the way *e* is specified. Thus essentialism holds for individual concepts.

Why this discriminatory treatment? Why accept essentialism for individual concepts and reject it for individuals? The point of doing so is this: my arguments against essentialism for concrete things rested not on general logical considerations, but on considerations that apply specifically to concrete things. I argued that it makes no sense to talk of a concrete thing as fulfilling a condition ϕ in every possible world—as fulfilling ϕ necessarily, in other words—apart from its designation. Essentialism, then, is false for concrete things because apart from a special designation, it is meaningless to talk of the same concrete thing in different possible worlds.

For this last, I had two arguments, both of which apply specifically to concrete things. First I considered the clay statue example, gave reasons for saying that *Goliath* is identical to Lumpl, and showed that the same statue in a different situation would not be the same piece of clay. Second, in Section III, I gave a theory of identity of concrete things across certain possible worlds, according to which such identity made sense only with respect to a kind. These arguments applied only to concrete things.[8]

It makes good sense, on the other hand, to speak of the same individual concept in different possible worlds. An individual concept is just a function which assigns to each possible world in a set an individual in that world. There is no problem of what that function would be in a possible world different from the actual one. Whereas, then, there is no good reason for rejecting essentialism indiscriminately, there are strong grounds for rejecting essentialism for concrete things.

VIII

An objection broached in Section V remains to be tackled. There is, according to the system here, no such thing as *de re* modality for concrete things: in a formula of the form $\Box Fx$, the variable ranges over individual concepts rather than concrete things. Now without *de re* modality for concrete things, the objection goes, our tongues will be tied: we will be left unable to say things that need to be said, both for scientific and for daily purposes.

In fact, though, the system here ties our tongues very little. It allows concrete things to have modal properties of a kind, and those permissible modal properties will do any job that *de re* modalities could reasonably be asked to do. To see how such legitimate modal properties can be constructed, return to the statue example.

According to the theory given here, the concrete thing *Goliath* or Lumpl has neither the property of being essentially humanoid nor the property of being possibly non-humanoid. There is a modal property, though, which it does have: it is essentially humanoid *qua* statue. That can be expressed in the Carnapian system I have given. Let S be the predicate "is a statue-rigid individual concept". S is intensional, then, in the sense that it applies to individual concepts, so that variables in its scope take individual concepts as values, just as they do in the scope of a modal operator. The sentence

x is essentially humanoid *qua* statue,

then, means this:

$$(\exists y)\left[y = x \,\&\, S\,y \,\&\, \Box(Ey \rightarrow Hy)\right].^{9} \tag{14}$$

Here the variable y is free within the scope of a modal operator, and hence ranges over individual concepts; but x occurs only outside the scope of modal operators, and hence ranges over individuals. In '$y = x$', then, the predicate '=' makes a compensating shift of the kind shown in Section V, but only in its left argument. Thus '$y = x$' here means that y is a concept of an individual identical to x—in other words, y is a concept of x. (14), then, says the following: "There is an individual concept *y* which is a statue-concept, and is a concept of something humanoid in any possible world in which it is a concept of anything." That gives a property which applies to concrete things: only the variable *x* is free in (14), and since it occurs only outside the scope of modal operators, it ranges over individuals. (14), then, gives a property of the concrete thing Lumpl, a property which we might call 'being essentially humanoid *qua* statue'.

Concrete things, then, in the system given here, have no *de re* modal properties—no properties of the form $\Box F$. They do, however, have modal properties of a more devious kind: modal properties *qua* a sortal. Such properties should serve any purpose for which concrete things really need modal properties.

IX

Dispositional properties raise problems of much the same kind as do modal properties. At least one promising account of dispositions is incompatible with the system given here.

Here is the account. A disposition like solubility is a property which applies to concrete things, and it can be expressed as a counterfactual conditional: '*x* is soluble' means "If *x* were placed in water, then *x* would dissolve." This counterfactual conditional in turn means something like this: "In the possible world which is, of all those worlds in which *x* is in water, most like the actual world, *x* dissolves."[10]

Now this account is incompatible with the system I have given, because it requires identity of concrete things across possible worlds. For without such cross-world identity, it makes no sense to talk of "the possible world which is, of all those worlds in which *x* is in water, most like the actual world." For such talk makes sense only if there is a definite set of worlds in which *x* is in water, and there is such a definite set only if for each possible world, either *x* is some definite entity in that world—so that it makes definite sense to say that *x* is in water in that world—or *x* definitely does not exist in that world. The account of dispositions I have sketched, then, requires identity of concrete things across possible worlds, which on the theory in this paper is meaningless.

The point is perhaps most clear in the statue example. It makes no sense to say of the concrete thing *Goliath*, or Lumpl, that if I squeezed it, it would cease to exist. If I squeezed the statue *Goliath, Goliath* would cease to exist, but if I squeezed the piece of clay Lumpl, Lumpl would go on existing in a different shape. Take, then, the property "If I squeezed *x*, then *x* would cease to exist," which I shall write

$$\text{I squeeze } x \;\Box\!\!\rightarrow\; x \text{ ceases to exist.} \qquad (15)$$

That is not a property which the single concrete thing, *Goliath* or Lumpl, either has or straightforwardly lacks.

Counterfactual properties, then, have much the same status as modal properties. A concrete thing—a piece of salt, for instance—cannot have the counterfactual property

$$x \text{ is in water} \;\Box\!\!\rightarrow\; x \text{ dissolves},$$

or as I shall write it,

$$Wx \;\Box\!\!\rightarrow\; Dx. \tag{16}$$

Put more precisely, the point is this: a concrete thing can have no such property if, first, the account of counterfactuals which I have given is correct and, second, identity of concrete things across possible worlds makes no sense. Call a property of the form given in (15) and (16) a *straightforward counterfactual property*; then on the theories I have given, concrete things can have no straightforward counterfactual properties.

Individual concepts, in contrast, can perfectly well have straightforward counterfactual properties, since they raise no problems of identity across possible worlds. Indeed we can treat the connective '$\Box\!\!\rightarrow$' as inducing the same shifts as do modal operators: making the variables in its scope range over individual concepts, and shifting the predicates appropriately. On that interpretation, (15) is true of the *Goliath*-concept but false of the Lumpl concept; (15) says, "In the possible world which, of all those worlds in which I squeeze the thing picked out by concept x, is most like the actual world, the thing picked out by x ceases to exist." That holds of the *Goliath*-concept but not of the Lumpl-concept. Likewise on this interpretation, (16) is true not of a piece of salt, but of a piece-of-salt individual concept. (16) now says the following: "In the possible world which is, of all those worlds in which the thing picked out by x is in water, most like the actual world, the thing picked out by x dissolves."

So far the situation is grave. The moral seems to be this: concrete things have no dispositional properties, but individual concepts do. Water-solubility, or something like it, may be a property of a piece-of-salt individual concept, but it cannot be a property of the concrete thing, that piece of salt. That is a sad way to leave the matter. On close examination, many seeming properties look covertly dispositional—mass and electric charge are prime examples. Strip concrete things of their dispositional properties and they may have few properties left.

Fortunately, though, individuals do turn out to have dispositional properties of a kind. The device used for modal properties in the last section works here too. A concrete thing like a piece of salt cannot, it is true, have the straightforward counterfactual property $Wx \Box\!\!\rightarrow Dx$. Only an individual concept could have that property. A piece of salt does, though, have the more devious counterfactual property given by "*Qua* piece of salt, if x were in water then x would dissolve," which I shall write

$$(x \text{ } qua \text{ piece})\left[Wx \Box\!\!\rightarrow Dx\right]. \tag{17}$$

This expands as follows: let $\mathcal{P}$ mean "is a piece-rigid individual concept"; then (17) means

$$(\exists y)\left[y = x \,\&\, \mathcal{P}y \,\&\, \left(Wy \Box\!\!\rightarrow Dy\right)\right]. \tag{18}$$

As in the corresponding formula (14) for modal properties, 'x' here is free of modal entanglements, and so it ranges over concrete things. (18) seems a good way to interpret water solubility as a property of pieces of salt.

Concrete things, then, can have dispositional properties. The dispositional property *is water-soluble* is not the straightforward counterfactual property given by (16), but the more devious counterfactual property given by (18). A system with contingent identity can still allow dispositions to be genuine properties of concrete things.

X

From the claim that *Goliath* = Lumpl, I think I have shown, there emerges a coherent system which stands up to objections. Why accept this system? In Section II, I gave one main reason: the system lets concrete things be made up in a simple way from entities that appear in fundamental physics. It thus gives us machinery for putting into one coherent system both our beliefs about the fundamental constitution of the world and our everyday picture of concrete things.

Another important reason for accepting the system is one of economy. I think I have shown how to get along without *de re* modality for concrete things and still say what needs to be said about them. That may be especially helpful when we deal with causal necessity; indeed the advantages of doing without *de re* causal necessity go far beyond mere economy. What I have said in this paper about plain necessity applies equally well to causal necessity, and the notion of causal necessity seems especially unobjectionable—even Quine thinks it may be legitimate. (See Quine, 1961, pp. 158–9.) Causally necessary truths are what scientists are looking for when they look for fundamental scientific laws, and it surely makes sense to look for fundamental scientific laws. Now we might expect fundamental scientific laws to take the form $\Box_c \phi$, "It is causally necessary that ϕ," where ϕ is extensional—contains no modal operators. If so, then scientific laws contain *de dicto* causal necessity, but no *de re* necessity. To get significant *de re* causal necessities, we would need to make metaphysical assumptions with no grounding in scientific law. If we can get along without *de re* physical necessity, that will keep puzzling metaphysical questions about essential properties out of physics. The system here shows how to do that.

None of the reasons I have given in favor of the system here are conclusive. The system has to be judged as a whole: it is coherent and withstands objections; the remaining question is whether it is superior to its rivals. What, then, are the alternatives?

Kripke gives an alternative formal semantics (1963), but no systematic directions for applying it. To use Kripke's semantics, one needs extensive intuitions that certain properties are essential and others accidental. Kripke makes no attempt to say how concrete things might appear in a theory of fundamental physics; whether such an account can be given in Kripke's system remains to be seen.

One other alternative to the theory in this paper is systematic: statues and pieces of clay can be taken, not to be "individuals" in the Carnapian sense of the term which I have been using, but to be Carnapian "individual concepts". They may be regarded, that is, as functions from possible worlds, whose values are Carnapian individuals. (See Thomason and Stalnaker, 1968). On such a view, a Carnapian individual would be regarded as a sort of "proto-individual" from which concrete things are constructed.

Such a view has its advantages: it allows standard quantification theory, with no Carnapian shift of the range of variables in modal contexts. Indeed as Quine points out, a Carnapian semantics can be interpreted so that variables always range over individual concepts. (Letter in Carnap, 1947, p. 196.)

One reason for preferring the Carnapian system is this. I expect that the variables used in expressing fundamental laws can most simply be interpreted as ranging over Carnapian individuals. If so, then I would be reluctant to regard those Carnapian individuals as mere proto-individuals, with genuine individuals as functions which take these proto-individuals as values at possible worlds. Fundamental physics, I would like to say, deals with genuine individuals.

If the system I have given is accepted, the ramifications are wide. Take just one example: the question of whether a person is identical with his body. If there is no consciousness after death, then, it would seem, a person ceases to exist when he dies. A person's body normally goes on existing after he dies. Ordinarily, then, a person is not identical with his body. In some cases, however, a person's body is destroyed when he dies. In such cases, according to the system in this paper, there is no purely logical reason against saying the following: the person in this case is identical with his body, but had he died a normal death, he would have been distinct from his body. If there are reasons against such a view, they must be non-logical reasons.

Whether or not the system I have advocated is the best one, I have at least done the following. First, I have shown that there is a problem with identity across possible worlds, even in the simple case of possible worlds which branch after the entity in question begins to exist. In such cases, I have shown, certain assumptions, not easily refuted, lead to contingent identity. Second, I have given a theory of proper names which fits much of what Kripke says about proper names when he considers examples, and which, in rare cases, allows contingent identity. Finally, I have shown how, while accepting contingent identity and rejecting *de re* modality for concrete things, we can still allow concrete things to have modal and dispositional properties.

The system I advocate is worked out in more detail in the appendix. In that system, I think, concrete things and possible worlds lose some of their mystery: they arise naturally from a systematic picture of the physical world.

Appendix

The goal of this appendix is to construct a semantics which will explain such expressions as "x in world W is necessarily humanoid *qua* statue" as used in this paper. The rough motivations for the semantics are these. A fundamental physical theory can be interpreted as giving a metaphysics, which says what sorts of fundamental entities, or "elements", there are, and what fundamental relations may hold among them. (I use 'relation' here in a broad sense that includes properties.) The elements, for example, might be point-instants or particle-instants, and the fundamental relations might include distance, time-order (or causal accessibility), mass density, electromagnetic field, and the like. I suppose the following. (a) A concrete thing, or "entity", is a set of elements. (b) All relations depend on fundamental relations: for any relation, whether it holds among given entities is fixed by which fundamental relations hold among which elements in the universe. (c) A relation *internal* to an entity is a relation whose holding depends on which fundamental relations hold among the various elements in that entity.

A model structure for the system will consist of the following. (1) A non-empty set D, called the domain of *elements*. A subset of D is called an *entity*; an entity, then, is a set of elements. I shall identify each element x with the entity $\{x\}$; an element, then, is an entity of a special kind (cf. Quine, 1963, p. 31). (2) A transitive reflexive relation $\leqslant$ on D. It should be thought of as a time relation, "is before or simultaneous with", or in special relativity, as a relation of causal accessibility. Besides transitivity and reflexivity, we might, in order to model a specific physical theory, want to impose additional restrictions on the relation $\leqslant$. (3) A non-empty set $\mathcal{W}$, to be read eventually as the set of all possible worlds. (4) A sequence R = $\mathcal{R}_1$, $\mathcal{R}_2$, . . . characterized as follows. An *n-place relation* is a function F whose domain is $\mathcal{W}$

and whose values are sets of n-tuples of entities. A one-place relation is called a property, where a 1-tuple is defined simply as the individual x. For each n, $\mathcal{R}_n$ is a set of n-place relations among elements, and a member of $\mathcal{R}_n$ is called a *fundamental relation*. We postulate that $\leqslant$ is a fundamental relation; that is, that one fundamental relation assigns the extension of $\leqslant$ to every possible world.

A *qualitative temporal-modal model structure*, or *QTM structure*, will be defined by first defining a "*proto-QTM structure*". A *proto-QTM structure* is an ordered 4-tuple $\langle D, \leqslant, \mathcal{W}, \mathcal{R}\rangle$ which satisfies the above conditions.

Next, some matters of notation. Variables x, y, and z will be used for elements; X, Y, and Z for entities. Variables j and k will be used for members of $\mathcal{W}$. When used as superscripts, they will indicate ordered pairs on the pattern $X^k = \langle X, k\rangle$; when used as subscripts, they will indicate the value of a function, on the pattern $F_k = F(k)$.

Given a proto-QTM structure, a relation of exact internal similarity is defined as follows. An isomorphism under R between X^j and Y^k is a relation :: between elements which maps the set X one-to-one onto the set Y and meets this condition: For any n-place fundamental relation F, and for any n-tuple $\langle x_1, \ldots, x_n\rangle$ of elements of X and n-tuple $\langle y_1, \ldots, y_n\rangle$ of elements of Y such that $x_1 :: y_1, \ldots, x_n :: y_n$, we have

$$\langle X_1, \ldots, X_n\rangle \in F_j \text{ iff} \langle Y_1, \ldots, Y_n\rangle \in F_k.$$

We shall write $X^j \approx Y^k$ iff there is an isomorphism under R between X^j and Y^k. This should be read as saying that X in j is *internally exactly similar* to Y in k—or *exactly like.*

As things stand, members of $\mathcal{W}$ cannot be treated as possible worlds, but only as specifications of possible worlds: j and k might be distinct and yet be just different specifications of the same possible world. That would be the case if the entire domain D were exactly alike in j and k—if $D^j \approx D^k$. One way out of this problem would be to define a possible world as a maximal subset $\mathcal{W}'$ of $\mathcal{W}$ such that whenever $j \in \mathcal{W}'$ and $k \in \mathcal{W}'$, then $D^j \approx D^k$. Later definitions will be more simple, however, if we merely represent each possible world by a single specification: if we allow in $\mathcal{W}$ just one specification of each possible world. That will be accomplished if the following condition is satisfied.

Condition of Unique Specification: For all j and k in $\mathcal{W}$, $D^j \approx D^k$ iff $j = k$.

A *QTM structure* is a proto-QTM structure which satisfies the Condition of Unique Specification.

We are now in a position to construct a notion that approximates identity across possible worlds with respect to a property. The *past* $\mathcal{P}x$ of an element x is the entity $\{y: y \leqslant x\}$. A "past" of an entity will be defined to include the combined past of the elements at the beginning of its existence.

DEFINITION. Z is *a past of* X iff

(i) Z is hereditary under $\leqslant$; that is,

$$\forall_z \forall_y (z \in Z \,\&\, y \leqslant z \rightarrow y \in Z)$$

(ii) For every element $x \in X$, $\mathcal{P}x \cap X \cap Z$ is non-empty.

This will be written $Z \lll X$.

Entities in two possible worlds will be "*F*-counterparts" if they have property F in their respective worlds and pasts which are exactly alike.

DEFINITION. X in j is an *F-counterpart of Y in k* iff $X \in F_j$, $Y \in F_k$, and there are pasts X_0 of X and Y_0 of Y such that there is an isomorphism under R between X_0 and Y_0 which is also an isomorphism between $X \cap X_0$ and $Y \cap Y_0$. This will be written $X^j =_F Y^k$.

An *individual concept* c is a function whose domain is a subset of $\mathcal{W}$ and whose values are entities.

DEFINITION. Individual concept c is *rigid with respect to* property F iff for any k in the domain of c and for any i,

(1) $c_k \in F_k$,
(2) If j is in the domain of c, then $c_j^j =_F c_k^k$,
(3) if j is not in the domain of c, then there is no Y such that $Y^j =_F c_k^k$.

Given a QTM structure, we now construct a Carnapian modal language with an additional special feature. Let ϕ be a wff with free variable α, so that ϕ can be said to ascribe a property F to α. Then $(\alpha * \phi)$ will be a one-place predicate which is true of those individual concepts which are rigid with respect to F. It can be read informally, then, as "is rigid with respect to the property which ϕ ascribes to α." For example, let S be "is a statue"; H, "is humanoid"; and let l be Lumpl. Then '$(y{*}Sy)$' means "is statue-rigid", and

$$\forall x\big[x = l \,\&\, \big(y{*}Sy\big)x \rightarrow \Box\big(Ex \rightarrow Hx\big)\big]$$

means that any statue-rigid concept of Lumpl is necessarily, if a concept of anything at all, a concept of something humanoid. Indeed that, as I shall explain, is how I shall gloss "Lumpl is essentially humanoid *qua* statue." The construction of this language $\mathcal{L}$ goes as follows.

The syntax of $\mathcal{L}$ is that of a predicate calculus with two additions, '□' and '*'. 'E' is a one-place predicate (for *exists*), and '=' and '⊆' are two-place predicates. If ϕ is a wff, then $\Box\phi$ is a wff. The use of '*' is peculiar to the system. Let α be a variable and ψ a wff. α is *extensional* in ψ iff α does not occur free in ψ within the scope of a predicate containing '*'. Then where α is extensional in ψ, $(\alpha * \psi)$ is a one-place predicate in which α is bound. All other variables free in ψ are free in $(\alpha * \psi)$. Where π is a predicate, $(\alpha * \pi\alpha)$ will be abbreviated $\pi *$.

A *value-assignment* $\mathcal{V}$ is a function which assigns (i) an n-place relation to each *ordinary predicate*—predicate other than 'E', '=', and '⊆' and the *-constructions, (ii) an individual concept to each individual constant in $\mathcal{L}$, and to each member of a set X of variables in $\mathcal{L}$. If the set X is empty, then $\mathcal{V}$ is called an *interpretation*. Where α is a variable, the α/c *variant* of $\mathcal{V}$ is a value assignment $\mathcal{V}'$, such that $\mathcal{V}'\alpha = c$ and for every term or predicate $\gamma \neq \alpha$, if $\mathcal{V}\gamma$ is defined, then $\mathcal{V}'\gamma = \mathcal{V}\gamma$, and otherwise, $\mathcal{V}'\gamma$ is undefined. The α/c variant of $\mathcal{V}$ will be written $\mathcal{V}\alpha/c$.

The truth-conditions for locutions without the sign '*' are the natural ones.

1. An atomic wff $\pi\alpha_1 \ldots \alpha_n$ is not true in k for $\mathcal{V}$ if for any term α_i in the wff, α_i is not in the domain of $\mathcal{V}$ or k is not in the domain of $\mathcal{V}\alpha_i$. Otherwise:

(a) $E\alpha$ is true in k for $\mathcal{V}$.
(b) $\alpha = \beta$ is true in k for $\mathcal{V}$ iff $(\mathcal{V}\alpha)k = (\mathcal{V}\beta)k$.
(c) $\alpha \subseteq \beta$ is true in k for $\mathcal{V}$ iff $(\mathcal{V}\alpha)k \subseteq (\mathcal{V}\beta)k$.
(d) Where π is any other atomic n-place predicate, $\pi\alpha_1 \ldots \alpha_n$ is true in k for $\mathcal{V}$ iff
$\langle(\mathcal{V}\alpha_1)k, \ldots, (\mathcal{V}\alpha_n)k\rangle \in (\mathcal{V}\pi)k$.

2. $\sim\phi$ is true in k for $\mathcal{V}$ iff ϕ is not true in k for $\mathcal{V}$, and $\phi_1 \vee \phi_2$ is true in k for $\mathcal{V}$ iff ϕ_1 is true in k for $\mathcal{V}$ or ϕ_2 is true in k for $\mathcal{V}$.

3. $(\forall x)\phi$ is true in k for $\mathcal{V}$ iff for every individual concept c, ϕ is true in k for $\mathcal{V}\ \alpha/c$.

4. $\Box\phi$ is true in k for $\mathcal{V}$ iff ϕ is true in every j for $\mathcal{V}$.

The truth conditions for expressions with '*' are specified as follows. Where α is extensional in ψ, the *property ascribed by* ψ *to* α *for* $\mathcal{V}$ is the function which assigns to each possible world k the set of all entities X for which the following holds: for some individual concept c, $X = c_k$ and ψ is true in k for $\mathcal{V}\ \alpha/c$. This will be written $\mathit{Prop}\ \mathcal{V}\colon \psi/\alpha$. Then $(\alpha * \psi)\beta$ is true in k for $\mathcal{V}$ iff the individual concept $\mathcal{V}\beta$ is rigid with respect to $\mathit{Prop}\ \mathcal{V}\colon \psi/\alpha$.

The logic of $\mathcal{L}$, it would seem, will be S5 with the Barcan formula and its converse, plus certain axioms concerning =, $\subseteq$, *E*, and *. What follows is not a report of results obtained, but what I expect to be true of the system. Consider first the symbol '*'. Closures of wffs on the following schemas will be valid. First, an individual concept which is rigid with respect to a property is always a concept of an entity with that property, if of anything at all.

$$(\alpha{*}\psi)\alpha \rightarrow \Box(E\alpha \rightarrow \psi), \qquad \text{(Ax.S.1)}$$

where α is extensional in ψ. Where ψ is $\pi\alpha$, this becomes

$$\pi{*}\alpha \rightarrow \Box(E\alpha \rightarrow \pi\alpha).$$

Second, if an entity has a given property, then it falls under an individual concept which is rigid with respect to that property.

$$\psi \rightarrow \exists\beta[\beta = \alpha \,\&\, (\alpha{*}\psi)\beta], \qquad \text{(Ax.S.2)}$$

where α and β are distinct variables, α is extensional in ψ, and β is not free in ψ. Where ψ is $\pi\alpha$, this becomes

$$\pi\alpha \rightarrow \exists\beta[\beta = \alpha \,\&\, \pi{*}\beta].$$

Identity of individual concepts α and β will be given by

$$\Box(E\alpha \vee E\beta \rightarrow \alpha = \beta),$$

and this will be written $x \equiv y$. The closures of wffs on the pattern of Leibniz' Law will be valid for extensional contexts. We will have, that is, the closure of

$$\alpha = \beta \rightarrow (\psi \rightarrow \phi),$$

where ϕ is obtained from ψ by substituting free occurrences of β for free occurrences of α in positions where α is extensional in ψ. The closures of wffs on the pattern of Leibniz' Law for $\equiv$ will be valid. That is,

$$\alpha \equiv \beta \rightarrow (\psi \leftrightarrow \phi)$$

wherever ϕ is obtained from ψ by substitution of free occurrences of β for free occurrences of α.

Now to explain such terms as 'qua', 'essentially', and 'sortal'. Take first sortal properties: there is no guarantee as matters stand that a thing which has property *F* falls under exactly one individual concept that is rigid with respect to F; that will be so, indeed, for very few properties F. A strict sortal will be a predicate for which there is such a guarantee: predicate π is a *strict sortal* under interpretation $\mathcal{V}$ iff

$$\Box\forall x\forall y\,(\pi{*}x \,\&\, \pi{*}y \rightarrow x \equiv y \vee \Box x \neq y)$$

is true under $\mathcal{V}$ for some k (or equivalently, for all k). In roughly Bressan's language (1972, p. 94), π is a strict sortal iff π^* is a quasi-absolute concept.

Probably most everyday sortals like 'statue' and 'lump' are not strict sortals in this sense. Consider a possible world k which is radially symmetrical until a time t. In k, distinct statues may well have exactly like pasts. Take a statue X in k, away from the axis of symmetry, which comes into existence before t; X has a twin X' in k across the axis of symmetry, with an exactly like past. Now let j branch from k at or after t; then two statues in j will each equally well be statue-counterparts in j of X in k. 'Statue', then, is not a strict sortal.

'Statue', though, is well behaved in another respect: it divides its reference, in the sense that necessarily, no two things which fall under it overlap. That is enough to guarantee that there will be multiple statue-counterparts only in strange cases of symmetry. π is a predicate of divided reference under interpretation $\mathcal{V}$ iff

$$\Box\forall x\forall y[\pi x \,\&\, \pi y \rightarrow x \text{ disjoint from } y]$$

is true under $\mathcal{V}$, where 'x disjoint from y' abbreviates

$$\forall z_1\forall z_2[z_1 \subseteq x \,\&\, z_2 \subseteq x \,\&\, z_1 \subseteq y \,\&\, z_2 \subseteq y \rightarrow z_1 = z_2].$$

(That is, only the empty set is a subset of both). The predicate π^*, I suspect, will be useful when and only when π is a predicate of divided reference.

Now for the use of '*qua*'. It is an abbreviation of a device for giving extensional modal properties. Tag a wff with [α *qua* π] where π is a one-place predicate, and the expansion will be as follows.

$$\ldots x \ldots [x \textit{ qua } \pi]$$

abbreviates

$$\pi x \,\&\, \forall y[y = x \,\&\, \pi{*}y \rightarrow \ldots y \ldots].$$

For example,

$$\Box(Ex \rightarrow Hx)\,[x \textit{ qua } S]$$

abbreviates

$$Sx \,\&\, \forall y[y = x \,\&\, S{*}y \rightarrow \Box(Ey \rightarrow Hy)];$$

that is, x is a statue, and any statue-rigid concept of x is necessarily, if a concept of anything, a concept of something humanoid. This ascribes an extensional property to x, which I shall call the property of being *essentially* humanoid *qua* statue.

Notes

1. I am grateful for the comments and criticisms of many people. I was helped in the early stages of revision by discussion at the University of Pittsburgh philosophy colloquium, by the written comments of Richard Gale and Paul Teller, and by discussion with Allen Hazen, Robert Kraut, and Storrs McCall. I am especially grateful to Anil Gupta for his extensive help, both in the early and the late stages of revision.

2. This fits the view put forth in Quine, 1950, Sec. 1.

3. David Lewis (1971) gives a theory very much like this. There are, according to Lewis, a diversity of counterpart relations which hold between entities in different possible worlds—the "personal" counterpart relation and the "bodily" counterpart relation are two (p. 208). The counterpart relation appropriate to a given modal context may be selected by a term, such as 'I' or 'my body', or it may be selected by a phrase, "regarded as a ___", which works like one of my "qua" phrases. In these respects, then, my theory fits Lewis's. In other respects, it differs. My relation of being an *F*-counterpart (see the appendix) is an equivalence relation, and it holds between any two entities in different worlds which are both *F*'s and which share a common past. Lewis's counterpart relations "are a matter of overall resemblance in a variety of respects" (p. 208), and are not equivalence relations (p. 209).

4. Geach (1962, Sec. 34) contends that a proper name conveys a "nominal essence"—"requirements as to identity" that can be expressed by a common noun. [Cf. p. 307 of this volume.] The name 'Thames', for instance, conveys the nominal essence expressed by the common noun 'river'. In this respect, my theory follows Geach's. Geach, however, (Sec. 31) thinks that even in the actual world, identity makes no sense except with respect to a general term. [Cf. p. 306 of this volume.] According to the theory in this paper, non-relative identity makes sense in talk of any one possible world; it is only cross-world identity that must be made relative to a sortal.

5. See especially Carnap, 1947, Sec. 41. I shall not follow Carnap in detail, nor, for the most part, shall I try to say in what precise ways I follow him and in what ways I deviate from what he says.

6. The talk of "shifts" here is not Carnap's; it is part of my own informal reading of Carnap's semantics. Carnap does think "that individual variables in modal sentences . . . must be interpreted as referring, not to individuals, but to individual concepts" (1947, p. 180). He does not, however, allow variables to shift their ranges of values within a single language. Rather, he constructs two languages, a non-modal

language S_1 in which variables range over individuals, and a modal language S_2 in which variables range over individual concepts. Any sentence of S_1 is a sentence of S_2, and is its own translation into S_2 (See pp. 200–202.) The semantics I give in the appendix is roughly that of Carnap's S_2. (See Carnap, 1947, pp. 183–4). Variables in the appendix always range over individual concepts; hence they never explicitly shift *to* a range of individual concepts from a range of individuals. In informal discussion in the body of this paper, though, I take a variable to range over individuals whenever such an interpretation is possible. That means I take the values of a variable to be individuals whenever the variable occurs in a formula *extensionally*, in the sense defined in the appendix.

Carnap does not talk of predicates' shifting in the way I describe, but once variables are taken to range over individual concepts, such a reinterpretation of predicates allows a straightforward reading of Carnap's semantics. Quine discusses this point in his letter to Carnap (Carnap, 1947, p. 197).

7. For other characterizations of essentialism, see Parsons, 1969, Sec. II.

8. Quine objects to essentialism even for abstract entities. "Essentialism," he writes, "is abruptly at variance with the idea, favored by Carnap, Lewis, and others, of explaining necessity by analyticity" (1961, p. 155). That, however, cannot be true: Carnap does explain his system in terms of analyticity, and his system involves essentialism, as I have explained. Carnap's system is thus a counterexample to Quine's claim; it shows that one can consistently both accept essentialism for individual concepts and explain necessity by analyticity.

9. Anil Gupta has shown me a formula similar to this one, which he attributes to Nuel Belnap.

10. See Stalnaker (1968) and Stalnaker and Thomason (1970). For a somewhat different theory which raises similar problems, see Lewis (1973).

References

Bressan, Aldo, *A General Interpreted Modal Calculus*, Yale University Press, New Haven and London, 1972.

Carnap, Rudolph, *Meaning and Necessity*, University of Chicago Press, Chicago, 1947.

Frege, Gottlob, 'On Sense and Reference' (trans. by Max Black), in Peter Geach and Max Black, *Translation from the Philosophical Writings of Gottlob Frege*, Blackwell, Oxford, pp. 55–78, 1966 (1892).

Geach, Peter, *Reference and Generality*, Cornell University Press, Ithaca, N.Y., 1962.

Kripke, Saul, 'Semantical Considerations on Modal Logic', *Acta Philosophica Fennica* 16 (1963) 83–94.

Kripke, Saul, 'Identity and Necessity', in Milton K. Munitz (ed.), *Identity and Individuation*, New York University Press, New York, pp. 135–64, 1971.

Kripke, Saul, 'Naming and Necessity', in Donald Davidson and Gilbert Harman (eds.), *Semantics of Natural Language*, D. Reidel Publishing Company, Dordrecht, 1972.

Lewis, David K., 'Counterparts of Persons and their Bodies', *Journal of Philosophy* 68 (1971) 203–11.

Lewis, David, K., *Counterfactuals*, Blackwell and Harvard University Press, 1973.

Parsons, Terrence, 'Essentialism and Quantified Modal Logic', *Philosophical Review* 78 (1969) 35–52.

Quine, W. V. O., 'Identity, Ostension, and Hypostasis', In *From a Logical Point of View*, Harper and Row, New York, pp. 65–79, 1961 (1950).

Quine, W. V. O., 'Reference and Modality', *From a Logical Point of View* (Second Edition), pp. 139–59, 1961.

Quine, W. V. O., *Set Theory and Its Logic*, Harvard University Press, Cambridge, Mass., 1963.

Russell, Bertrand, 'On Denoting', in Robert Marsh (ed.), *Logic and Knowledge*, Macmillan, New York, pp. 41–56, 1956 (1905).

Stalnaker, Robert, 'A Theory of Conditionals', in *Studies in Logical Theory*, American Philosophical Quarterly Monograph Series, No. 2, 1968.

Stalnaker, Robert and Thomason, Richmond, 'A Semantic Analysis of Conditional Logic', *Theoria* 36 (1970) 23–42.

Thomason, Richmond and Stalnaker, Robert, 'Modality and Reference', *Noûs* 2 (1968) 359–72.

7

Counterparts or Double Lives? (Selections)

David Lewis

4.1 Good Questions and Bad

Peter van Inwagen has written that anyone who is rightly taught—that is, anyone who has read Plantinga—

> will see that there is no problem of trans-world identity. He will find that all attempts he knows of to formulate the supposed problem are either incoherent or else have such obvious 'solutions' that they do not deserve to be called problems. He will realize that it was all done with mirrors—that is, with empty words and confused pictures. There is, therefore, no longer any excuse for talking as if there were a 'problem of trans-world identity'. ('Plantinga on Trans-World Identity', page 101.)

Nevertheless, I shall devote the whole of this final chapter to the problem of trans-world identity.

Still, to a great extent I agree with van Inwagen's harsh judgement. Very often we do meet formulations that probably manifest confusion, and that are apt to cause it. I shall begin by separating questions. I think there are some good ones to be found, as well as the incoherent ones and the ones with uncontroversial 'solutions'.

The first thing to say is that our topic, like the Holy Roman Empire, is badly named; we may continue to use the customary name, but only if we are careful not to take it seriously. In the first place we should bear in mind that Trans-World Airlines is an intercontinental, but not as yet an interplanetary, carrier. More important, we should not suppose that we have here any problem about *identity*.

We never have. Identity is utterly simple and unproblematic. Everything is identical to itself; nothing is ever identical to anything else except itself.

There is never any problem about what makes something identical to itself; nothing can ever fail to be. And there is never any problem about what makes two things identical; two things never can be identical. There might be a problem about how to define identity to someone sufficiently lacking in conceptual resources—we note that it won't suffice to teach him certain rules of inference—but since such unfortunates are rare, even among philosophers, we needn't worry much if their condition is incurable.

We *do* state plenty of genuine problems in terms of identity. But we *needn't* state them so. Therefore they are not problems about identity. Is it ever so that an F is identical to a G? That is, is it ever so that the same thing is an F, and also a G? More simply, is it ever so that an F is a G? The identity drops out. Thus it is a good question whether a river is something you can bathe in twice; or whether a restaurant is something that can continue to exist through a simultaneous change in ownership and location and name; or whether numbers are von Neumann ordinals; or whether there is something that all charged particles have in common; or whether there could be a time traveller who meets his younger self; or whether there was ever a genuine nation that included both Austria and Hungary. All of these questions could be stated in terms of identity—harmlessly, unless that way of stating the questions confused us about where to seek for answers.

Likewise for the question whether worlds ever overlap; that is, whether two worlds ever have a common part; that is, whether any part of one world is ever part of another as well; that is, whether there is ever identity between parts of different worlds. This is a good question, but not a question about identity. Or rather, it is a good question for genuine modal realists;[†] it makes little sense as a question for ersatzers. I consider this question in section 4.2, where I shall defend a qualified negative answer.

[†]Editor's note: *Genuine modal realism*, according to Lewis, is the view that there are other worlds and individuals inhabiting those worlds. These worlds are concrete objects that are spatiotemporally related to all and only their own parts. They are spatiotemporally unrelated to one another, and there are enough of them so that "absolutely *every* way a world could possibly be is a way that some world *is*" (Lewis 1986, p. 2; italics in original). These worlds are unactualized possibilities; but, on Lewis's view, to say that is not to deny that they exist. Rather, it is simply to deny that they are *actual*, which is just to deny that they are parts of *our* world, the world we inhabit.

Ersatz modal realism is an alternative to Lewis's view. It is the view that "instead of an incredible plurality of concrete worlds, we can have one world only, and countless abstract entities representing ways that this world might have been" (Lewis 1986, p. 136). Different kinds of ersatzism correspond to the different kinds of abstract entities that might be taken to represent *possibilia*. 'Linguistic ersatzism' refers to those views that take worlds to be maximal consistent sets of sentences—

It is also a good question, but it is a different good question, whether there is anything that overlaps two different worlds, and so is in both in the way that a highway may be in two different states. Again, I could state it in terms of identity: is there ever identity between things that are (partly) in different worlds? Really it is not a question about identity, but about mereology: is there any reason to restrict mereological summation so that several things have a mereological sum only if all of them are parts of a single world? The follow-up question concerns semantics: if summation is unrestricted, so that indeed there are trans-world individuals, are these mere oddities? Are they nameless, do they fall outside the extensions of ordinary predicates and the domains of ordinary quantification? Or do they include things of importance to us, such as ourselves? I consider these questions in section 4.3, where I shall acknowledge the existence of trans-world individuals but dismiss them as oddities.

It is yet another good question, and this time it is a good question for genuine modal realists and ersatzers alike, whether it ever happens that anything exists according to two different (genuine or ersatz) worlds. If you like, I can state this question too in terms of identity: does it ever happen that something which exists according to one world and something which exists according to another are identical? The answer to that ought to be uncontroversial: yes, that very often happens. Take our worldmate Hubert Humphrey, for instance. The Humphrey who exists according to our world and the Humphrey who exists according to some other worlds are identical. (It is too bad that grammar demands the plural.) That is, Humphrey exists according to many different (genuine or ersatz) worlds. According to ours, he exists and he lost the presidential election; according to others, he exists and he won. This is a question that, as van Inwagen says, does not deserve to be called a problem.

---

complete consistent "stories" about how things might have been. Linguistic ersatz worlds represent possible objects or states of affairs by containing sentences that describe those objects or states of affairs. 'Pictorial ersatzism' refers to those views that take worlds to be more like pictures, or scale models. Such worlds represented by isomorphism. A pictorial ersatz world represents possible objects or states of affairs by containing parts, properties, and relations that correspond to the parts, properties, and relations of the relevant object or state of affairs. (For example, such a world represents a cat's being on a mat by containing parts, properties, and relations that correspond to the cat's parts and properties, the mat's parts and properties, and the relations between the cat and the mat.) 'Magical ersatzism' refers to those views that take worlds to be abstract simples (where a simple is anything that lacks proper parts, or internal structure) and that offer no account of how worlds represent possible objects and states of affairs. Under linguistic and pictorial ersatzism, representation depends in some way upon the internal structure of the relevant abstract entities; but because magical ersatz worlds have no internal structure, it remains a mystery how they represent.

But what *does* deserve to be called a problem is the follow-up question: what is it for Humphrey to exist according to a world? What is representation *de re*? How does a world, genuine or ersatz, represent, concerning Humphrey, that he exists? This one is *not* a question for genuine modal realists and ersatzers alike. Or rather, it is not *one* question for both. The available answers for genuine and for ersatz worlds will look quite different.

A genuine world might do it by having Humphrey himself as a part. That is how our own world represents, concerning Humphrey, that he exists. But for other worlds to represent in the same way that Humphrey exists, Humphrey would have to be a common part of many overlapping worlds, and somehow he would have to have different properties in different ones. I reject such overlap. There is a better way for a genuine world to represent, concerning Humphrey, that he exists. Humphrey may be represented *in absentia* at other worlds, just as he may be in museums in this world. The museum can have a waxwork figure to represent Humphrey, or better yet an animated simulacrum. Another world can do better still: it can have as part a Humphrey of its own, a flesh-and-blood counterpart of our Humphrey, a man very like Humphrey in his origins, in his intrinsic character, or in his historical role. By having such a part, a world represents *de re*, concerning Humphrey—that is, the Humphrey of our world, whom we as his worldmates may call simply Humphrey—that he exists and does thus-and-so. By waving its arm, the simulacrum in the museum represents Humphrey as waving his arm; by waving his arm, or by winning the presidential election, the other-worldly Humphrey represents the this-worldly Humphrey as waving or as winning. That is how it is that Humphrey—our Humphrey—waves or wins according to the other world. This is counterpart theory, the answer I myself favour to the question how a world represents *de re*.[1]

(The same goes in reverse. Our Humphrey is a counterpart of many Humphreys of many other worlds. I deny that the counterpart relation is always symmetrical, but surely it often is. So here are many other-worldly Humphreys who win the presidency, but who lose according to this world. They are represented as losing by the presence here of Humphrey the loser.)

There are various ways that an ersatz world might represent, concerning Humphrey, that he exists, or that he waves, or that he wins. It depends on what sort of ersatz world we are dealing with. A linguistic ersatz world might include English sentences that mention Humphrey by name: 'Humphrey exists', 'Humphrey waves', 'Humphrey wins'. Or it might include sentences of some other worldmaking language, which mention Humphrey by some other name. Or it might instead include sentences of the worldmaking language which say explicitly that there is someone of a certain description who exists, and waves, and wins; and this could qualify as representation *de re* concerning Humphrey if the description sufficiently resembles the description of Humphrey as he actually is. Or, instead of saying explicitly that there is someone of the appropriate description, a linguistic ersatz world might say it implicitly, by means of many sentences having to do with the vacancy or occupation of spacetime points, or with the instantiating of various elementary universals by various elementary particulars. A pictorial ersatz world might have a part which is a picture, made out of stuff that is in some mysterious sense abstract, of Humphrey waving and winning. A magical ersatz world might represent that Humphrey exists and waves and wins by having some ineffable distinctive intrinsic nature. Or it might do it by means of brute necessary connections: necessarily, if some simple element stands in some unanalysable relation to the concrete world then Humphrey exists and waves and wins.

It is sometimes thought that ersatzism is better off than counterpart theory in respecting certain intuitions: intuitions that *de re* modality has to do with the *res* itself, not some imitation or substitute or counterpart. Thus Kripke makes his famous complaint that on my view

> . . . if we say 'Humphrey might have won the election (if only he had done such-and-such),' we are not talking about something that might have happened to *Humphrey*, but to someone else, a 'counterpart'. Probably, however, Humphrey could not care less whether someone *else*, no matter how much resembling him, would have been victorious in another possible world. (*Naming and Necessity*, page 45.)

Coming from an advocate of genuine modal realism with overlap, this complaint might have some force. But here it comes only a page away from Kripke's equally famous remark that

> A possible world isn't a distant country that we are coming across, or viewing through a telescope. (Page 44.)

Joking aside (he does say that 'another possible world is too far away'), Kripke's point seems to be that we are supposed to respect Humphrey's intuition that it is *he himself* who would have been victorious in another world, and we are supposed to do this by declining to think of that other world as the sort of thing that he himself could even be part of! What is going on?

I think counterpart theorists and ersatzers are in perfect agreement that there are other worlds (genuine or ersatz) *according to* which Humphrey—he himself! (stamp the foot, bang the table)—wins the election. And we are in equal agreement that Humphrey—he himself—is not *part* of these other worlds. Somehow, perhaps by containing suitable constituents or perhaps by magic, but anyhow not by containing Humphrey himself, the other world represents him as winning. If there were any genuine modal realists who believed in overlap of worlds, they would indeed be in a position to insist that at another world we have Humphrey himself winning the presidency. That might indeed be a point in their favour. But it is not a point in favour of any other view but theirs, and in particular it is not a point in favour of any kind of ersatzism.

Counterpart theory does say (and ersatzism does not) that someone else—the victorious counterpart—enters into the story of how it is that another world represents Humphrey as winning, and thereby enters into the story of how it is that Humphrey might have won. Insofar as the intuitive complaint is that someone else gets into the act, the point is rightly taken. But I do not see why that is any objection, any more than it would be an objection against ersatzism that some abstract whatnot gets into the act. What matters is that the someone else, or the abstract whatnot, should not crowd out Humphrey himself. And there all is well. Thanks to the victorious counterpart, Humphrey himself has the requisite modal property: we can truly say that *he* might have won. There is no need to deny that the victorious counterpart also makes true a second statement describing the very same possibility: we can truly say that a Humphrey-like counterpart might have won. The two statements are not in competition. Therefore we need not suppress the second (say, by forbidding any mixture of ordinary modal language with talk of counterparts) in order to safeguard the first.[2]

I said that counterpart theory and ersatzism are alike in denying that Humphrey himself is part of the other world which represents him as winning. But that was a little too quick. Counterpart theory and ersatzism are also alike in having trick ways to dodge the conclusion. In both cases there is a loophole to exploit, but exploiting the loophole does nothing to satisfy the alleged intuition that it must be Humphrey himself who wins. For the counterpart theorist, the trick is to say that 'Humphrey' names not the Humphrey of our world, and not the Humphrey of another, but rather the trans-world individual who is the mereological sum of all these local Humphreys. If that is what Humphrey is, then indeed he himself is partly in this world and partly in that and not wholly in any. Part of him loses and part of him wins. But presumably the losing part cares what might have happened to *it*; it could not care less what happens to some *other* slice off the same great salami—unless, of course, the world containing that otherworldly slice of Humphrey can be taken as a world that represents the this-worldly slice as winning.

For the ersatzer (of the linguistic persuasion) the trick is to remember that anything you please can serve as a word of the worldmaking language. Humphrey might as well be used as his own name, in Lagadonian fashion. Then he will be, if not a part, at least a set-theoretic constituent of the ersatz world which is a set of sentences saying *inter alia* that he wins. So what? Presumably he could not care less what words of what languages are assembled with him into what set-theoretic structures—unless, of course, we get a linguistic structure that represents him as winning. Let him by all means care how he can be consistently represented, but not about the words of the representation. It is perfectly arbitrary whether he serves as a word. And if he does, it is perfectly arbitrary what he means. If Humphrey is to be made a word, there is no need to make him be his own name. He would do just as well as a name for Checkers, or as a preposition or adverb. Or he could be the negation sign in a sentence that denies his existence.

There are at least two more good questions that can be extracted from the topic of trans-world identity, though again they have nothing special to do with identity. I merely state these questions here; I shall take them up in section 4.5. Again they are questions for genuine modal realists and ersatzers alike. For the sake of neutrality, I shall formulate them in terms of representation *de re*; that is, in terms of truth according to a world, genuine or ersatz, concerning some actual individual such as Humphrey.

One is the question of haecceitism. We can distinguish representation of the way things are qualitatively (in a broad sense of that world) from representation *de re*. It may be the case according to a world that there are things of certain kinds, arranged in certain ways, and with certain causal relationships; these are matters of qualitative character. But also it may be the case, according to a world, concerning the individual Humphrey, that he exists and waves and wins. Can these two kinds of representation vary independently? Or does what a world represents concerning matters of qualitative character determine what that world represents *de re*?

The other is the question of constancy. Do we have a settled answer, fixed once and for all, about what is true concerning a certain individual according to a certain (genuine or ersatz) world? Or can different answers be right in different contexts? Can two opposed answers even be right together, in a single context? Can it happen sometimes that no answer is determinately right?

• • •

4.5 Against Constancy

The Great Western Railway ought to have absorbed two other railways early on: the Bristol and Gloucester, and the Birmingham and Gloucester. But it tried to drive too hard a bargain. In 1845 the line from Bristol to Gloucester to Birmingham fell into rival hands. Therefore, after the grouping of railways in 1923, the post-grouping Great Western lacked a part that it might have had. What we know as the Great Western, without the missing line, was the whole of the Great Western; not, as it so easily might have been, a part of a still Greater Western.

This is an instance of a much-discussed paradox.[3] Most versions involve what I would take to be temporal parts, or temporal parts of spatial parts, that something might have had or might have lacked. Such versions are all very well for me, since I believe in arbitrary spatiotemporal parts; but to bring home the problem to those who do not believe in temporal parts, I have preferred a purely spatial example. The missing line was at no time a part of the post-grouping Great Western; whereas with better luck in 1845, the line would have been part of it for the entire quarter century of its existence.[4]

Here is the paradox. Let GWR– be the Great Western as it actually was without the missing line. Let GWR be the Great Western. Let GWR+ be the sum of GWR– and the missing line. Here is GWR, in other words GWR–; they are identical. But the plural is a nonsense of grammar: 'they' are one thing, and *it* is self-identical. What might have happened to *it*? It is GWR; so it would have been greater, in fact it would have been identical to GWR+. It is GWR–; so it would have been only a part of GWR, not the whole, and hence not identical to GWR, which would instead have been identical to GWR+. Most certainly it, that is GWR–, would not have been identical to GWR+. We contradict ourselves about what would have become of this one thing which we can refer to in two ways: as GWR or as GWR–.

It is incredible to say, under the circumstances, that GWR and GWR– are, after all, two different things: that they are really not identical or that they are only 'relatively identical'. ('Relative identity' is not identity, as may be seen from the fact that it sometimes holds between things which differ in their other relative identities.) We have one thing. What we have two of, besides names for it, are ways of representing. There is some kind of equivocation built into representation *de re*, and the equivocation shows up when we get conflicting answers. We have a suitable (genuine or ersatz) world according to which the Bristol-Gloucester-Birmingham line was absorbed, and we have the actual thing that is called GWR and also called GWR–. That one world manages to represent that one thing as including the line, and also manages to represent that one thing as excluding the line. Evidently the way the representing works is not constant. One name evokes one way of representing, and the other another. At least in this way the difference of names matters, though they differ not at all in what they name.

You might think that what is going on is simpler than I have made out: the names are non-rigid, they amount to abbreviated definite descriptions, they differ in what they would have named if history had been different in the way supposed. (I mean that they differ in what they would have named under their actual interpretation—it is irrelevant what different interpretation they might have been given in the different history.) You might think we're not dealing with representation *de re* at all, still less with a peculiarly equivocal form of it, but merely with a difference in what would have been named by names with different non-rigid senses. This might be partly right.

Perhaps my introduction of the names did give them different non-rigid senses, so that the names would not have named the same thing if history had been different. Perhaps I also failed in my attempt to word the crucial sentences so as to favour *de re* readings. That hypothesis solves our original problem. But that doesn't get us far. For I can restate the problem so that the difference-between-non-rigid-names solution will not apply.

I ask you: think of this thing we've been talking about under two names—now, what would have happened to *it* if the line had been absorbed? Now you're stuck. I haven't used either name. You know well enough what thing is in question, and you know well enough what sort of (genuine or ersatz) world is in question, you know that I'm asking *de re* what happens to that thing according to such a world—and you have no unequivocally right answer. Your trouble, I think, is that two ways of representing have been evoked just previously, and now I'm giving you no guidance to help you choose between them. The fact (if it is a fact) that the two ways were evoked by two non-rigid names is irrelevant.

Here is another way to recover our problem, blocking the difference-of-non-rigid-names solution. Let's introduce new names which definitely are abbreviated descriptions:

GWR/Jupiter $=^{\mathrm{df}}$ that which is GWR if the line was not absorbed, otherwise the planet Jupiter;

GWR–/Jupiter $=^{\mathrm{df}}$ that which is GWR– if the line was not absorbed, otherwise the planet Jupiter.

These contrived names are non-rigid for sure; but in a way that blocks the solution. Had the line been absorbed, they would not have differed in what they named; because then they would both have named (a counterpart of) Jupiter. And in actuality also they do not differ in what they name; because the line was not absorbed, so they both name the same thing, namely the thing we have called sometimes GWR and sometimes GWR–. So consider this thing. What might have happened to *it*? *It* is GWR/Jupiter, namely by being GWR; so if the line had been absorbed, *it* would have included the line, *it* would have been GWR+. *It* is GWR–/Jupiter, namely by being GWR–; so if the line had been absorbed, *it* would not have included the line, *it* would still have been GWR–. In no case would *it* have been the planet Jupiter, right?—If you agree with that, you must agree that my wording with the stressed pronouns succeeded in setting up a *de re* reading and making it irrelevant what our non-rigid names would have named. (This may not be a firm matter; if my life depended on it I could probably manage to hear the question in the other way and give an honest answer 'It would have been Jupiter'. Perhaps some people could hear it that way more easily than I. It is enough that the reading I have described is possible, it needn't be inevitable.) So we have back our inconstancy in representation *de re*. And the difference between the contrived names which makes them evoke different ways of representing is not a difference in what they would have named if the line had been absorbed, because there is no such difference. Instead, our contrived names borrowed the evocative powers of the original names 'GWR' and 'GWR–' that appeared so conspicuously within them and within their definitions. I admit I helped them along when I reminded you that GWR/Jupiter was GWR, and that GWR–/Jupiter was GWR–. But as those identities are true, I do not see how it can have been unfair to say so.

I think there is a great range of cases in which there is no determinate right answer to questions about representation *de re*, and therefore no right answer to questions about modality or counterfactuals *de re*.[5] Could Hubert Humphrey have been an angel? A human born to different parents? A human born to different parents in ancient Egypt? A robot? A clever donkey that talks? An ordinary donkey? A poached egg? Given some contextual guidance, these questions should have sensible answers. There are ways of representing whereby some worlds represent him as an angel, there are ways of representing whereby none do. Your problem is that the right way of representing is determined, or perhaps under-determined, by context—and I supplied no context.

You could do worse than plunge for the first answer to come into your head, and defend that strenuously. If you did, your answer would be right. For your answer itself would create a context, and the context would select a way of representing, and the way of representing would be such as to make your answer true. (If at all possible. Perhaps not if you gave an especially silly answer, such as that Humphrey could have been a poached egg, yet he could not have been a human born to different parents.) That is how it is in general with dependence on complex features of context. There is a rule of accommodation: what you say makes itself true, if at all possible, by creating a context that selects the relevant features so as to make it true. Say that France is hexagonal, and you thereby set the standards of precision low, and you speak the truth; say that France is not hexagonal (preferably on some other occasion) and you set the standards high, and again you speak the truth.[6] In parallel fashion, I suggest that those philosophers who preach that origins are essential are absolutely right—in the context of their own preaching. They make themselves right: their preaching constitutes a context in which *de re* modality is governed by a way of representing (as I think, by a counterpart relation) that requires match of origins. But if I ask how things would be if Saul Kripke had come from no sperm and egg but had been brought by a stork, that makes equally good sense. I create a context that makes my question make sense, and to do so it has to be a context that makes origins not be essential.

Attend to the variety of what we say about modality and counterfactuals *de re*, and I think you will find abundant evidence that we do not have settled answers, fixed once and for all, about what is true concerning a certain individual according to a certain (genuine or ersatz) world. The way of representing is not at all constant. Different answers are often right in different contexts, as witness the comfort with which we adhere to, or presuppose, opposed answers. '*It* would have included the Bristol-Gloucester-Birmingham line.' '*It* would have been only part of a still Greater Western.'—Can you really take this as a dispute? It can very well happen that no answer is determinately right, for lack of the contextual guidance that normally does the determining.

Even within a single context, we can find opposed answers that are right together. That could happen in the case of the Great Western and the missing line. But it happens more prominently in familiar puzzles about how a bit of stuff constitutes the thing that is made of it. To dodge strife about temporal parts, it will be best to begin with a case where the stuff constitutes the thing for all the time that either the stuff or the thing exists: the plastic is synthesised right in the mold, so it no sooner exists at all than it constitutes the dishpan; and the dishpan is destroyed just when the plastic is incinerated. But suppose the factory had received its order for plastic dishpans a day later. The same bit of plastic would have been made; for the raw materials were already divided into portions just right to fill one mold. But it would have been made in another mold, and it would have constituted a wastebasket. The dishpan would have been made the next day out of different plastic. It reeks of double counting to say that here we have a dishpan, and we also have a dishpan-shaped bit of plastic that is just where the dishpan is, weighs just what the dishpan weighs (why don't the two together weigh twice as much?), and so on. This multiplication of entities is absurd on its face; and it only obfuscates the matter if we say that the plastic and the dishpan are 'relatively identical' while implying that they are absolutely *not* identical.

But if the plastic and the dishpan are identical, what would have happened to 'them', or rather to *it*, if the plastic had been made in the form of a wastebasket, and the dishpan had been made the next day out of different plastic? *It* would have been a wastebasket; *it* would have been a dishpan made the next day—those answers, I submit, are both correct. The (genuine or ersatz) world in question represents the one thing twice over, in two different ways, once as a bit of plastic in the form of a wastebasket, and once as another bit of plastic in the form of a dishpan made the next day. Both ways of representing work together in one context to make good sense of the statement that the plastic does constitute the dishpan but it might not have done; in fact, it *is* the dishpan ('is' of identity) but it might not have been. It and the dishpan—it and itself—might have coexisted without being identical! This sounds outrageous. It sounds like doublethink—I concede the identity of the plastic and the dishpan, yet when it suits me I still distinguish them. Not so. I only distinguish what everyone must distinguish: two different references, in different words, to the one thing. And I say that these different references tend to evoke two different ways of representing, whereby one world can make conflicting representations *de re* concerning that one thing. You can double up the ways of representing, here within one context, for one world, concerning one plastic dishpan. Or else you can double up entities, somehow distinguishing the dishpan from its plastic after all. I submit that the first doubling is more credible than the second.

I think the more common case of temporary constitution is no different. This time, make a statue of wax. The wax exists before and after the statue does, but for a time—for all the time the statue exists—the wax constitutes it. The statue and a temporal part of the wax are identical. Under other circumstances it would have been a statue made of different wax; and it would have been formed into a nondescript lump sitting next to the statue. A certain world represents it twice over in different ways, once as the statue and once as the lump. Likewise for the still more temporary constitution of a wave by ever-changing water, or a flame by ever-changing gas.

Notice the one thing I can't say: I can't pull out the subject and conjoin the predicates, saying in the first case 'it would have been both a wastebasket and a dishpan made the next day' or in the second case 'it would have been both a statue made of different wax and formed into a nondescript lump'. For whatever the world represents *de re*, in the two different ways, it does not represent that anything satisfies the conjoined predicates.

I do not see how the resources of quantified modal logic can draw the distinction we need. Let A specify the circumstances in question; let F and G be the two predicates not to be conjoined. We have two formulas:

> necessarily, if A then F(X), and necessarily, if A then G(X);
> necessarily, if A then both F(X) and G(X).

But they will be equivalent, under any standard treatment. So we cannot say that the first is true and the second false if the A-worlds represent X in one way as satisfying F and in another way as satisfying G. But if the resources of quantified modal logic, unless improved in some non-standard way, do not know how to draw the distinction we need, the more fools they. *We* know how to draw it.

The inconstancy of *de re* representation can easily be explained in counterpart theory. We have many and varied relations of comparative similarity. Some differ from others because they put different weights or priorities on different respects of (intrinsic or extrinsic) qualitative similarity; and even if they are alike in the respects of comparison they stress, they can still differ because one is more stringent than another. Any of these relations is a candidate to be expressed by the word 'counterpart'. Likewise many different relations, some more stringent and some less, some stressing some respects of comparison and others stressing others, have a claim to be called 'similarity'. The exact meaning of 'counterpart' or 'similar' is neither constant nor determinate. These words equivocally express a range of different semantic values, and the limits of the range are subject to pressures of context. Two things may be counterparts in one context, but not in another; or it may be indeterminate whether two things are counterparts. Inconstancy in representation *de re* is exactly what we should expect under the hypothesis that it works by comparative overall similarity of complex things. What would be hard to understand, had it been found, would be constancy.

(If counterpart theory is right, the language of *de re* modality is governed by relations of similarity. And of course the language in which we say explicitly that things are similar or different also is governed by relations of similarity. Suppose we mix the two; then the mixed language will be governed by similarity twice over. Then it is vulnerable twice over to indeterminacy, and subject twice over to contextual pressures that push the resolution of indeterminacy one way or another. Should we expect uniform resolution, so that the *de re* modality is governed by exactly the same relations of similarity that govern explicit predications of similarity or difference? Or should we expect a messier situation, in which one sort of similarity gets played off against another? If we had uniform resolution then, as Feldman and others have observed, it would be contradictory to say such things as that I might have been very different from the way I actually am. (Worse yet: I might have been very different from the way I actually am while at the same time someone else was very similar to the way I actually am.) That certainly does not *sound* contradictory. It sounds true. And what makes it true, I suggest, is a counterpart of mine who is very similar to me under one similarity relation that governs the *de re* modality, but very dissimilar to me under another similarity relation that governs the explicit predications. For instance, someone might be my counterpart in virtue of close match of origins, but differ very much from me in later life. (I don't mean to suggest that either similarity relation is fully determinate; or that one sort of similarity relation is assigned permanently to one job and another to the other.) We have the messy situation, with different similarity relations playing off against each other in a single context. And that should be no surprise: the same thing happens even when all talk of similarity is explicit and *de re* modality is out of the picture. I can say that Ted and Fred are very much alike, yet very different. Uniform resolutions would make that a contradiction—so much the worse for them! The fundamental principle of contextual resolution of indeterminacy is that what makes a resolution right is that it makes good sense of what has been said. It is no good making what has been said come out flagrantly contradictory, so any uniform resolution gets disqualified at once. As for the narrowing down of non-uniform resolutions, most likely that must wait on what gets said next.)

A world where the Bristol-Gloucester-Birmingham line was absorbed provides two rivals to serve as counterparts of the this-worldly Great Western Railway. The larger candidate is better in one way: like the this-worldly Great Western Railway, it is the whole of a railway. The smaller candidate is better in other ways: it matches the geographical extent of the this-worldly Great Western, and also its parts can be put into correspondence with the parts of the this-worldly Great Western in such a way that corresponding parts are excellent counterparts of one another. Stress the respects of comparison in which the first candidate has the advantage, and we get a counterpart relation whereby the world in question represents the Great Western as including the line. Stress the respects in which the second has the advantage, and we get a counterpart relation whereby the world in question represents the Great Western as being no more extensive than it actually is, and as being less than the whole of a railway. It is understandable that the first counterpart relation should be evoked by the name 'GWR' for the this-worldly Great Western, and that the second should be evoked by the alternative name 'GWR–' for the very same thing. Likewise it is understandable that the contrived names 'GWR/Jupiter' and 'GWR–/Jupiter' also should evoke the first and second counterpart relations respectively, thanks to the appearance within them of the original names. If the contrived names are less decisively evocative, that too is only to be expected.[7]

When discussing the case in a more neutral setting, I dodged the question whether the names 'GWR' and 'GWR–' were rigid. In the setting of counterpart theory, I can return to that question. Rigidity in the strict sense means naming the same thing at all worlds, or at least all worlds where that thing exists. That's all very well for numerals and the like, but without overlap of worlds we wouldn't expect an ordinary proper name of a person or a thing—of a railway, say—to be strictly rigid. However, an ordinary proper name might well be *quasi-rigid*: that is, it might name at another world the counterpart there of what it names here.

(Complications. (1) What if there is no counterpart at the other world?—Then let the name be denotationless there. (2) What if there are two?—Then let the name be indeterminate in denotation between the two. (3) What if, despite all that wording and context may do to help, it remains indeterminate which inhabitant of the other world is the counterpart of the thing named here?—Then again let the name be indeterminate in denotation. (4) So far, I have been saying what it means for a name to be quasi-rigid with respect to this world; but it can likewise be quasi-rigid with respect to other worlds, and quasi-rigid *simpliciter* iff it is so with respect to every world where it names anything.)

Given inconstancy of counterpart relations, we may have to say that a name is quasi-rigid under some counterpart relations but not under others. For instance, a name may be quasi-rigid under the counterpart relation it tends to evoke, but not under the counterpart relation that another name of the same thing tends to evoke. I think that is the case for the names 'GWR' and 'GWR–', given the way I introduced them. (However the contrived names 'GWR/Jupiter' and 'GWR–/Jupiter' are not quasi-rigid under any reasonable counterpart relation.) When a name is quasi-rigid under the counterpart relation it tends to evoke, then it doesn't matter whether or not we take its occurrence in a modalised predication as *de re*. We might ask whether the this-worldly denotation of 'GWR' is such that its other-worldly counterpart, under the relation evoked by 'GWR', is the whole of a railway. Or we might ask whether the other-worldly denotation of 'GWR', which is to be the counterpart of the this-worldly denotation under the relation evoked by 'GWR', is the whole of a railway. It's the same question either way. There are three ways for the choice of a name to make a difference to the proposition expressed by a sentence: (1) by a difference in this-worldly denotation, (2) by a difference in other-worldly denotation, and (3) by a difference in what counterpart relation tends to be evoked. If a name is quasi-rigid under the counterpart relation it tends to evoke, then (2) and (3) merge. To isolate the effect of (3)—and thereby see the need for inconstancy of counterpart relations—we must blank out (2), as I did in introducing the contrived names 'GWR/Jupiter' and 'GWR–/Jupiter'.

A parallel treatment applies to our case of a thing and the matter that constitutes it. Here at this world we have the plastic made in the form of a dishpan out of a certain portion of raw materials; and at another world, the plastic made out of the counterpart of that portion of raw materials was made in the form of a wastebasket, and a dishpan was made the next day out of different plastic. Let us suppose that counterparthood for the portion of raw materials is unproblematic: perhaps the raw materials already were divided into separate portions before there was any divergence between the alternative world and ours. We have two candidates to be the counterpart of the plastic which is the dishpan. If we stress match of origins, the other-worldly wastebasket is the better candidate. So we have a counterpart relation—that is, a way of representing—whereby the world in question represents the plastic, that is the dishpan, as being made in the form of a wastebasket instead. But if we stress similarity of form, and perhaps also such matters as the order it fills and the place to which it goes, the other-worldly dishpan is the better candidate. So we have another counterpart relation—another way of representing—whereby the world in question represents the dishpan, that is the plastic, as being made a day later out of different raw materials. Here at this world (the only world it is part of) the dishpan just is the plastic; but different ways of referring to this single thing tend to evoke different counterpart relations.

Likewise for our case of temporary constitution: the statue is a temporal part of the wax; but under one counterpart relation a certain world represents it as a nondescript lump, whereas under another counterpart relation that same world represents it as a statue made of different wax. Calling it the wax evokes the first counterpart relation, calling it the statue evokes the second.[8]

I distinguish two different ways that something might have multiple counterparts in another world. The first way is that there are different counterpart relations, differing in the comparative weights or priorities they give to different respects of comparison, which favour different candidates. This is the inconstancy of counterparts that we have been considering. The second way is that there might be a single counterpart relation, given by a single system of weights or priorities, which on occasion is one-many: it delivers multiple counterparts because of ties—say, the tie between a pair of twins. It is not that one system of weights and priorities favours one twin, and another favours the other. (Indeed that might be so, but take a case where it is not.) Rather, any reasonable system results in a tie. It was this second way of having multiple counterparts that forced us to acknowledge different individual possibilities within a single world, lest we be tempted to demand haecceitistic differences between the worlds themselves. But we need to allow for both ways of having multiple counterparts. The first cannot take the place of the second, because sometimes the candidates will be tied under any reasonable standards. The second cannot take the place of the first, because it does not provide a way for influence of context to tilt the decision one way or the other.

So far I have simplified the discussion of inconstancy by ignoring my previous proposal that accessible individual possibilities, not worlds, are what represent *de re*. But now we should merge the two topics, to acknowledge that inconstancy and ties might occur together. Take first the case of the Great Western and the missing line. We have the this-worldly individual, excluding the line, which we call GWR or GWR–. A world where the line was absorbed gives us two individuals, that is, two individual possibilities: the one that includes the line and the one that doesn't. It is not at all equivocal what these two possibilities, if accessible, would represent *de re* concerning the this-worldly individual. The first would represent it as including the line; whereas the second would represent it as excluding the line and being less than the whole of a railway. What *is* in question is which one is accessible. This question is the same as the question which individual is the counterpart. Translating what I said before: there are two accessibility relations for individual possibilities, both based on comparative similarity. The name 'GWR' (or 'GWR/Jupiter') for the this-worldly individual tends to evoke the accessibility relation that stresses similarity in respect of being the whole of a railway. The name 'GWR–' (or 'GWR–/Jupiter'), though it names the same thing, tends to evoke the accessibility relation that stresses similarity in geographical extent and correspondence of parts. If nothing is said that decisively evokes one rather than the other, we might fall into indecision. Or perhaps by default we get an accessibility relation that makes *both* individual possibilities accessible. In that case—as in the cases of twin counterparts that tempt us into haecceitism—one world gives us two different individual possibilities for the same thing. But there is another way to get multiple individual possibilities: suppose that every epoch of a world of eternal recurrence contains a Great Western that succeeds in absorbing the line. This world provides two rival infinite classes of counterparts—that is, of individual possibilities—for the this-worldly Great Western. Stress one respect of similarity, and it provides infinitely many accessible individual possibilities of including the line; stress another, and it provides infinitely many accessible individual possibilities of excluding the line and being less than the whole of a railway; do nothing to evoke one stress or the other, and either it becomes indeterminate which kind of individual possibilities that world affords or else it affords a mixture of both kinds.

Along with individual possibilities, we had joint possibilities for sequences; for instance, pairs. These include identity pairs and non-identity pairs; and so we get, if not exactly a sense in which one thing might have been two (or *vice versa*), at least a sense in which an identity pair might have been a non-identity pair (or *vice versa*). I don't know whether it is wise to call this 'contingent identity'. Perhaps so; or perhaps that phrase should be reserved either for the unproblematic phenomenon of contingent co-referentiality of descriptions, or else for the absurd notion that one thing has an individual possibility of not being self-identical. At any rate, call the phenomenon what you will, we have the this-worldly identity pair of GWR and GWR–, that is of one thing twice over; and we have the other-worldly non-identity pair of GWR and GWR–, two different things. The second pair, if it were an accessible joint possibility for the first pair, would provide the identity pair with a possibility of being non-identical. But to give the requisite accessibility of pairs, we need to stress different respects of similarity for the first terms of the pairs and for the second; and besides, we have to play down the respect of similarity in which identity pairs are *ipso facto* alike and non-identity pairs are *ipso facto* alike. That may seem an implausibly complicated way for accessibility of pairs to work. Yet unless this sort of accessibility relation is available, what accounts for our inclination to say that one thing might have been two? I suppose the relation is available; and it is evoked when it must be, that is when it is required if what has been said is to be true.

It is well for my preferred theory—genuine modal realism, without overlap, and with qualitative counterpart relations‡—that it has no trouble making

‡Editor's note: A *qualitative counterpart relation* relates distinct individuals in different worlds on the basis of their qualitative features—that is, on the basis of common properties shared by those individuals. A *non-qualitative counterpart relation*

representation *de re* come out inconstant. But I cannot claim this as an advantage of my approach over its leading rivals, because they too—with one partial exception—can provide for inconstancy with equal ease.

Suppose we preferred the haecceitistic sort of counterpart theory: genuine modal realism, no overlap between worlds, representation *de re* by means of non-qualitative counterpart relations. As noted in the previous section [section 4.4, not reprinted here], a non-qualitative counterpart relation would be a very mysterious thing to have to take as primitive. But I don't see that many of them would be significantly more mysterious than one, and if we had many counterpart relations of whatever sort, we would have the resources for inconstancy. (Or perhaps we could have mixed counterpart relations, conjoining one fixed non-qualitative relation with various different qualitative similarity relations. The non-qualitative part provides the desired haecceitistic differences, the qualitative part provides the inconstancy.) The mysteries of this theory are severe, but provision for inconstancy does nothing to make them worse.

Suppose next that we preferred linguistic ersatzism in an anti-haecceitistic version: we have maximal consistent descriptions in qualitative terms—qualitative ersatz individuals—and an ersatz world represents *de re* by means of ersatz counterpart relationships among these ersatz individuals. For instance, we have one ersatz individual that describes Humphrey as he actually is, we have a second that is a counterpart of the first but differs by including the description 'wins the presidency', we have an ersatz world according to which that second ersatz individual is actualised; and thereby that ersatz world represents Humphrey *de re* as winning. (Or we might prefer to say that it is the counterpart ersatz individual itself—an accessible individual possibility—that does the representing *de re*.) If so, it is as easy as ever to have many respects of comparison. For instance, we have one ersatz individual that describes the Great Western as it actually is, without the Bristol-Gloucester-Birmingham line; and we have two others, both actualised according to a certain ersatz world, which are rival candidates to be counterparts of the first. One of them purports to describe a Greater Western that includes the line; whereas the other purports to describe something that is less than the whole of a railway and that excludes the line. Which candidate is favoured depends on how much weight we give to different respects of comparison; and that is how one ersatz world represents the Great Western in two conflicting ways (alternatively, that is how one ersatz world affords two conflicting individual possibilities for it).

---

is one that relates distinct individuals in different worlds on the basis of non-qualitative facts about them. As Lewis notes, it is rather mysterious what such facts might be. (Indeed, Lewis thinks that the very label "non-qualitative counterpart relation" is itself a contradiction in terms.) All that is clear is that individuals so related are not identical and that the reason they are counterparts of one another has nothing to do with the qualitative resemblance they bear to one another.

Suppose next that we preferred linguistic ersatzism in its haecceitistic version, in which representation *de re* works by naming. A linguistic ersatz world represents *de re*, concerning the Great Western, that it does or doesn't include the line, by containing or implying a sentence which says of the Great Western, by name, that it does or doesn't include the line. But then we can have inconstancy if our worldmaking language includes two different names for the Great Western: 'GWR' and 'GWR–', for instance. An ersatz world can represent the Great Western under one name as more inclusive, under the other name as being less than the whole of a railway. In order to make sure that when the names go their separate ways, the difference between them will be in the right direction, the names must have some descriptive content; axioms that distinguish the names will have to figure in the definitions of consistency and thence of ersatz worlds.

As we might expect, the one theory that has some trouble providing for inconstancy is genuine modal realism with overlap, in which representation *de re* works by trans-world identity. It was easy to see how we could have many rival candidates to be the counterpart relation, differing both in stringency and in the stress given to various respects of comparison. Not so for identity. There is only one candidate to be the relation of (numerical) identity: it can only be the relation that everything bears to itself and nothing bears to anything else. There is no room for different contexts to go different ways about which relation is to be called identity; and there is no room for indeterminacy caused by indecision between rival candidates.

(The truth value of an identity *sentence* may indeed depend on context, or remain indeterminate. But when that happens, the fault lies not with identity but elsewhere. If the singular terms that flank the identity sign have inconstant or indeterminate denotation, that is apt to make the truth value of the sentence inconstant or indeterminate. But that is not a case of inconstant or indeterminate identity between two different things denoted by those terms; nor yet is it a case of inconstant or indeterminate self-identity. The relevant things are one and all thoroughly self-identical, and none of them is at all identical to anything except itself. What's left murky is the question which exactly are the relevant things.)

Then to the extent that representation *de re* works by trans-world identity, understood as overlap, there is no room for it to be inconstant or indeterminate whether a given world represents a given thing as existing; or, if it does, which part of that world it is whose properties are those that the given thing has according to that world. And that makes it difficult for matters of *de re* modality to be inconstant or indeterminate. Suppose we ask whether Humphrey might have been exactly spherical in shape. Suppose we stipulate that we have in mind the broadest sort of possibility, without any accessibility restrictions. Suppose, *per impossibile,* that spherical shape is not the intrinsic property it seems to be, but rather is a relation that things sometimes bear to worlds of which they are parts—so really we are asking whether Humphrey spheres any of the worlds he lives in. And yet suppose that 'exactly spherical' remains as precise and unequivocal as we are accustomed to think. Now *all* openings for inconstancy and indeterminacy are gone. Our question has to have a right answer, constant and determinate.

But that is only so long as the question concerns absolutely unrestricted possibility. I've argued that modal realism with overlap is congenial to extreme haecceitism, and uncongenial to essentialist constraints. If so, then we could be content to agree that, speaking absolutely unrestrictedly, Humphrey could indeed have been exactly spherical in shape. That is quite definitely so—no inconstancy, no indeterminacy. And he could have been stranger things than that! But on an extreme haecceitist overlap theory, absolutely unrestricted modality loses much of its interest. To capture more commonplace modal opinions, we bring on the accessibility restrictions—and these *are* matters of the qualitative character of things, therefore they are ideally suited to go inconstant and indeterminate. It may be absolutely settled that a world represents Humphrey as spherical—but it may be completely unsettled whether that world is a not-too-far-out world where things are not too different from the way they actually are, and therefore completely unsettled whether that world is one that we should ignore as inaccessible when we say what might have happened to Humphrey.

Counterpart theory treats the question whether Humphrey might have been spherical as follows. Some other-worldly spheres are rather distant counterparts of Humphrey, none are very close counterparts of him, and how close the closest of them are depends on which respects of comparison you stress. So the question whether Humphrey might have been spherical, that is whether any sphere is his counterpart, takes the form: how close is close enough? An extreme haecceitist overlap theory treats the same question as follows. Some other worlds where Humphrey is a sphere are rather distantly accessible from our world, none are very closely accessible, and how close the closest of them are depends on which respect of comparison you stress. So the question whether Humphrey might have been spherical, that is whether any world where he is spherical is accessible from ours, takes the form: how close is close enough? In the unclear cases as in the clear ones, this theory runs parallel to counterpart theory. Restricted modality *de re* can be as inconstant and indeterminate as we please.

Our initial example of inconstancy turns not on stringency but on different respects of comparison. Here again, *mutatis mutandis*, an extreme haecceitist overlap theory runs parallel to counterpart theory. We have the individual GWR, in other words GWR–; under the overlap theory, it is absolutely settled which worlds do and do not represent that individual as including the missing line; but it is not settled whether that individual might have included the missing line until it is settled which are the worlds we ought not to ignore. And that is a matter of how we weigh similarity in respect of being a whole railway versus similarity in respect of geographical extent and correspondence of parts. There context matters, and different names might evoke different accessibility relations. And that is how GWR and GWR– are identical, yet we want to say, speaking *de re* (since the Jupiter trick would block the alternative solution), that GWR would have included the line and GWR– would have been less than the whole of a railway.

So far, so good. But there is one thing that I think we want to say that cannot be provided in the overlap theory, and that is one more reason why some other view should be preferred. Take the case of the plastic that constitutes the dishpan for the whole of the time that either one exists. (The case of GWR and GWR– would do as well.) I say that the plastic and the dishpan are identical. I also say they might not have been, namely if the plastic had been made in the shape of a wastebasket and the dishpan had been made the next day from different plastic. What I mean is not the uncontroversial truth that 'the plastic' and 'the dishpan' (used exactly as I use them, say by an other-worldly duplicate of me) might not have referred to the same thing. And what I mean is not the absurd falsehood that something, namely the plastic which is the dishpan, has a *de re* possibility of failing to be self-identical. What I mean is that an identity pair has the *de re* possibility of being a non-identity pair. Is there a way to make sense of this? Counterpart theory obliges, once we provide for pairs to be counterparts of pairs. But the overlap theory will not oblige, and that is a point against it.

To oblige, the overlap theory would have to say that the very same pair is an identity pair at one world and a non-identity pair at another world. This is not a difference in how the pair is represented, as an ersatzer would say. It is not a difference between counterpart pairs, as I would say. Only one alternative remains: it must be a difference in the relations that the one pair bears to different worlds. But how could that be true? Being an identity pair is an intrinsic matter. That is just the way the pair is in itself, not an external relation of the pair to this world. It is hard enough to understand the idea that intrinsically shapeless things are differently shape-related to different worlds (or times) but it is harder still to understand how something could bear a being-an-identity-pair relation to some worlds and not to others. This just cannot be so. If the pair is wholly present in many worlds, then if it's an identity pair anywhere then it's an identity pair everywhere. At no world is it anything else. Then it is determinately and unrestrictedly necessary that it be an identity pair. That is inescapable: nothing we might do with inconstant accessibility restrictions can undo it.

'Contingent identity' is a tricky business. It isn't clear what should be meant by the phrase: some things it might mean are uncontroversial, some are absurd. But one thing to mean by it which seems neither trivial nor absurd is that an identity pair has the *de re* possibility of being a non-identity pair. Some theories, for instance counterpart theory, can make good enough sense of that. But the overlap theory, to its discredit, cannot.

Notes

1. See my 'Counterpart Theory and Quantified Modal Logic'; 'Counterparts of Persons and Their Bodies'; and *Counterfactuals*, pages 39–43; also David Kaplan, 'Transworld Heir Lines'.

2. Here I am indebted to Mondadori; see his 'Counterpartese, Counterpartese*, Counterpartese$_D$.' But I disagree with him at one point. He grants that I may truly say that Humphrey himself might have won; but then he insists that if we ask 'who would have had the property of *winning*,' my answer must be 'not Humphrey, but one of his counterparts' (page 81). Not so. The modal predicate 'would have had the property of winning' is on a par with the modal predicate 'might have won'. I can apply either predicate in one sense to Humphrey, in another sense to the victorious counterpart. If there is an objection to be raised, it must be that I *can* say *un*wanted things, not that I *cannot* say *wanted* things. I reply that the unwanted things are not seriously objectionable in the way that lack of the wanted things would be.

3. See Wiggins, 'On Being in the Same Place at the Same Time'; my 'Counterparts of Persons and Their Bodies'; Gibbard, 'Contingent Identity', Geach, *Reference and* Generality (third edition), pages 215–18 [this volume, pp. 309–12] van Inwagen, 'The Doctrine of Arbitrary Undetached Parts'; and Robinson, *The Metaphysics of Material Constitution.*

4. To dodge strife about temporal parts, it is important that the post-grouping Great Western should have been in some sense a new and different railway from the pre-grouping Great Western. On this I take the word of O. S. Nock; 'It is sometimes lightly remarked that the Great Western was hardly affected at all. This is very far from the case, and it was a new Great Western Railway that came into being from 1923 onwards. The old company did not absorb the local lines in Wales. Although the old Great Western Railway Company was not wound up the leading Welsh lines came into the new organisation as *constituents*, not absorbed companies or subsidiaries'. (*History of the Great Western Railway*, volume III, pages 1–2.)

5. However, attitudes *de re* are a very different story. There is still indeterminacy, but it arises in other ways. See the final section of my 'Attitudes *De Dicto* and *De Se*'.

6. See my 'Scorekeeping in a Language Game'.

7. I claim that in this case and many others, different names of the same thing tend to evoke different counterpart relations, thereby reducing the semantic indeterminacy of modal idioms governed by counterpart relations. But I do not claim (1) that evocative names eliminate all indeterminacy, or (2) that an evocative name favouring one sort of counterpart relation always outweighs other contextual pressures favouring another, or (3) that every name without exception—still less, every referring expression—tends to evoke some counterpart relations rather than others, or (4) that the semantic indeterminacy of modal idioms governed by counterpart relations is so severe as to render those idioms meaningless except when something—as it might be, an evocative name—is present to reduce the indeterminacy. Compare Gibbard's treatment of contingent identity, which resembles mine but does make these claims; thus it seems to me fundamentally right, but exaggerated. ✓

8. See Robinson for a general discussion of constitution in terms of inconstancy of counterparts; and my 'Counterparts of Persons and Their Bodies' for discussion of a special case, the permanent or temporary constitution of a person by his body.

8

Identity and Time

George Myro

I

It is not uncommon to encounter difficulties in trying to understand philosophically the relationship between the concept of time and the concept of identity. In this essay I should like to set out and recommend a proposal—which was, within my ken, first made by H. Paul Grice—concerning one group of such difficulties. The main idea of the proposal, as I see it, is that temporal qualifications—such as: today, a year ago, at noon on Saturday, 17 January 1981, and so on—should be regarded as applying systematically and uniformly (though, perhaps, in some cases, 'trivially') to all statements, including statements of identity.

What are the difficulties in question? I shall try to make them emerge from some examples (none of which is novel or exciting).

Suppose that on Monday morning I take a piece of wax and fashion it into a vase, which I then put on my mantelpiece to stand there in lonely splendour. It is no doubt admired by my friends and myself throughout Monday. But in the middle of the night I become dissatisfied. I get up, crush the vase, mould the piece of wax into a bust of Aristotle, and put it back on the mantelpiece to be admired by my friends and myself throughout Tuesday. Now, what is the relationship between the vase, the bust of Aristotle, and the piece of wax?

Suppose that a wooden ship which once sailed around the world is put into the centre of a market-place as a public monument to the world-circumnavigation. For one reason or another, various planks and pieces of wood are gradually removed from the ship and replaced by new ones—until one day not a single bit of the original wood remains in the old ship. Meanwhile, the original planks and pieces of wood have been transported to Texas and reassembled there into a ship very much like the one which stands in the centre of the market-place. Now, what is the relationship between the two ships and the wood which has been transported?

It is easy to come up with further examples of this sort. We ourselves are rather like the ship in the market-place. For we are told that in the course of time our own planks are replaced by others, and the ones which are removed from us no doubt go into other ships. Invite a group of people to a party, and in all probability at the end each will contain some atoms from each.

The second example—about the ship—raises a special problem which I am *not* going to discuss. And that is: which of the two ships—the one in the market-place or the one in Texas (if either)—is the 'original' ship—the one which sailed around the world? I shall suppose that it is the ship in the market-place which is the 'original' one. But I think that the points which I shall be making can be made *mutatis mutandis* if one opts for any other plausible alternative.

The example about the ship can be extended a bit to raise a question which appears to be another instance of the sort I want to discuss. Suppose the ship in the market-place (in spite of the replacement of wood) deteriorates beyond repair. So that the city may not lose a famous public monument and tourist attraction, the city fathers arrange to have the other ship transported back from Texas and set up in the market-place in place of the decayed one. Now, what is the relationship between the two ships and the tourist-attracting monument?

Well, what is difficult about these questions? Let us confine ourselves to the piece of wax. It would have been natural for me to say on Monday: this piece of wax is a vase (if for some reason this is not obvious to my friends). And also: this vase is a piece of wax (though of course cunningly shaped). For this and other reasons, it seems not unnatural to conclude that the vase is *identical* with the (cunningly shaped) piece of wax. And on Tuesday it would have been equally natural to say: this piece of wax is a bust of Aristotle—and also: this bust of Aristotle is a (in a different way cunningly shaped) piece of wax—and to conclude in a parallel fashion that the bust of Aristotle is *identical* with the (in a different way cunningly shaped) piece of wax. But it would be not at all natural to say that my vase is *identical* with my bust of Aristotle (unless by way of aesthetic judgement). Let us review: the vase is *identical* with the piece of wax, and the bust is *identical* with the piece of wax, but the vase is *not identical* with the bust. Do we have a break-down of the transitivity of identity? Again, the piece of wax is to be found on the mantelpiece on Tuesday, but the vase is not. Do we have a more general break-down of Leibniz's Law? Or is it that, contrary to appearances, we do not have cases of identity here? Or what?

I believe there is some tendency, when confronted with examples and questions such as these, to take refuge in one or another of several familiar philosophical positions, some extreme ones among which are:

(1) Change is an illusion. Nothing really changes.
(2) The world really consists of imperishable substances or substrata, which in the course of change acquire and lose characteristics.
(3) The world really consists of momentary entities (events?) none of which exists, or, perhaps, even *can* exist, over a period of time, and change consists in the succession of some of these by others.

Perhaps one a little less extreme is:

(4) The world really consists of space-time 'worms' which overlap here and then, share 'temporal slices'.

I am sure there are others. Indeed, there are two more which have a certain contemporary appeal. One of these is:

(5) There is no concept of identity *tout court*. Identity is always relativized to a concept.

When we think of things as being the same, we must always be going on to specify: the *same what*. Thus we should not either affirm or deny that the vase is just identical with the bust. Rather, we should affirm that the vase is the *same piece of wax* as the bust, and of course deny that the vase is the *same vase* or the *same bust* or the *same artifact* as the bust. Something like this position has been advocated by Peter Geach (who, incidentally, regards Frege as an ally in this). And the other of the two positions is:

(6) In spite of appearances, the relationships between the vase and the piece of wax, and the bust and the piece of wax, are not relationships of *identity*. Rather, they are relationships of '*constitution*'. The vase is only constituted, or made out of, the piece of wax, and so is the bust. There are other cases in which we might be misled into thinking that we have a relationship of identity. Thus in the extension of my example about the ship, one might be inclined to think that the tourist-attraction is *identical* with the first ship, and also with the second ship. And then be baffled by the fact that the two ships are not identical and have different characteristics. (And perhaps to escape the bafflement be enticed into position (5), confining oneself to saying that the two ships are the *same tourist-attraction* but of course not the *same ship*.) But what we should realize is that each ship only functions as, or

> plays the role of, the tourist attraction. The various difficulties arise out of mistaking either of two special relations—that of *constitution* and that of *function*—for the relation of identity. Something like this position has been advocated by David Wiggins (who, incidentally, suggests that this view is an interpretation of Aristotle).

I shall not be able to discuss even these last two positions—Geach's and Wiggins's—systematically. I shall simply summarize some results of reflection on them and then go on to outline Grice's approach to the difficulties. I am not *fully* convinced that Grice's approach is completely correct or completely adequate, but I find it the most attractive of those familiar to me. And perhaps in the end it is not really incompatible with the others but only emphasizes something which they do not.

In his book *Identity and Spatio-Temporal Continuity*, Wiggins, in setting out his own position, criticizes Geach's. I am not convinced that Wiggins succeeds in showing Geach's theory to be untenable; but he does succeed, I think, in calling attention to difficulties within it. I think he makes three main points in connection with this.

1. The concept of identity is strongly linked with Leibniz's Law, and this connection cannot be seriously weakened without winding up with a concept of something other than identity.
2. Geach's notion of concept-relative identity is in various ways at odds with Leibniz's Law and so is a poor candidate for a notion of identity.
3. Cases of the sort which might be regarded as supporting Geach's position—my examples are of this sort—can be better accounted for by an alternative theory—Wiggins's—which is not at odds with Leibniz's Law.

It is common ground between the two theories that we do, and perhaps must, use constructions of the sort: A is the same F as B. But whereas Geach holds that such constructions express identity relative to the concept F between A and B (and that there is no relation of just plain identity), Wiggins maintains that such constructions express just plain identity—and also something else—(and that there is no relation of concept-relative identity). Let us take a brief look at how Wiggins proposes to interpret constructions of this sort. I think his proposal for my examples amounts to the following:

> The vase is the same piece of wax as the bust

should be understood as tantamount to:

> The piece of wax of which the vase is constituted is identical with the piece of wax of which the bust is constituted

and

The first ship is the same tourist-attraction as the second ship

should be interpreted somewhat as follows:

> The tourist-attraction as which the first ship functions is identical with the tourist-attraction as which the second ship functions.

(Note that 'the tourist-attraction' must be regarded as picking out not a *type* of tourist-attraction—e.g. '(a ship which is the) centre-piece of a public place', but a particular *instance* of a tourist-attraction—e.g. 'the centre-piece of *that* market-place, *to wit*, the ship or replica of the ship which circumnavigated the world'. For the city in question might contain a further ship in the centre of a second market-place, commemorating whatever you please; and even come later to contain a still further ship in the centre of the first market-place commemorating, say, a naval victory.)

The point I want to stress is that on Wiggins's view, we have in each of the two cases three distinct objects, none of which is identical with either of the other two. In the first case: the vase, the bust, and the tourist-attraction; in the second case: the first ship, the second ship, and the tourist-attraction. It will also be seen that in parallel fashion we have two further distinct objects: the 'original' wood, and the 'new' wood.

It seems to me that Wiggins's proposal has four major objectionable features:

1. It multiplies senses. A statement of the form: A is B—has besides the predicative interpretation, five others, namely:

   A is identical with B
   A constitutes B
   A is constituted of B
   A functions as B
   A is something which B functions as

   But a statement of the form: A is the same F as B—has in principle (in addition to Wiggins's special sense (roughly): A is identical with B, and A is 'essentially' F) twenty-five different interpretations. For the general form of analysis of such a statement is (if I am right):

   > The F thing which stands in relation W to A is identical with the F thing which stands in relation W′ to B

   and we have a choice of five relations for W and for W′, namely the five just enumerated as senses of: A is B. Such opportunity for ambiguity and equivocation is to be avoided if possible.

2. It multiplies entities. And this in two ways. First, there is a multiplicity of *types* of particulars:[1] there are familiar objects, such as vases and ships; and there are pieces of stuff which constitute these objects, such as pieces of wax and masses of wood; and then there are role- or function-particulars which familiar objects play or perform, such as landmarks, monuments, and tourist-attractions. And, second, there is a potentially indefinite multiplicity of *particulars* in any given place at a given time. In the centre of the market-place at a given time there is the tourist-attraction, and also the ship, and also the collection of planks. On my mantelpiece on Monday there is the vase, and also the piece of wax. But what if the piece of organic matter which is wax on Monday and Tuesday is transformed (through my switching from art to chemistry) into plastic by Wednesday? We should have to say that the piece of organic matter was on my mantelpiece on Monday—in company with the vase and the piece of wax. And what if (through advancing to nuclear physics) I transmute the piece of solid stuff from organic matter into metal by Thursday? Then the piece of solid stuff must have been there in company with the vase, the piece of wax, and the piece of organic matter. Is there here a stopping point beyond which one could not conceive of going? Such multiplicity seems undesirable.
3. Though Wiggins succeeds in preserving the link between identity and Leibniz's Law, he fails to account for a connection between Leibniz's Law and the supposed relations of constitution and function. For they seem to behave with respect to Leibniz's Law very much like identity. If my vase weighs two pounds, has a tulip-shape, is pale yellow, smells nice, and is located in the centre of the mantelpiece, so, on Monday, does the piece of wax—and not, it seems, by a possibly surprising law of nature. On a given day, the wood, the ship, and the tourist-attraction cast the same shadow, skin the same knees, and feed the same termites. It would further complicate Wiggins's theory if we were to account for these facts along the following lines:

   > 'weighs two thousand pounds' sometimes means: (literally) weighs two thousand pounds—sometimes means: is constituted out of something which (literally) weighs two thousand pounds—sometimes means: is something as which something which (literally) weighs two thousand pounds functions—etc.

   More dubiously and with various restrictions, something analogous seems to hold for the relation of being the same F. If the vase is the same piece of wax as the bust, then if the vase weighs two pounds, so does the bust. But here we are perhaps prepared to see that this is so only given the law of nature to the effect that, normally, a piece of wax does not (appreciably) change in weight over an approximately short period of time. And certainly, it is not the case that if the vase has a tulip shape, so does the bust.

4. It fails to explain how the wood fails to be a ship—even though the wood is shaped like a ship, floats like a ship, conveys cargo like a ship, etc. The wood is *awfully* ship-like!

At this point I must say that both Geach's and Wiggins's theses appear to be designed to account also for various types of cases other than those of my examples. To take one instance, if Jones is both the mayor of the city and the dean of the college, we might be at first tempted into holding that the mayor is identical with the dean and then be baffled by our willingness to say that the mayor declared a city-wide curfew together with our reluctance to say that the dean did. Geach would propose to help us out by distinguishing between two identity relations: being the *same man* (which the mayor and dean are) and being the *same official* (which the mayor and the dean are not). Wiggins would propose to help us out by holding that there are three *distinct* particulars here: Jones, the mayor, and the dean, of which the first *functions* as each of the other two. Both proposals are supposed to account for the apparent break-down of Leibniz's Law.

Now it seems that for cases such as this one, also, something very much like (a restricted) Leibniz's Law does hold for the relations between any two of: Jones, the mayor, and the dean. If any one of these is blond, plays tennis, and has three daughters, so does each of the other two—and not, it seems, as the result of any law of nature.

I mention cases of *this* sort mainly to point out that the proposal which I shall espouse is not designed to deal with them. Very roughly, there are various sorts of cases in which our inclination to attribute identity comes into conflict with our inclination to accept Leibniz's Law without qualification. In some of these cases, the difficulty can be traced to *time*; in others it cannot. The proposal I shall espouse is designed to deal only with the former.

With respect to *such* cases—let us return to my vase made out of wax—Wiggins's acceptance of Leibniz's Law in an unrestricted and, in particular, unqualified-with-respect-to-time form forces him to deny identity between the vase and the piece of wax. For they (and similarly for other cases involving time) have different life histories. The vase exists for only one day. The piece of wax, longer. But now special provision must be made so that the 'new' alleged relation between the vase and the piece of wax exemplifies some principle rather like Leibniz's Law. For the vase and the piece of wax *must* share a great many properties. Geach relativizes identity to concepts right from the start and, along with this, proposes a form of Leibniz's Law relativized to concepts. The relation between the vase and the piece of wax continues to appear to be something *like* identity.

The scope of this essay precludes further discussion of ways[2] of dealing with the difficulties different from the way proposed by Grice.

It was, if I recollect correctly, in the summer of 1971 that a group met weekly in Berkeley to discuss Wiggins's then new book and the issues it raised. We kept running into difficulties. Towards the end of one of the later meetings (perhaps the last), Paul Grice said he thought the solution (to the difficulties raised by cases involving *time*) was that A could be identical with B at one time and fail to be identical with B at another. My own (unspoken) reaction to this was that this was 'one of those ideas of Paul's', ingenious and boldly simple in initial conception and incapable of being coherently worked out in full detail. I set to reflecting just where the attempt at a full working out would break down. To my surprise, no such point came into view. So I continued, now with the growing conviction that the proposal might be viable. As the shape of a fairly full coherent working-out became clear, insuperable paradoxes came into view. But further scrutiny showed not only that they were superable, merely apparent, but that they were clues to further insights. In all of this I was immeasurably helped by Paul Grice's generosity with his ideas and in other ways, as well as by suggestions of students, both here, at Berkeley, and at the University of Minnesota in Minneapolis. It now seems to me that this 'one of those ideas of Paul's' is correct and an idea of great philosophical fruitfulness. Since I have, over the years, had relevantly similar experiences with quite a number of ideas Paul Grice has put forth, I have formed a 'Grice Rule': If what he says strikes me initially as 'can't be right', then it is almost certainly right; if what he says strikes me initially as 'almost certainly right', then it can't be right. The correctness of this rule has been borne out over and over again. Obviously, it would not be in good taste for me to reveal whether Paul Grice has ever said anything that struck me initially as 'almost certainly right'.

Let us, then, try to deal with the difficulties which emerge from the examples with which I began by deploying Grice's idea that A can be identical with B at one time and fail to be identical with B at another. I think that we should not regard this as a 'new' notion of identity, relativized, identity-at-a-time—any more than we should, in dealing with an object changing from being red to being green, regard outselves as needing a 'new' notion of being red, relativized, being-red-at-a-time. The idea is simply that we should regard statements—*not excluding statements of identity*—as subject to temporal qualifications in a systematic and uniform way. Thus, we are to envisage having in a 'regimented' sort of way:

at t, A is red
at t′, A is green (not red)

and:

at t, A = B
at t′, A ≠ B

such that, in suitable circumstances, *both* members of each pair are true.

For my example of the vase and the bust of Aristotle made, at various times, from the same piece of wax, we should have as true:

on Monday, the piece of wax = the vase
on Monday, the piece of wax is on the mantelpiece
on Monday, the vase is on the mantelpiece
on Tuesday, the piece of wax is on the mantelpiece
on Tuesday, the vase is not on the mantelpiece
on Tuesday, the piece of wax ≠ the vase
on Tuesday, the piece of wax = the bust of Aristotle
at *all* times, the vase ≠ the bust of Aristotle

This raises at once questions about Leibniz's Law. Well, we are envisaging imposing temporal qualifications on statements in general, systematically and uniformly. We would, for example, say:

at *all* times, if A is red, then A is not green.

Why should we not treat Leibniz's Law in the same way:

at *all* times, if A = B, then A is F if and only if B is F

We might call this 'Leibniz's Law subject (like other statements) to temporal qualification'. We now see why, *on Monday*, the vase and the piece of wax *must* share properties, such as being on the mantelpiece, weighing two pounds, having a tulip-shape, being pale yellow, and smelling nice.

But we *do* encounter a complication. For it seems that, *on Monday*, the piece of wax has the property of going to be, on Tuesday, on the mantelpiece, whereas the vase lacks this property. But also we see what to do about this complication. For the property in question, representable by the open sentence:

on Tuesday, x is on the mantelpiece

is one the possession of which *at any time* is *dependent* on the possession of another property—namely, being on the mantelpiece—at a certain time or times—namely, on Tuesday. And this is reflected in the open sentence representing the property in question by the actual occurrence of a temporal qualification—namely, 'on Tuesday'.

So the general way of dealing with the complication is to divide properties into those which are '*time-free*'—like being on the mantelpiece—which are represented by open sentences *not* containing temporal qualifications, and those which are '*time-bound*'—like being on the mantelpiece on Tuesday—which are represented by open sentences which do contain temporal qualifications. And what must be done is that 'Leibniz's Law subject (like other statements) to temporal qualification' is to be, in addition, *restricted* to properties which are '*time-free*'—properly represented by open sentences (or 'predicates') which do not (relevantly) contain temporal qualifications.[3]

One may reasonably feel that this additional restriction is *no* addition within the spirit of the original idea but only an addition within the letter. For the original idea envisages that on Monday, the piece of wax is identical with the vase, while on Tuesday the piece of wax is, but the vase is not, on the mantelpiece. Should we, then, not, in all consistency, envisage that on Monday the piece of wax is, but the vase is not, *going to be on Tuesday* on the mantelpiece? The additional restriction on 'Leibniz's Law subject (like other statements) to temporal qualification' is merely a reflection of this point.

It now appears that it may very well be the case that at any given time A and B are identical even though their life-histories differ.

What can be done to make clear whether this is or is not the correct account of the matter? This itself is not clear. One thing that can be done is to set out a general theoretical account of the logical relationships among statements, with studied attention to temporal qualification. If no hitches develop, one can then attempt to survey how well the general theoretical account concords with what we seem to see with respect to particular cases and topics.

II

Nowadays, a favourite method of setting out a general theoretical account of logical relations among statements is to describe a 'formal' or 'formalized' 'system' and then give more or less detailed hints for correlating suitable elements of this system with statements expressed in the vernacular. A system of this sort—let us call it System G—which incorporates Grice's idea that statements of identity, along with other statements, are to be subject to temporal qualification, and, indeed, in such a way that in some cases at t, $A = B$, while at t′, $A \neq B$, can, indeed, be described. I shall here try to convey a general idea of the system and give a more precise characterization elsewhere.

System G is really a rather minor modification of a standard Predicate Calculus with Identity (PCI) designed to fulfil three desiderata:

1. it permits us to express the idea that so-and-so is the case at one time but not at another, and, in particular,
2. permits us to express the idea that a particular thing exists at one time but not at another, and
3. permits us to express the idea that thing A and thing B are identical at one time but not at another.

No doubt, these desiderata can be attained in a number of alternative ways. Indeed, Grice himself has registered to me his strong dislike of various features of the way I have chosen. But I find it the most attractive and so steam ahead.[4]

1. Syntactically, that so-and-so is the case at time t will be represented by prefixing a symbol for time t to a formula which is, in the first instance, simply one of the familiar ones of PCI or augmented by Parsons' Operator discussed below, separating the two, for ease of reading with a bar. For example:

$$t\,|\,(Fa \,\&\, \exists x(Gx \,\&\, Hxa)),\; t\,|\,[b]\,Fb$$

Such expressions are, of course, to be subject to truth-functions. But it also proves convenient to allow quantifiers occurring outside of the scope of a time-symbol but binding variables within that scope, predication with respect to and quantification over time-symbols themselves, and subjecting such expressions, in turn, to temporal qualification. Thus, for example:

$$\exists t\; t\,|\,\exists x(\exists t'\exists t''\,(t < t'' \,\&\, t'\,|\,Fx \,\&\, t''\,|\,{\sim}Fx))$$

Such expressions are to be called 'proto-formulae' and are to be divided into two kinds: those in which any individual variables and constants have occurrences outside the scope of any time-symbol are to be *merely proto-formulae* and *proto-sentences*, and only those in which this feature is not found are to be *formulae* and *sentences*.

2. Syntactically, that a particular object *exists* at time t will be represented by a device which is a modification of an idea of Paul Grice's put forward in another connection.[5]

This idea drives a wedge between the notions of 'some' and 'all', represented by quantification, on the one hand, and the notion of existence, represented by an additional device, on the other. It allows (or can be easily adapted to allow) us to say truly that *something* (i.e. Pegasus) is a winged horse—even though Pegasus does not exist, and, indeed, there do not exist any winged horses—without 'ontological commitment' to Pegasus or winged horses. Similarly, we might want to say that *someone* (say Plato) is now admired, exerts influence, and excels every living philosopher—even though he no longer exists and there does not now and, indeed, could not now exist anyone excelling (in philosophy) every living philosopher.

The main idea of Grice's proposal can be explained briefly thus. He wishes to extend the notion of '*scope*' to individual-symbols and truth-functional connectives, and thereby distinguish, for example:

It is not the case that Pegasus is in the San Francisco Zoo.

from:

Pegasus is not in the San Francisco Zoo.

In the former, negation has the largest 'scope', the existence of Pegasus is not required for the truth of the whole, and the whole is in fact true. Whereas in the latter, the name 'Pegasus' has the largest scope, the existence of Pegasus is, consequently, required for the truth of the whole, and so the whole is false (or, some might want to say: has no truth-value).

The details of Grice's actual proposal are rather complicated. But the idea important for our purposes is that there should be a way to indicate 'scope' of individual-symbols. And this idea can be easily exploited by adopting a simplifying suggestion of Charles Parsons'. So let us introduce a device (call it *Parsons' Operator*) consisting of an individual-symbol within square brackets to be prefixable to formulae and proto-formulae, so that we may distinguish between, for example,

$$Fb$$

and

$$[b]\ Fb$$

The former does not require for its truth the existence of b, whereas the latter does. The 'inference rules' governing this device are essentially:

$$[\beta]\phi \vdash \phi$$
$$\phi, [\beta]\psi \vdash [\beta]\phi$$

It will be seen that one proto-formula which is true if and only if a exists is: [a] a = a—but there are infinitely many others.

3. Syntactically, that A is identical with B at t has already been provided for:

$$t\,|\,a = b$$

I trust that a good enough idea of the 'formation rules' of System G has been conveyed. The details are to be published elsewhere.

In matters of this kind, it is customary to turn one's attention to the 'semantics' of the system being described. About this I will keep mum at the present. I shall make some remarks which, I hope, will be helpful, and a fairly precise discussion of two different 'semantics' will be published elsewhere.

Instead, I shall here try to give a general idea of the 'inference-rules' of System G.

The 'inference-rules' are really a rather minor modification of standard 'natural deduction' rules for PCI. I shall briefly sketch the main differences. The details are in a discussion to be published elsewhere.

1. Only *sentences* (i.e. not expressions which are merely *proto-sentences*) are to form lines in a derivation.

2. All but one (the 'introduction of premisses (suppositions) rule') of the familiar 'rules' have both 'Internal' and 'External' versions—depending upon whether the 'inferential transformation' takes place *within* the scope of a time-symbol or *not*—but are with an exception to be noted, otherwise unchanged. I think the idea is best got across by illustration:

'Internal'	*'External'*
k | (Fa & Fb) ∴k | Fa	k | Fa & k | Fb k | Fa
k | ∀xFx ∴k | Fa	∀t t | Fa ∴ k | Fa
k | ∀t t | Fa ∴k | k | Fa	
k′ | Fa ∴k′ | ∀xFx	k | Fb ∴ ∀t t | Fb
k′ | k | Fb ∴k′ | ∀t t | Fb	

For the last three: *provided* 'the constant in question':—'a' or 'k', as appropriate—does not occur in the 'inferred' line or any of the 'premisses (suppositions)' of the 'given' line.

3. The exception of a familiar 'rule' which undergoes a further modification is—as may be expected from previous discussion—the 'Internal' version of Leibniz's Law. The idea is that given, for example,

$$k \mid a = b$$

and any formula,

$$k \mid \ldots\ldots\ldots$$

one may infer any formula

$$k \mid ---------$$

which results from replacing occurrences of 'a' by occurrences of 'b' or *vice versa—provided no such replacement has taken place at an occurrence which is within the scope of an occurrence of some time-symbol other than 'k'*. This is the 'formal' upshot of our discussion of 'time-free' and 'time-bound' properties/predicates.

4. Some 'rules' are needed to govern the new devices. The two needed for Parsons' Operator have already been discussed. Three are needed for temporal qualification.

$k \mid \phi \vdash \phi$—*provided* ϕ is a *sentence*
$\phi \vdash k \mid \phi$—(ϕ is already required to be a *sentenc*
$\sim k \mid \phi \dashv\vdash k \mid \sim \phi$

5. Presumably, 'rules' (or 'axioms') will be wanted to characterize the 'nature of time', for example:

$$\wedge \vdash (k < k' \,\&\, k' < k'') \supset k < k''$$
$$\wedge \vdash k < k' \supset \exists t(k < t \,\&\, t < k')$$

and/or others, though these may be regarded as outside the 'formal' development of the system.

It may be helpful to give as an illustration a derivation correct both downwards and upwards (if taken to be not part of a larger derivation):

$k \mid \forall x Fx$
$k \mid Fa$
$k' \mid k \mid Fa$
$k' \mid \forall x\, k \mid Fx$

This completes the sketch of the 'syntax' of System G. We must now try to tackle matters 'semantical'.

III

There is a familiar way, or cluster of ways, of describing the 'semantics' of a system such as System G. It is said to be done in a 'meta-language', which is usually a more or less 'regimented' (sometimes *very much* 'regimented') version of English (or some other 'natural language'). But the problems with which we have started are, in part, problems about the nature of English (and similar languages). Are statements of identity subject to temporal qualification in such a way that A can be identical with B at one time but not at another? If so, then one might want, in describing in English the 'semantics' of System G, to bring into prominence those features of English which are relevantly related to this fact. This seems to amount to saying that in using English as the 'meta-language' for this purpose, one might want to 'regiment' it into, in effect, an interpreted version of System G. For, perhaps, only thus can one describe the 'semantics' of System G in a clear and coherent way. It seems to me, reasonably clearly, that at least one *can* do this by proceeding in this way.

Supposing it is so, one may still harbour worries about what it shows. One cannot help having some lingering feeling that one is pulling oneself up by one's boot-straps. Still, doing the job may be illuminating and thought-provoking.

Fortunately, however, it is possible to describe a sort of 'semantics' for System G in a version of English 'regimented' in such a way as to keep entirely out of prominence those features with which System G is designed to deal. This may convince one of the viability of System G (whatever exactly that may mean). But because of the way this job is done, it carries with it a pressure to think that the viability of System G thus demonstrated does not show that identity is variant with respect to time, but, rather, the opposite. For, in this way of describing the 'semantics' of System G, the objects 'semantically correlated' to the elements of the system are not—at least, explicitly regarded as—capable of being identical at one time and not at another. Some form of mildly recondite tinkering brings it about that expressions of System G which notationally suggest time-variant identity come out, or turn out to be capable of coming out, true.

Thus we are caught between two fires: either describing the 'semantics' in what might appear to be a question-begging way or describing it in a way which might make it appear that the system fails to represent time-variant identity.

My own opinion is that the first approach does give the 'correct', intended 'semantics' of System G in its application to the vicissitudes of things in the course of time. The second approach gives only a *simulated* 'semantics' by attending to an assemblage of objects *at one time*, or unchanging over time, which is in a way isomorphic to the vicissitudes in the course of time. But the second approach, being more familiar, is still capable of making clear important features of System G.

My procedure will be to discuss some issues, clarity concerning which seems to help with the first approach, and then to sketch its gist. A concise formulation of it and of the second approach is in a discussion to be published elsewhere.

I have suggested that regarding Leibniz's Law as subject to temporal qualification—including the restriction to 'time-free' conditions—clears the way for the thesis that identity—like all other 'time-free' properties and relations—is subject to time. But there is another obstacle, or cluster of obstacles, in the way. I believe that a discussion of this will throw light on a plethora of puzzles and discomforts.

The business with Leibniz's Law may be granted to make clear how it might be that, today, the ship is identical with the wood, even though, a year ago, the ship was (still) in the market-place, but the wood was not (was in the lumber-yard). But (it may be said) if, today, the ship is truly identical with the wood, then, today, there is just *one*—relevantly prominent—object in the centre of the market-place, and what about *this object*, a year ago—was it in the market-place or was it not (was it in the lumber-yard)? We seem to have a paradox.

I would like to make a general suggestion for dealing with this sort of difficulty. The suggestion summarily put, is that in order to consider (in a familiar way) with respect to an object whether it is at time t such-and-such, one must identify or single-out the object by means of a condition which the object satisfies *at t* uniquely. And for this purpose, a condition which an object satisfies *at some other time* uniquely may prove insufficient.

The application of the suggestion to the illustrative puzzle is as follows: if we wish to discuss the whereabouts *a year ago* of an object, it is not enough to identify the object as the *one* which is *today* in the centre of the market-place. We must identify the object as the *one* which was *a year ago* such-and-such. It does not matter *what* condition we use, *provided* it is one which the object satisfied *a year ago* uniquely. For example, all three conditions: being today in the centre of the market-place, being a ship which is today in the centre of the market-place, being (a mass of) wood which is today in the centre of the market-place—are candidates for identifying conditions. But, in our example, the first of these conditions was *not*, and only the other two *were*, uniquely satisfied a year ago. So the first condition *will not do* for discussion of the whereabouts a year ago of any object, while the other two *will*. And now we have a non-paradoxical answer to our question—or, rather non-paradoxical answers to our answerable questions: the ship which is today in the market-place was in the market-place a year ago; the wood which is today in the market-place was not (was in the lumber-yard).

It is tempting to see the situation in a different light. Someone says to us: where was that (pointing?) object (which is now in the centre of the market-place) a year ago? We do not know how to answer, knowing that the ship was (still) in the market-place, but the wood was in the lumber-yard. We say: what do you mean—the ship in the market-place or the wood in the market-place? Only when he answers, can we, in turn, answer. It is tempting to interpret this as our asking *which of two different objects* in the centre of the market-place does he mean (or is he or might he be interested in).

But this is not the only way to see the situation. We can think of our asking him what he means not as asking which of two different objects he means, but, rather, as asking which of two different answerable questions he (is or might be interested in) posing:

> A year ago: the object which was (*then*) uniquely a ship which is today uniquely in the market-place, where was it?

> A year ago: the object which was (*then*) uniquely (a mass of) wood which is today uniquely in the market-place, where was it?

The suggestion is that we must try to find out which of these questions he (is or might be interested in) posing because his spoken question, taken *au pied de la lettre*, is:

> A year ago: the object which was *then* uniquely an object which is today uniquely in the market-place, where was it?

and as such is unanswerable, since (*ex hypothesi*) there was *not* a year ago any uniquely such object. The condition of being in the centre of the market-place *is* uniquely satisfied *today*. But the condition of being today uniquely in the market-place was *not* uniquely satisfied a year ago.

The suggestion I am making is this. A statement which can be regarded as of the form:

> The A thing is at t B

is to be further regarded as being of the form:

> At t, the (then) uniquely A thing is B

allowing for suitable reworking of the phrase represented by 'A'. If we make the supposition that a Russellian treatment is to be accorded to such forms, and use '1xAx' to represent[6]: x is uniquely A—we shall have:

$$t \mid \exists x(1xAx \,\&\, Bx)$$

We may illustrate this with respect to our example in, one may hope, suggestive notation:

The ship in the market-place (today) was last year in the market-place.
1 | ∃x (1x (Sx & t | 1xMx) & Mx)
The wood in the market-place (today) was last year not in the market-place
1 | ∃x (1x (Wx & t | 1xMx) & ~ Mx)
These form a consistent[7] set with:
t | ∃x 1xMx

that is: today there is just *one* object in the market-place.

Notice that the two statements:

t | ∃x (1xMx & 1|Mx)
t | ∃x (1xMx & 1|~ Mx)

which generate an air of paradox are actually mutually consistent and, indeed, are (in our example) both true. Because of the proposed reinterpretation of Leibniz's Law, they do not generate the inconsistent:

t | ∃x (1x Mx & 1|Mx & 1|~ Mx)

and—it is being suggested—they are *not* to be read as:

The object (today) in the market-place was last year in the market-place.
The object (today) in the market-place was last year not in the market-place.

These would be represented by:

1 | ∃x (1x t|1xMx & Mx)
1 | ∃x (1x t|1xMx & ~ Mx)

and these are (since we are adopting the Russellian treatment) both false, because

1 | ∃x 1x t|1x Mx

is false.

I believe that if we reject the supposition that a Russellian treatment is to be accorded to statements of the sort under discussion, we shall be able to give a more elaborate account which will, nevertheless, dispel the air of paradox more or less along the same lines.[8]

I have said that for a discussion whether a certain object is at t such-and-such, the object must be identified or singled out by some condition which *at t* it satisfies uniquely. I have said that, in general, it does not matter what this condition is, *provided* the requirement is fulfilled. But one should expect that we would want to have available to us conditions which would allow us to discuss the state of an object at any and every time by being satisfied by that object uniquely at any and every time—and, indeed, '*a priori*'. Such conditions are available as conjunctions of conditions which (as an '*a priori*' matter) an object satisfies at *all* times with conditions which an object satisfies uniquely at some time. Thus, some object is at all times uniquely an object which (as an '*a priori*' matter) at all times[9] is a ship and today is uniquely in the market-place. And so we can discuss the vicissitudes in the course of time of *the ship which is today in the market-place* and of *the (mass of) wood which is today in the market-place* and make such remarks as that the ship in question is at some time identical with and at other times distinct from the (mass of) wood in question.

One may see here room for a notion of being 'essentially' a ship or being 'essentially' a (mass of) wood. And in a discussion to be published elsewhere I have set out a compressed account of an attempt to spell out such a notion.

IV

I believe that attention to matters of the sort discussed above will help to resolve similar puzzles which may arise when we move to more explicitly 'semantical' considerations. For example, one may wish to consider for what values of the variable 'x' the formula '1| Mx' (in the intended interpretation) comes out true (within the context of our example). And one may come to feel that the variable cannot be regarded as taking (*inter alia*) as value the alleged *single*—relevantly prominent—object which is today in the centre of the market-place. For would the formula come out true or false for that value of the variable—in view of the fact that the ship was, while the wood was not, in the market-place last year? One is moved to hold that the formula comes out true for the ship as value of 'x' and comes out false for the wood as value of 'x'. And then one is further moved to hold that there are, therefore after all, *two* objects involved.[10]

The point to keep in mind is that, just as in the puzzle previously discussed to consider whether the formula '1| Mx' comes out true for a particular value of 'x'—since it involves considering whether that value of 'x' was in the market-place a year ago—requires that the value of 'x' in question be identified or singled out in some way such that it is determinate which of the objects *a year ago* it is. And simply specifying that it is the object which is *today* in the centre of the market-place is insufficient, since, though there is only one such object today, *a year ago* there were *two* objects which satisfied this condition.

We must rethink the notion of value of variable with attention to temporal qualification. The following may be suggestive, if not quite philosophically rigorous. When a variable 'takes as value' an object, then *at each time* some one object is uniquely such that *at every time* that object is the unique value of the variable. So we may speak with respect to any time, of the object which the variable 'has as value' *at that time*. Now we may consider two such 'cases' of 'taking as value'. It may happen that at some times t, the object which the variable 'has as value' in the one 'case' at t is identical at t with the object which the variable 'has as value' in the other 'case' at t; while at other times t′, the object which the variable 'has as value' in the one 'case' at t′ is *not* identical at t′ with the object the variable 'has as value' in the other 'case' at t′. Thus, for two 'cases' of 'taking as value', there may be times such that the values of the variable are at those times identical, and times such that at those times the values of the variable are distinct. But the differences between the two 'cases' of 'taking as value' should not be promoted into a temporally unqualified distinctness of the objects 'taken as value'. The object 'taken as value' in one 'case' is at some times identical with, at other times distinct from, the object 'taken as value' in the other 'case'. Or, at any rate, so we should think if we allow that the ship is at some times identical with and at other times distinct from the (mass of) wood.

Now, we can see through our puzzle. In one 'case' the variable 'x' 'takes as value' the ship, in another 'case' it 'takes as value' the wood. The object which 'x' 'has as value' *today* in the first 'case' is *today* identical with the object which 'x' 'has as value' today in the second 'case'—it is, indeed, the single thing in the centre of the market-place today. But the object which x 'had as value' *last year* in the first 'case' was *not last year* identical with the object 'x' 'had as value' *last year* in the second 'case'. And the formula '1| Mx' comes out true for that object as value of 'x' which 'x' 'had as value', last year in the *first* 'case'—namely the ship—and comes out false for that object as value of 'x' which 'x' 'had as value' last year in the second 'case'—namely the wood—even though the former and the latter are *today* identical.[11]

But, perhaps, it is more philosophically rigorous to regard a 'case' of a variable 'taking as value' an object as an *ordered couple* of that variable and that object. Now it is even easier to see that (if we hold on to the view that the ship and the wood are identical today) the ordered couple ('x', the ship) and the ordered couple ('x', the wood) have *the same* second term *today*, but had *distinct* second terms *last year*. If we hold on to a principle of extensionality, we should hold that the ordered couples themselves are identical *today*, but were distinct *last year*. (And, similarly, we should hold that the 'cases' in terms of which we were thinking before were two at some times but only one at others.)[12]

This brings to mind that we must re-think our notions of *set* with attention to temporal qualification before we can employ that notion in describing the intended 'semantics' of System G. First, the relation of set-membership is to be subjected to temporal qualification: $t \mid x \in y$. So which objects belong to a set may change over time. For example, one would expect that an object belongs to the set of things which are red at all and only those times at which the object is red. But if we want to allow such sets as, for example, the set of things which were red at *some specific time t*, we encounter a complication. Let us return to our ship s and our wood w and consider the set of things which were in the market-place last year, $\hat{x}1 \mid Mx$. What belongs to this set *today*? It seems that the ship does, for it was in the market-place last year. But today the ship is identical with the wood, so the wood belongs to the set, even though the wood was *not* in the market-place a year ago. That is, if:

$$t \mid s \in \hat{x}\, 1 \mid Mx$$
$$t \mid s = w$$

then,

$$t \mid w \in \hat{x}\, 1 \mid Mx$$

but,

$$\sim t \mid 1 \mid Mw$$

Is this an insurmountable paradox? We, certainly, would get a contradiction if we maintained (even with some adaptation of the usual provisions to preclude the ***familiar*** set-theoretic paradoxes), for any time t:

$$t \mid (x \in \hat{y} \ldots y \ldots \equiv \ldots x \ldots)$$

unless we artificially exempted the set-membership relation from substitutivity in accordance with our formulation of Leibniz's Law—artificially, because the set-membership relation does not seem '*time-bound*' and, certainly, notationally is not. But a small modification suffices to preclude contradiction. We should maintain (with some adaptation of the usual provisions to preclude the familiar set-theoretic paradoxes), instead, for all times t:

$$t \mid (x \in \hat{y} \ldots y \ldots \equiv \exists z\, (x = z \,\&\, \ldots z \ldots))$$

The only unpleasant consequence of this is that sets $\hat{x} \ldots x \ldots$ and $\hat{x}\sim \ldots x \ldots$ are not in every case exclusive: they may fail to be when ... x ... is '*time-bound*'. So the ship, that is, the wood, is today a member both of the set of things which were in the market-place a year ago and also of the set of things which were not in the market-place a year ago. But this seems not to cause any serious difficulties. As we have already seen, ordered couples and other entities, such as functions, construed as certain kinds of sets in more or less the usual ways may be identical at some times and distinct at others. For example, if today but not at other times all and only philosophers are wise, then the set of philosophers and the set of the wise are identical today but not at other times.

Because the membership of sets changes over time, it will be useful to counter-act this feature, as we move to more explicit consideration of matters 'semantical'. For example, it will be useful to have a notion of a set of ordered *n*-tuples such that all their terms are *at one time or another* members of a certain set. For example, {⟨the ship, the wood⟩} was even last year a set of ordered couples all of whose terms are *at one time or another* (namely today) members of the set of things in the market-place, even though the wood was not last year a member of that set. Another notion that is useful is that of a '*temporally rigid*' function: one which, loosely speaking, has 'same' arguments and values at all times. But words fail me here. A '*temporally rigid*' function f is one that satisfies the condition:

$$\forall t\, t \mid \forall x \forall y \big(f(x) = y \supset \exists z\, \exists u \big(x = z \,\&\, y = u \,\&\, \forall t' t' \mid f(z) = u\big)\big)$$

We are now ready to turn our attention to the intended 'semantics' of System G.

We could give one or another 'definition of truth' for sentences (and, as it turns out, *proto-sentences*) of System G, thereby *fixing* the interpretation of its non-logical constants. It is more customary and, in various ways, more useful to give a once-and-for-all 'definition of truth with respect to a model', which leaves the interpretation of the non-logical constants *unfixed*. The intended interpretation then can be given later simply by selecting a particular 'model' as the intended one. I shall sketch a 'definition with respect to a model'.[13]

A model of the intended sort is to be any ordered quintuple of a non-empty set of objects, a non-empty set of times, a temporally-rigid function from predicates of degree *i* to sets of ordered *i*–tuples all of whose terms are at one time or another members of the domain of objects (and from sentential letters to 'T' or 'F'), a temporally rigid function from individual constants to objects which are at one time or another members of the domain of objects, and a temporally-rigid function from time-constants to objects which are at one time or another members of the domain of times. A γ-variant of a model is, as usual, a model which differs from the first at most in the value which the appropriate function has for γ as argument.

If we pay attention to temporal qualification, we will expect that explicit definitions will be of the form:

$$\forall t\, t \mid \forall x_{1\ldots} \forall x_n \left(Fx_{1\ldots}\, x_n \equiv ---x_{1\ldots}\, x_n---\right)$$

and inductive definitions will be of the form: $\forall t\, t \mid$, followed by the clauses of the inductive definition. The definition of 'truth with respect to a model' is not to be an exception. We would thus define in effect 'truth with respect to a model m *at time t*'—though the proper expression of this would be of the form: $t \mid T\phi m$. A consequence of this is that we define 'truth with respect to a model' also for *proto-sentences* such as 'Mw'. But these will, in general, be true with respect to a model *at some times but not at others*. This is, of course, just what we should expect. For 'the wood is in the market-place' (temporally unqualified) is true today but was false a year ago. *Sentences* of System G, on the other hand, will, as one should expect, retain the same truth-value at all times, just as (read tenselessly) 'In year *k* the wood is in the market-place' does not change its truth-value over time.

Well, what about the inductive clauses of the definition of 'truth with respect to a model'? They are *exactly* the usual ones—*including* the clause for identity-sentences of the form: a = b! Except, of course, that additional clauses are needed for the devices of temporal qualification and the device used to represent existence. Of these, the novel ones are, in effect:

if ϕ is $\kappa < \kappa'$, then $T\phi m$ iff the time assigned by m to κ is earlier than the time assigned by m to κ'

if ϕ is $\kappa \mid \psi$, then $T\phi m$ iff at the time assigned by m to κ, $T\psi m$

if ϕ is $[\beta]\ \psi$, then $T\phi m$ iff $T\psi m$ and the object assigned by m to β exists.

Of course, we are to remember that we are supposing that our meta-language deals with temporal qualification and existence in the ways being recommended and so itself has an overall structure like that of System G.

A further observation may be of interest. If we choose to interpret some time-constant, say 'n', as having the meaning of 'now', then we should regard as an interpretation of System G a set S of models m differing only in what time is assigned to 'n' and *correlated* with t if and only if m assigns t to 'n'. Then, at any time a proto-sentence is to be true with respect to this *correlation* of the set of models if and only if the proto-sentence is true at that time with respect to the model correlated to that time. This may help us to think about McTaggartian problems about time.

I see a last bit of support for Grice's proposal concerning time and identity in the systematic consideration that, whereas the atemporal, 'absolute', notion of identity can be introduced into System G '*by definition*' as: $\forall t\, t \mid x = y$,

Grice's conception of identity as subject to temporal qualification cannot be thus recovered from 'absolute identity'.[14]

But, *perhaps*, on the other hand, . . .

Notes

1. This multiplicity seems to remain in Grice's proposal as well.

2. For a recent discussion and references, see Griffin, N., *Relative Identity*, Clarendon Press, Oxford, 1977.

3. Obviously, quite a bit more could be said about this. One can easily get worried about the quasi-metaphysical notion of the possession of a property at all times being *dependent* on the possession of another property at a certain time or times. And one may have Goodmanesque (*à la 'grue'*) worries about corresponding open sentences or 'predicates'. The starting point would seem to be that being 'time-free' is intimately connected with being a property such that it is possible to have it at one time and fail to have it at another, independently of any purely temporal ordering of the times in question.

4. It may be worth noting that a number of the other ways, including a 'tense-logic', may be obtained from the one I have chosen essentially as *notational variants*, 'by definition'. (At least, if enough 'rules' or 'axioms' characterizing the 'nature of time' are incorporated.)

5. Grice, H. P., 'Vacuous Names' in Davidson, D. and Hintikka, J., *Words and Objections*, Dordrecht, D. Reidel, 1969. I am also attracted by the idea of simply representing existence by a predicate: t | Ex—instead of: t | [x] x = x. This is a saving of one syntactical construction and two 'inference-rules'. For I have been so far unable to discern any distinctive logical features of an existence-predicate within a system of the present general sort.

6. Notation of the form: 1x . . . x . . . may be regarded as abbreviating: ∀y (. . . y . . . ≡ y = x)—where the dotted lines represent any proto-formulae differing only in the replacement of the variables at all free occurrences. An inductive procedure is needed to specify such abbreviations with full strictness and generality, if elimination of such abbreviation is to be unique. I suppress Parsons' Operator as inessential to the discussion.

7. Though in the absence of 'semantics' for System G, consistency would be undefined—except 'syntactically', e.g. not generating both ϕ and $\sim\phi$ *via* the 'rules of reference'.

8. I venture to suggest that more or less the same approach is to be adopted with respect to statements involving (alethic) modality. Roughly, a statement of the form:

> The A thing could have been B.

is to be construed along the lines:

> In some possible world, the object which is ('there') uniquely A is B.

again allowing for suitable reworking of the phrase represented by 'A'. For example:

> In some possible world, today, the object which is ('there', 'now') uniquely [a ship which is *in this world*, today, uniquely in the market-place] is (made of/identical with a mass of) steel.

9. Or, at any rate, at all times at which it *exists*. There seem to be options as to how to construe remarks about the state of objects at times at which they do not exist.

10. This feeling is reinforced by taking a glance at what I have labelled as *simulated* 'semantics' for System G. But that is just because such 'semantics' *is simulated*. It can be described within a framework within which temporal qualifications can be suppressed, identity does not vary with respect to time, and, consequently, variation of identity with respect to time has to be *mimicked* by a certain sort of non-identity. A discussion at Stanford of the general topic of this paper prompted the first six paragraphs of this section and a reordering of the exposition. Thanks, in particular, to John Etchemendy.

11. The failure of substitutivity in accordance with our formulation of Leibniz's Law suggests that we are dealing with '*time-bound*' notions as our reflections and a scrutiny of the 'definition of truth' confirm.

12. Rather analogous remarks, *mutatis mutandis*, can be made about the value of a variable being at t something which does not exist at t.

13. It is not clear to me, but it *may* be that this way of proceeding will not turn out to be as useful as one might expect it to be. For it may, perhaps, turn out that some 'possible' models of the intended sort will not be 'actual'. For example, it is quite likely that no 'two' objects are repeatedly identical and distinct over exactly five billion times (intervals). So there will not *be* a model of the sort described with such objects 'in it'. And this will make the 'truth in a model' approach useless for definitions of such logical notions as consequence and consistency. Perhaps this can be mitigated by adding an artificial time-ordering which will 'rearrange the times'. But, in any case, we can have recourse to the *simulated* 'semantics' for the definition of the logical notions.

14. I venture to suggest that the same point, *mutatis mutandis*, can be made concerning identity *vis-à-vis* (alethic) modality. Indeed, System G can be easily reinterpreted as a 'modal logic without tears', and by repeating the moves whereby System G was obtained from PCI one can obtain a 'modal temporal logic with tiers without tears'. It is also not unlikely that the formal structure of system G can be useful for detailed investigation of propositional attitudes.

PART III

Eliminativism and Dominant Kinds

9

I Do Not Exist

Peter Unger

It seems utterly obvious that the question 'Do I exist?' may be correctly answered only in the affirmative; of course the answer must be 'Yes.' Descartes, it may be said, made this idea the keystone of his philosophy, he found it so compelling. Hume, however, in his characteristically sceptical style, at least at times questioned the propriety of an affirmative reply. My teacher, Professor Sir Alfred Jules Ayer, to whom this essay is dedicated, customarily expressed himself in a conditional manner, which I find quite congenial:

> The sentence 'I exist', in this usage, may be allowed to express a statement which like other statements is capable of being either true or false. It differs, however, from most other statements in that if it is false it can not actually be made. Consequently, no one who uses these words intelligently and correctly can use them to make a statement which he knows to be false. If he succeeds in making the statement, it must be true.[1]

Of course Ayer is right in pointing to the absurdity of a person's trying to deny his own existence. Prepared to pay this price, in this brief essay I mean to deny my own putative existence, a position which I take to be even more radical than Hume's. This is owing not to a desire to be more perverse than any of my predecessors, but, rather, to certain arguments which have occurred to me, and which seem quite far from any of their thoughts. As may be expected of a student of Ayer's, and as I have indicated, I appreciate the utterly paradoxical position into which these arguments lead me. But I venture to suppose that this does not reflect badly on my reasonings in any relevant regard. Rather, it may show their great scope, thus highlighting obscure defects in prevalent conceptions. With this understanding, I mean to present herein the main lines of reasoning against my own existence.

I offer my arguments as a challenge to any others that there may be, so that they may dissuade me from the path of extreme nihilism that reason appears to require. Accordingly, I shall present my ideas as forcefully as possible, not to indicate any enormous confidence on my part, but rather to provoke others to reply most promptly and effectively. For my own part, I can find nothing importantly wrong with the uncomfortable thoughts I shall thus boldly put forth. The more I reflect upon them, the more I become convinced of their essential truth or justice, for any errors I ever find are superficial mistakes, requiring at most only minor changes in formulation. As a consequence, there appears to be growing within me an inclination to expend much effort toward developing the required nihilism in great detail, no matter how painfully laborious the attempt may be. Perhaps this growth had best be stopped, but then only by an appropriate rational argument.

To compound my dilemma, I notice that, in general outline, the same view lately has been conjectured by another writer, Samuel Wheeler, or so it appears. In a pioneering paper, 'Reference and Vagueness', Wheeler conjectured that there may not be any people; I should suppose he meant to include himself.[2] While he does not offer a positive argument for the nihilistic surmise, he does disarm prevalent ideas which would point the other way. Appearing to find a similar current in another, but no adequate compelling force in the opposite direction, the situation encourages my thoughts to move, however slowly and painfully, toward their properly destructive denial. Perhaps a response to my challenge may save me from the ultimately fruitless labours I seem required to undertake.

The challenging position is this: I do not exist and neither do you. The scientific perspective, especially as developed over the last few centuries, compels this result. Now, there is nothing especially unfortunate in this as regards the human condition. For, as regards almost everything which is commonly alleged to exist, it may be argued, in like manner, that it in fact does not. There are, then, no tables or chairs, nor rocks or stones or ordinary stars. Neither are there any plants or animals. No finite persons or conscious beings exist, including myself Peter Unger: I do not exist. So much for this challenging position. To the main arguments for it, rather briefly presented, I now turn.

I. The Sorites of Decomposition

Tables, as well as chairs, have often been believed to be paradigms of existing things or entities, but I shall argue that they do not exist at all. They are, if you will, only fictions, though nothing whatever depends on my use of such a term of convenience. My argument will be in the form of an indirect proof, wherein I reduce to absurdity the supposition of their existence.

According to our modern scientific view, if there are any tables, then each of them is constituted of, or is composed of, or comprises, or consists of, or whatever, many atoms, and still more 'elementary particles', but only a finite number of each. Now, nothing here depends on the expression 'is constituted of', or on any similar expression. Baldly put, the point is this: where and when there are no atoms present, there and then there is no table. This idea is not crucial to the argument; a 'less scientific' analogue will work as well, so far as the purer logical features go. But it is good to have nature apparently so co-operative.

Now, at the same time, according to our common-sense view of the matter, which for something like a *table* is, of course, all but definitive, one atom, or only a few, removed, or added, quite innocuously, will not make a relevant difference. If you have a table at the start, then, after an atom has been gently ticked off the edge somewhere, there will still be a table present. These simple ideas, when brought into combination, leave nothing for reason but to conclude that there really are no tables. It takes no great acumen to see this, as the reasoning is utterly simple, and most just and suitable to the subject before us.

For, if there is a table there, then it has only a finite number of atoms—say, a billion billion; it does not matter. The net removal of one, then, leaves us with a supposed table of a billion billion minus one atoms; after two are removed, the supposed table has a billion billion minus two; and so on. After a billion billion atoms have been removed, we have a table consisting of no atoms at all. In this simple fashion, I suggest, we have reduced to an absurdity the supposition that the table in question exists, or ever did exist. As this argument may be most readily generalised, we may conclude that there really are no such things as tables.

To advance discussion, it may be helpful if I give the argument just presented something like a formal shape or presentation. We begin with a supposition of existence:

(1) There exists at least one table.

But, from our scientific perspective, we may add this second premiss:

(2) For anything there may be, if it is a table, then it consists of many atoms, but only a finite number.

From these two premisses, we may deduce that there is at least one table which consists of many atoms, but a finite number of them. The crux and bite of my argument, however, may be supposed to come with a third and final premiss:

(3) For anything there may be, if it is a table (which consists of many atoms, but a finite number), then the net removal of one atom, or

> only a few, in a way which is most innocuous and favourable, will not mean the difference as to whether there is a table in the situation.

These three premisses, I take it, are inconsistent. The assessment of this inconsistency, I submit, leads one to reject, and to deny, the first premiss, whatever one may subsequently think of the remaining two propositions.

Discounting minor matters of formulation, I doubt that many would deny our second premiss. Many more, I imagine, are liable to deny our third and final proposition. It has, I must admit, been stated in a way which leaves matters less than completely clear and evident. Accordingly, I shall try to provide some clarificatory interpretation, to the extent that this seems merited even in a very brief treatment.

I have said that an atom is to be removed in a way which is most innocuous and favourable. What do I mean by such a way? First, I mean for the removal to be *net*, of course, and in the fullest way. The process which removes an atom does not put something else in its place, or in anywhere else; nor does such a thing happen in any other way. And, what is removed is randomly cast aside, so to speak. Secondly, I mean for the net removal to take place with as little disruptive effect as possible on what remains, especially as regards the question, if it really has any substance, as to whether or not any table remains. In other words, we might say, it is most unlikely that an atom will ever be blasted out of a central position; rather, one will be gently dislodged from an outside spot. Additionally, we are to conceive of the most favourable, or least disruptive, conditions, as regards temperature, pressure, electricity, magnetism, and so on. Further, if an occasion arises where, vary conditions as we may, a single atom cannot be removed without substantial relevant disruption, then we remove as few as possible, balanced against a disruptive effect. Finally, I close this interpretation with a remark on the alleged matter of whether an entity may be *as much as possible*, or be *as well off toward being, a table*. I am supposing this matter to have substance, of course, but only on way toward exposing its absurdity. This is an indirect argument.

Thus clarified, perhaps we may profitably divide what our premiss is saying under two heads. First, it makes a 'causal' claim: there is no relevant breaking point where, no matter what is done to be gentle and to retain things, the whole business, or a substantial portion thereof, collapses, or turns into an apparent donkey, or disappears, or whatever. Rather, things are relevantly quite gradual. To deny this, I believe, is to cast aside science, and even common sense as well. And, secondly, our premiss claims that, in this rather gradual way of things, the difference made by the small removals encountered, by one atom, more or less, is never nearly so much as the difference, merely alleged as it may be, between a table's being there and not being there. To deny this premiss, then, is as much as to affirm that there comes a place where, by taking away an atom or so, presumably *any one or few of millions* still, one makes a table cease to exist. And this, I suggest, is as much as to expect a miracle.

Now, as it is stated, of course, our final premiss points to conditions, and a way, that are quite ideal. That is no fault. It may make one think, however, that the whole argument has an 'airy-fairy' character, and is quite unrealistic. But conditions close enough to those which are most favourable do occur almost all the time. And, very small bits, if not nearly so small as an atom, can be removed in stepwise fashion, for an argument to similar effect. Whatever 'airy-fairy' features are there, then, cannot be basic to the argument.

Within fine points of formulation, our third premiss thus fairly compels belief. As a move to escape our just but uncomfortable conclusion, it remains only to deny the reasoning employed. In this vein, some may object that 'the logic' I have used is what is at fault. If some 'alternative logic' is chosen, they may respond, instead of the system of rules and formulae I have employed, the integrity of our tables may be secured. But I do not believe that good reasoning can ever be captured or frozen into any such system, or that the matter is really one of choosing one or another optional pieces of logical apparatus, like so many hammers or wrenches. There is not, I suggest, here a question of this logic or that one. Without my now being less than sceptical, it is a question of whether my reasoning has been sound, and has been just and appropriate to the topic before us. Now, if I have been in error in my reasoning, or unjust to my subject matter, then such an error or injustice should be made manifest. But, excepting small points of formulation, and with a proper sceptical hesitancy, I doubt that this will be done. Of course, I am no mathematician. But, I think that a fair appraisal of the matter by those more mathematically inclined will find them to view things in much the way that I here recommend.

In a somewhat deeper vein, perhaps, it should be re-emphasised that my argument is not dependent upon the existence of atoms, at least not in any fundamental way. Perhaps there are no atoms, and in 'removing an atom' what really happens is something involving, say, an underlying plenum, which is the only existing (physical) reality. If so, then perhaps the argument presented is acceptable only provisionally; perhaps it operates only on a superficial level. But, whatever changes or profundities may be compellingly envisioned, I hardly think that the reinstatement of tables is among them.

As a related, already anticipated point, while the gradual nature of things is needed for my argument, no deep theories about material reality are important. While it is nice to have ready-made units there to remove—molecules, atoms and particles—the slightest contrivance will work about as well. Thus, from an alleged table, one may remove a tiny chip or splinter, until not a single one remains.

In the manner of G. E. Moore, some will object to my argument along the following lines. First, they will claim to be *more certain* of the existence of tables than of *anything* which I am bringing to bear against such alleged existence. And, then, they will say, with apparent caution and modesty, that, while they are *not sure which* of the things I advance is in error, there *must be at least one* weak link, or fault, in my reasoning. Now, it well may be that this Moorian reply is often, or even usually, a proper answer to a philosophical attack on common sense. But, is it *always* proper, appropriate or correct? Is common sense *always* to be believed, while philosophy, along with science, is *always* to yield? I cannot believe that this is so, and that *no exceptions* can be made to this popular Moorian doctrine. What of the *present case*, then: may not *that* be just such an exception? We have seen, I suggest, that to deny my argument amounts to supposing a miracle: the gentle, innocuous removal of a single atom, or only a few, *which is not even perceptible to the unaided senses*, takes us from a situation where a table is present to one where there is no table at all. Indeed, the removal of *any one*, or *any few*, of *millions* of removable atoms or groups, will be enough to work the trick. This is, after all, where the issue does lie. Can common sense be so powerful as to sustain such a miraculous supposition as this? I do not think so.

In contrast to its employment with tables and chairs, our argument does not seem nearly so compelling, if at all, against *physical objects*. Intuitively, we have the idea that if we consider a biggish physical object, consisting of many atoms, as we take one away and then another, and so on, what we have left is always a physical object, so long as any object at all remains. The last atom, particle or whatever, it may be supposed, is as well off toward being a physical object as is the biggish thing at the start.

Let us be a bit particular as regards the differences between our sorites against tables, or any other ordinary things, and a similar attempt against physical objects. In the first place, we cannot say, in parallel with (2), that, for anything there may be, if it is a physical object, then it consists of many atoms but only a finite number. For an atom itself is a physical object and it does not consist of atoms, let alone many of them. Nor will matters improve if we look for a finer component than atoms, for what we find may also be regarded, I suppose, as a physical object if it is any proper component at all. Nor can a parallel with (3) be accepted readily. Unlike with a table, if you have a physical object and remove an atom, you may have left no physical object at all. For that atom, now removed, may have been the only physical object there to be removed. Now, none of this is to suppose that physical objects do exist. But, as the present argument does not compellingly disprove their existence, they appear to be a somewhat extraordinary thing, whether truly existent or only alleged for all that.

All in all, it may be said, I hope, that the argument I have employed is a rather *simple* piece of reasoning. I call this sort of argument the *sorites of decomposition*. A parallel argument, going the other way, suggests itself, *the sorites of accumulation*, as well as variations upon, and combinations of, both of these forms of reasoning. In particular, counterfactual variations should be of interest to many contemporary writers.

We employed our argument against tables, which, if they exist at all, have certain more or less special features. They are in some sense functional things; they are typically man-made; and so on. But none of this, it will be easily recognised, has anything to do with the matter at hand. Our argument may be employed equally well to deny the existence of such alleged things as sticks and stones, mountains and lakes, planets, (ordinary) stars and galaxies, ships and carriages, pieces of hair and of money, bodies of horses and of generals, and so on, and so forth. Such things as are not susceptible to decomposition withstand this form of argument: certain sub-atomic particles may provide an example. More importantly, decomposible things which are in a relevant way 'defined with precision' escape the present reasonings. Accordingly, I shall not now deny the existence of most molecules, even some 'quite large' ones, nor, perhaps, even certain crystal structures. However, something such as a blue 1968 Chevrolet four-door sedan, while according to most accounts not something vaguely described, will fall prey to our sorites. While much of physics and chemistry thus *might* remain relatively unscathed, biological entities, above the molecular level, appear to be nothing but fictions. I deny, then, not only the bodies of animals, including human beings, but also their organs, such as livers, hearts and brains, their tissues, and even individual cells, such as neurons.

Similar decomposition arguments make it clear, as well, that many alleged substances in fact do not exist at all. Unlike water and gold, which may be real, but which do not come in drops or hunks, juice and brass are only fictions. Also among the sorts of stuff that do not exist are, I should think, air and earth, meat and flesh, wood and rock, cloth and paper, and so on.

None of the things so far placed in the range of our reasonings, however, is of nearly so great an interest, I imagine, as we ourselves. Accordingly, I now turn to begin a new section, devoted to this topic, wherein I explicitly reason to deny, not without paradox, but perhaps with success, the very thing that Descartes would have me consider *certain*: my own present existence.

II. A Disproof of My Own Existence

The developing scientific perspective, especially owing to gains in biology and chemistry over the last few centuries, renders it exceedingly likely, at least, that no finite people or beings exist. In particular, and more conservatively, this perspective indicates that I myself do not exist; that I never have and never shall.

To achieve this paradoxical result, I shall again employ the sorites of decomposition. Now, the 'normal growth of the human being from conception' also provides, I believe, a sound sorites of accumulation. That sorites is naturally instanced, we might say, even though, with cellular growth not being clearly arithmetic, a unit of increment may have to be contrived: what happens during the first second; what happens during the next; and so on. But, the very artificiality of a gradual decomposition may better jar the mind. Thus, it may increase the chances for acceptance of the uncomfortable conclusion. Now, the most compelling decompositions are not yet attainable. We cannot remove, for example, one cell at a time, while keeping the remainder alive and functioning impressively. While it is not strictly relevant, I should think that this ability is not too far off for us, perhaps no more than a few centuries. In any case, if and when it can be done, I hope that it will not be. What is most relevant is that nature allow for the decompositions herein to be imagined.

As I have indicated, the unit of decrement which I shall choose is the cell. It is instructive for us now to argue at this level. As a cell consists of millions of atoms, a sorites of decomposition based on the atom can show that cells do not exist. Thus, the success of an argument against myself, or even my body, based on the cell, makes it quite clear that, in our argument against tables, the reliance on atoms was far from fundamental.

To mirror our previous argument, against tables, I now display the following three premisses:

(1) I exist.
(2) If I exist, then I consist of many cells, but a finite number.
(3) If I exist (and consist of many cells, but a finite number), then the net removal of one cell, or only a few, in a way which is most innocuous and favourable, will not mean the difference as to whether I exist.

As before, these three propositions form an inconsistent set. They have it that I am still there with no cells at all, even while my existence depends on cells. To escape this inconsistency realistically, we must suppose this. Even under conditions most favourable to me, the removal of a single cell, or only a few, *any* one or few of those in the situation, will mean the difference between my existence and no me at all. But, if I do exist, can my existence really be that tenuous? I think not. Therefore, I do not exist.

A bit more informally, the idea is this. One cell, more or less, will not mean the difference between my being there and not. So, take one away, and I am still there. Take another away; again, no problem. But after a while there are no cells at all. Indeed, as they have been replaced by nothing, in the relevant structures, it is unclear what will be there: perhaps, some salty water. Supposedly, I am still there. But given anything like the developed perspective of science, this is really quite absurd. Thus, the supposition of my existence has been reduced to an absurdity.

As before, it is important to discuss our third and final premiss. Because of the previous parallel discussion, various points may now be safely passed over. But a few new things arise in the present context which, even in a brief essay, are worthy of some consideration.

In the first place, it should be noted that, in the previous reasoning, about tables, we did not become involved in matters of identity, or persistence. There, I argued that *no* table, the same or any other, survived the decremental changes, and so *no* table existed in the first place. In contrast, the present argument does involve identity and, except for its counterfactual form, even persistence through time: I myself must survive. No new problems of importance are, I suggest, thus introduced for us. Indeed, we may abandon questions of identity entirely, and construct a general argument, upon the alleged existence of finite persons or beings, to parallel more completely our argument about tables. To play it safe with respect to such various forms as there may be of 'extra-terrestrial beings', we should then make our unit the atom, or even the particle, instead of the cell. It was to honour Descartes, so to say, and to pack the punch of particularity, that I focused the argument on myself, quite directly, thus becoming involved with identity. But that involvement is not essential.

In the second place, it will be maintained, I suppose, that my argument about tables did not involve considerations of life, or of consciousness. Let us grant this point. But how might such involvements as are now upon us serve to promote my own existence, or that of any finite being? I think there is no realistic way. Let us try to interpret our third premiss quite graphically, now, to clarify its import. On its most relevant interpretation, I suggest, life and consciousness, as well as the 'capacity' for them, will be present for as long as anyone might need to appreciate our argument's point. For it is supposed, in our third premiss, that the 'way' in which a cell is removed is one which is most innocuous and favourable—that is, with respect to me, or to my own identity. How might that happen?

At the present level of reasoning, the following scenario, I suggest, is more or less appropriate. At a certain stage in the decremental process, not very far along, it seems clear, life-support systems will be brought in to keep me going as well as possible. I shall be placed *in vitro*; nourishing fluids will be pumped into me; electrical stimulation will be provided, but not in such a way that any apparatus 'does my experiencing or thinking for me'; and so on. Cell after cell is pulled away. The remaining ones are kept alive, and kept functioning 'at the highest level of achievement of which they are capable'. The added apparatus has not, in the case here described, replaced the removed cells as part of me. In this present case, an electric wire will only be a means of support, much as a cardiac pacemaker serves even now.

While *other cases* may be construed as involving the replacement of natural parts by synthetic ones, this present one is not correctly understood in such terms. Sticking to what might here most plausibly be considered myself, then, at a certain point we are down to a brain in a vat and, then, half a brain. So far, so good; but then we get down to a third of a brain, then a sixteenth. Still later, there are only fifty-three neurons in living combination. Where at the end, there is but one living nerve cell, and then it too is gone. Where will I disappear from the scene? Realistically, now, will the removal of a single cell ever, under such favourable conditions, mean my disappearance from reality? While that may be a 'logical possibility', it does not compel belief. The conclusion of our argument, in contrast, is quite compelling: I do not disappear at any time, because I was never around in the first place.

We may agree that at one time it may have been a very compelling thought that there were souls, or individual essences, one for each person. Many people even now believe in such things, and in minds, a life force, if not entelechies, ghosts, spirits, and so on. Many of these believers, I imagine, think that a person is not only real, but an immaterial, indivisible entity. Thus, I expect, they lay the ground for a hope in survival of bodily death, and perhaps even immortality. At the time of Descartes, for example, it may be that all of these suppositions fairly demanded or compelled credence. But they do not sit well, I suggest, with our developed scientific perspective. For that reason, I believe, they offer no compelling alternative now to the bleak conclusions drawn herein.

My sorites of decomposition, against my own existence, has, to be sure, required some speculative effort. But such speculation as there may be is, I submit, far from wild. Further, it does jar the mind, and lets us look anew at the process of cellular development. We may reason justly, then, about the embryo growing from a fertilised egg, and we may conclude again, less speculatively, that, just like you, I do not exist. Against this more 'natural' argument, some would object, I suppose, that I myself was once nothing but a fertilised egg. Now, while I admire attempts to be consistent, I think that, in the present case, the attempt has little to recommend it, and is in any case erroneous. If someone persists in such a thought, however, I should bid him consider whether even a sperm, or an egg, was any existing entity, much less a fertilised egg. Accumulation and decomposition arguments, it seems, may also be used to refute the supposed existence of any of them.

III. The Substance of the Argument and the Irrelevance of Logical Inventions

The main thrust of this argument is, in light of our scientific perspective, the same in my own case and in those of a table, a stone and, for that matter, even of a yo-yo. Let us reconsider the matter, then, with respect to alleged yo-yos, for they give us an example which is refreshingly light and calmly unemotional. Again the main issues seem to turn on a suitable third premiss:

> For anything there may be, if it is a yo-yo (which consists of many atoms, but a finite number), then the net removal of one atom, or only a few, in a way which is most innocuous and favorable, will not mean the difference as to whether there is a yo-yo in the situation.

Now, how could such a premiss as this be false, and untrue, and inaccurate and unacceptable? Apart from minor matters of formulation, there are, it seems clear, only two ways in which things might go wrong for it.

First, and more on 'the side of things in the world', it might be that nature protected yo-yos, or at least one of them, by giving it a place of its own in the world, set apart from other things, an essence if you please. But how might anything like this actually obtain? The matter is, I think, very important, so, even if we repeat some of our previous words, let us try to outline the possibilities. First, yo-yos would be protected if, either at the start or at some later point, we just could not take out any atoms from them. Or, being realistic, and supposing that that way is not available, they might still be saved if new atoms were to rush in whenever crucial old ones were extracted. Or if that is out, as it surely appears to be, it might be that at some point, even under the most favourable conditions for relevant gradualness, a spontaneous explosion should take place, a yo-yo's previous existence thus being preserved by such sudden destruction. Or, failing that, which does seem more in line with any actual experience of the world, a god on high, or a suitable natural law, might turn an endangered dwindling yo-yo into a sousaphone, perhaps upon the removal of the four million and twelfth atom, so that our concepts themselves would never have to be tested on its behalf. And so on; and so forth. There are, then, many logical possibilities for nature to conspire, as it were, so that things would fit our term 'yo-yo'. But we are confident that none of them actually obtain. To think otherwise, I should say, is to expect a miracle: if you will, a *miracle of metaphysical illusion.*

With the world being so unfavourable for them, as it surely seems to be, the only chance for yo-yos lies on 'the side of our terms and concepts'. But what can be expected here? At the very least, we need the concept of a yo-yo to be atomically precise. Certain concepts of molecules seem to be thus precise: when you snip a hydrogen atom off the end somewhere, and do not replace it, you no longer have in the situation a molecule of that original kind. But is the concept of a yo-yo relevantly like that? I think we ask too much of ourselves if we expect ourselves to be working here in such a precise manner. Accordingly, to suppose this much for ourselves and 'yo-

yo' is to expect another miracle, perhaps a *miracle of conceptual comprehension*. On either hand, then, yo-yos require a miracle; for any who do not believe in miracles, there is no rational belief in yo-yos.

Our reasonings turn up for us an implicit contradiction in our beliefs. To strive to be reasonable we must give up one at least. To deny a suitable second premiss is to have yo-yos floating around with no atoms at all, nor any matter in the situation, and that is yet more miraculous than the two apparent wonders we have just considered. The only path to consistency, then, which is even remotely reasonable or realistic is to deny existence for alleged yo-yos, for we have just covered the whole story as to what wonders a commitment to them means. If this is appreciated we may see the irrelevance of remarks about clear cases, paradigms, family resemblances, and other soothing remedies, lately influential but now happily well on the wane. Perhaps more importantly, in these more technical times, we may also thus see the emptiness in the suggestion, currently favoured by certain philosophers, that we escape the argument by assigning to relevant sentences truth values other than truth and falsity.[3] For, whatever these values may be, they do not reduce one bit the miracles that yo-yos require; at most they occasion only a mildly different description of them.

Let us suppose we have before us a yo-yo. As atoms are removed one at a time, without replacement, we keep considering singular propositions each to the effect that at the appropriate new time a yo-yo is before us. We begin, as in any *reductio*, by assigning truth. As things progress, at some particular point, atomically counted, we are for the first time no longer to assign truth! Instead, when some peripheral atom is gently removed, and there would appear to be at least virtually no significant difference in what is before us, we are for the first time to depart from our initial kind of assignment, and to assign *some other* value. Perhaps the new value will not be falsity; it may be indefiniteness, or some numerical value just a shade less than unity, say 0.999, or some other newly invented candidate. But whatever else it is, there will be just as much of a miracle for us to expect. For, given that we have no miracle of metaphysical illusion to help us—that is, the world is indeed relevantly gradual—it will take a miraculous sensitivity on the part of 'yo-yo' to generate the difference, however we should choose to label such a wonderful discrimination. So sensitive is our concept of a yo-yo that, as a single atom goes away at the periphery, truth or unity or whatever is suddenly left behind! To expect that is, I submit, still to expect a miracle of conceptual comprehension. Hence, any new values, as well as the logical inventiveness they may occasion, are utterly irrelevant to the issues here.

Nor will it help matters to invoke a distinction between propositions and sentences, which may express or fail to express relevant propositions. Let us focus on the sentence 'There is a yo-yo before us now.' We may begin as before, with a putative paradigm yo-yo, and may then judge that our sentence expresses a proposition which is true. We then take off peripheral atoms, one at a time, and ask whether the sentence does something else, for the first time, with the removal of each single one. The supposition that with a single atom something else is for the first time done appears quite incredible, as well it should; it is but another form of our miracle of conceptual comprehension. But if this miracle may not be expected, then, if the sentence is not to express a truth with no atoms before us, we must conclude that our sentence never expresses a truth.[4]

Concerning the question of our putative yo-yos, then, it appears that only two responses are relevant: a belief in the miraculous or else an acceptance of nihilism. And the same choice, I submit, is there with alleged tables, and stones, and even my very own self. No matter how it is looked at, there is not much of a choice here. Habit and emotion appear on one side, while reason seems to be on quite the other.

IV. The Scope of these Problems

The argument I have employed derives, of course, from 'the paradox of the heap', an ancient problem devised by Eubulides, the great Megarian thinker. In way of reconstruction, we might say that Eubulides showed that there were and are no heaps. First, we may suppose the existence of heaps. Secondly, we note that, if any heap exists, it consists of various other entities—of grains of sand, or of beans, for example. Finally, we note that, if one bean is removed without replacement, and this is done most favourably and innocuously, what remains will be a heap. Thus, given anything like our view of reality, heaps, which many suppose to be ordinary existing things, are only fictions: there are no heaps.

I shall not here bother to detail the differences and similarities between Eubulides's original argument and my own variations upon it. So far as the compelling force goes, though, suffice it to say that our modern scientific perspective means that there is little difference between a heap and almost anything else, so to say, including myself. As far as repercussions or consequences are concerned, however, my own arguments are of course enormously more effective than the original version. While this is rather obvious, the details may be worth some presentation.

First, virtually all of our common-sense beliefs are untrue, and even as to nothing. Moreover, most of our learned studies are similarly unfortunate, at least in anything like their present formulations. Samuel Wheeler begins to put the point in a manner which is conjectural, and perhaps somewhat ironic: 'If there is no objective difference between possible persons and possible non-persons, much of what we believe about morality, psychology, etc., is in trouble.'[5] We may say, now, that the matter is not very conjectural, and that all of moral reasoning, as well as psychological understanding, looks to be in deep trouble indeed. This holds as well, of course, for the other studies concerning man. History, law and medicine are all a tissue of fictions, as are economics, linguistics and politics. Various related areas of philosophy, such as epistemology, the philosophy of language and the philosophy of mind, can contain nothing sound and true. Unless mathematics is clearly severed from connections with human beings, it too must fall prey to our sorites. Various other studies look to fare poorly. Biology, for example, is a tissue of nonentities and untruth, except as it becomes biochemistry perhaps, or something much of that sort. Astronomy too, except as it becomes astrophysics, or something similar, looks to be about anything but our universe.

Under a second head, we may notice that, while they may in some respects involve language importantly, our sorites arguments undermine all natural languages, while the argument of Eubulides hardly begins to do anything here. In the first place, as there are no human beings, there is no human language or thought. Waiving that basic point, and supposing the opposite, we shall notice that our existing expressions, at least by and large, fail to make any contact with whatever is there. For example, the proper names so far given do not refer to anything real. We may confirm this by a sorites argument directly involving such famous nonentities as Cicero, Descartes, Venus, Everest, and so on. Should someone name an individual atom 'Adam', things might be different on this score. The personal pronouns, we have seen, fare little better. Except for atoms, and so on, none of our referential devices look to be of much distinction.

But then, too, the picture looks bleak for the question of whether atoms exist, and so for any other things. For we cannot, in good faith, long waive the point that there is no human language or thought, nor even any human or other finite beings. And from such a standpoint even simple arithmetic looks to be beyond comprehension, there being none of us to grasp any realities or truth which might be there. Finally, the existence of any sorites arguments themselves cannot be relevantly affirmed, there being not a one of us ever to consider any such piece of reasoning. The chain of nihilistic propositions appears to come full circle.

This undeniable absurdity is, I suggest, no blameworthy fault of our Eubulidean reasonings. On the contrary, by such means, our sorites arguments allow us to perceive the truly thoroughgoing inconsistencies in our available language and thought. Continuing to speak in the paradoxical manner they expose, we might say this. For anything like truth's sake, these arguments counsel us to begin a radical reconstruction of our means of thought and expression. No available earthly means, which is sufficiently rich for many of our purposes, fares any better than does English. I have been disclosing no peculiar subtleties of our language which may be absent in Chinese, or in ancient Greek. But what steps should we take to make things better?

With something like a heap, and sticking to Eubulides's original level of argument, moderately good steps can be taken quickly and easily. For, if there are no heaps, we can define the word 'hoap', for example, so that a hoap may consist, minimally, of two items: for example, beans or grains of sand, touching each other. But, if there are no tables, trees or cats, what are we supposed to define, and, even very roughly, what is to be the definition of it? If I do not exist, then what does exist in which, so to speak, I should have an appropriate and rather intense interest? If you do not exist, as is here argued, what does exist over there which must not be inappropriately interfered with, or harmed? I am truly in darkness on these momentous matters, with no light at all to guide me.

These problems are, I believe, of the first importance for any who value philosophy and the traditional quest after truth. But I am far from sanguine that my challenge, from which they flow, will be met with an attempt to reply which is properly serious, let alone rationally effective. For it is easiest to shun the most pervasive difficulties in philosophy, to leave it to others, in times long to come, to explain their solutions. It is easiest to presume we know in advance, without knowing the details, which way the answer *must* go, letting the social acceptance of others serve as our assurance and even foundation, rather than anything like the light of one's own reason. But I am hopeful that one or two thoughtful souls may break the common easy pattern. Perhaps they will allow me to avoid the labours, apparently painful and fruitless, involved in developing an adequate philosophy of nihilism, which it now appears is the only adequate philosophy there can be. Or perhaps, on the contrary, they will provide me with further reason for thinking that this challenge is too powerful to be met adequately, and that there is no rational hope at all for the thought that anyone might be real. That might not be cheerful, but at least it would be something. Either way, I doubt that Eubulides ever had it so good.[6]

Notes

1. A. J. Ayer, *The Problem of Knowledge* (London: Macmillan, 1956) p. 50.
2. Samuel C. Wheeler III, 'Reference and Vagueness', *Synthèse*, XXX (1967) no. 3–4 367–79.
3. A recent example of a philosopher who would treat of vagueness by means of exotic truth values is David H. Sanford in his 'Borderline Logic', *American Philosophical Quarterly*, XII, (1975) no. 1, 29–39. Sanford provides references to other writers of a similar persuasion.
4. On these matters, I am indebted to discussion with David Sanford.

5. Wheeler, in *Synthese*, xxx (1967), no. 3–4, 371.

6. I have been helped in writing this paper by discussion with various people; Ralph Silverman and Samuel Wheeler deserve special thanks.

For a discussion of related matters, I refer the reader to my paper, 'There are No Ordinary Things'. *Synthese*, xli (1979), 117–54. For a detailed analysis of sorites arguments, see my 'Why There are No People', *Midwest Studies in Philosophy*, vol. IV: *Studies in Metaphysics*. And, for a discussion of relations between the nihilistic approach of this present paper and the sceptical approach in epistemology, see my 'Skepticism and Nihilism', *Noûs*, xiv (1980), 517–45.

10

The Doctrine of Arbitrary Undetached Parts

Peter Van Inwagen

1.

Many philosophers accept what I shall call the Doctrine of Arbitrary Undetached Parts (DAUP). Adherents of this doctrine believe in such objects as the northern half of the Eiffel Tower, the middle two-thirds of the cigar Uncle Henry is smoking, and the thousands (at least) of overlapping perfect duplicates of Michelangelo's *David* that were hidden inside the block of marble from which (as they see it) Michelangelo liberated the *David*. Moreover, they do not believe in only *some* "undetached parts"; they believe, so to speak, in *all* of them. The following statement of DAUP, though it is imperfect in some respects, at least captures the *generality* of the doctrine I mean to denote by that name:

> For every material object[1] M, if R is the region of space occupied[2] by M at time *t*, and if sub-R is *any* occupiable[3] sub-region of R *whatever*, there exists a material object that occupies the region sub-R at *t*.

(It should be obvious that DAUP, so defined, entails the existence of the northern half of the Eiffel Tower[4] and the other items in the above list.) This definition or statement or whatever it is of DAUP has, as I have said, certain imperfections as a statement of the doctrine I wish to describe certain philosophers as holding. One was mentioned in footnote 4. Another is this: there are philosophers who hold what is recognizable as a version of DAUP who would not be willing to admit regions of space into their ontologies.[5] Here is a third: this statement entails that material objects have boundaries so sharp that they occupy regions that are sets of points; and no adherent of DAUP that I know of would accept such a thesis about material objects.

I think the second one turns out to be crucial.

But these defects are irrelevant to the points that will be raised in the sequel and I shall not attempt to formulate a statement of DAUP that remedies them. For our purposes, therefore, DAUP may be identified with my imperfect statement of it.

What I want to say about DAUP involves only two components of that doctrine: (i) the arbitrariness of the parts—a *part* of an object is of course an object that occupies a sub-region of the region occupied by that object—whose existence it asserts (". . . *any* occupiable sub-region of R *whatever* . . .") and (ii) the concreteness and materiality of these parts. The second of these features calls for a brief comment. A philosopher might hold that, e.g., the northern half of the Eiffel Tower exists, but identify this item in his ontology with some *abstract* object, such as the pair whose first term is the Eiffel Tower and whose second term is the northern half of the region of space occupied by the Eiffel Tower. (If this idea were to be applied to moving, flexible objects or to objects that grow or shrink, it would have to be radically elaborated; I mean only to provide a vague, general picture of how one might identify parts with abstract objects.) This paper is not addressed to that philosopher's doctrine. It is addressed to DAUP, which holds that, e.g., the northern half of the Eiffel Tower is a concrete material particular in the same sense as that in which the Eiffel Tower itself is a concrete material particular.

2.

The Doctrine of Arbitrary Undetached Parts is false. It is also mischievous: it has caused a great deal of confusion in our thinking about material objects. But I shall not attempt to show that it is mischievous. I shall be content to show that it is false.

As a first step towards showing this, I shall show that DAUP entails a thesis very close to *mereological essentialism*: it entails the thesis that it is impossible for an object to lose any of its parts; that is, it entails the thesis that if a part is removed from an object, and no new part is added to the "remainder," then that object must therewith cease to exist. This is a weaker thesis than mereological essentialism proper, which entails that if a part is removed from an object, then that object must therewith cease to exist *whether or not* any part is added to the remainder.[6] We may call this weaker doctrine *Mereological Near-Essentialism* (MNE). I shall not raise the question whether DAUP entails mereological essentialism proper; it will do for my purposes to show that it entails MNE. (A parenthetical note. We are speaking at a very high level of abstraction. I have not said what it would be for an object to "lose" a part. An adherent of DAUP may very well believe in the existence of "scattered objects," that is, objects that are not "in one piece."[7] Whether he does or not will depend on which regions he takes to be occupiable in the sense of note 3. Someone who accepts the existence of scattered objects might very well accept the following account of cutting a cake. If I cut a cake and separate the newly cut piece from the remainder, I have not caused anything to "lose a piece"; I have merely changed a certain cake from a non-scattered to a scattered object. Thus, in this context and at this level of generality, it is not clear just what "losing a part" may come down to. Still, the *annihilation* of a part would seem to be sufficient for the losing of it. In any case, the loss of parts is possible or it isn't. If it is, then MNE refers to just those possible cases that count as losses of parts, whether by separation or annihilation. If it isn't, MNE is a vacuously necessary truth and is thus entailed by DAUP.)

I shall now show that DAUP entails MNE. Assume that DAUP is true and MNE false. It follows from the falsity of MNE that there is a time (which for simplicity's sake I shall assume to be the present) such that there could be objects O and P such that P is a part of O at that time and such that O could survive the subsequent loss of P. Suppose such objects exist. By DAUP there is an object that occupies just that region of space that is the set-theoretic difference between the region occupied by O and the region occupied by P.[8] Call this object O-minus, O-minus is numerically diverse from O, since they occupy different regions of space and have different parts. Now suppose O were to lose P; for good measure let us suppose P to be annihilated, all other parts of O remaining unchanged, except for such changes in them as may be logically necessitated by the annihilation of P. It would seem that O-minus would still exist. Admittedly, this is not a formally demonstrable consequence of DAUP. Nevertheless, the proposition that a thing cannot cease to exist *simply* because something that was *not* a part of it is "detached" from it seems to be a sufficiently obvious conceptual truth that we may in good conscience use it as a premise. We have seen that O could (logically) have survived the annihilation of P. Let us suppose it has. What is the relation (now) between O and O-minus? Only one answer would seem to be possible: identity. "Each" is a material object, after all, and "they" now have the same boundaries, and, in fact, share all their "momentary" physical properties. Someone *might* say that O and O-minus are two material objects that now have the same size, shape, position, weight, orientation in space, linear velocity, angular velocity, and so on, these two objects being numerically distinct simply in virtue of their having different histories. But this *I* cannot conceive of; if the meaning of 'material object' is such as to allow the conceptual possibility of this, then I do not understand 'material object' and therefore do not understand DAUP. We have reached the conclusion that O is now O-minus. But O and O-minus were once diverse (when P was a part of O) and thus we have arrived at a violation of the principle of the transitivity of identity. Hence we must reject our assumption that MNE is false, and we have shown that DAUP entails MNE.[9]

I should be the last to deny that there are disputable steps in this argument. In the next section we shall apply this general argument to a particular case, and I shall try to leave no disputable contention undefended. What I shall say may, I hope, be applied to the general case.

Let us agree for the nonce that I have shown that DAUP entails MNE. So what? Why shouldn't the proponent of DAUP simply accept MNE? No reason, I suppose. Unless there is some object that is known to be capable of surviving the loss of a part.

3.

There is. We ourselves, we men and women, are such objects. Or at least we are if we *have* parts; whether or not we have parts is a question the correct answer to which depends on the correct answer to the general, theoretical questions raised in this paper. But, at any rate, we all too frequently undergo, and often survive, episodes of the sort that it is correct to describe in ordinary speech as "losing a finger" or "losing a leg." I wish to examine in detail one such episode—a fictional one involving a real person—on the assumption that DAUP is true. (We shall reach an absurd result—that identity is not transitive—and we shall therefore have to conclude that DAUP is false.) We have already seen, in the preceding section, in abstract outline, what our examination of this episode will reveal.

Consider Descartes and his left leg.[10] (The adherent of DAUP is going to have a certain amount of trouble with Descartes's left leg: there are, according to DAUP, an enormous number of objects that are equally good candidates for the office of "Descartes's left leg." I shall not address this problem. I shall assume in the sequel that some one of these candidates has been chosen, by fair means or foul, to fill this office.) If DAUP is true, then at any moment during Descartes's life, there was a thing (problems of multiplicity aside) that was his left leg at that moment. Let us pick some moment, call it t_0, during Descartes's life, and let 'L' designate the thing that was his leg at the moment. There *also* existed at that moment, according to DAUP, a thing we shall call *D-minus*, the thing that occupied at t_0 the region of space that was the set-theoretic difference between the region occupied by Descartes and the region occupied by L. Obviously, Descartes and D-minus were not the same thing (at t_0), since, at t_0 they were differently shaped. Now suppose that at t (shortly after t_0), L and D-minus became separated from each other; for good measure, let us suppose that L was then annihilated.

It would seem that after this episode—which I assume could be correctly described in the idiom of everyday life like this: Descartes's left leg was cut off and then destroyed—D-minus still existed. The survival by D-minus of its separation from L is not a formal consequence of DAUP. Still, how can we avoid this conclusion? It seems simply *true*, an inescapable consequence of the requirement of DAUP that the undetached parts of material objects be themselves, in the same sense, material objects. What "material objects" are may not be altogether clear. But if you can cause a thing to cease to exist by detaching from it (or even by destroying) something that was *not* one of its parts but simply part of its *environment*, while leaving the arrangement of all *its* parts wholly unchanged, if you can do *that*, then, I maintain, you have not got anything that can properly be called a material object.

It would seem that after this episode, Descartes still existed. One can, after all, survive the loss of a leg.

But if both Descartes and D-minus survived the severance of L from D-minus at *t*, what was the relation between them immediately after *t*? Only one answer is possible: they were then identical. If they were not, then we should have to admit that there was a time at which there were two material objects having the *same* size, shape, position, orientation, attitude, mass, velocity (both linear and angular), and color. Someone *might* say this, I suppose, but I should not understand him and I suspect that no one else would either.

We may also reach the conclusion that Descartes and D-minus were identical after *t* by a slightly different route. Before *t*, D-minus was *ex hypothesi* a part of Descartes. At *t*, Descartes lost L and lost no other parts (save parts of him that overlapped L). Therefore, after *t* Descartes had D-minus as a part. But, clearly, after *t*, no part of Descartes was "larger" than D-minus—that is, no part of Descartes had D-minus as a *proper* part. Therefore, Descartes (after t) had D-minus as an improper part. Therefore, after *t*, Descartes and D-minus were identical.

Our argument has led us to this conclusion: that there was a time at which Descartes and D-minus were identical. And, as we have noted, there was an earlier time at which they were *not* identical. But if this is correct, then there was once an object that had earlier been two objects, which is a plain violation of the principle of the transitivity of identity. I mean it is a violation of the principle of the transitivity of identity *simpliciter*, by the way, and not of a principle that claims transitivity for some "specialized" version of identity like "identity through time." So far as I can see, there is no relation called "identity through time," unless those words are simply another name for identity *simpliciter*. We may represent explicitly the violation of the transitivity of identity I contend we have arrived at as follows. If our argument is correct then all four of the following propositions are true:

> The thing that was D-minus before t = the thing that was D-minus after t
> The thing that was D-minus after t = the thing that was Descartes after t
> The thing that was Descartes after t = the thing that was Descartes before t
> The thing that was D-minus before $t \neq$ the thing that was Descartes before t.[11]

Thus our *reductio* has been accomplished, and we must conclude that there was never any such thing as D-minus. Therefore, DAUP is false, for DAUP entails that there was such a thing as D-minus.

We can, in fact, easily reach an even more striking conclusion: L does not exist either: there was never any such thing as Descartes's left leg. We need only one premise to reach this conclusion, namely that if L existed, D-minus did too. And this premise seems quite reasonable, for it would seem wholly arbitrary to accept the existence of L and to deny the existence of D-minus. In more senses than one, L and D-minus stand or fall together. If these things existed, they would be things of the same sort. Each would be an *arbitrary* undetached part of a certain man.[12] This fact may be disguised by our having (problems of multiplicity and vagueness aside) what is a customary and idiomatic name for L if it is a name for anything: "Descartes's left leg." But this is a linguistic accident that reflects our interests. (We may imagine a race of rational beings who raise human beings as meat animals. Suppose these beings, for religious reasons, never eat left legs. They might very well have in their language some customary and idiomatic phrase that stands to D-minus in the same relation as that in which the English phrase 'Descartes's left leg' stands to L.)

If our argument against DAUP also leads to the conclusion that there never was any such thing as Descartes's left leg (which I am willing to grant), this may lead some people to think that there *must* be something wrong with the argument. Here is a leg (one is tempted to say) and here is another leg, and therefore van Inwagen is wrong. I am not entirely out of sympathy with this reaction. If a philosophical argument leads us to deny something that every human being in history has believed, then it is a pretty good bet that something is wrong with the argument. But I doubt that in saying that there never was any such thing as Descartes's left leg[13] I am denying anything that has been believed, as the Church says, *ubique et ab omnibus*.[14] The proposition I mean to express by the words 'There never was any such thing as Descartes's left leg' does not, as I see it, entail the falsity of, e.g., the proposition that Descartes scratched his left leg on the morning of his eleventh birthday. I think I could show this. To make good this claim, I should at least have to provide some reason for thinking that sentences that apparently involve reference to or quantification over the limbs of animals can be translated into sentences that don't even apparently involve such reference or quantification. I believe I could do this, but this is not the place for it. My purpose in the present paragraph is to explain what sort of position my position on the nonexistence of Descartes's left leg is, and not to defend that position. (My position is comparable to that of many other philosophers who have denied the existence of various objects in order to escape the paradoxical consequences that they thought, rightly or wrongly, would follow from the existence of such objects. Philosophers who have denied the existence of the material substrate have not, in general, denied the existence of tables and chairs; philosophers who have denied the existence of sense-data have not, in general, denied the existence of perception or even the existence of a distinction between appearance and reality; philosophers who have denied the existence of pains have not, in general, denied the existence of pain.) -

Nonetheless, an argument that leads to the conclusion that there never was any such thing as Descartes's left leg is at least *prima facie* objectionable. But all the objections to this argument I know of involve principles or lead to conclusions that, in my view at least, are more objectionable than the proposition that Descartes's left leg did not exist. In the remainder of this section and in the two sections that follow I shall examine these objections.

There are four objections, or types of objection, that I shall simply dismiss.

I shall simply dismiss any objection that involves a denial of the principle of the transitivity of identity. People who take this line are, as Professor Geach would say, "not to be heard." Anyone who rejects the principle of the transitivity of identity simply does not understand the difference between the number one and the number two.

I shall simply dismiss any objection that involves the contention that it would have been logically impossible for Descartes to survive the loss of a leg.[15] I do not know if anyone would say this, but if anyone would, he too is not to be heard.

I shall simply dismiss any objection that involves the contention that it would have been impossible for D-minus to survive being separated from L.

I shall simply dismiss any objection that involves the contention that it was possible for Descartes and D-minus to have been numerically distinct material objects having the same momentary physical properties. (I would not go so far as to say that such objections are not to be heard. I dismiss them because I cannot understand them and therefore have nothing to say about them.)

I know of two objections to my argument that are worthy of extended consideration. I shall call them the *Chisholm Objection* and the *Lewis Objection*. I will discuss them in the two sections that follow.

4.

The Chisholm Objection. It will not have escaped the reader's attention that my argument assumes that Descartes was a flesh-and-blood object that, when unmutilated, was shaped like a statue of Descartes. Many philosophers, including Descartes, would reject this assumption. Though I am myself convinced of its truth beyond all doubt and beyond all possibility of conversion by philosophical argument, I admit that it is highly controversial. To be sure, few philosophers would deny either that there was once a flesh-and-blood object shaped like a statue of Descartes or that that object was somehow intimately related to Descartes. But many philosophers would deny what seems evident to me: that he (that thing that thought) *was* that object. These philosophers would say that that object was not Descartes but rather his *body*. The philosopher who thus distinguishes between Descartes and his body and who wishes to accept the existence of D-minus may reply to the argument of Section 3 as follows:

> I can accept the existence of D-minus, and I can accept the proposition that Descartes was capable of surviving the loss of a leg, and I can accept the principle of the transitivity of identity, and your arguments do not show that my acceptance of these things forces upon me the desperate expedient of admitting that it is conceptually possible for there to be two conterminous material objects. I need only say—and I *do* say it—that D-minus was not a part of Descartes but only a part of Descartes's *body*.

And this response is perfectly proper. But this is not the end of the matter, for certain consequences follow upon it.

First, though my imaginary philosopher has escaped the consequences of the assumption that D-minus was a part of Descartes, he must nonetheless face the consequences of conceding that D-minus was a part of Descartes's body. Here is one: that Descartes's body (that is, the thing that at any given moment was the body Descartes had *then*) could not have survived the loss of a part. This could be easily shown by a trivial modification of the argument of Section 3. Moreover, since, as a matter of empirical fact, human bodies are (to speak with the vulgar) constantly exchanging matter with their surroundings, he must concede that Descartes is continually "changing bodies"; and not just every now and then, but hundreds of times every second. Well, perhaps he will be willing to say this. We have shown independently of any considerations involving persons and their bodies that DAUP entails MNE, and the continual changing of one's body is a consequence of the proposition that at any given time one has some body or other, together with MNE and certain empirical facts about the human organism.

There is, however, a much more serious and far-reaching consequence of our imaginary philosopher's objection to the argument of Section 3. Of those philosophers I know of who have thought about these matters, only Roderick Chisholm has seen the inevitability of this consequence.[16] I therefore call the above objection to the argument of Section 3 the *Chisholm Objection*, provided that it is understood to include the consequence I shall set forth in the following paragraphs.

If DAUP is true, then a human being, if he lasts from one moment to the next, cannot during that interval lose any parts. This is simply a consequence of the fact that DAUP entails MNE. Now there may be some "everyday" material objects that endure for appreciable periods of time according to the strict standards of endurance entailed by MNE. The Hope Diamond, say, or a fly in amber. But none of these observable, enduring material things is you or I. Therefore, if DAUP is true, and if you and I last from one moment to the next, we cannot be everyday material objects. I concede that there are observable material things other than the statue-shaped flesh-and-blood objects that *I* think you and I are that, according to reputable philosophers, are what you and I are. For example, some reputable philosophers think that you and I are living human brains. But such views are no more consistent with DAUP than is my own, for no such view is consistent with MNE and, therefore, no such view is consistent with DAUP. (Suppose for example that I am a brain. Surely I can survive the loss of some part of myself; a single cell, say. Let P be a part of me I can survive the loss of. Let B-minus be the object that occupies the region that is the set-theoretic difference between the region occupied by my brain—that is, by me—and the region occupied by P . . .)

It would seem, therefore, that (given our persistence through time, the transitivity of identity, and so on) it follows from DAUP that we are not observable material things, or, at any rate, that we are not material things of any sort that *has* so far been observed. Therefore, anyone who accepts DAUP must either accept the thesis that we are not material things or else accept the thesis that we are material things of a kind very different from any kind that has ever been observed.

The difficulties with the thesis that we are, contrary to all appearances, immaterial things, are well known.

Let us examine the thesis that we are material things of a sort that has never been observed. Anyone who accepts this may reasonably be expected to answer the question. *Why* have we so far gone unobserved? It cannot be for want of people's poking and prying inside human bodies. There are, I think, three possible answers.

(i) We have gone unobserved because we are very small; perhaps as small as or smaller than a single cell. Presumably an object that small, or even a bit larger, might be located inside our bodies—inside our brains if anywhere, I should think—and have escaped the attention of the most assiduous physiologists.

(ii) We have gone unobserved because we are made of some sort of subtle matter (the "nameless and unknown" soul-stuff of Epicurus and Lucretius) that can affect gross, everyday matter—or else we should not have charge of our bodies—but which affects it to such a small degree that physicists have not yet taken note of its effects.

(iii) We have gone unobserved because we are far from our bodies, with which we interact at a distance.

We may note that (i), (ii) and (iii) are not exclusive alternatives: perhaps we are at once tiny, subtle, and far away.

Let us call an object a *Chisholm Object* if it is a concrete particular that thinks and wills and is the cause of the voluntary movements of a human body and is in practice unobservable, either because it is immaterial (a Cartesian ego) or, if material, tiny or made of subtle matter or remote from the human body it controls.

We may now state the Chisholm Objection more adequately:

> Your argument has a false premise: that D-minus was a part of Descartes. Moreover, there is no true proposition that you could use in place of the proposition that D-minus was a part of Descartes in some reconstructed argument against DAUP, for Descartes was a Chisholm Object; if he ever lost a part, he lost it in 1650 (the year of his death) or later. Moreover, in the strict, philosophical sense (to borrow Bishop Butler's fine phrase) of *same* it is very unlikely that there was any appreciable interval throughout which Descartes had the same body.

I think that this is the only possible objection to my argument that is not demonstrably wrong. I have nothing to say against it except that I do not believe a word of it. But that is a psychological report, not an argument. Doubtless there are philosophers who find equally incredible my contention that, in the strict, philosophical senses of *was* and *thing*, there never was any such thing as Descartes's left leg.

I think that the arguments of this section and the preceding section show that anyone who accepts DAUP should also accept the proposition that every person is a Chisholm Object. For my part, I say so much the worse for DAUP. At any rate, I am fairly sure that few philosophers would find acceptance of the propositions the Chisholm Objection commits its adherents to an acceptable price to pay for DAUP.

5.

The Lewis Objection. One philosopher who balks at paying this price and who is nevertheless attracted to DAUP is David Lewis.[17] Lewis argues, *à la* Gaunilon, that my reasoning must be faulty since parallel reasoning leads to an obviously false conclusion.[18]

Consider the Austro-Hungarian Empire in, say, 1900. In 1900, Austria existed and Hungary existed and these two countries composed the Empire. That is, they did not overlap and the portion of the earth's surface occupied by one or the other was just exactly the portion of the earth's surface occupied by the Empire. Thus in a very obvious sense, these two countries stood to the Empire as L and D-minus (if such there were) stood to Descartes. Now (the Lewis Objection runs) consider the following argument:

> Suppose that the Martians had totally destroyed Hungary and had left the territory occupied by Austria untouched. We can only suppose that Austria would have

> survived this destruction of Hungary. We can only suppose that the Austro-Hungarian Empire (whose capital at Vienna of course escaped destruction) would also have survived the destruction of Hungary. (True, "the Austro-Hungarian Empire" might not have been a very good *name* for it thereafter; but the example of the Holy Roman Empire shows that the name of an empire need not be a *good* name.) Empires and other states can increase and decrease in extent and can gain and lose parts without losing their identities (consider, for example, the fact that the United States survived the admission into the Union of Alaska and Hawaii). The act we have supposed the Martians to have performed would have caused the Empire to lose a part without causing it to cease to exist. Now what would have been the relation between Austria and the Empire after the destruction of Hungary? We can only suppose that it would have been identity, for what distinction would there have been between them? Moreover, Austria would have been the largest part of the Empire, and, according to any acceptable mereology, the largest part of a thing is its sole improper part, itself. But this is to suppose that the Empire might have been Austria at one time and not at another, which would be a violation of the principle of the transitivity of identity. Since the principle of the transitivity of identity is a necessary truth, only one conclusion is possible: Austria did not exist in 1900. Moreover, since Hungary existed in 1900 if and only if Austria did, Hungary did not exist in 1900 either.

Since the conclusion of this argument is absurd, there must be something wrong with the argument. But the argument is sound if and only if our earlier *reductio* arguments are sound. Therefore they are not sound.

I reject the Lewis Objection. I believe it contains a false premise: that after the destruction of Hungary, Austria and the Empire would have been identical. I say they would merely have occupied the same territory. They would have differed in many of their properties. Two examples would be historical properties (the Empire would have had the property *having had Hungary as a part*; Austria would not have had it) and modal properties (the Empire would have had the property *possibly having Bavaria as a part*; Austria would not have had it).

As to the "largest part" argument, though one politico-geographical entity may correctly be said to be "part" of another, "part" in this sense does not obey the laws of any mereology I know of.[19] Call this relation the *PG-part relation*. It would seem that it should be defined as follows: A is a PG-part of B if the territory occupied by A is a part (in the standard, spatial sense) of the territory occupied by B. If this definition is accepted—and what are the alternatives?—then there would seem to be only one natural definition of 'A is a larger PG-part of B than C is' and only one natural definition of 'A is a proper PG-part of B'; in fact, these definitions are so natural it would be pedantic to state them. But it follows from these natural definitions that there need be no such thing as the largest PG-part of a politico-geographical entity, and, moreover, that a politico-geographical entity may have improper PG-parts other than itself. Take, for example, the City of Washington and the District of Columbia. Each of these is an improper PG-part of the other, and yet, by the principle of the non-identity of discernibles, they are numerically diverse. For example, the District of Columbia has the properties *having been the same size throughout its existence, not being a city,* and *having had Georgetown as a PG-part in 1850;* Washington has none of them. If matters had gone as we imagined with Austria and the Austro-Hungarian Empire, then this would have been just their situation: each would have been an improper PG part of the other.

Therefore, the Lewis Objection fails, since the "parallel" argument Lewis produces, though it indeed has an absurd conclusion, is not really parallel to the *reductio* arguments of sections 2 and 3. In a nutshell, the reason is this: "parts" of material objects and "parts" of politico-geographical entities do not work the same way. If an "improper part" of a material object is a material object that occupies the same region of space as that object, then every material object has exactly one improper part: itself. If an "improper part" of a politico-geographical entity that occupies the same territory as that entity, then every politico-geographical entity has *at least* one improper part: itself; but some have more.

6.

The Chisholm Objection I cannot accept. The Lewis Objection fails. I therefore find no reason to doubt the soundness of our *reductio* arguments, and I conclude that, though (I have no doubt) there are undetached parts, there are not "just any" undetached parts. That is, I conclude that DAUP is false. In this, the final section, I will show how what has been said in the earlier sections may be applied to another sort of "part."

Some philosophers would call "parts" of the sort we have been talking about, 'spatial parts'. They would oppose them to *temporal* parts. I fully accept the arguments of Chisholm and Geach for the conclusion that the idea of a temporal part is incoherent.[20] I simply do not understand what these things are supposed to be, and I do not think this is my fault. I think that no one understands what they are supposed to be, though of course plenty of philosophers think they do. (If anyone who thinks he does understand temporal parts feels inclined to charge me with conceptual arrogance, I invite him to consider the following list: the Absolute Idea; impossible objects; Cartesian egos; bare particulars; things-in-themselves; pure acts of will; simple, non-natural properties; logically perfect languages; sense-data. I think it very likely that he will find that there is at least one item on this list that he has no glimmering of an understanding of. Yet each of them has been believed in by great philosophers. Anyone, therefore, who fails to understand some item on this list is no less conceptually arrogant than I.) But if I do not understand temporal parts, I at any rate understand what parameters are supposed by most philosophers who say they believe in them to individuate them: to each persisting object and each occupiable interval of time such that that object exists at every moment in that interval, there corresponds a *concrete* particular that is a temporal part of that object.[21] (Of course if some philosopher wishes to call an object-interval pair a "temporal part" of its first term, I have no objection.) So far as I know, no philosopher who believes there are *any* temporal parts thinks that there could be some occupiable sub-interval of the interval during which a given object exists that is *not* occupied by a temporal part of that object. That is to say, all philosophers who accept the existence of (proper) temporal parts, would accept what might be called the Doctrine of Arbitrary Temporal Parts (DATP)[22]:

> For every persisting object P, if I is the interval of time occupied by P and if sub-I is *any* occupiable sub-interval of I *whatever*, there exists a persisting object that occupies the interval sub-I and which, for every moment *t* that falls within sub-I, has at *t* exactly the same momentary properties[23] that P has.

This doctrine is formally very similar to DAUP. (The differences in structure can, I think, be traced to the fact that there are three spatial dimensions and only one temporal dimension.)

There is at least one philosopher, the author of this paper, who thinks that while there *are* undetached spatial parts, comparatively few of the occupiable regions that fall wholly within a given material object are occupied. (See footnote 9.) *I* think this because I think that the cells living things are made of are, in a sense I cannot here explore, *unitary* things, things having an entelechy; in this respect they are like the men, women, and dogs (Thurber's list) of which they are parts. It is very hard to see how anyone could take a similar attitude toward temporal parts. I reject the Doctrine of Arbitrary Undetached (Spatial) Parts. But if there were temporal parts, then they would *all* be "arbitrary": there are no temporal analogues of cells.

Or perhaps this is wrong. Perhaps there is one sort of temporal part such that one could affirm the existence of parts of this sort and, without appearing to be placing wholly arbitrary restrictions on one's ontology, deny the existence of all other (proper) temporal parts. I am thinking of *instantaneous* temporal parts, those that occupy a mathematical instant of time, an interval of measure 0. In what follows, I am going to adopt the arguments that were employed earlier in this paper against DAUP to the task of showing that DATP is false. I think that anyone who, perhaps impressed by my argument, rejects DATP and who wants to believe in *some* temporal parts has only one possibility open to him: he must believe in the improper temporal part of an object (i.e., the object itself) and he must believe in all the instantaneous parts of the object and in no other parts. He must, for example, believe in Descartes and he must believe in the part of Descartes that occupied *t*, where *t* is any *instant* of time at which Descartes existed, and he must *not* believe in the part of Descartes that occupied the year 1625. I shall offer no arguments against *this* doctrine of temporal parts.

I said in the preceding paragraph that I should argue that DATP was false. I spoke loosely. DATP is not false. It is meaningless because the notion of a temporal part is meaningless. Or, at any rate, *I* don't understand it. But I *can* give an argument that *would* be an argument for the falsity of DATP if that doctrine made any sense. I can do this because, as I said above, though I do not understand the notion of a temporal part, I know what parameters are supposed to individuate temporal parts. Moreover, I can justifiably assume that discourse about temporal parts must satisfy certain formal constraints that I am familiar with from my understanding of parts *simpliciter.* But this self-justification is too abstract to convey much. Let us turn to the argument.

Our argument against DAUP depended on its being possible for a thing to lose its parts, or, more accurately, for its parts to become separated or to be annihilated. Nothing like this can figure in an argument about temporal parts: no one would suppose that two "adjoining" temporal parts of a thing might become separated or that a temporal part of a thing might cease to exist. (I *think*. I'm feeling my way about in the dark, you understand. The chair I'm sitting on is supposed to be a temporal part of itself and *it* could cease to exist.) At any rate, I won't assume this is possible. But one can assume, I think, that adjoining temporal parts of a thing might not have been in "contact"; not, perhaps, that there might have been an interval between them, but, at any rate, that one of them might not have existed. Take Descartes, for example. Let L be the temporal part of Descartes that occupied the last year of Descartes's existence.[24] Let D-minus be the temporal part of Descartes that occupied the interval from Descartes's birth (or conception or whenever it was he began to exist) to the moment exactly one year before Descartes ceased to exist. Though L and D-minus were in fact "joined" to each other, there would not seem to have been any necessity to this; there are surely possible worlds in which D-minus exists and L does not, either because *no* temporal part of Descartes adjoins D-minus or because some part other than L does.

Now if this is so, then it is easy to adapt our earlier methods to the task of deducing an absurdity from the proposition that there was such a thing as D-minus. If there was such a thing as D-minus, then there was such a thing as L, and the relations that held between D-minus, L, and Descartes are those that were described in the preceding paragraph. In that case, obviously, D-minus and Descartes were not identical. But suppose, as seems possible, that Descartes had ceased to exist exactly one year earlier than he in fact did; or, if you like, suppose, as seems possible, that D-minus had not been "attached to L" or "continuous with L" (or however one should put it). What then would have been the relationship that held between D-minus and Descartes? What could it have been but identity? To suppose otherwise is to suppose that a thing might have had two improper temporal parts. But if D-minus and Descartes could have been identical, then there are two things that could have been one thing. This is not only a violation of an obvious *modal* principle about identity ('$x \neq y \supset \Box x \neq y$'), it is a violation of the principle of the transitivity of identity *simpliciter*. This may be seen from inspection of the following four propositions (in which '*t*' denotes the moment exactly one year before the moment at which Descartes ceased to exist):

D-minus = the thing that would have been D-minus if Descartes had ceased to exist at *t*
The thing that would have been D-minus if Descartes had ceased to exist at *t* = the thing that would have been Descartes if Descartes had ceased to exist at *t*
The thing that would have been Descartes if Descartes had ceased to exist at *t* = Descartes
D-minus ≠ Descartes.[25]

I have not presented any explicit argument for the conclusion that all four of these propositions can be derived from the assumption that D-minus exists (and would have existed if Descartes had ceased to exist at *t*). I should do so if this paper consisted solely of an attack on DATP. But I have devoted a good deal of space to an argument showing that DAUP entails a violation of the principle of the transitivity of identity, and I believe the reader will find it an easy task to construct the arguments I *would* give (if pressed) for the conclusion that DATP entails a violation of that principle.

I conclude that DATP fails for much the same reason that DAUP fails. More exactly, I conclude that if anyone ever does provide some explanation of the notion of a temporal part (thus bringing DATP into existence: at present there is no such doctrine), then DATP *will* fail for much the same reason that DAUP fails.[26]

Notes

1. I shall not define *material object*.

2. I shall assume that the space we inhabit is a three-dimensional continuum of *points*. A *region* is any set of points. Suppose we agree that we know what it means to say that a given point in space *lies within* a given material object at a given moment. Then an object *occupies* a certain region at a certain moment if that region is the set containing all and only those points that lie within that object at that moment.

3. A region of space is *occupiable* if it is possible (in what Plantinga calls "the broadly logical sense") for it to be occupied by a material object. Presumably not all

regions of space are occupiable. Consider a spherical region S; consider that sub-region of S that consists of just the points within S that are at distances from the center of S that have irrational measures: it is certainly hard to see how this sub-region could be occupied by a material object. I shall not discuss occupiability further, however, since its exact nature is not relevant to the issues that we shall be taking up. For an interesting proposal about occupiable regions, see Richard Cartwright's fine paper "Scattered Objects" in *Analysis and Metaphysics* ed. by Keith Lehrer (Dordrecht: D. Reidel, 1975). If we accept Cartwright's account of what it is for a region to be occupiable (to be what he calls a "receptacle"), then DAUP is an immediate consequence of (though it does not entail) what he calls the *Covering Principle*.

4. More precisely: DAUP entails that, for any time *t*, if the Eiffel Tower exists at *t*, and if the northern half of the space it occupies at *t* is then occupiable—and I think no one would want to deny *that*—then there exists an object at *t* that occupies that space, an object it would certainly be natural to call "the northern half of the Eiffel Tower." There is a thesis that DAUP intuitively "ought" to entail that my statement of it does *not* entail. Consider two times *t* and *t′*. Suppose that the Eiffel Tower exists and has the same location and orientation in space at both these times. Suppose that at both these times it consists of the same girders, struts, and rivets, arranged in the same way. The thesis: the thing that is the northern half of the Eiffel Tower at *t* is identical with the thing that is the northern half of the Eiffel Tower at *t′*. I regard the failure of my statement of DAUP to entail this thesis as a defect in that statement. (I *think* this entailment fails to hold. It certainly cannot be shown formally to hold. For all I know, however, there may be some feature of the concept of a material object in virtue of which it *does* hold.)

5. Argle for example. See "Holes" by David and Stephanie Lewis, *The Australian Journal of Philosophy*, 48 (1970).

6. Mereological essentialism proper also entails that a thing could not have "started out with" different parts, which is not a consequence of the weaker thesis. For general discussions of mereological essentialism, see Roderick M. Chisholm, "Parts as Essential to Their Wholes." *The Review of Metaphysics* XXVI (1973) and *Person and Object: A Metaphysical Study* (La Salle: Open Court, 1976), Appendix B.

7. Scattered objects' is Cartwright's term. See his article of that title (cited in note 3, above) for a precise definition of 'scattered object'.

8. Here I assume the following principle: if A is a material object and B is (a material object that is) a part of A and if R_A is the region occupied by A and R_B is the region occupied by B, then R_A minus R_B is occupiable. If there is any doubt about this principle, it could be proved as follows. Imagine that B was annihilated and that all else remained the same. Then R_A *would be* occupied by a material object (even if it hadn't been before the annihilation of B). This principle is, strictly speaking, false if certain views about occupiability are correct, since it assumes that both "closed" and "open" regions are occupiable. (This is an implicit assumption of our little proof.) Those who care about such things will see that this assumption could be removed at the cost of a little elaboration that would not materially affect the use made of the principle in the body of the paper. Those who wish to deny the existence of "scattered objects" may wish to append the clause 'if topologically connected' to the principle.

9. A very similar argument can be found in Cartwright, *op. cit.*, pp. 164–166. Someone might argue that if the above argument is sound, then it can be extended in the following way to prove not simply that MNE follows from DAUP but that MNE is true *simpliciter:* Either there are undetached parts or there aren't: if there aren't, then MNE is vacuously true: if there are, then our argument can be used to show that MNE is true. This reaction conflates DAUP with the thesis that there are undetached parts. Any argument like the one I have presented in the text would have to employ some principle that allowed the arguer pass from the existence of the object O and the part P to the existence of the object O-minus. This is just what DAUP allows one to do. (Of course there are weaker principles that would legitimize this inference.) Therefore, if one rejects DAUP (and if one accepts no other principle that would legitimize the inference of the existence of O-minus from the existence of O and P), one can consistently believe in the existence of undetached parts that are not essential to their wholes. I, for example, believe that there exists a cell in my right hand that is an undetached part of me and such that I could survive the loss of it. I can consistently believe this because I do not think that there is any such object as "I-minus-that-cell"; that is, if R is the region of space I occupy and r is the region of space that cell occupies, I do not think that there exists any object that occupies the region R-r.

10. The following reflections on Descartes and his left leg supersede those contained in my paper "Philosophers and the Words 'Human Body'," in *Time and Cause: Essays Presented to Richard Taylor* (Dordrecht: D. Reidel, 1980).

11. The first and third of these four propositions I take to be trivial logical truths. Or, at least, to follow trivially from the propositions that D-minus existed before and after *t* and that Descartes existed before and after *t*.

12. Perhaps I am wrong about this. If I am, if a leg is like a cell (say), and unlike the left half of a cell, in being a non-arbitrary part of a human being, then I am wrong about something that is of no great import, since I am not saying that there are *no* undetached parts (cf. n. 9). But whether or not there was such a thing as L, there was certainly no such thing as D-minus. And the non-existence of D-minus is sufficient to refute DAUP. Nevertheless, I think I am right and that L did not exist. I will assert this rather than suspend judgment because I think that if my thesis about parts entails that L did not exist, then my thesis has an extremely counter-intuitive consequence and I do not wish to make my thesis look more plausible than it is by glossing over its more implausible consequences.

13. There's the bit where you say it.

14. There's the bit where you take it back.

15. Some philosophers distinguish between survival and identity. I have no idea what they mean by this. When I say that a certain person survived a certain adventure, what I say entails that a person who existed before the adventure and a person who existed after the adventure were the same person.

16. My knowledge of Chisholm's views on this question comes entirely from a paper I heard him read in 1978. He has recently told me, however, that I have not misrepresented him.

17. Lewis holds that "persons and their bodies are identical." See his "Counterparts of Persons and Their Bodies," *The Journal of Philosophy* LXVIII (1971).

18. This argument was communicated to me in a letter. The wording of the argument in the text is mine. It is my fault and not Lewis's that the political details of the

example are inaccurate. I should like to apologize to anyone who cares about the constitution of the Dual Monarchy.

19. By a 'politico-geographical entity', I mean an entity that (i) is a political entity—is brought into existence by human beings' entering into political relations with one another—and (ii) extends over part of the Earth's surface. (Strictly speaking, this is a definition of a *terrestrial* politico-geographical entity). Thus the Caspian Sea is not a politico-geographical entity because it fails to satisfy condition (i). The Congress of the United States fails to satisfy condition (ii). The United States, the British Commonwealth, Paris, Nova Scotia, and the territorial waters of Peru are politico-geographical entities.

20. See Geach's British Academy Lecture "Some Problems about Time," reprinted in *Logic Matters* (Oxford: Blackwell, 1972) and Appendix A to Chisholm's *Person and Object.*

21. An object *occupies* a set of moments of time if it exists at every moment in that set and at no other moments. A set of moments of time is an *occupiable interval* if it is possible in the broadly logical sense for there to be some object that occupies it. Presumably not all sets of moments of time are occupiable intervals. Cf. n. 3.

22. I do not say '*undetached* temporal parts'. A detached temporal part of a thing, presumably, would be something that *used to be* a temporal part of that thing. None of the friends of temporal parts, so far as I know, has found any use for such a notion.

23. It is well known that grave difficulties attend the notion of a "momentary" property. But I do not see how to state DATP without using it. I shall not exploit these difficulties in what follows, however, and thus *I* am under no obligation to explain momentary properties.

24. Some people believe that Descartes has never ceased to exist. The argument I shall present does not really require that we assume that Descartes has ceased to exist but only that we assume that it is *possible* for him to cease to exist.

25. The first and third of these four propositions I take to be trivial logical truths. Or, at least, to follow trivially from the propositions that D-minus existed and would have existed if Descartes had ceased to exist at *t* and that Descartes existed and would have existed if he had ceased to exist at *t*. Cf. n. 11.

26. This paper was read at philosophy colloquia at the University of Western Ontario, Brown University, Rutgers University, and New York University. I should like to thank the audiences at these colloquia for their stimulating objections and comments.

I have benefited from criticism of this paper by David Armstrong, Mark Brown, Roderick Chisholm, Richard Feldman, Eli Hirsch, Jennifer Hornsby, Michael Levin, David Lewis, Stephanie Lewis, Lawrence Brian Lombard, Philip Quinn, Michael Tye, James Van Cleve, and, especially, Peter Unger.

11

Identity Through Time

Roderick M. Chisholm

The identity of a person is a perfect identity; wherever it is real, it admits of no degrees; and it is impossible that a person should be in part the same, and in part different . . . For this cause, I have first considered personal identity, as that which is perfect in its kind, and the natural measure of that which is imperfect.

Thomas Reid[1]

1. The Ship of Theseus

To understand the philosophical problems involved in persistence, in the fact that one and the same thing may endure through a period of time, we will begin with what Reid would have called the 'imperfect' cases and remind ourselves of some ancient philosophical puzzles. One such puzzle is suggested by the familiar dictum of Heraclitus: 'You could not step twice in the same river; for other and yet other waters are ever flowing on.'[2] Another is the problem of the Ship of Theseus.[3]

Updating the latter problem somewhat, let us imagine a ship—the Ship of Theseus—that was made entirely of wood when it came into being. One day a wooden plank is cast off and replaced by an aluminum one. Since the change is only slight, there is no question as to the survival of the Ship of Theseus. We still have the ship we had before; that is to say, the ship that we have now is identical with the ship we had before. On another day, another wooden plank is cast off and also replaced by an aluminum one. Still the same ship, since, as before, the change is only slight. The changes continue, in a similar way, and finally the Ship of Theseus is made entirely of aluminum. The aluminum ship, one may well argue, is the wooden ship we started with, for the ship we started with survived each particular change, and identity, after all, is transitive.

But what happened to the discarded wooden planks? Consider this possibility, suggested by Thomas Hobbes: 'If some man had kept the old planks as they were taken out, and by putting them afterwards together in the same order, had again made a ship of them, this, without doubt, had also been the same numerical ship with that which was at the beginning; and so there would have been two ships numerically the same, which is absurd.'[4] Assuming, as perhaps one has no right to do, that each of the wooden planks survived intact throughout these changes, one might well argue that the reassembled wooden ship *is* the ship we started with. 'After all, it is made up of the very same parts, standing in the very same relations, whereas that ugly aluminum object doesn't have a single part in common with our original ship.'

To compound the problem still further, let us suppose that the captain of the original ship had solemnly taken the vow that, if his ship were ever to go down, he would go down with it. What, now, if the two ships collide at sea and he sees them start to sink together? Where does his duty lie—with the aluminum ship or with the reassembled wooden ship?

'The carriage' is another ancient version of the problem. Socrates and Plato change the parts of their carriages piece by piece until, finally, Socrates's original carriage is made up of all the parts of Plato's carriage and Plato's carriage is made up of all the parts of Socrates's original carriage. Have they exchanged their carriages or not, and if so, at what point?

Perhaps the essence of the problem is suggested by an even simpler situation. Consider a child playing with his blocks. He builds a house with ten blocks, uses it as a garrison for his toy soldiers, disassembles it, builds many other things, then builds a house again, with each of the ten blocks occupying the position it had occupied before, and he uses it again as a garrison for his soldiers. Was the house that was destroyed the same as the one that subsequently came into being?

These puzzles about the persistence of objects through periods of time have their analogues for the extension of objects through places in space. Consider the river that is known in New Orleans as 'the Mississippi'. Most of us would say that the source of the river is in northern Minnesota. But what if one were to argue instead that the source is in Montana, where it is known as 'the Missouri'? Or that its source is in Pittsburgh, where it is known as 'the Ohio', or that its source is farther back where it is called 'the Allegheny', or in still another place where it is called 'the Monongahela'?[5]

The accompanying diagram provides us with a schematic illustration.

```
(a)         (b)         (c)
 x           x           x
       x     x     x
            xxx
             x
             x
             x
            (d)
```

Of the river that has its central point at (d), one might wonder whether it flows south-easterly from (a), or due south from (b), or south-westerly from (c). (For simplicity, we ignore the Allegheny and the Monongahela.) If we are puzzled about the beginning of the Mississippi, we should be equally puzzled about the end of the Rhine. Reading our diagram from bottom to top (and again oversimplifying), we could say that if the Rhine begins at (d), then it ends either with the Maas at (a), or with the Waal at (b), or with the Lek at (c).[6]

Perhaps we can imagine three philosophers looking down at the river(s) that end(s) at (d). One insists that the river flows between (a) and (d), another that it flows between (b) and (d) and the third that it flows between (c) and (d); and each insists that, since the arms (or tributaries) to which the other two philosophers refer are distinct not only from each other but from the river itself, neither of the other two can be right. Their dispute, clearly, would be analogous in significant respects to the problem of the Ship of Theseus.

What are we to say of such puzzles? We might follow the extreme course that Carneades took and simply deny the principle of the transitivity of identity.[7] In other words we might say that things identical with the same thing need not be identical with each other. But if we thus abandon reason and logic at the very outset, we will have no way of deciding at the end what is the most reasonable thing to say about ourselves and *our* persistence through time.

We might be tempted to deny the possibility of alteration. Thus one could say: 'Strictly speaking, nothing alters—nothing is such that at one time it has one set of properties and at another time it has another set of properties. What happens is, rather, that at one time there is a thing having the one set of properties and at the other time there is another thing having the other set of properties.' But this supposition, if we apply it to ourselves, is inconsistent with the data with which we have begun. Each of us knows with respect to himself that he now has properties he didn't have in the past and that formerly he had properties he doesn't have now. ('But a thing *x* isn't identical with a thing *y* unless they have all their properties in common. And if the present you has one set of properties and the past you another, how can they be the same thing?') The answer is, of course, that there aren't two you's, a present one having one set of properties, and a past one having another. It is rather that you *are* now such that you have these properties and lack those, whereas formerly you *were* such that you had those properties and lacked these. The 'former you' *has* the same properties that the 'present you' now has, and the 'present you' *had* the same properties that the 'former you' then had.[8]

Bishop Butler suggested that it is only in 'a loose and popular sense' that we may speak of the persistence of such familiar things as ships, plants and houses. And he contrasted this 'loose and popular sense' with 'the strict and philosophical sense' in which we may speak of the persistence of *persons*.[9] Let us consider these suggestions.

2. Playing Loose with the 'Is' of Identity

We will not pause to ask what Butler meant in fact. Let us ask what he could have meant. He suggested that there is a kind of looseness involved when we say that such things as the Ship of Theseus persist through time. What kind of looseness is this?

It could hardly be that the Ship of Theseus, in contrast with other things, is only loosely identical with itself. Surely one cannot say that, while some things are only loosely identical with themselves, other things are tightly identical with themselves.[10] The statement 'This thing is more loosely identical with itself than that thing', if it says anything at all, tells us only that the first thing is more susceptible than the second to loss of identity, and this means only that the first is more readily perishable than the second.

We should construe Butler's remark as saying, not that there is a loose kind of identity, but rather that there is a loose sense of 'identity'—a loose (and popular) use of the 'is' of identity.

What would be a *loose* sense of 'A is B', or 'A is identical with B'—a sense of 'A is B' which is consistent with a denial of the *strict* sense of 'A is B'? I suggest this: we use the locution 'A is B', or 'A is identical with B', in a *loose* sense, if we use it in such a way that it is consistent with saying 'A has a certain property that B does not have' or 'Some things are true of A that aren't true of B'.

Do we ever use the locution 'A is B' in this loose way? It would seem, unfortunately, that we do.

I will single out five different types of such misuse.

(1) One may say: 'Route 6 is Point Street in Providence and is Fall River Avenue in Seekonk.' Here we would seem to have the 'is' of identity, since it is followed in each occurrence by a term ('Point Street' and 'Fall River Avenue') and not by a predicate expression. But since Point Street and Fall River Avenue have different properties (one is in Providence and not in Seekonk and the other is in Seekonk and not in Providence), the statement may be said to play loose with 'is'.

As our brief discussion of the rivers may make clear, this use of 'is' is readily avoided. We have only to replace 'is' by 'is part of' and then switch around the terms, as in: 'Point Street in Providence is part of Route 6 and Fall River Avenue in Seekonk is part of Route 6.' Or we could also say, of course: 'Point Street is part of Route 6 in Providence and Fall River Avenue is part of Route 6 in Seekonk.'[11]

(2) One may say 'This train will be two trains after Minneapolis', or, travelling in the other direction, 'Those two trains will be one train after Minneapolis'. In the first case ('fission'), we are not saying that there is one thing which will subsequently be identical with two things. We are saying, rather, that there is one thing which will be divided into two things, neither of them being identical with the original thing, but each of them being a part of the original thing. And in the second case ('fusion'), we are not saying that there are two things which are subsequently to become identical with each other, or with a third thing. We are saying rather that there are two things which will both become parts of a third thing. (Why not cite an amoeba as an instance of 'fission'? There is the off-chance that amoebas are persons, or at least may be thought to be persons, and in such a case, as we shall see, our treatment would have to be somewhat different.)

(3) One may say: 'The President of the United States was Eisenhower in 1955, Johnson in 1965 and Ford in 1975.'[12] Here one may seem to be saying that there is, or was, something—namely, the President of the United States—which was identical with Eisenhower in 1955, with Johnson in 1965 and with Ford in 1975. And so, given that Eisenhower, Johnson and Ford were three different people, one may seem to be saying that there is one thing which has been identical with three different things. But this talk, too, is readily avoided. We have only to reformulate the original sentence in such a way that the temporal expression ('in 1955', 'in 1965' and 'in 1975') may be seen to modify, not the verb 'was', but the term 'the President of the United States'. Thus we could say: 'The President of the United States in 1955 (the person who officially presided over the United States in 1955) was Eisenhower; the President of the United States in 1965 was Johnson; and the President of the United States in 1975 was Ford.'[13]

(4) Pointing to a musical instrument, one man may say to another: 'What you have there is the same instrument that I play, but the one that I play isn't as old as that one.' The first 'is' might be taken to be the 'is' of identity, for it would seem to be followed by a term ('the same instrument that I play'), but the man is saying, of the thing designated by the first term ('what you have there'), that it is older than the thing designated by the second. But of course he didn't need to talk that way. He could have said: 'What you have there is an instrument of the same sort as the one that I play.'

We note a second example of this way of playing loose with 'is'—not because the example introduces any new considerations (for it doesn't), but because it has attracted the attention of philosophers.

Consider the following list:

Socrates is mortal.
Socrates is mortal.

How many sentences have been listed? We could say either 'exactly one' or 'exactly two'. That these incompatible answers are both possible indicates that the question is ambiguous. And so it has been suggested that, to avoid the ambiguity, we introduce the terms 'sentence-token' and 'sentence-type' and then say 'There are two sentence-tokens on the list and one sentence-type'. But if we say this, then we can say: 'The first item on the list is the same sentence-type as the second (for they are syntactically just alike and say the same thing), but the two are different sentence-tokens (for they are two, one being in one place and the other in another).' Here, once again, we are playing loose with 'is'.[14] We *needn't* speak this way in order to deal with the ambiguity of 'How many sentences are there?' We could say there *are* two sentence-tokens and they are tokens *of* the same (sentence-) type. The example does not differ in principle, then, from 'The instrument Jones plays is the same as the one Smith plays but is somewhat older'.

It is sometimes said that we should distinguish the two locutions 'A is identical with B and A is a so-and-so' and 'A is the same so-and-so as B'. It has even been suggested that, for purposes of philosophy, the first of these two locutions should be abandoned in favour of the second.[15] According to this suggestion, we should never say, simply and absolutely, 'A is identical with B'; we should 'relativise the ascription of identity to a sortal' and say something of the form 'A is the same so-and-so as B', where the expression replacing 'so-and-so' is a count-term, or sortal, such as 'man', 'dog', 'horse'. But this suggestion has point only if we can find instances of the following:

> A is the same so-and-so as B, and A is a such-and-such but is not the same such-and-such as B.

Are there really any such As and Bs?

What would be an instance of the above formula? In other words, what would be an instance of an A which is 'the same so-and-so' as something B, but which is not 'the same such-and-such' as B? The only instances which have ever been cited, in defending this doctrine of 'relativised identity', would seem to be instances of one or the other of the four ways of playing loose with 'is' that we have just distinguished. For example: 'Different official personages may be one and the same man' or 'This is the same word as that'. What the suggestion comes to, then, is that we abandon the strict use of 'is' and replace it by one or more of the loose uses just discussed. There may be advantages to this type of permissiveness, but it will not help us with our philosophical problems.[16]

Do these ways of playing loose with 'is' suggest a true interpretation of the thesis we have attributed to Bishop Butler—the thesis according to which it is only in 'a loose and popular sense' that we may speak of the persistence through time of such familiar physical things as ships, plants and houses? Is it only by playing loose with 'is' that we may say, of the Ship of Theseus, that it is one and the same thing from one period of time to another?

We *can*, of course, play loose with 'is' in one or another of these ways when we talk about the Ship of Theseus. Knowing that it is going to be broken up into two ships, we might say: 'It's going to be two ships.' Or knowing that it was made by joining two other ships, we might say: 'Once it had been two ships.' Or knowing that it makes the same ferry run as does the Ship of Callicles, we might say: 'The Ship of Theseus and the Ship of Callicles are the same ferry.' But the Ship of Theseus doesn't have to be talked about in these loose and popular ways any more than anything else does.

(5) It may be that the Ship of Theseus and the carriage and other familiar things involve still another way of playing loose with 'is'. Thus Hume said that it is convenient to 'feign identity' when we speak about things which, though they 'are supposed to continue the same, are such only as consist of succession of parts, connected together by resemblance, contiguity, or causation'.[17] What Hume here has in mind by 'feigning' may have been put more clearly by Thomas Reid. (Though Reid and Hume were far apart with respect to most of the matters that concern us here, they seem to be together with respect to this one.) Reid wrote:

> All bodies, as they consist of innumerable parts that may be disjoined from them by a great variety of causes, are subject to continual changes of their substance, increasing, diminishing, changing insensibly. When such alterations are gradual, because language could not afford a different name for every different state of such a changeable being, it retains the same name, and is considered as the same thing. Thus we say of an old regiment that it did such a thing a century ago, though there now is not a man alive who then belonged to it. We say a tree is the same in the seed-bed and in the forest. A ship of war, which has successively changed her anchors, her tackle, her sails, her masts, her planks, and her timbers, while she keeps the same name is the same.[18]

I believe that Reid is here saying two things. The first is that, whenever there is a change of parts, however insignificant the parts may be, then some old thing ceases to be and some new thing comes into being. This presupposes that, strictly speaking, the parts of a thing are essential to it, and therefore when, as we commonly say, something loses a part, then that thing strictly and philosophically ceases to be.[19]

The second thing I take Reid to be saying is this. If, from the point of view of our practical concerns, the new thing that comes into being upon the addition of parts is sufficiently similar to the old one, then it is much more convenient for us to treat them as if they were one than it is for us to take account of the fact that they are diverse. This point could also be put by saying that such things as the Ship of Theseus and indeed most familiar physical things are really 'fictions', or as we would say today, 'logical constructions'. They are logical constructions upon things which *cannot* survive the loss of their parts.

If Reid is right, then, 'The Ship of Theseus was in Athens last week and will be in Kerkyra Melaina next week' need not be construed as telling us that there *is* in fact a certain ship that was in Athens last week and will be in Kerkyra Melaina next week. It does not imply that any ship that was in the one place is identical with any ship that will be in the other place. And so if this is true, and if all the same we say 'A ship that was in Athens last week is identical with a ship that will be in Kerkyra Melaina next week', then, once again, we are playing loose with the 'is' of identity.

3. An Interpretation of Bishop Butler's Theses

We have found a way, then, of interpreting Bishop Butler's two theses.

According to the first, familiar physical things such as trees, ships, bodies and houses persist 'only in a loose and popular sense'. This thesis may be construed as presupposing that these things are 'fictions', logical constructions or *entia per alio*. And it tells us that, from the fact that any such physical thing may be said to exist at a certain place P at a certain time t and also at a certain place Q at a certain other time t', we may *not* infer that what exists at P at t is identical with what exists at Q at t'.

According to the second thesis, persons persist 'in a strict and philosophical sense'. This may be construed as telling us that persons are not thus 'fictions', logical constructions or *entia per alio*. And so it implies that, if a person may be said to exist at a certain place P at a certain time t and also at a certain place Q at a certain other time t', then we *may* infer that something existing at P at t is identical with something existing at Q at t'.

We now consider the two theses in turn.

4. Feigning Identity

Could we think of familiar physical things, such as ships and trees and houses, as being logical constructions? Let us consider just one type of physical thing, for what we say about it may be applied, *mutatis mutandis*, to the others.

Mon	AB
Tue	BC
Wed	CD

Consider the history of a very simple table. On Monday it came into being when a certain thing A was joined with a certain other thing B. On Tuesday A was detached from B and C was joined to B, these things occurring in such a way that a table was to be found during every moment of the process. And on Wednesday B was detached from C and D was joined with C, these things, too, occurring in such a way that a table was to be found during every moment of the process. Let us suppose that no other separating or joining occurred.

I suggest that in this situation there are the following three wholes among others: AB, that is, the thing made up of A and B; BC, the thing made up of B and C; and CD, the thing made up of C and D. I will say that AB 'constituted' our table on Monday, that BC 'constituted' our table on Tuesday and that CD 'constituted' our table on Wednesday. Although AB, BC and CD are three different things, they all constitute the same table. We thus have an illustration of what Hume called 'a succession of objects'.[20]

One might also say, of each of the three wholes, AB, BC and CD, that it 'stands in for' or 'does duty for' our table on one of the three successive days. Thus if we consider the spatial location of the three wholes, we see that the place of the table was occupied by AB on Monday, by BC on Tuesday, and by CD on Wednesday. Again, the table was red on Monday if and only if AB was red on Monday, and it weighed 10 pounds on Monday if and only if AB weighed 10 pounds on Monday. And analogously for BC on Tuesday and for CD on Wednesday.

The situation may seem to involve two somewhat different types of individual thing. On the one hand, there is what might be called the *ens successivum*—the 'successive table' that is made up of different things at different times.[21] And on the other hand, there are the things that do duty on the different days for the successive table: namely, AB, BC and CD. But any *ens successivum* may be viewed as a logical construction upon the various things that may be said to do duty for it.

Considering, then, just the simple situation I have described, can we express the information we have about the *ens successivum* in statements that refer only to the particular things that stand in or do duty for it? It should be clear that we can, but let us consider the situation in some detail.

Looking back to our diagram, we can see that Monday's table evolved into Tuesday's table and that Tuesday's table evolved into Wednesday's table. We began with AB; then A was separated from B and replaced by C, but in such a way that there was a table to be found at every moment during the process; then, in a similar way, B was separated from C and replaced by D. We could say, then, that BC was a 'direct table successor' of AB, and that CD was a 'direct table successor' of AB.

Making use of the undefined concept of *part*, or *proper part*, we may define the concept of 'table successor' in the following way:

D.III.1 *x* is at *t* a direct table successor of *y* at *t′* = Df (i) *t* does not begin before *t′*; (ii) *x* is a table at *t* and *y* is a table at *t′*; and (iii) there is a *z*, such that *z* is a part of *x* at *t* and a part of *y* at *t′*, and at every moment between *t′* and *t*, inclusive, *z* is itself a table.

Thus *z* is a table which is a proper part of a table. (If we cut off a small part of a table, we may still have a table left. But if the thing that is left is a table, then, since it was there before, it was then a table that was a proper part of a table.) The concept *part*, as it is understood here, will be discussed in detail in Appendix B ('Mereological Essentialism') [not reprinted here].

We may also say, more generally, that the CD of Wednesday is a 'table successor' of the AB of Monday, even though CD is not a *direct* table successor of AB. The more general concept is this:

D.III.2 *x* is at *t* a table successor of *y* at *t′* = Df (i) *t* does not begin before *t′*; (ii) *x* is a table at *t* and *y* is a table at *t′*; and (iii) *x* has at *t* every property P such that (a) *y* has P at *t′* and (b) all direct table successors of anything having P have P.

The definition assures us that a direct table successor of a direct table successor is a table successor; so, too, for a direct table successor of a direct table successor . . . of a direct table successor.[22]

We may now say that things that are thus related by table succession 'constitute the same successive table'.

D.III.3 *x* constitutes at *t* the same successive table that *y* constitutes at *t′* = Df Either (a) *x* and only *x* is at *t* a table successor of *y* at *t′*, or (b) *y* and only *y* is at *t′* a table successor of *x* at *t*.

Each such thing may be said to 'constitute a successive table'.

D.III.4 *x* constitutes at *t* a successive table = Df There are a *y* and a *t′* such that *y* is other than *x* and *x* constitutes at *t* the same table that *y* constitutes at *t′*.

We are on the way, then, to reducing our successive table to those things that are said to constitute it.

Certain propositions, ostensibly about the successive table, may be reduced in a straightforward way to propositions about the things that are said to constitute it. For example:

D.III.5 There is exactly one successive table at place P at time *t* = Df There is exactly one thing at place P at time *t* that constitutes a successive table at *t*.

Our definition of 'constituting the same successive table' (D.III.3) assures us that nothing will constitute more than one successive table at any given time.

Some of the properties that the table has at any given time are thus such that the table borrows them from the thing that constitutes it at that time; but others are not. An example of a property of the first sort may be that of *being red*; an example of a property of the second sort may be that of *having once been blue.* How are we to mark off the former set of properties?

Some properties may be said to be 'rooted outside the times at which they are had'. Examples are the property of *being a widow* and the property of *being a future President.* If we know of anything that it has the former property at any given time, then we can deduce that the thing existed prior to that time. And if we know of anything that it has the latter property at any given time, then we can deduce that the thing continues to exist after that time. Let us say:

D.III.6 G is rooted outside times at which it is had = D*f* Necessarily, for any *x* and for any period of time *t*, *x* has the property G throughout *t* only if *x* exists at some time before or after *t*.

Some properties may—but need not—be rooted outside the times at which they are had. An example is the property of *being such that it is or was red.* Our successive table may derive this from its present constituent—if its present constituent is red. But it may derive it from a former constituent—if its present constituent is not red. The definition of this type of property is straightforward:

D.III.7 G may be rooted outside times at which it is had = D*f* G is equivalent to a disjunction of two properties one of which is, and the other of which is not, rooted outside times at which it is had.

Some properties, finally, are *not* such that they may be rooted outside the times at which they are had.[23] An example is *being red.*

Of the properties that our successive table has at any given time, which are the ones that it borrows from the thing that happens to constitute it at that time? The answer is: those of its properties which are *not* essential to it, and those of its properties which are *not* such that they may be rooted outside the times at which they are had. But the essential properties of the successive table—e.g. that it *is* a successive table—and those of its properties which may be rooted outside the times at which they are had—e.g. that it was blue or that it was or will be blue—are not such that, for any time, they are borrowed from the thing that constitutes the successive table at that time.

We may say, more generally, of the *ens successivum* and the thing that constitutes it at any given time, that they are exactly alike at that time with respect to all those properties which are such that they are not essential to either and they may not be rooted outside the times at which they are had.

Consider now the following definitional schema:

D.III.8 The successive table that is at place P at time *t* is F at *t* = Df There is exactly one thing at place P at *t* that constitutes a successive table at *t* and that thing is F at *t*.

This definition is applicable only if the predicates that replace the schematic letter 'F' are properly restricted. For the properties designated by such predicates should be those which are not essential to either and are not such that they may be rooted outside the times at which they are had. Hence acceptable replacements for 'F' would be: 'red', '10 feet square', and 'such that it weighs 10 pounds'.

But not all the properties of the successive table are derivable in this straightforward way from the properties of things that constitute it. For example, if AB ceased to be after Monday, we could say of the successive table on Monday, but not of AB, that it was going to persist through Wednesday. Or if CD came into being on Wednesday, we could say of the successive table on Wednesday, but not of CD, that it is at least two days old. Moreover, on Monday, the successive table, but not AB, was such that it would be constituted by CD on Wednesday; while on Wednesday, the successive table, but not CD, was such that it was constituted by AB on Monday.

Nevertheless all such truths about the successive table may be reduced to truths about AB, BC and CD. That this is so should be apparent from these definitions.

D.III.9 The successive table that is at place P at time *t* has existed for at least 3 days = Df There is exactly one *x* such that *x* is at place P at time *t* and *x* constitutes a successive table at *t*; there are a *y* and a time *t′* such that *x* is at *t* a table-successor of *y* at *t′*; and *t* and *t′* are separated by a period of three days.

This definition tells us, then, what it is for a successive table to persist through time. And the following definition suggests the way in which, at any time, the successive table may borrow its properties from things that constitute it at *other* times:

D.III.10 The successive table that is at place P at time t is constituted by x at t' = Df There is a y such that y is at place P at time t; y constitutes a successive table at t; and either x is identical with y and t is identical with t', or y constitutes at t the same successive table that x constitutes at t'.

It should now be obvious how to say such things as 'the successive table is red on Monday and green on Wednesday'.

One may object, 'You are committed to saying that AB, BC, CD, and our table are four different things. It may well be, however, that each of the three things AB, BC, CD satisfies the conditions of any acceptable definition of the term 'table'. Indeed your definitions presuppose that each of them is a table. Hence you are committed to saying that, in the situation described, there are *four* tables. But this is absurd; for actually you have described only *one* table.'

We will find a reply to this objection, if we distinguish the strict and philosophical sense of such expressions as 'There are four tables' from their ordinary, or loose and popular, sense. To say that there are four tables, in the strict and philosophical sense, is to say that there are four different things, each of them a table. But from the fact that there are four tables, in this strict and philosophical sense, it will not follow that there are four tables in the ordinary, or loose and popular, sense. If there are to be four tables in the ordinary, or loose and popular, sense, it must be the case that there are four things, not only such that each constitutes a table, but also such that no two of them constitute the same table. In other words, there must be four *entia successiva*, each of them a table.

We may, therefore, explicate the ordinary, or loose and popular, sense of 'There are n so-and-so's at t' (or 'The number of so-and-so's at t is n') in the following way:

D.III.11 There are, in the loose and popular sense, n so-and-so's at t = Df There are n things each of which constitutes a so-and-so at t, and no two of which constitute the same so-and-so at t.

The term 'so-and-so' in this schematic definition may be replaced by any more specific count-term, e.g. 'table' or 'ship'. And the definiendum could be replaced by 'The number of successive so-and-so's at t is n'.

Hence the answer to the above objection is this: in saying that there are exactly *three* tables in the situation described one is speaking in the strict and philosophical sense and not in the loose and popular sense. In saying that there is exactly *one* table one is speaking in the loose and popular sense and not in the strict and philosophical sense. But the statement that there are *four* tables—AB, BC, CD and the successive table—is simply the result of confusion. One is trying to speak both ways at once.[24] The sense in which we may say that there *is* the successive table is not the sense in which we may say that there *is* the individual thing AB, or BC, or CD.[25]

The foregoing sketch, then, makes clear one way in which we may feign identity when what we are dealing with is in fact only a 'succession of related objects'. The ways in which we do thus feign identity are considerably more subtle and complex. Playing loose with 'is' and 'same', we may even speak of the sameness of a table when we are dealing with successions of objects which are related, not by what I have called table succession, but in much more tenuous ways. Nevertheless it should be clear that if we are saying something we really know, when we thus speak of the sameness of a table, what we are saying could be re-expressed in such a way that we refer only to the related objects and not to the ostensible entities we think of them as making up. And so, too, for other familiar things—ships and trees and houses—that involve successions of related objects that stand in or do duty for them at different times.

We could say, then, that such things are *entia per alio*. They are ontological parasites that derive all their properties from other things—from the various things that do duty for them. An *ens per alio* never is or has anything on its own. It is what it is in virtue of the nature of something other than itself. At every moment of its history an *ens per alio* has something other than itself as its stand-in.

But if there are *entia per alio*, then there are also *entia per se*.

5. The Persistence of Persons through Time

Am I an *ens per alio* or an *ens per se*?

Consider the simplest of Cartesian facts—say, that I now hope for rain. Hoping for rain is one of those properties that are rooted only in the times at which they are had. And so if I am an *ens per alio*, an *ens successivum*, like our simple table or the Ship of Theseus, then I may be said to hope for rain only in virtue of the fact that my present stand-in hopes for rain. I borrow the property, so to speak, from the thing that constitutes me now.

But surely *that* hypothesis is not to be taken seriously. There is no reason whatever for supposing that *I* hope for rain only in virtue of the fact that some *other* thing hopes for rain—some stand-in that, strictly and philosophically, is not identical with me but happens to be doing duty for me at this particular moment.

If there are thus two things that now hope for rain, the one doing it on its own and the other such that its hoping is done for it by the thing that now happens to constitute it, then I am the former thing and not the latter thing. But this is to say that I am *not* an *ens successivum.*[26]

But might I not be a constituent of an *ens successivum*?

If I am a constituent of an *ens successivum*, then there have been other things that once constituted the same person that I do now and presumably there will be still others in the future. But if this is so, then the things I think I know about my past history may all be false (even though they may be true of the person I happen now to constitute) and I may have no grounds for making any prediction at all about my future. *Is* this the sort of thing I am?

Let us recall the data with which we began, the list of things we have a right to believe about ourselves. Among those things, we said, is the fact that we do undergo change and persist through time. Each of us is justified in believing a great variety of things about his past. We are justified in believing these things until we have found some reason to doubt them. It is reasonable to treat these beliefs as being innocent, epistemically, until we have found some positive reason for thinking them guilty.

What would such a positive reason be?

It is important to remind ourselves that we do *not* find any such positive reason in the writings of those philosophers who have professed to be sceptical about the persistence of persons through time.

Consider, for example, Kant's discussion of what he calls 'the third paralogism of transcendental psychology'. For all I can know, Kant there says, the thing that calls itself 'I' at one time may be other than the thing that calls itself 'I' at another time. There might be a series of different subjects which make up my biography, each of them passing its thoughts and memories on to its successor—each subject would 'retain the thought of the preceding subject and so hand it over to the subsequent subject'.[27] The relation between the successive subjects, he says, could be like that of a set of elastic balls, one of which impinges on another in a straight line and 'communicates to the latter its whole motion, and therefore its whole state (that is, if we take account only of the positions in space)'. Kant goes on to say: 'If, then, in analogy with such bodies, we postulate substances such that the one communicates to the other representations together with the consciousness of them, we can conceive a whole series of substances of which the first transmits its state together with its consciousness to the second, the second its own state with that of the preceding substance to the third, and this in turn the states of all the preceding substances together with its own consciousness and with their consciousness to another. The last substance would then be conscious of all the states of the previously changed substances, as being its own states, because they would have been transferred to it together with the consciousness of them. And yet it would not have been one and the same person in all these states'.[28]

Does *this* give us a reason for wondering whether we have in fact persisted through time? Surely not. What Kant has pointed out to us, in these speculations, is simply that the following is logically possible: instead of there being just one person who makes up my biography, there was a succession of different persons, all but the first of them being deluded with respect to its past. It is also logically possible, as Russell pointed out, that the universe came into being three seconds ago with all its ostensible traces and relics of the past. And it is logically possible that a malicious demon is deceiving each of us with respect to what we think are the external physical things around us. But the fact that these are logically possible is itself no reason for thinking that they actually occur.

'Given the transitory nature of the ultimate particles that make up the physical universe, isn't it reasonable to suppose that, if I do persist through time, then my consciousness may be transferred, as John Locke seemed to suggest, from one substance or individual thing to another? And if my consciousness is thus transferred, wouldn't I, too, be transferred from one substance to another?'

The supposition, I am certain, is not only untenable but also incoherent. Philosophers have taken it seriously, however, and so we should consider it briefly.

Is it possible to transfer my consciousness from one substance to another with the result that, whereas the former substance but not the latter was I, the latter substance but not the former is now I? In such a case, I could truly say: 'This is other than that, but once I was that and now I'm this.'

Locke said that, 'it being the same consciousness that makes a man be himself to himself, personal identity depends on that only, whether it be annexed solely to one individual substance, or can be continued in a succession of several substances'.[29] The same consciousness, he said, *could* be thus continued in a succession of several substances, if it were 'transferred from one thinking substance to another', and if this does happen then the different 'thinking substances may make but one person'[30] And these different thinking substances will all be 'the same self'.[31] (In fairness to Locke, we should note that he does not quite bring himself to say that I might now be identical with this but not with that and then later identical with that but not with this. Although he suggests that it is possible to transfer my consciousness from one substance to another, he does not explicitly say that, whereas the former substance *was* I, the latter substance is *now* I. It may very well be that he, too, was playing loose with 'is'.)

A *part* of a thing or an *appendage* to a thing may be transferred to another thing, as an organ may be transplanted from one body to another. The *contents* of a thing may be transferred to another thing, as apples may be moved from one bag to another.

Speaking somewhat more metaphorically, we might also say that the *properties* of one thing may be transferred to another thing. If you are infected by my contagious disease and if I then recover, one *could* say that my sickness *including my aches and pains* has been transferred from me to you. But the disease or sickness will not be transferred in the literal sense in which, say, its carriers might be transferred.

My personality traits could be said to be transferred to you if you acquire the kind of complexes and dispositions that are characteristic of me. My beliefs could be said to be transferred to you, if you begin to believe the same things I do. And my memories could even be said to be transferred from me to you, if you remember, or think you remember, the same things I do. (But if I remember or think I remember *my* doing the deed, the content of that memory could *not* be transferred to you.)[32] By thus acquiring my properties—or, more accurately, by thus instantiating some of the properties that I do—you may become so much like me that others will have difficulty in telling us apart—in that they are unable to decide, with respect to certain things that have happened, whether they belong to your biography or to mine. Perhaps the courts will have to make a decree. Perhaps it will even be reasonable for them to decide, with respect to some of the things that only I did in the past, that you and not I are responsible for them, and then they might decide, with respect to the name I formerly had, that you should be the one who bears it.

But none of these possibilities, perplexing as they may be, justifies us in saying that there could be *two* different substances which are such that *I* am transferred from one to the other.[33]

There is still another type of transfer which is quite naturally described in the way in which Locke described 'transfer of self'. This is illustrated in the transfer of a shadow ('the shadow of his hand moved from the wall to the table and became larger but more faint in the process'). But a shadow is an *ens per alio*; it borrows its properties from other things (most notably from shadowed objects). The kind of transfer that is involved in the passage of a shadow from one object to another, to the extent that it differs from the types of transfer we distinguished above, is typical of *entia per alio*. But persons, we have seen, are *entia per se*.

What could it mean, after all, to say that I might be 'annexed to' or 'placed in' a thinking thing or individual substance?

Whatever it might mean, either I am identical with the thinking substance in which I am thus placed or I am not identical with it.

If I am identical with the thinking substance in which I am thus placed, then I cannot be transferred *from* that substance to another thinking substance.

But if I am placed in a certain thinking substance and am not identical with that thinking substance, then there are *two* different things—the thinking substance and I. But if there are two things, which of us does the thinking? There are exactly four possibilities.

(1) Neither of us does the thinking—that is to say, neither of us thinks. But this we know is false.

(2) I think but the thinking substance does not think. Why call the latter a 'thinking' substance, then? (It would be like calling an elevator a thinking substance because it contains someone who thinks.) And what relation do I bear to this thinking substance? I'm not a *property* of it, since properties do not think. Am I a proper *part*, then, of the thinking substance? But proper parts of substances are themselves substances. And so if I am myself a thinking substance, what is the point of saying there is *another* thinking substance in which I am 'placed' or to which I am 'annexed'?

(3) The thinking substance thinks but I do not. But isn't this absurd? 'It's not really I who think; it is some *other* thing that thinks in me—some other thing that does what I mistakenly take to be my thinking.' (Or should the latter clause have been: 'some other thing that does what *it* mistakenly takes to be my thinking'?)

(4) Both the thinking substance and I think. Isn't this multiplying thinkers beyond necessity? If I want my dinner, does it follow that two of us want my dinner? Or does the thinking substance want its dinner and not mine?

I think we may reasonably conclude that there is no significant sense in which we may speak of the transfer of a self from one substance or individual thing to another.

6. 'Will I Be He?': Truth-Conditions and Criteria

Suppose that there is a person *x* who happens to know, with respect to a certain set of properties, that there is or will be a certain person *y* who will have those properties at some future time, and *x* asks himself: 'Will I be he?' Either *x* is identical with *y*, or *x* is diverse from *y*.

We cannot find the *answer* to the question, 'Is *x* identical with *y*?', merely by deciding what would be practically convenient. To be sure, if we lack sufficient evidence for making a decision, it may yet be necessary for the courts to *rule* that *x* is the same person as *y*, or that he is not. Perhaps the ruling will have to be based upon practical considerations and conceivably such considerations may lead the court later to 'defeat' its ruling. But one may always ask of any such ruling 'But is it *correct*, or *true*?' For a ruling to the effect that *x* is the same person as *y* will be correct, or true, only if *x* is identical with *y*.

We should remind ourselves, however, that the expression '*x* is the same person as *y*' also has a use which is not this strict and philosophical one. Thus there are circumstances in which one might say: 'Mr Jones is not at all the same person he used to be. You will be disappointed. He is not the person that you remember.' We would not say this sort of thing if Mr Jones had changed only slightly. We would say it only if he had undergone changes that were quite basic and thorough-going—the kind of changes that might be produced by psychoanalysis, or by a lobotomy, or by a series of personal tragedies. But just *how* basic and thorough-going must these changes be if we are to say of Mr Jones that he is a different person? The proper answer would seem to be: 'As basic and thorough-going as you would like. It's just a matter of convention. It all depends upon how widely it is convenient for you to construe the expression "He's the same person he used to be". In so far as the rules of language are in your own hands, you may have it any way you would like.'[34] (Compare 'Jones is not himself today' or 'Jones was not himself when he said that'.)

This, however, is only playing loose with 'same'—or, more accurately, it is playing loose with 'not the same'. When we say, in the above sense, 'Jones is no longer the person he used to be', we do not mean that there is, or was, a certain entity such that Jones was formerly identical with that entity and is no longer so. What we are saying does not imply that there are (or have been) certain entities, x and y, such that at one time x is, or was, identical with y, and at another time x is not identical with y. For this is incoherent, but 'Jones is no longer the person he used to be' is not.

Nor do we mean, when we say 'Jones is no longer the person he used to be', that there *was* a certain entity, the old Jones, which no longer exists, and that there is a certain *different* entity, the new Jones, which somehow has taken his place. We are not describing the kind of change that takes place when one President succeeds another. In the latter case, there is a clear answer to the question 'What happened to the old one?' But when we decide to call Jones a new person, we are not confronted with such questions as: 'What happened, then, to the old Jones? Did he die, or was he annihilated, or disassembled, or did he retire to some other place?'

The old Jones did not die; he was not annihilated or disassembled; and he did not retire to any other place. He *became* the new Jones. And to say that he 'became' the new Jones is *not* to say that he 'became identical' with something he hadn't been identical with before. For it is only when a thing comes into being that it may be said to become identical with something it hadn't been identical with before. To say that our man 'became the new Jones' is to say that he, Jones, *altered* in a significant way, taking on certain interesting properties he had not had before. (Hence we should contrast the 'became' of 'Jones then became a married man', said when Jones ceased to be a bachelor, with that of 'The President then became a Republican', said when President Johnson retired.) When we say of a thing that *it* has properties that *it* did not have before, we are saying that there is an x such that x formerly had such-and-such properties and x presently has such-and-such other properties.

It will be instructive, I think, to consider two somewhat different examples.

The first is suggested by C. S. Peirce.[35] Elaborating upon his suggestion, let us assume that you are about to undergo an operation and that you still have a decision to make. The utilities involved are, first, financial—you wish to avoid any needless expense—and, secondly, the avoidance of pain, the avoidance, however, just of *your* pain, for pain that is other than yours, let us assume, is of no concern whatever to you. The doctor proposes two operating procedures—one a very expensive procedure in which you will be subjected to total anaesthesia and no pain will be felt at all, and the other of a rather different sort. The second operation will be very inexpensive indeed; there will be no anaesthesia at all and therefore there will be excruciating pain. But the doctor will give you two drugs: first, a drug just before the operation which will induce complete amnesia, so that while you are on the table you will have no memory whatever of your present life; and, secondly, just after the agony is over, a drug that will make you completely forget everything that happened on the table. The question is: given the utilities involved, namely, the avoidance of needless expense and the avoidance of pain that *you* will feel, other pains not mattering, is it reasonable for you to opt for the less expensive operation?

My own conviction is that it would *not* be reasonable, even if you could be completely certain that both amnesia injections would be successful. *You* are the one who would undergo that pain, even though you, Jones, would not know at the time that it is Jones who is undergoing it, and even though you would never remember it. Consider after all, the hypothesis that it would *not* be you. What would be your status, in such a case, during the time of the operation? Would you have passed away? That is to say, would you have *ceased to be*, but with the guarantee that you—you, yourself—would come into being once again when the agony was over?[36] And what about the person who *would* be feeling the pain? Who would he be?

It may well be that these things would not be obvious to you if in fact you had to make such a decision. But there is one point, I think, that ought to be obvious.

Suppose that others come to you—friends, relatives, judges, clergymen—and they offer the following advice and assurance. 'Have no fear', they will say. 'Take the cheaper operation and we will take care of everything. We will lay down the convention that the man on the table is not you, Jones, but is Smith.' What *ought* to be obvious to you, it seems to me, is that the laying down of this convention should have no effect at all upon your decision. For you may still ask, 'But won't that person be I?' and, it seems to me, the question has an answer.

I now turn to the second example. Suppose you know that your body, like that of an amoeba, would one day undergo fission and that you would go off, so to speak, in two different directions. Suppose you also know, somehow, that the one who went off to the left would experience the most wretched of lives and that the one who went off to the right would experience a life of great happiness and value. If I am right in saying that one's question 'Will that person be I?' or 'Will I be he?' always has a definite answer, then, I think, we may draw these conclusions. There is no possibility whatever that *you* would be *both* the person on the right and the person on the left. Moreover, there *is* a possibility that you would be *one or the other* of those two persons. And, finally, *you* could be one of those persons and yet have no memory at all of your present existence. In this case, there may well be no *criterion* by means of which you or anyone else could decide which of the two halves was in fact yourself. Yet it would be reasonable of you, if you were concerned with *your* future pleasures and pains, to hope that you would be the one on the right and not the one on the left. It would also be reasonable of you, given such self-concern, to have this hope even if you knew that the one on the right would have no memory of your present existence. Indeed it would be reasonable of you to have it even if you know that the one on the *left* thought he remembered the facts of your present existence. And it seems to me to be absolutely certain that no fears that you might have, about being the half on the left, could reasonably be allayed by the adoption of a convention, even if our procedure were endorsed by the highest authorities.[37]

In trying to *decide* which one of the two persons, if either, you will be, you will, of course, make use of such *criteria* that you have and are able to apply. As we all know, there are intriguing philosophical questions about the criteria of the identity of persons through time. ('How are we to make sure, or make a reasonable guess, that that person at that time is the same as that person at the other time?')[38] What are we to do, for example, when bodily criteria and psychological criteria conflict? Suppose we know that the person on the left will have certain *bodily* characteristics that we have always taken to be typical only of you—and that the person on the right will have certain *psychological* characteristics that we have always taken to be typical only of you. In such a case there may be no sufficient reason at all for deciding that you are or that you are not one or the other of the two different persons. But from this it does not follow that you *will* not in fact be one or the other of the two persons.

We should remind ourselves of a very simple and obvious point. When you ask yourself, 'Will I be the person on the right?' your question is *not* 'Will the person on the right satisfy such criteria as I have, or such criteria as someone or other has, for deciding whether or not a given person is I?' To be sure, the best you can do, by way of answering the first question, is to try to answer the second. But the answers to the two questions are logically independent of each other.

What is a *criterion* of personal identity? It is a statement telling what constitutes evidence of personal identity—what constitutes a good reason for saying of a person *x* that he is, or that he is not, identical with a person *y*. Now there is, after all, a fundamental distinction between the *truth-conditions* of a proposition and the *evidence* we can have for deciding whether or not the proposition is true. The *truth-conditions* for the proposition that Caesar crossed the Rubicon consist of the fact, if it is a fact, that Caesar did cross the Rubicon. The only *evidence* you and I can have of this fact will consist of certain *other* propositions—propositions about records, memories and traces. It is only in the case of what is self-presenting (that I hope for rain or that I seem to me to have a headache) that the evidence for a proposition coincides with its truth-conditions. In all other cases, the two are logically independent; the one could be true while the other is false.[39]

The question 'Was it Caesar?' is not the same as the question: 'Do we have good evidence for thinking it was Caesar?' (or 'Have the criteria for saying that it was Caesar been fulfilled?'). This is true despite the fact that the most reasonable way of trying to find the answer to the first question is to try to answer the second.

And analogously for 'Will I be he?'

What I have said may recall this observation made by Leibniz: 'Suppose that some individual could suddenly become King of China on condition, however, of forgetting what he had been, as though being born again, would it not amount to the same practically, or as far as the effects could be perceived, as if the individual were annihilated, and a King of China were at the same instant created in his place? The individual would have no reason to desire this.'[40]

If I am being asked to consider the possibility that there is an *ens successivum* of which I happen to be the present constituent and which will subsequently be constituted by someone who will then be a King of China, then the fate of the later constituent may well be no special concern of mine. But what if Leibniz were not thus playing loose with 'is'?

In such a case, the proper reply to his question is suggested by the following observation in Bayle's *Dictionary*: 'The same atoms which compose water are in ice, in vapours, in clouds, in hail and snow; those which compose wheat are in the meal, in the bread, the blood, the flesh, the bones etc. Were they unhappy under the figure or form of water, and under that of ice, it would be the same numerical substance that would be unhappy in these two conditions; and consequently all the calamities which are to be dreaded, under the form of meal, concern the atoms which form corn; and nothing ought to concern itself so much about the state or lot of the meal, as the atoms which form the wheat, though they are not to suffer these calamities, under the form of wheat.' Bayle concludes that 'there are but two methods a man can employ to calm, in a rational manner, the fears of another life. One is, to promise himself the felicities of Paradise; the other, to be firmly persuaded that he shall be deprived of sensations of every kind.'[41]

Notes

1. *On the Intellectual Powers of Man*, Essay III, Chapter 14 in Sir William Hamilton, ed., *The Works of Thomas Reid, D.D.* (Edinburgh: Maclachlan & Stewart, 1854), p. 345.

2. Fragment 41-2, as translated in Milton C. Nahm, *Selections from Early Greek Philosophy* (New York: F. S. Crofts, 1934), p. 91.

3. See Plato, *Phaedo*, 58A and Xenophon, *Memorabilia*, 4, 8, 2. Leibniz speaks of the Ship of Theseus in the *New Essays Concerning Human Understanding*, Book II, Chapter 27, Section 4, noting that any ordinary physical body may be said to be 'like a river which always changes its water, or like the ship of Theseus which the Athenians were always repairing' (Open Court edition), p. 240.

4. Thomas Hobbes, *Concerning Body*, Chapter XI ('Of Identity and Difference'), Section 7.

5. Cf. W. V. Quine: 'Thus take the question of the biggest fresh lake. Is Michigan-Huron admissible, or is it a pair of lakes? . . . Then take the question of the longest river. Is the Mississippi-Missouri admissible, or is it a river and a half?' *Word and Object* (New York: John Wiley, 1960), p. 128.

6. Using terms not commonly applied to rivers, we may note for future reference that when our diagram is read from top to bottom it illustrates *fusion* and when it is read from bottom to top it illustrates *fission*.

7. See Note c of the article 'Carneades' in Pierre Bayle's *A General Dictionary: Historical and Critical*, trans. Rev. J. P. Bernard, Rev. Thomas Birch, John Lockeman *et al.* (10 vols; London: James Bettenham, 1734–41): 'He found uncertainty in the most evident notions. All logicians know that the foundation of the syllogism, and consequently the faculty of reasoning, is built on this maxim: Those things which are identical with a third are the same with each other (*Quae sunt idem uno tertio sunt idem inter se*). It is certain that Carneades opposed it strongly and displayed all his subtleties against it.'

8. Further aspects of this kind of problem are discussed in Appendix A ('The Doctrine of Temporal Parts') [not reprinted here].

9. Dissertation I, in *The Whole Works of Joseph Butler, LL.D.* (London: Thomas Tegg, 1839), pp. 263–70. But compare Locke's third letter to the Bishop of Worcester: 'For it being his body both before and after the resurrection, everyone ordinarily speaks of his body as the same, though, in a strict and philosophical sense, as your lordship speaks, it be not the very same.'

10. I have heard it suggested, however, that (a) whereas the evening star is strictly identical with the evening star, nevertheless (b) the evening star is identical but not strictly identical with the morning star. The facts of the matter would seem to be only these: the evening star (i.e. the morning star) is necessarily self-identical; it is

not necessarily such that it is visible in the evening or in the morning; it would be contradictory to say that the evening star exists and is not identical with the evening star, or that the morning star exists and is not identical with the morning star; but it would not be contradictory to say that the morning star exists and the evening star exists and the morning star is not identical with the evening star; and whatever is identical with the evening star (i.e. with the morning star) has all the properties that it does.

11. This example of the roads, like that of the rivers above ('the Mississippi-Missouri'), may suggest that the key to our puzzles about identity through time may be found in the doctrine of 'temporal parts'. According to this doctrine, every individual thing *x* is such that, for every period of time through which *x* exists, there is a set of parts which are such that *x* is made up of them at that time and they do not exist at any other time. (Compare: every individual thing *x* is such that, for every portion of space that *x* occupies at any time, there is at that time a set of parts of *x* which then occupy that place and no other place.) I consider this doctrine in detail in Appendix A (not reprinted here). I there conclude that it will not help us with our problems about identity through time and that there is no sufficient reason for accepting it.

12. Contrast P. T. Geach, *Reference and Generality* (Ithaca: The Cornell University Press, 1962), p, 157: '. . . different official personages may be one and the same man'. Possibly an illustration would be: 'The fire-chief isn't the same personage as the Sunday-school superintendent (for one is charged with putting out fires and the other with religious instruction); yet Jones is both.' But here one seems to be playing loose with 'isn't', for what one has in mind, presumably, is something of this sort: 'Being the fire-chief commits one to different things than does being the Sunday-school superintendent, and Jones is both.'

13. There may be temptations in thus playing loose with 'is'. Suppose there were a monarchy wherein the subjects found it distasteful ever to affirm that the monarch vacated his throne. Instead of saying that there have been so many dozen kings and queens in the history of their country, they will say that the monarch has now existed for many hundreds of years and has had so many dozen different names. At certain times it has been appropriate that these names be masculine, like 'George' and 'Henry', and at other times it has been appropriate that they be feminine, like 'Victoria' and 'Elizabeth'. What, then, if we knew about these people and were to hear such talk as this: 'There has existed for many hundreds of years an *x* such that *x* is our monarch; *x* is now feminine, though fifty years ago *x* was masculine, and fifty years before that *x* was feminine'? We should not conclude that there was in that land a monarch who is vastly different from any of the people in ours. We should conclude rather that the speakers were either deluded or pretending.

14. Other examples are suggested by: 'He has a copy of *The Republic* on his desk and another on the table and he doesn't have any other books. How many books does he have?' 'He played the *Appassionata* once in the afternoon and once again in the evening, but nothing further. How many sonatas did he play?'

15. Compare P. T. Geach in *Logic Matters* (Berkeley and Los Angeles: The University of California Press, 1972), pp. 238–49; and *Reference and Generality* (Ithaca: Cornell University Press, 1962), pp. 149*ff*. The suggestion is criticised in detail by David Wiggins, in *Identity and Spatio-Temporal Continuity* (Oxford: Basil

Blackwell, 1967), pp. 1–26. Compare W. V. Quine in a review of *Reference and Generality* in *Philosophical Review*, LXXIII (1964), 100–4, and Fred Feldman, 'Geach and Relativised Identity', *Review of Metaphysics*, XXII (1968), 547–55.

16. Compare P. T. Geach: 'Even if the man Peter Geach is the same person as the man Julius Caesar, they are certainly different men; they were for example born at different times to a different pair of parents.' P. T. Geach, *God and the Soul* (London: Routledge & Kegan Paul, 1969b), p. 6. John Locke says very similar things; see the Fraser edition of the *Essay Concerning Human Understanding*, pp. 445, 450*ff.*

17. *A Treatise of Human Nature*, Book I, Part IV, Section VI; L. A. Selby-Bigge edition, p. 255.

18. Thomas Reid, *Essays on the Intellectual Powers of Man*, Essay III, Chapter IV. In *The Works of Thomas Reid, D.D.*, ed. Sir William Hamilton (Edinburgh: Maclachlan & Stewart, 1854), p. 346.

19. This thesis is discussed and defended in Appendix B ('Mercological Essentialism') [not reprinted here].

20. See *A Treatise of Human Nature*, Book I, Part iv, Section 6 (Selby-Bigge edition, p. 255): 'all objects, to which we ascribe identity, without observing their invariableness and uninterruptedness, are such as consist of a succession of related objects'. In this same section. Hume affirms a version of the principle of mereological essentialism.

21. We could define an *ens successivum* by saying, with St Augustine, that it is 'a single thing . . . composed of many, all of which exist not together'; see *Confessions*, Book IV, Chapter XI. St Thomas says in effect that a *successivum* is a thing such that some of its parts do not coexist with others of its parts ('una pars non est cum alia parte'); see the *Commentary on the Sentences*, Book I, Dist. VIII, Q. II, Art. I, ad 4. The term '*ens successivum*' has traditionally been applied to such things as periods of time (e.g. days, weeks, months) and events; compare Aristotle's *Physics*, Book III, Chapter VI, 206a.

22. Definition D.III.2 thus makes use of the general device by means of which Frege defined the ancestral relation; see G. Frege, *The Foundations of Arithmetic* (Oxford: Basil Blackwell, 1950), section 79. A more intuitive reading of clause (iii) might be: '(iii) x belongs at t to every class c which is such that (a) y belongs to c at t' and (b) all direct table successors of anything belonging to c belong to c'.

23. The distinction among these several types of property will be used in the following chapter to mark off those states of affairs that are *events*. (We had noted in the previous chapter that, although 'John is walking' refers to an event, 'John will walk' and 'John is such that either he is walking or he will walk' do not refer to events.)

24. Compare Hume: 'Tho' we commonly be able to distinguish pretty exactly betwixt numerical and specific identity, yet it sometimes happens that we confound them, and in our thinking and reasoning employ the one for the other.' *A Treatise of Human Nature*, Book I, Part IV, Section vi ('Of Personal Identity'), Selby-Bigge edition, pp. 257–8.

25. It may be noted that we have defined the loose and popular sense of the expression, 'There are n so-and-so's at t' and not the more general 'The number of so-and-so's that there ever will have been is n'. For the loose and popular sense of this latter expression is not sufficiently fixed to be explicated in any strict and philo-

sophical sense. The following example may make this clear. In the infantry of the United States Army during World War II each private carried materials for half a tent—something like one piece of canvas, a pole and ropes. Two privates could then assemble their materials and create a tent which would be disassembled in the morning. On another night the two privates might find different tent companions. Occasionally when the company was in camp the various tent parts were collected, stored away, and then re-issued but with no attempt to assign particular parts to their former holders. Supposing, to simplify the matter considerably, that all the tents that there ever will have been were those that were created by the members of a certain infantry company, how, making use of our ordinary criteria, would we go about answering the question 'Just how many tents *have* there been?' Would an accounting of the history of the joinings of the various tent parts be sufficient to give us the answer?

26. And so if we say that men are mere *entia per alio* and that God is the only *ens per se*, it will follow that I am God and not a man. Compare Bayle's refutation of Spinoza's doctrine according to which men are modifications of God: '. . . when we say that a man denies, affirms, gets angry, caresses, praises, and the like, we ascribe all these attributes to the substance of his soul itself, and not to his thoughts as they are either accidents or modifications. If it were true then, as Spinoza claims, that men are modalities of God, one would speak falsely when one said, "Peter denies this, he wants that, he affirms such and such a thing"; for actually, according to this theory, it is God who denies, wants, affirms; and consequently all the denominations that result from the thoughts of all men are properly and physically to be ascribed to God. From which it follows that God hates and loves, denies and affirms the same things at the same time . . .'. From note N of the article 'Spinoza'; the passage may be found in R. H. Popkin, ed., Pierre Bayle, *Historical and Critical Dictionary: Selections* (Indianapolis: Bobbs-Merrill, 1965) 309–10.

27. *Critique of Pure Reason*, Kemp Smith edition, p. 342. The passage is from page 363 of the first edition of the *Kritik*.

28. Page 342 of the Kemp Smith edition; pp. 363–4 of the first edition.

29. *Essay Concerning Human Understanding*, Book II, Chapter xxiii ('Our Complex Ideas of Substance'), A. C. Fraser edition, p. 451.

30. *Op. cit.*, Fraser edition, p. 454.

31. *Op. cit.*, Fraser edition, p. 458.

32. The defence of this observation may be found in Section 4 of Chapter I.

33. Kant at least was clear about this point. When he states that the 'consciousness' of one substance may be transferred to another, as the motion of one ball may be transferred to another, and notes that the last of a series of such substances might be conscious of all the states of the previous substances, he adds that 'it would not have been one and the same person in all these states'; *Critique of Pure Reason*, Kemp Smith edition, p. 342 (first edition of *Kritik*, p. 364).

34. Compare Bernard Williams, *Problems of the Self* (Cambridge: The University Press, 1973), pp. 2*ff.*

35. '"If the power to remember dies with the material body, has the question of any single person's future life after death any particular interest for him?" As you put the question, it is not whether the matter ought rationally to have an interest but

whether as a fact it has; and perhaps this is the proper question, trusting as it seems to do, rather to instinct than to reason. Now if we had a drug which would abolish memory for a while, and you were going to be cut for the stone, suppose the surgeon were to say, "You will suffer damnably, but I will administer this drug so that you will during that suffering lose all memory of your previous life. Now you have, of course, no particular interest in your suffering as long as you will not remember your present and past life, you know, have you?" ' *Collected Papers*, Vol. V (Cambridge, Mass.: Harvard University Press, 1935), p. 355.

36. See Locke's *Essay*, Book II, Chapter xxvii, Section i: 'One thing cannot have two beginnings of existence.' Compare Thomas Reid, *Essays on the Intellectual Powers of Man*, Essay III, Chapter 4.

37. Some philosophers who have considered this type of situation have not presupposed, as I have, that persons are *entia per se*. Thus Derek Parfit has suggested it is a mistake to believe that in such cases the question 'Will I be he?' has a true answer. He writes: 'If we give up this belief, as I think we should, these problems disappear. We shall then regard the case as like many others in which, for quite unpuzzling reasons, there *is* no answer to a question about identity. (Consider "Was England the same nation after 1066?")' Derek Parfit, 'Personal Identity', *Philosophical Review*, LXXX (1971), 3–27; the quotation is on page 8. P. F. Strawson has expressed a similar scepticism: 'Perhaps I should say, not that I do not understand Professor Chisholm's notion of strict personal identity, but rather that I understand it well enough to think there can be no such thing.' P. F. Strawson, 'Chisholm on Identity through Time', in H. E. Kiefer and M. K. Munitz, eds, *Language, Belief, and Metaphysics* (Albany: State University of New York Press, 1970), pp. 183–6; the quotation is on page 186. I think that the conception of persons set forth in Strawson's *Individuals* coheres more readily with the view that persons are *entia per se* than with the view that they are ontological parasites or *entia per alio*.

38. Compare Godfrey Vesey, *Personal Identity* (London: Macmillan, 1974), pp. 8*ff.*, 80*ff.*; Bernard Williams, *Problems of the Self* (Cambridge: The University Press, 1973), pp. 8*ff.*, 15*ff.*; and Anthony Quinton, 'The Soul', *Journal of Philosophy*, LIX (1962), 393–409, and *The Nature of Things* (London and Boston: Routledge & Kegan Paul, 1973); and Richard Taylor, *With Heart and Mind* (New York: St Martin's Press, 1973), pp. 122–33.

39. I have attempted to throw light upon these distinctions in Chapter IV ('The Problem of the Criterion') of *Theory of Knowledge* (Englewood Cliffs, N.J.: Prentice-Hall, 1966). Compare the discussion of criteria of self-identity in Sydney Shoemaker, *Self-Knowledge and Self-Identity* (Ithaca: Cornell University Press, 1963), pp. 35–8, 211–12, 255–60.

40. G. W. Leibniz, *Discourse on Metaphysics*, Section XXXIV (Open Court edition, p. 58). Sydney Shoemaker cited this passage in criticising an earlier formulation of my views. This earlier formulation, Shoemaker's criticism, and my rejoinder may be found in Norman S. Care and Robert H. Grimm, eds, *Perception and Personal Identity* (Cleveland: Case Western Reserve Press, 1969), pp. 82–139.

41. Pierre Bayle, article 'Lucretius', Note Q, *A General Dictionary, Historical and Critical*, trans. Rev. J. P. Bernard, Rev. Thomas Birch, John Lockeman *et al.* (10 volumes: London, James Bettenham, 1734–41)

12

Preserving the Principle of One Object to a Place: A Novel Account of the Relations Among Objects, Sorts, Sortals, and Persistence Conditions

Michael B. Burke

I. Introduction

It is common for the whole of one object and the whole of another to occupy just the same place at just the same time. So say many identity theorists, partly on the basis of reasoning such as this:

Before us lies a copper statue. In just the same place, presumably, there is some *copper* and a *piece* of copper. Now what are the relations among the statue, the copper, and the piece of copper? They can't all be the same one thing, since they differ in their persistence conditions. Suppose that tomorrow we are going to hammer the statue flat and then break what remains into bits. Both the copper and the piece of copper, but not the statue, will survive the flattening. And the copper, but not the piece of copper, will survive the subsequent shattering. So before us there are three objects occupying just the same place. Or if the copper is not an object, there are two such objects: the statue and the *piece* of copper. Of course, it is only because the statue and the piece of copper consist of the same particles of matter that they are able to occupy the same place.

Supporters of such reasoning propose that the commonsense principle of one material object to a place be restricted so as to apply only to objects of the same sort. They would allow place-sharing by a statue and a piece of copper, although not by two statues or by two pieces of copper.

Let's reserve the term 'coincidence' and its cognates for cases in which the whole of one object wholly occupies the place wholly and simultaneously occupied by the whole of another. Note that as here defined, 'coincidence' denotes an irreflexive relationship. We will use 'coextension' and its cognates for the corresponding reflexive relationship.

The idea that material objects commonly coincide with others is widely accepted.[1] Indeed, it is a corollary of what may be considered the standard account of the relations among objects, sorts, sortals, and persistence conditions. But to many the idea seems preposterous.[2] And I (1992) have argued that the idea is incoherent. Presumably, those who accept coincidence do so only because they see no congenial way to avoid it. In this paper, I will present and defend a novel alternative to the standard account, one which dispenses with coinciding objects and which may prove more widely agreeable than the other ways of preserving the principle of one object to a place. A quick look at those other ways, followed by a preview of what lies ahead, will take up the remainder of this introductory section.

One way we could avoid coincidence in the statue case is by denying that statues are *essentially* statues. We could say that there is before us but a single object, one which at present is both a piece of copper and a statue and which after tomorrow's flattening will remain a piece of copper but no longer be a statue. Thus today's statue will continue to exist after ceasing to be a statue, just as prime ministers often continue to exist after ceasing to be prime ministers. There are two drawbacks to this solution. One is simply that many of us are unwilling to allow that a work of art (or a functional artifact, such as a car) *would* survive a flattening. The other drawback is that the solution is inapplicable to certain other putative cases of coincidence, such as that of Tibbles the cat. (Tibbles is discussed in Section VI.) In such a case, in which one of the putatively coinciding objects is initially a large proper part of the other, what would help would be some basis for ruling that at least one of the objects ceases to exist. What would be no help at all would be a ruling that some seemingly essential property actually is accidental. That might *prolong* a career; it could not foreshorten one.

Some theorists have sought to avoid coincidence by invoking the doctrine that material objects have temporal as well as spatial parts.[3] On this doctrine, it is not the whole of the piece of copper, but at most a part of it, a temporal part, that is present during any period shorter than the entire period throughout which the piece of copper exists. The relation between the piece of copper and the shorter-careered statue is like the relation between a pipe and its bowl. The bowl is a spatial part of the pipe; the statue is a temporal part of the piece of copper. In both cases it is only a part of the second object, not the whole of it, that is coextensive with the first object. And because the part in question is numerically identical with the object with which it is coextensive, coincidence is avoided. For genuine coincidence it would be necessary for different objects to occupy the same place at every time at which either exists.

The insufficiency of the temporal-parts solution emerges when we notice that there indeed are putative cases of career-long place-sharing. Such a case is described by Allan Gibbard (1975) [this volume, chapter 6]. A clay statue was brought into being by the conjoining of separately fashioned halves and will be destroyed by being broken into bits. The statue is spatially *and temporally* congruent with the piece of clay that was thereby brought into being and will thereby be destroyed. Even so, it can be argued that the statue and the piece of clay are diverse: It seems true of the piece of clay, but not of the statue, that it *could* survive being hammered flat. To block this argument it would be necessary to supplement the already heavy baggage of temporal parts with some such device as the rejection of *de re* modal properties (this is Gibbard's choice), the claim that the property denoted by a modal predicate varies with the sense of the subject to which it is attached (Noonan 1985, 202–6), the claim that objects have their size and shape essentially (Heller 1990, 53–55), or a doctrine of *modal* parts (Schlesinger 1985).

The need for such supplements substantially diminishes the appeal of the temporal-parts solution. Furthermore, the doctrine of temporal parts is at odds with our ordinary ways of thinking. This creates a presumption against the doctrine that could be overcome only by showing that there are problems for whose solution the doctrine is required. My aim is to show that putative cases of coincidence do not constitute such a problem.

Yet another way to avoid coincidence is to hold, with Geach (1967), that it is common for objects to be numerically identical relative to one sortal but numerically diverse relative to another. With regard to our statue case, the sortal relativist might say something like this. The statue here now and the piece of copper here now are identical relative to all sortals and, in that sense, are absolutely the same one object. Will this one object still exist after tomorrow's hammering? Relative to the sortal 'piece of copper', the answer is yes. But relative to the sortal 'statue', the answer is no. Tomorrow there will be an object spatiotemporally continuous with today's object, but tomorrow's object is neither absolutely identical with today's object nor absolutely diverse from it.

Another form of relativism, one advocated by Myro (1985) [this volume, chapter 8] and suggested by Stalnaker (1986), makes numerical identity relative to time. On this theory, our statue is presently identical with the piece of copper: so we have before us just one object. Will this object survive tomorrow's hammering? The answer of the temporal relativist is that the hammering will destroy the statue, but not the piece of copper with which the statue is temporarily identical.

Most of us, I believe, find these relativist theories uncongenial, if not unacceptable. I will show how we can comfortably avoid coincidence without surrendering the absoluteness of identity.

Now the statue case is but one of several commonly cited as examples of coincidence. The others feature such pairs as a person and his or her body, a tree and the aggregate of the molecules of which it is composed, and a tailless cat and its "puss" (that part of a normal cat which consists of all of the cat but the tail). Probably it is the latter case, the case of Tibbles the cat, that lately has received the most attention. In seeking a way to avoid coincidence we will want to be mindful of the entire range of putative cases. Some philosophers have paid a steep price to avoid coincidence in one type of case, evidently without noticing that their costly solution is inapplicable to cases of other types. Following a discussion of the Tibbles case, William Carter (1983) reluctantly recommends consideration of the doctrine of mereological essentialism. But that radical doctrine would be unhelpful in cases such as that of the statue, in which the spectre of coincidence arises from something other than the loss or gain of a part. Peter van Inwagen (1981), who also focuses exclusively on Tibbles-type cases, avoids both coincidence and mereological essentialism by the expedient of denying that there are such things as undetached legs, tails, and pusses. But this desperate move contributes nothing to the handling of cases not involving the loss or gain of a part.

In Section II of this paper, I will show how we can dispense with coincidence in the statue case without resorting to temporal parts, sortal relativism, temporal relativism, mereological essentialism, a denial of the essentiality of statuehood, or any other theory that conflicts with our ordinary ways of thinking. In Section III, I will challenge the arguments in support of the standard account of the relations among objects, sortals, and persistence conditions, an account on which coincidence is unavoidable. In Sections IV and V, I will outline and defend an alternative to the standard account, an alternative that will accommodate Section II's treatment of the statue case. In Section VI, I will show how the alternative account enables us to dispose of other putative cases of coincidence, including, notably, the case of persons and their bodies.

II. The Statue and the Piece of Copper

In this section, I will present my own account of the statue case. I will do so in the context of responding to a persuasive pretheoretical argument for the diversity of the statue and the piece of copper, a variant of the argument presented at the beginning of Section 1. (The *theoretical* argument for the same conclusion will be examined in Section III.)

Before us today lies a statue fashioned a week ago from the whole of a single piece of copper acquired a year ago. Let's call the statue "Statue" and the original piece of copper "Piece 1." In the place occupied by Statue, it seems true to say, we have a piece of copper. To give it a name that leaves open its relation to Statue and to Piece 1, let's call this piece of copper

This leads me to think of P_1 and P_2 as temporal parts of the copper.

"Piece 2." Now there are two things that seem hard to deny: first, that Piece 2 is the same piece of copper as Piece 1; second, that Statue has existed only for a week and therefore is not to be identified with Piece 1. Thus are we pushed toward the surprising conclusion that Statue and Piece 2 are different objects simultaneously occupying the same place.

The argument's main line is this:

Premise 1: Piece 2 is Piece 1.
Premise 2: Statue is not Piece 1.
Conclusion: Statue is not Piece 2.

How might we resist this unwelcome conclusion? Given our ambition of reconciling the principle of one object to a place with the essentiality of statuehood, with the absoluteness of identity, and with our ordinary conception of objects as enduring (rather than perduring) through time, there appear to be only two ways of challenging the argument.

One is to deny that there is such a thing as Piece 2, to deny, that is, that when Piece 1 has been used to make a statue we still have a piece of copper. Of course, we still have some *copper*. And we have a copper statue. But, it might be said, the term 'piece of copper' cannot correctly be applied to a finished product. Before last week's hammering we had a piece of copper. Today, it might be said, we do not. Therefore, Piece 1, which was a piece of copper *essentially*, has ceased to exist. So far as I am aware, no one has advanced this objection to the argument. And while I have some sympathy for the objection, I wouldn't care to rely on it. For one thing, it is far from clear that the extension of 'piece of copper' is restricted in the way the objection assumes. For another, this sort of objection would be implausible as applied to certain other cases, such as that of Tibbles the cat. So, I will not dispute the assumption that there is such a thing as Piece 2.

The other way for us to challenge the argument is to grant the existence of Piece 2 but to deny the identity of Piece 2 with Piece 1. In my judgment, the best account of the statue case is this: Piece 2 is numerically identical with Statue. That is, we have here just one object. It is (predicatively) both a piece of copper and a statue. This object has existed only a week. It is not to be identified with Piece 1. Although there is here a piece of copper, it is not the one with which we began. We have the same *copper*, but not the same *piece* of copper.[4]

What is novel in my account, and what is likely at first to seem counterintuitive, is my denial of Premise 1. In what follows I will explain why this premise is false and try to break its hold on our intuitions.

How could Premise 1 fail to be true? How could Piece 2, the piece of copper here now, fail to be Piece 1, the piece of copper that we had to begin with? After all, Piece 2 is qualitatively and spatiotemporally continuous with

Piece 1 under the sortal 'piece of copper'. And it consists of just the same copper atoms. Surely a piece of copper retains its identity while undergoing a continuous change in shape. (We'll suppose that the statue was made by hammering rather than by casting.)

The answer is simple. The reason that Piece 2 is not Piece 1 is that Piece 1 was merely a piece of copper, whereas Piece 2 is also a *statue*. Given the assumption that a mere piece of copper cannot *become* a statue (and it is only this essentialist assumption that warrants Premise 2 of my opponents' argument), Piece 2 cannot be identified with Piece 1. But why do I say that Piece 2 is (predicatively) a statue? Because Piece 2 is Statue. Providing we make this commonsensical assumption, we can see *that* Piece 2 is not Piece 1. And we can see *why* Piece 2 is not Piece 1.

In effect, of course, we are standing our opponents' argument on its head. If we begin by assuming that there is just one object before us, that the piece of copper here and the statue here are one and the same, and if we then join our opponents in assuming that statues are statues *essentially*, we can conclude straight away that Premise 1 is false.

The problem is that denying the identity of Piece 2 and Piece 1 seems as much a violation of common sense as does denying the identity of Statue and Piece 2. I have explained why Premise 1 is false. But if it is false, why does it have such strong intuitive appeal? In the remainder of this section, I will offer three explanations.

(1) "Surely," say believers in coincidence, "the piece of copper here now is the piece of copper we had to begin with." Unless we have our wits about us we will be quick to agree. By referring to each object as a "piece of copper" they encourage us to ignore the objects' difference in sort. They deflect attention from the point that the object here now is also a statue. If we consider only that the objects are pieces of copper consisting of the same copper, then of course we will agree that they are the *same* piece of copper. I believe this goes far toward explaining why Premise 1 strikes us as unexceptionable.

(2) A further explanation, I believe, is found in the ease with which one can overlook the distinction between a piece of copper and the copper of which it consists. It is true that the *copper* here now is the *copper* we had to begin with. And one might think that this is to say that the *piece* of copper here now is the *piece* we had to begin with. That the claims are different ones, that the copper and the piece of copper are not to be identified, is shown by the fact that the copper and the piece of copper have different persistence conditions. The copper, but not the piece of copper, could survive the cutting of the piece into five smaller pieces.

Of course, the copper and the piece of copper occupy just the same place. So if the copper differs from the piece of copper, don't we have coincidence after all? No, we don't. But the reason why not can't be given until

Section VI, where we will consider putative cases of coincidence that feature quantities of matter.

(3) Oversights are not the whole explanation for the appeal of Premise 1. Perhaps some would accept Premise 1 simply because they would reject Premise 2. If one is inclined even to identify *Statue* with Piece 1, to say that the original piece of copper has become a statue, then one will be inclined to identify Piece 2 with both Statue and Piece 1. Of course, my opponents must reject this conception of the case: It involves rejecting both the second premise and the conclusion of their argument.

In sum: If we keep clearly in mind that 'Piece 2' refers not to the *copper* here, but to the *piece* of copper, and that this piece of copper is also a statue, whereas Piece 1 was *merely* a piece of copper, then we will feel much less inclination to identify Piece 2 with Piece 1. Such inclination as remains is simply the inclination, felt by some, to identify *Statue* with Piece 1, to say that Piece 1 has become a statue. But if Premise 1 is accepted only because Premise 2 is rejected, the verdict on the argument under discussion will be the same.[5]

We have seen that denying Premise 1 is not the violation of common sense it initially seems. So far as common sense is concerned, we are free to deny the identity of Piece 2 with Piece 1 and to identify Piece 2 with Statue instead. But there remains an obstacle to doing so: The diversity of Statue and Piece 2 is entailed by a widely accepted philosophical theory. Let's proceed to examine that theory.[6]

III. The Standard Account

The following doctrines constitute the heart of what may be considered the standard theoretical account of the relations among objects, sortals, and persistence conditions.[7] (1) Associated with every sortal is a set of persistence conditions. (2) Objects that satisfy a given sortal invariably have the persistence conditions associated with that sortal.[8] (3) Two sortals are cosatisfiable (as are 'kitten' and 'cat') only if the persistence conditions associated with one are the same as the persistence conditions associated with the other.[9]

With regard to (2), let's give the long definite description it contains a Russellian interpretation. (Let's *not* take that description to mean 'whatever persistence conditions, *if any*, are associated with that sortal'.) Thus understood, doctrine (2) entails doctrine (3).

Now from the conjunction of doctrine (3) and the proposition that 'statue' and 'piece of copper' are sortals associated with different persistence conditions, it follows that nothing is both a statue and a piece of copper. Since 'Statue' is our name for a certain statue and 'Piece 2' our name for a certain piece of copper, it follows that Statue is not Piece 2.

Might we deny that 'statue' and 'piece of copper' are sortals associated with different persistence conditions? I believe not. I regard both 'statue' and 'piece of copper' as sortals, for reasons that will soon be apparent. I see no reason to deny doctrine (1), the doctrine that every sortal is associated with some set of persistence conditions. And for reasons given toward the end of Section IV, I agree that the persistence conditions associated with 'statue' are incompatible with those associated with 'piece of copper'. What we should deny, if we want to maintain the identity of Statue and Piece 2, and if, more generally, we want to avoid coinciding objects, are doctrines (2) and (3). But since arguments for (3) invariably rely on (2) (we'll soon see some examples), we will directly challenge only the arguments for (2).

Before doing so we must consider the notion of a sortal, that is, the notion of a term that denotes a sort. And we must consider what is meant by 'the persistence conditions *associated* with a sortal'.

Of the many criteria of sortalhood that have been suggested, the relatively precise criteria come in three varieties: grammatical, mereological, and numerative. Unfortunately, to all of these relatively precise criteria there are fairly clear counterexamples.[10] Of the criteria currently on offer, my preference is for Wiggins': A sortal is a term that can be used to answer the question 'What is it?' There is an object on my coffee table. If I tell you only that it is a red object, you will not know what it is. But if I tell you that it is an apple, you will. 'Apple' is a sortal. 'Red object' is not.

The Wiggins criterion of sortalhood seems to accord well with our judgments concerning which terms do and do not denote sorts, in the appropriate sense of 'sorts'. (More on this in Section IV.) Of course, the criterion (like sortalhood itself) is somewhat vague. There are cases where we would be able to say with confidence neither that a term does answer the *what is it* question nor that it doesn't. Certainly we would prefer a more precise criterion—and a more illuminating one. But I don't know of such a criterion that isn't otherwise unsatisfactory. In Section IV we will discover an important merit of the Wiggins criterion. Here we may note that it is agreeably liberal: It accepts as sortals all terms billed as such by those who believe in coincidence. On some criteria, 'piece of copper' doesn't qualify. On Wiggins', it does: There are objects (such as copper scraps) for which 'piece of copper' clearly does answer the *what is it* question.

Identity theorists speak both of the persistence conditions of *objects* and of the persistence conditions *associated with sortals*.[11] By 'the persistence conditions of the object *o*' is meant 'the conditions necessary and sufficient for the persistence of *o*'. These conditions determine the changes that *o* can and cannot undergo while continuing to exist. But what might be meant by 'the persistence conditions *associated with the sortal F*'? One way to define this expression is to equate it with 'the persistence conditions *that any object will have if it satisfies the sortal F*'.

The problem with this definition is that it makes doctrine (1), the doctrine that for every sortal there is an associated set of persistence conditions, equivalent to doctrine (2). (Given the definition, doctrine (1) says that for every sortal there is a single set of persistence conditions that is had by any object that satisfies that sortal. Given the same definition, and given the Russellian interpretation of definite descriptions, doctrine (2) says the same thing.) For my purposes such a definition would be inconvenient: I want both to accept doctrine (1) and to reject doctrine (2).

I grant that every sortal has an associated set of persistence conditions. But I want to claim that an object can satisfy sortals associated with different persistence conditions. In such a case, I want to say, the object has the persistence conditions associated with just one of the (groups of) sortals it satisfies. It is quite possible, I want to contend, for some *F*'s to have the persistence conditions associated with *F* while other *F*'s, *F*'s which are *G*'s, have the persistence conditions associated with *G*.[12] To avoid excluding this possibility by definition (which would merely force a reformulation of my claims), let's understand 'the persistence conditions *associated with the sortal F*' to mean 'the persistence conditions *that any object has if it has the persistence conditions it has in consequence of satisfying the sortal F*'.[13] This will leave it an open question, even for those who accept doctrine (1), whether objects satisfying a given sortal invariably have the persistence conditions associated with that sortal. That is, it will leave open whether doctrine (2) is true.

Let's proceed, then, to take up that very question. The first thing to be said is that the burden of proof rests with the doctrine's proponents. No one, I believe, would suggest that doctrine (2) is self-evident. It will be accepted, if at all, on the basis of some philosophical argument. And precisely because accepting the doctrine would force us to accept that there often is a multiplicity of objects where we ordinarily suppose there to be just one, or else to avoid this extravagance by resort to theories that many philosophers find more disagreeable still, the argument will need to be a rather convincing one.

Does such an argument exist? Despite the importance of doctrine (2), one is hard pressed to find in the literature on identity a *statement* of the doctrine, never mind a defense of it. Generally the doctrine serves as an unstated assumption in arguments for doctrine (3), as in the passages below.

> Because sortals have criteria for reidentification built into them [doctrine (1)], one object cannot fall under two sortals having different criteria for reidentification [doctrine (3)]. Still, we want to locate objects falling under different sortals at the same place. For example, the car and the lump of plastic occupy the same volume of space but cannot be identified with one another because of the different criteria for reidentifying cars and lumps of plastic (Pollock 1974, 160–61)
>
> Wherever an individual x belongs to each of two different sorts ϕ and ψ, these sorts cannot . . . have different criteria of identity [doctrine (3)] . . . The point quite simply is that, if C_ϕ and C_ψ are the respective criteria of identity and they are *different*, then if x were to belong to both ϕ and ψ we could not in general

> rule out *a priori* the possibility that there should arise circumstances in which, according to C_ϕ (say), x would cease to exist, whereas according to C_ψ it would not; so that anyone asserting that x instantiates both ϕ and ψ would lay himself open to the intolerable possibility that circumstances should arise in which he would have to say that x *both does and does not* cease to exist. (Lowe 1983, 54)

Pollock assumes that any object satisfying a given sortal is to be reidentified by the criterion "built into" that sortal. Lowe assumes the same thing: that the criterion of identity associated with a sort is applicable to any object of that sort. In our terms, both assume doctrine (2): Any object satisfying a given sortal has the persistence conditions associated with that sortal. But nowhere does Pollock or Lowe defend, or even formally *state*, doctrine (2). Neither considers the possibility I suggested earlier: When an object satisfies sortals associated with different identity criteria, *one* of these criteria is privileged to serve as the criterion by which the object is properly reidentified. (*Which* one will be discussed in Section V.)

Now there are persuasive arguments for doctrine (2), if it is granted that physical objects commonly coincide with others. In the present context, of course, those arguments are inadmissible. To speed us on our way I'll relegate them to a note.[14]

What other arguments are there? So far as I can determine, there is just one. And I know of no statement of the argument less sketchy than this one by Wiggins (1980, 62):

> . . . to fulfil its office and constitute an answer to the *what is it* question, a genuinely sortal predicate must stand for a concept that implicitly or explicitly determines identity, persistence, and existence conditions for members of its extension.

Neglecting the reference to identity and existence conditions, and making explicit both the implicit premise (IP) and the implicit conclusion (IC), Wiggins' argument for doctrine (2) (IC) might be laid out as follows:

P If every sortal answers the *what is it* question, then every sortal stands for a concept that determines persistence conditions for every member of its extension.

IP Every sortal answers the *what is it* question.

IC Every sortal stands for a concept that determines persistence conditions for every member of its extension.

The problem with the argument is that it depends on the ambiguity of the sentence (IP) that serves both as the implicit premise and as the antecedent of the explicit premise: Every sortal answers the *what is it* question. IP might mean either IP1 or IP2.

IP1 Every sortal is such that there are or could be objects for which it answers the *what is it* question.

IP2 Every sortal is such that it answers, *for every member of its extension*, the *what is it* question.

Now for the argument to be valid, IP must have a consistent meaning. But in order for IP to be warranted, IP must mean IP1. And in order for P to be warranted, IP must mean IP2. Let me try to substantiate the latter two claims.

If IP is taken to mean IP1, then IP is unexceptionable. Indeed, IP1 is simply a more precise formulation of what I meant earlier in this section when, following Wiggins, I defined sortals as terms that can be used to answer the *what is it* question. A quite different claim, and one I see no good reason to accept, is IP2. Consider the sortal 'piece of copper'. For some objects, *mere* pieces of copper, 'piece of copper' answers the *what is it* question. But what would stop us from saying, contrary to IP2, that there are other pieces of copper, Statue, for example, for which 'piece of copper' fails to answer that question? Indeed, this is precisely the sort of account that I will develop and defend in sections IV and V. (To make IP2 an implicit *definition* of 'sortal' would merely force a reformulation of the issues.)

Now certainly it would make sense for those who accept doctrine (3), the doctrine that sortals are cosatisfiable only if they are associated with the same sets of persistence conditions, also to accept IP2. Given doctrine (3), there is a convincing argument for IP2.[15] But as remarked earlier, the only support I know (or can imagine) for doctrine (3) is doctrine (2). Since IP2 is employed here in support of doctrine (2), IP2 cannot here be supported by reference to a doctrine for which doctrine (2) is the only support. And since there is no apparent argument for IP2 that *doesn't* rely on doctrine (3) (or else on doctrine (2) itself), I conclude that IP2 is unwarranted.[16]

Unfortunately for Wiggins' argument, IP2 is the interpretation of IP required by the stated premise, P. If IP means only IP1, then there is no apparent basis for inferring the consequent of P from its antecedent. Given only that sortals answer the *what is it* question for *some* members of their extensions, we cannot infer that sortals stand for concepts that determine persistence conditions for *all* members of their extensions.

Accordingly, Wiggins' argument, the only argument for doctrine (2) that doesn't depend explicitly on the thesis that material objects commonly coincide with others, may be rejected. Of course, the failure of arguments for the doctrine does not mean that the doctrine is false—or even that it cannot reasonably be accepted. Doctrine (2) is the linchpin of the standard account of the relations among objects, sortals, and persistence conditions. Despite the implausible implications of that account, there will be an understandable reluctance to reject it until there is an appealing alternative.

IV. An Alternative Account

In this section, I will offer an alternative to the standard account. In Section V, I will defend my account against a likely objection. And in Section VI, I will show that my account permits us to dispose of other putative cases of coincidence in the same way we disposed of the statue case.

First, a terminological matter. For ease of expression I will hereafter treat sortals associated with the same persistence conditions as the same sortal. Thus 'puppy', 'injured dog', and 'dog', which all have the same associated persistence conditions, will count as a single sortal.

Also to be treated as a single sortal is any group of sortals that are associated with sets of persistence conditions that are different but not incompatible. Such groups exist, I believe, just in case it is possible for one substance sortal to restrict another.[17] A possible example of such a group: 'collie', 'dog', 'mammal', 'animal'. The persistence conditions associated with these terms are not incompatible. That is, it is possible for a single individual to have the persistence conditions associated with all four terms. But if all of these terms are substance sortals (which is very much open to question), then they all differ slightly in their associated persistence conditions.[18] In any event, I will use 'the same sortal' as short for 'sortals associated with persistence conditions that are identical or, at least, not incompatible'. And I will use 'different sortals' as short for 'sortals associated with incompatible persistence conditions'.

Now for my account, of which we have had partial previews, of the relations among objects, sorts, sortals, persistence conditions, and answers to the *what is it* question. Of the three doctrines listed at the beginning of Section III, I accept (1) but reject (2) and (3). I agree that every sortal has an associated set of persistence conditions, but I hold that every composite object that is not a mere aggregate satisfies at least two sortals, one being 'aggregate'.[19] For example, Piece 2 (= Statue) is (predicatively) a piece of copper, a statue, and an aggregate of copper atoms. I also hold that among the sortals satisfied by an object, one is the object's "dominant" sortal.

Let's say that sortal *F* is object *o*'s *dominant sortal* just in case *o* has the persistence conditions it has in consequence of satisfying *F*. And let's say that sortal *F dominates* sortal *G*, with respect to *o*, just in case (1) *o* satisfies both *F* and *G*, and (2) *F*, not *G*, is *o*'s dominant sortal. With respect to Piece 2, for example, 'statue' dominates both 'piece of copper' and 'aggregate of copper atoms'. (The *basis* for this and other such claims will be made clear in the next section.)

These definitions raise a question: Is it possible for *F* to dominate *G* with respect to one object but for *G* to dominate *F* with respect to another? Suppose we have two gold statues. One is the creation of a master and is of interest primarily as a work of art. The other is an amateurish production of interest primarily as a piece of gold. Now certainly we *could* say that even in the latter case the object has the persistence conditions associated with 'statue'. We could simply add that our primary interest is not in the *object* but in the stuff of which it consists. The alternative, a plausible one, is to say that 'statue' dominates 'piece of gold' with respect to the first object but that 'piece of gold' dominates 'statue' with respect to the second.

Again, consider an example of "found art": a stone "statue" whose intrinsic properties are entirely the result of natural processes. Even assuming that the found object really is a statue, it is tempting to think that 'piece of stone' is its dominant sortal. It would be plausible to say that the statue once was a mere piece of stone and that it became a work of art, while remaining the same piece of stone, when it was found, appreciated, and displayed with certain intentions. It is an advantage of my account that it is able to accommodate this view of the case. (On the standard account, an object satisfies just one sortal. Given that 'statue' is a sortal, *every* statue must have the persistence conditions associated with 'statue'.) Without denying that found art really is art, without claiming that examples of found art are examples of art even before they are found, without claiming that all artworks are abstracta, and without taking any other controversial position within aesthetics, we are able to avoid saying that artists sometimes cause material objects to come into being merely by taking and inviting others to take a certain attitude. (I don't myself *mind* saying that. But some do.)

For ease of exposition, and contrary to what I am inclined to believe, I will sometimes speak as though *G* can never dominate *F* if *F* ever dominates *G*. Accordingly, it will be useful to have two additional definitions. They will permit us to speak of dominance and domination *simpliciter*, as well as dominance and domination with respect to a specified individual. Let's say that *F* is the dominant member of a set of cosatisfiable sortals just in case *F* dominates every other member of that set. And let's say that sortal *F* dominates sortal *G* just in case (1) it is possible that there be an object with respect to which *F* dominates *G*, and (2) it is not possible that there be an object with respect to which *G* dominates *F*.

Now what I propose is that we reject doctrine (2), the doctrine that objects satisfying a given sortal invariably have the persistence conditions associated with that sortal, in favor of doctrine (2′): Objects that satisfy at least one sortal invariably have the persistence conditions associated with one or another of the sortals they satisfy. In combination with the assumption that every object satisfies at least one sortal (not necessarily a *short* sortal), doctrine (2′) entails this: For every object there is a sortal such that the object has the persistence conditions it has in consequence of satisfying that sortal. Or, using our new terminology: Every object satisfies one or more sortals, one of which is its dominant sortal.

Furthermore, I submit that only an object's dominant sortal tells what the object is. The alternative, which I reject, is to say that any of the sortals satisfied by an object will suffice to answer the *what is it* question for that object, but the dominant sortal provides the *best* answer. Consider a copper statue, an object that satisfies both 'piece of copper' and 'statue'. The dominant sortal, I hold, is 'statue'. (How dominant sortals are to be identified is explained in Section V.) Now would 'piece of copper' provide even an inferior answer to the *what is it* question? I think not. What, after all, does 'piece of copper' mean? Given that the term applies (on my account) to copper statues, kettles, and bracelets, as well as to *mere* pieces of copper, 'piece of copper' means merely 'cohesive object formed by a quantity of copper'. And merely to be told what kind of stuff an object consists of (and that it is cohesive) is not to be told *what* that object is. (Unless, of course, the object is merely a piece of that kind of stuff.) I can no more tell you what the copper statue is by telling you that it is something copper than by telling you that it is something brown.

Still, one can imagine an argument for the alternative view. It runs as follows: (1) Every sortal denotes a sort. ('Sortal' was introduced by Locke as short for 'term denoting a sort'.) And it seems natural to say that (2) any object that satisfies a given sortal is an object of the *sort* denoted by that sortal. It follows that (3) every sortal answers, for every object that satisfies it, the question 'What *sort* of object is it?' even if some other sortal provides a *better* answer to that question. But surely, (4) the question 'What *sort* of object is it?' is logically equivalent to the question '*What* is it?' (It's only because of this equivalence that it is acceptable to use suitability for answering the *what is it* question as a criterion of *sortal*hood.) It follows that (5) every sortal answers, for every object that satisfies it, the question 'What is it?' even if some other sortal provides a better answer to that question.[20]

On the definition with which we are working, a sortal is a term such that there are or could be objects for which the term answers the *what is it* question. Accordingly, let's say that a *sort* is a classification such that there are or could be objects for which the information that they belong to that classification answers the *what is it* question. Now given these definitions, it is true that (1) every sortal denotes a sort. And it is true that (2) any object that satisfies a given sortal will be an object *of the sort* denoted by that sortal, in the sense that the object will belong to the classification with which the sort is identical. But does it follow that (3) every sortal answers, for every object that satisfies it, the question 'What *sort* of object is it?'

Certainly it *sounds* as though (3) follows from (2). That's because (3) *does* follow from (2), if the question 'What sort of object is it?' is taken to mean 'What is a sort such that the object is of that sort?' But if instead the question is understood (as is required for the truth of (4)) to be logically equivalent to '*What* is it?' then (3) does *not* follow from (2). To infer (3), thus understood, from (2) would be to rely on the assumption, call it "*A*," that for any sort and for any object, the information that the object is of that sort answers the *what is it* question for that object. Now *A* would be an entirely reasonable assumption, if there were reason to believe that every object is an object of just one sort. But, of course, I argued in Section III that there is *not* any reason to believe this. In any case, the argument's dependence on *A* renders the argument circular. *A* is essentially identical to the argument's conclusion: (5).

It is worth noting that our use of 'sort' has been a technical one. As is customary in philosophical writings, we have used it to refer to something like Aristotle's second substances, to classifications of objects according to their "forms." In ordinary contexts, the question 'What sort of object is it?' generally means 'What is a sort such that the object is of that sort?' And it requires for an answer nothing more than does the question 'What *manner* of object is it?' For answering the latter, both non-sortals and non-dominant sortals suffice. With respect to Statue, for example, the question can be answered by 'something heavy', 'something brown', or 'something copper'.

It is an important merit of the Wiggins criterion of sortalhood that it substitutes an unambiguous question—'What is it?'—for the ambiguous question 'What sort of object is it?' In my view, the latter is *doubly* ambiguous. It can mean (1) 'What is a sort, in the ordinary sense of "sort," such that the object is of that sort?' (2) What is a sort, in the Aristotelian sense of "sort", such that the object is of that sort?' or (3) 'What is the object?" On my account, unlike Wiggins', a correct answer to (2) is not necessarily a correct answer to (3).

In what follows, I will use 'of that sort' to mean 'of that Aristotelian sort'. (More precisely, I will use it in the sense indicated four paragraphs back.) And I will use such expressions as 'tell what sort of object it is' and 'tell the object's sort' to mean 'tell *what* the object is'. The latter, of course, is equivalent to 'answer the *what is it* question with respect to the object'.

To summarize my account: Every composite object that is not a mere aggregate satisfies at least two sortals, one of which is its *dominant* sortal, that is, the sortal from which it gets its persistence conditions. Although an object is *of* the sort denoted by each of the sortals it satisfies, only the object's dominant sortal *tells the object's sort*. That is, only the object's dominant sortal answers the *what is it* question for that object.

Before concluding this section, I will address a couple of questions concerning persistence conditions. The task of the theory of diachronic identity is that of identifying the general persistence conditions associated with broad *categories* of objects. Besides the specific persistence conditions associated with various *sorts* of objects (and the sortals that name them), it is commonly assumed that there are general persistence conditions associated with such broad categories as works of art, functional artifacts, hunks of stuff, aggregates, natural kinds, persons, and organizations. Despite helping myself freely to the language of "persistence conditions," I will undertake to identify neither these general persistence conditions nor the specific persistence conditions associated with the sortals that figure in my examples. how Convien

That, obviously, would require another long paper.[21] This much, however, can be said: The persistence conditions associated with a given sortal need be no different on my account than on the standard account, with one exception. On my account, an object that has the persistence conditions it has in consequence of satisfying *F* can persist only so long as it does not undergo changes that would cause it to satisfy a sortal that dominates *F*. Thus a mere piece of copper could not survive changes that would make it a statue. On my account, therefore, but not on the standard account, a mere piece of copper would be destroyed by changes that would cause it to be coextensive with a statue. (On the standard account, of course, such changes would cause the piece of copper to be *coincident* with a statue, not to *be* a statue.)

Earlier I said that if 'dog' and 'animal' are both substance sortals, then the persistence conditions associated with these terms are different but not incompatible, the difference lying solely in their levels of generality. (See note 18.) It might be thought that I ought, in consistency, to say the same thing with respect to 'copper statue' and 'piece of copper', since I hold that the former restricts the latter[22] just as 'dog' restricts 'animal'. But if there were no incompatibility of persistence conditions with respect to 'piece of copper' and '*copper* statue', then (contrary to what I have said) there also would be none with respect to 'piece of copper' and 'statue'.

The difference between the two cases is this: 'Piece of copper', unlike 'animal', applies (on my account) to objects of diverse *categories*. Its extension includes works of art and functional artifacts, as well as mere hunks of matter. These categories are associated with mutually inconsistent general persistence conditions. Functional artifacts are commonly thought to be capable of persisting despite the replacement of many or even all of their original parts, providing there is spatiotemporal continuity under a sortal. By contrast, works of art and mere hunks of matter can survive much less in the way of compositional change. There is no (non-trivial) set of persistence conditions, however general, that is possessed by all pieces of copper. That is why the persistence conditions associated with 'piece of copper' cannot differ simply in level of generality from those associated with 'copper statue'.

On my account, the persistence conditions associated with 'piece of copper' are the persistence conditions possessed by those objects for which that term answers the *what is it* question: *mere* pieces of copper. As already noted, I won't try actually to formulate those conditions. But I assume that they are incompatible with the persistence conditions associated with 'statue', which I, along with supporters of the standard account, assume to be much more restrictive with regard to changes in shape.

To reconnect with the paper's main line of development, the reader may wish to reread the summary of my account, six paragraphs back, before proceeding to Section V.

V. The *Which One* Problem

In Section IV, I outlined an account of the relations among objects, sorts, sortals, and persistence conditions. Among the advantages of my account over the standard account are its ontological economy,[23] its compatibility with the commonsense principle of one material object to a place, its flexibility in dealing with atypical cases of the sort discussed in the sixth and seventh paragraphs of section IV, and its freedom from two of the burdens of the standard account: that of avoiding (or else defending) a multiplication of *agents* (see the final two paragraphs of section VI) and that of explaining how coinciding objects could differ in *sort*, a problem that threatens the very coherence of the standard account.[24] Are there *dis*advantages to my account? Well, there is one *apparent* disadvantage.

On the account presented in Section IV, objects commonly satisfy two or more sortals but get their persistence conditions from just one. The obvious question is *which* one. If an object is both a statue and a piece of copper, how do we determine whether it has the persistence conditions associated with 'statue' or the persistence conditions associated with 'piece of copper'? In general, how do we identify an object's dominant sortal? On the standard account, of course, this awkward question does not arise, since every object satisfies just one sortal. (Recall that sortals associated with identical or compatible persistence conditions, such as 'collie', 'dog', 'mammal', and 'animal', aren't being counted as different sortals.) In this section, I will offer an answer to the *which one* question. And I will show that questions of essentially the same kind face proponents of the standard account. So whatever the merits of my answer, the *which one* problem puts my account at no significant disadvantage.

So, which of the sortals satisfied by an object is the object's dominant sortal? If we make the plausible assumption that an object's persistence conditions are determined by its sort (see note 13) the answer to this question is straightforward: An object's dominant sortal is the sortal that tells the object's sort, the sortal that tells what the object is.

Of course, this answer raises a new question, in response to which I offer (as a first approximation) the following criterion: Of the sortals satisfied by an object, the one that tells the object's sort is the one whose satisfaction entails possession of the widest range of properties.

Admittedly, the criterion is somewhat vague. But its vagueness seldom prevents a clear-cut decision. This will become clear as we consider a representative sample of cases. To keep things simple we'll limit ourselves to pairwise comparisons. But to make the comparisons appropriately challenging we'll consider some of the most troublesome pairs. After we see how the criterion works, we'll inquire into its justification.

Suppose, to begin with, that we are choosing between 'tree' and 'hunk of cells'. Which of these cosatisfiable sortals (is such that its satisfaction) entails possession of the wider range of properties? Well, both sortals entail possession of physical and chemical properties. But 'tree', unlike 'hunk of cells', also entails possession of a full range of biological properties. (Or if dead but undecomposed trees are still trees, what is entailed by 'tree' is possession at *some* time of a full range of biological properties.) Think of a hunk of fat cells just excised by a plastic surgeon. Every one of the cells constituting the hunk engages in a full range of biological activities. But the hunk itself, unlike those hunks of cells that are also organisms, probably does not engage (and probably never did engage) in any biological activities at all. Even if it does (or did), there are certain biological activities, such as reproduction, that are engaged in only by organisms, not by just any hunk of cells. So, 'tree' entails possession of a certain range of properties whose possession is not entailed by 'hunk of cells'. And since 'tree' is (on my account) a *restriction* of 'hunk of cells', the latter can entail nothing whatsoever not entailed by the former. Accordingly, my criterion selects 'tree' over 'hunk of cells'.[25]

Now consider a couple of cases involving artifacts: one a work of art satisfying both 'statue' and 'piece of copper', the other a functional artifact satisfying both 'typewriter' and 'hunk of metal'. This time the sortals competing for dominance are ordered neither by the restriction relation nor by any simple variant of it. ('Statue' doesn't restrict 'piece of copper'. It doesn't even restrict 'piece of stuff': There are statues made of two or more separated pieces. And there *could* be a two-piece typewriter, even if there isn't one.) Still, it is clear that 'statue' and 'typewriter' entail possession of the wider range of properties. Admittedly, there are specific physical and chemical properties entailed by 'piece of copper' and 'hunk of metal' that are not entailed by 'statue' and 'typewriter'. But that's not what counts. Any statue and any typewriter will be composed of *some* substance or substances and thus will *have* a full range of physical and chemical properties. What counts, on my criterion, is the entailed range of properties, not the range of specific properties entailed. So, 'piece of copper' and 'hunk of metal' enjoy no advantage with respect to physical and chemical properties. But 'statue', unlike 'piece of copper', entails possession of aesthetic properties, such as artistic genre and artistic style. And 'typewriter', unlike 'hunk of metal', entails possession of functional properties, such as function, degree of functionality, mode of operation, and quality of design. So the types of properties common to all statues or all typewriters exceed in range the types of properties common to all pieces of copper or all hunks of metal. Accordingly, my criterion chooses 'statue' and 'typewriter' over 'piece of copper' and 'hunk of metal'.

I can think of three types of case that call for special attention. Typical of one is the case of Tibbles the cat, which was mentioned in Section I. A "puss" is that part of a normal cat that includes all of the cat except its tail. So when a cat loses its tail, there is (on my account) an object satisfying both the sortal 'cat' and the sortal 'puss' (allowing, as I will, that 'puss' is a sortal). The question, then, is which of these sortals (supposing it to be one or the other) is the object's *dominant* sortal. Assuming that persistence conditions are a function of sort, the answer depends on whether it is 'cat' or 'puss' that tells the object's sort. That, in turn, depends on which of these sortals entails possession of the wider range of properties. As usual, the answer is clear. Both 'cat' and 'puss' entail possession of physical and chemical properties. But 'cat', unlike 'puss', entails possession of *behavioral* properties. (Most pusses aren't cats: most are proper *parts* of cats. So most pusses don't breathe, sleep, hunt, mate, or otherwise *act*.) Given my criterion, we can rule without hesitation, and with a sense of enhanced understanding, that the dominant sortal is 'cat' rather than the philosophical concoction 'puss'. (What we should go on to say about the Tibbles case is spelled out in Section VI.)

Also calling for special attention is the always troublesome case of persons and their bodies. To generate work for my criterion, let's make two assumptions, each disputable: (1) that persons are wholly physical and (2) that the persistence conditions associated with 'person' are nevertheless incompatible with those associated with 'human body'. On my account, of course, the assumed incompatibility of persistence conditions is no bar to the cosatisfiability of the two sortals. So let's assume that human persons satisfy both 'person' and 'human body'. The question now arises: Which term dominates? Given my criterion, the question is which term entails possession of the wider range of properties. Assuming it to be *necessary* not only that persons are wholly physical but that they are living or otherwise functioning organisms, whether biological, mechanical, or whatever, the answer is clear. Person entails present possession not only of physical properties and of chemical properties, but also of the properties of a biological or other sort of functioning organism. Since some human bodies are dead (and yet still exist), 'human body' does not. Furthermore, 'person' entails present or past possession of the capacity, or at least of the potential, for intellection. 'Human body' does not: Some genetically defective human bodies never have even the potential to function intellectually. It is clear, on the two assumptions made above,[26] that 'person' entails possession of the wider range of properties and, therefore, that my criterion chooses 'person' over 'human body'. (The implications of this are discussed in Section VI.)

Having just mentioned that it is a matter of controversy whether the persistence conditions associated with 'person' are incompatible with those associated with 'human body', probably it is opportune to remark that the general account presented in this paper, like the standard account of the relations among objects, sorts, sortals, and persistence conditions, is meant to be compatible with a variety of views concerning the properties essential to various sorts and categories of objects and, therefore, with any of a variety of views concerning the persistence conditions associated with various sortals and categorials. The aim of the present section is not to resolve controversies among essentialists. The aim, rather, is to provide a plausible and generally serviceable means of identifying an object's dominant sortal, and thus its persistence conditions, when it has been determined by other means (a combination of intuition, philosophical reasoning, and, at least on the causal theory of reference, empirical inquiry) what persistence conditions are associated with the various sortals satisfied by the object. The latter is a challenging task, but no more so on my account than on the standard one.

Finally, suppose we are choosing between 'piece of copper' and 'aggregate of molecules'. Here, for once, there is not a perfectly familiar category of property whose possession is entailed by one sortal but not by the other. This is not surprising, since pieces of copper are among the most primitive of the sorts of objects ordinarily recognized, while 'aggregate of molecules', in the intended sense (clarified in Section VI), does not denote an ordinarily recognized sort of object. But since I want to accommodate those who believe in arbitrary sums, here, very briefly, is what I suggest. A composite object is "strongly" unified, let us say, just in case there is something that unites its components, something that makes them the components of a single object, *beyond the mere fact that they exist.* (The latter *is* sufficient to make them the components of an "aggregate.") Now I assume (despite the nihilistic arguments of van Inwagen 1990) that there are quite a number of such uniting relationships, all easier to illustrate than to define, such as those possessed by the components of a piece of copper (roughly: cohesion), a solar system, the United States of America, a tree, a pile of dirt, and a disassembled trombone. Corresponding to each strongly uniting relationship is a strongly unifying property. 'Piece of copper' entails possession of a member of this category of properties. 'Aggregate of molecules' does not. And since 'piece of copper' is (on my account) a *restriction* of 'aggregate of molecules', the latter entails nothing not entailed by the former. Accordingly, my criterion selects 'piece of copper' over 'aggregate of molecules'. (More on aggregates in Section VI.)

We have seen that my criterion provides clear-cut rulings across a wide range of cases. And in general, I think its rulings are the ones we want. But we saw in Section IV that it is a potentially significant advantage of my general account that it can make provision for some *FG*'s to have the persistence conditions associated with *F* while other *FG*'s have the persistence conditions associated with *G*. This would provide options for dealing with atypical cases, such as those involving "found art" or amateurish art employing valuable materials. (On the standard account, *every* work of art must have the persistence conditions associated with 'work of art'.) To secure these options it would be necessary to modify my criterion of sortal dominance. I will not consider such modifications in this paper.

So, we have at least a rough answer to the *which one* question. But what *justifies* the answer? What justifies accepting my criterion? Two things do: its intrinsic reasonableness and, especially, the agreeableness of its rulings. Suppose that a number of objects have been identified merely by their places, without the aid of any of the sortals they satisfy. (It's only on the standard account, on which there can be more than one object to a place, that an object must be identified under a sortal.) And suppose we are asked what the identified objects are. As will be evident from the examples we have considered, the answers yielded by my criterion will be the same ones, except perhaps in atypical cases of the kind mentioned above, that we would give in the course of ordinary life. When asked to say what something is (perhaps by a child), we ordinarily produce, whenever possible, a dictionary entry, such as 'cat', 'desk', or 'mountain range'. We would select 'typewriter' over 'hunk of metal', at least if we were instructed to ignore any extraordinary features of the context. I assume that our ordinary answers are generally correct (when we have correct information about which sortals are satisfied by the objects in question). And since my criterion gives the same answers, I conclude that my criterion is accurate.

Of course, anti-essentialists would deny that there *are* uniquely correct answers to *what is it* questions. They would insist that an object's sort, like its essential properties and its persistence conditions, is always *relative* to something like an interest or a description. What sort of object is our brown copper statue? Would it continue to exist if hammered flat? If painted green? The answers, an interest-relativist would say, may differ for a curator, a metallurgist, and a decorator. The brown copper statue has no interest-independent persistence conditions and, in our sense of 'sort', no interest-independent sort. Ditto for the typewriter/hunk of metal.

Now the account offered in this paper, like the standard account of the relations among objects, sorts, sortals, and persistence conditions, is frankly essentialist. But my aim in this paper is not to defend essentialism. It is to present an essentialist alternative to the essentialist standard account. I do, however, want to emphasize one point. To be an essentialist is not necessarily to be a realist with regard to essentiality. (See Hooker 1978 and Sidelle 1989.) Neither is it necessarily to be a realist with regard to persistence conditions or sort. An object's essential properties, its persistence conditions, its sort, and its dominant sortal all are matters that can be viewed by an essentialist either as objective or as relative to our conceptual scheme.[27] (The anti-essentialist views them as relative to descriptions, contexts, interests, or other things similarly numerous and transitory.) A pleasing feature of conceptual-scheme relativism is that it provides relatively little basis for skepticism concerning our ability to determine an object's essential properties, persistence conditions, and dominant sortal (when we have answers to the relevant empirical questions): To make such determinations we need only be attuned to the features of our own conceptual scheme. For the conceptual-scheme relativist, at least, there is little question of the propriety of taking agreement between the rulings of my criterion and the informed judgments we make in ordinary life as evidence for the accuracy of my criterion.

To conclude this section, I want to argue that there would be little advantage to the standard account even if we did not have a satisfactory answer to the *which one* question. Although the standard account does not face the problem of identifying an object's dominant sortal, it does face problems of the same kind. We can identify an object's dominant sortal if we can decide, with respect to certain of the properties of the object, whether the object has them accidentally or essentially. If we are choosing among 'statue', 'piece of copper', and 'aggregate of molecules', it will be sufficient to decide whether the object is a statue essentially and, if not, whether it is a piece of copper essentially. Some will consider such decisions problematic. But on the standard account, too, as on any essentialist account, there are many decisions to be made, and justified, about the essential properties of objects.

Consider our copper statue. By denying that it is also a piece of copper and an aggregate of molecules, we could indeed ease the task of deciding whether the statue is a statue essentially. But the gain would be of little significance, since many decisions about the essential properties of the statue would remain: What changes in shape could the statue survive? How much of the statue could be destroyed without the statue's ceasing to exist? Could the original composition of the statue have been partially or wholly different? Could the statue have been the work of a different artist? Could it continue to exist if it ceased to be regarded, even by its creator, as a work of art?

In short, the problem of identifying an object's dominant sortal is the problem of determining which of the sortal properties of an object are had by the object essentially. If we lessened this problem by insisting that the sortal properties (i.e., the properties denoted by substance sortals) are instantiated by different (but coincident) objects, we would still have the problem of determining the essentiality or inessentiality to the various instantiating objects of many types of *non*-sortal properties. That we would be left after our ontological extravagance with slightly fewer decisions concerning the essentiality of properties is, I submit, a minor consideration that is far outweighed by the considerations enumerated in the first paragraph of this section.

In summary, I have presented an answer to the *which one* question, suggested a justification for the answer, and noted that questions of the same general kind arise on the standard account also, as on any essentialist account.

VI. Other Putative Cases of Coincidence

In sections III through V, I challenged the arguments supporting the standard account, proposed an alternative to that account, and defended my account against a predictable objection. In this section, I will show how my account handles putative cases of coincidence *other* than that of the statue and the piece of copper.

A. Ordinary Objects and Quantities of Matter

Sydney Shoemaker (Shoemaker and Swinburne 1984, 113), after noting that a copper statue is arguably diverse from the hunk of copper with which it is coextensive, writes, ". . . whatever we say of the hunk of copper, the statue does share its space with one entity that is incontestably non-identical with it, namely the quantity of copper of which it is composed."[28]

I agree with Shoemaker that the quantity of copper (i.e., the copper) is diverse from the statue, but only because I agree with Henry Laycock that the quantity of copper (unlike the piece of copper) is not a single object. Laycock (1972) would say that the copper is to be identified with the copper atoms of which the statue is composed[29] and thus is to be identified with objects, not with *an* object. If he is right, the congruence of the statue and the copper is not a case of coincidence because it is not a case of the congruence of one object with any one other.

But suppose the copper *is* a single object, as many would hold it to be. In that case, presumably, the copper is identical with the *aggregate* of the copper atoms (or with the aggregate of the particles of matter) of which the statue is composed. Putative cases of coincidence featuring aggregates are dealt with in subsection B.

B. Ordinary Objects and Aggregates

Among the most frequently cited examples of coincidence are those involving ordinary physical objects (such as ships and trees) and "aggregates" (or "collections") of particles, molecules, cells, planks, or whatever. Entirely representative is an example given by Wiggins [this volume, p. 4]:

> A certain tree T stands (leafless, suppose) at a certain spot . . . and occupies a certain volume . . . All and only [that volume] is also occupied by the aggregate W of the cellulose molecules which compose the tree. . . . Are [T and W] identical? . . . T = W only if T and W have exactly the same conditions of persistence and survival through change. But self-evidently they do not. . . . Suppose T is chopped down and then dismembered and cut up in such a way that no cellulose molecule is damaged. It seems that W then survives. And there is just as much wood in the world as there was before.[30] But T, the tree, cannot survive such treatment. Conversely, suppose the tree is pruned and the clippings are burned . . . Then the tree T survives but W, the aggregate defined as the aggregate of such and such particular cellulose molecules, does not survive.

To what, we need to ask, does Wiggins refer by 'the aggregate W of the cellulose molecules'? Is he referring to the *set* of the cellulose molecules? Presumably not. Sets, at least as standardly conceived, aren't physical objects and don't occupy space. Is he referring to the *aggregation* (or heap) of the cellulose molecules? Evidently not. It seems clear that Wiggins takes W to be capable of surviving the dispersal of its members. This is a capability not possessed by aggregations.

When speaking of "aggregates," Wiggins, and others who offer similar examples, evidently have in mind a category of object concerning which they evidently accept the following propositions. (1) For any set of two or more physical objects there is a physical object, an aggregate, that is composed of all and only the members of that set. (2) Every aggregate has the persistence conditions it has in consequence of being an aggregate. (3) An object that has the persistence conditions it has in consequence of being an aggregate will persist just so long as do all of the objects of which it is the aggregate. From the conjunction of (1), (2), and (3) it follows that for any set of two or more physical objects there is a physical object, an aggregate, which is composed of all and only the members of that set and which will persist just so long as do all of those members.

Now (1) is a doctrine of arbitrary sums and hence is very much open to question. But for the sake of argument, I am willing to allow arbitrary sums. Furthermore, I agree that (3) is approximately correct, when 'aggregate' denotes the category of object Wiggins evidently has in mind. What I deny, unsurprisingly, is (2). With respect to the case at hand, I deny that W, the aggregate of the cellulose molecules, has the persistence conditions associated with 'aggregate of cellulose molecules'.[31]

On my account, W satisfies 'tree' as well as 'aggregate of cellulose molecules'. Since 'tree' dominates 'aggregate of cellulose molecules', for the reasons indicated in Section V, W has the persistence conditions associated with 'tree'. Hence there is no reason to deny the identity of W with T, no reason to consider this a case of coincidence.

Let's use 'Z' to refer to the object that is constituted after the dismemberment of T by the cellulose molecules of which T had been composed. On my account, W and Z are different aggregates of molecules even though they are aggregates of the same molecules. This will not seem counterintuitive, so long as two points are kept firmly in mind: (1) An aggregate of molecules is to be distinguished from the molecules of which it is the aggregate: The molecules are *many* objects; their aggregate is *one* object. (2) W, unlike Z, is not *just* an aggregate of certain cellulose molecules: It is also a tree.

What, the reader may ask, do I take 'aggregate of cellulose molecules' to *mean*? The answer is that I consider the term a name for the (natural) *sort* of thing that Z is. (I'm allowing that there *is* such a thing as Z.) What one says about that sort of thing will depend upon whether one favors the standard account or my account of the relations among objects, sorts, sortals, and persistence conditions. On the standard account, an aggregate of cellulose molecules is any object that (a) is composed exclusively of cellulose molecules and (b) will persist just so long as do all of the cellulose molecules of which it is composed.[32] On my account, an aggregate of cellulose molecules is any object, whether an ordinary object or merely a sum, and whatever its persistence conditions, that is composed exclusively of cellulose molecules.[33] Such an object will have the persistence conditions associated with 'aggregate of cellulose molecules' just in case that sortal tells what the object is. An object that does have those persistence conditions, Z for instance, will persist just so long as (a) all of the cellulose molecules of which it is the aggregate persist, and (b) it does not undergo changes that would cause it to satisfy a sortal that dominates 'aggregate of cellulose molecules'.

C. Cats and Pusses

A "puss" is that part of a normal cat that includes all of the cat except its tail. Yesterday the cat Tibbles consisted of a 7-pound puss, named 'Tib', and a 1-pound tail. Earlier today Tibbles lost its tail. But Tibbles still exists. And so does Tib. Yesterday Tib occupied a proper part of the place occupied by Tibbles. Today Tib occupies the whole of that place. Still, Tib and Tibbles differ numerically, because they have different histories. Tibbles is a former 8-pounder; Tib is not. So, Tib and Tibbles are different objects that now occupy just the same place.[34]

In spite of all the attention this argument has received, there is a simple, commonsensical response that seems to have been overlooked: that of rejecting the premise that Tib still exists. We can agree that yesterday there was such a thing as Tibbles' puss. And we can agree that today there is a puss that is spatiotemporally continuous with that puss. But we can deny that today's puss is identical with yesterday's. Initially this sounds unpromising. But that is only because we tend to focus on what the two pusses have in common, especially their shape and their composition, and fail to attend to their difference in *sort*: Yesterday's puss, Tib, was *merely* a puss, while today's is also a cat. If we assume that cats are cats *essentially*, and thus *non*-cats are *non*-cats essentially, we can conclude that Tib has ceased to exist.[35]

I called this response "commonsensical" because I think that sortal essentialism is implicit in our ordinary ways of thinking. At least it doesn't represent a radical departure from those ways of thinking, as do the other theories by reference to which the case has been disposed. (For nine ways of dealing with Tib and Tibbles, see Simons 1987, 119.)

Of course, the suggested response assumes the cosatisfiability of 'cat' and 'puss'. But the cosatisfiability of different sortals is precisely what my account provides for. The response also assumes that 'cat' dominates 'puss', an assumption whose warrant was made clear in Section V.

D. Persons and Bodies

Perhaps the most frequently cited example of coincidence is that of persons and their bodies. Let's briefly consider the example from both dualist and materialist points of view.

On dualist theories of the human person, there is no threat of genuine coincidence. Dualist theories divide into those on which the body is a proper *part* of the person and those on which the body is something like a possession. On theories of the first type, it is true that a person occupies the place occupied by his body. But it's not the whole of the person that occupies that place; it's merely a part of him that does so. This is no more a case of coincidence than is the case of a pipe and its bowl. ('Coincidence' is defined in the fourth paragraph of Section I.) On theories of the second type, on which a person is a mind or soul that "possesses" a body, it is only in some non-literal sense that a person may be said to "occupy" the place occupied by her body. The sense is similar to that in which a general may be said to occupy the area occupied by his army, even if he commands the army from outside that area.

On materialist theories, the matter is more complicated. For materialists who identify persons with their bodies, there is no question of coincidence. But for supporters of (some version of) the brain criterion or the psychological criterion of personal identity, coincidence may seem unavoidable, except by the radical measures surveyed in Section I. Let's consider the matter just from the standpoint of the psychological criterion. Once we have done so, it will be sufficiently evident what might be said from the standpoint of the brain criterion.

Suppose that Jane and Jill have undergone a procedure that effected an exchange of the information in their brains. The result is this: There now is a person who has the psychological properties originally had by Jane, but whose body is qualitatively and compositionally identical to the body originally had by Jill. And *vice-versa.* Proponents of the psychological criterion will say that the former is Jane and the latter Jill. And no doubt they will view this as a case of body switching. If we call Jill's original body "Body 1" and Jane's present body "Body 2," no doubt they will say that Body 2 is Body 1, that Jane now has the body originally had by Jill. But if they do say this, then (unless they hold that persons are abstracta—or invoke one of the radical theories canvassed in Section I), they will have to say that Jane and Body 2 are different physical objects that now occupy the same place.

My suggestion for materialists who accept the psychological criterion is to deny that Body 2 is Body 1. On what grounds might they do so? Well, we have found no general bar to the cosatisfiability of different sortals. And it would seem entirely natural for materialists to insist on the cosatisfiability of 'person' and 'human body'. Materialists who accept the psychological criterion can say that Body 1 and Body 2 are persons as well as human bodies, that 'person' dominates 'human body' (for the reasons given in Section V), and that psychological continuity is required for personal identity. They can conclude that Body 2 is not Body 1, on the grounds that Body 2 lacks psychological continuity with Body 1. They can add that reference to persons as "bodies" is as an invitation to consider them in abstraction from their psychological properties and that this is part of what accounts for our readiness to misidentify Body 2 (Jane) with Body 1 (Jill).

But isn't this bizarre? Body 2 consists of the same head, the same neck, the same torso, and the same limbs as did Body 1. How could it fail to *be* Body 1? Actually, the suggestion should elicit little surprise. We are accustomed to cases, such as that of the ship of Theseus, in which the same parts in the same arrangement arguably fail to make the same object. Just as one can argue that spatiotemporal continuity is necessary for the diachronic identity of ships, one can argue that psychological continuity is necessary for the diachronic identity of those human bodies (the psychologically functioning ones) that are persons.

Considerations of the sort presented in the preceding two paragraphs will serve also to make it plausible (to materialists who favor the psychological criterion) that Jane's present body is none other than the body she had to begin with.[36]

To conclude this subsection, I want to indicate, although I won't here develop, a line of reasoning that suggests that coincidence is especially worth resisting precisely in the case of persons and their bodies. Suppose that Pete, a person, coincides with his body, Bob. Then Pete, like Bob, is a physical object. (It is only on theories on which persons are purely physical objects that persons are literally coextensive with their bodies.) Indeed, Pete consists of just the same particles of matter as does Bob.

Now here is the problem. Suppose that Pete is thinking. On both type-type and token-token versions of materialism, Pete's thinking is identifiable with some physical event taking place within Pete. But any physical event taking place within Pete is taking place also within Bob. Does this mean that Bob, also, is thinking? If not, why not? If a person and his body are different physical objects composed of just the same particles of matter, the only differences between them, it would seem, lie in their persistence conditions and, perhaps, in their early histories. (No doubt it would be said that death without dismemberment would terminate the existence of Pete but not that of Bob. And perhaps it would be said that Bob came into existence some months or years earlier than Pete.) But there is no apparent way to explain, simply by reference to *those* differences, why thinking (or talking or walking) is something done by persons *but not by their bodies*. Unless an explanation can be provided, or unless materialists are willing to accept the multiplication and coincidence of *agents*, they had better find a way to avoid saying that persons and their bodies are different physical objects wholly present in just the same place. To materialists who favor the psychological criterion (or the brain criterion) of personal identity, I commend the sort of account presented above.

VII. Conclusion

I have presented and defended a novel account of the relations among objects, sorts, sortals, and persistence conditions. Among its advantages over the standard account (all listed at the beginning of Section V) is its compatibility with the commonsense principle of one material object to a place. My account enables us to dispose of the full range of putative counterexamples to that principle. And it enables us to do so without resorting to anti-essentialism, temporal parts, sortal relativism, temporal relativism, mereological essentialism, or other theories that conflict with our ordinary ways of thinking about the world.[37]

Notes

1. Among those prepared to accept coincidence are Chappell (1990), Chisholm (1973, 587–91), Doepkė (1982) [this volume, Chapter 2], Forbes (1987, 142–44), Hirsch (1982), Johnston (1992) [this volume, Chapter 4], Kripke (1971, 163–64, fn. 19), Lowe (1983), Pollock (1974, 157–66), Salmon (1981, 224–29). Shorter (1977, 399), Simons (1987, 212–15, 221–24), Thomson (1983) [this volume, Chapter 3], Yablo (1987), and, most influentially, Wiggins (1967, Part One; 1968 [this volume, Chapter 1]; 1980, chap. 1).

2. Peter van Inwagen calls it a "desperate expedient" (1981, 129) [this volume, p. 198]. Harold Noonan says that it "manifests a bad case of double vision" (1988, 222). David Lewis, speaking of the idea that plastic dishpans coincide with dishpan-shaped pieces of plastic, writes, "This multiplication of entities is absurd on its face" (1986, 252) [this volume, p. 135].

3. See Cartwright 1987, 168–70 and Heller 1990, 19.

4. There will be more on the relation between the copper and the piece of copper later in this section.

5. I want here to add two points of clarification (1) I would not deny the analogue of Premise 1 in just *any* case that might be substituted for the one under discussion. In general, I would deny the analogue of Premise 1 just in those cases in which I accepted the analogue of Premise 2. In a case in which I considered the analogue of 'statue' not to be a "substance sortal" (defined in note 17), probably it is the analogue of Premise 2 that I would want to reject. And although I consider 'statue' to be a substance sortal, I might have considered rejecting Premise 2 itself if Statue

had been an example of "found art" or extremely amateurish art. The theory to be outlined in Section IV, unlike standard sortal essentialism, allows for substance sortals to apply essentially to some objects and accidentally to others. (2) The argument mentioned at the beginning of Section I differs from the argument discussed in this section in attributing to the statue and the piece of copper divergent *modal* properties. I would deal with the former argument in the same way I have dealt with the latter: I would deny that the piece of copper *could* survive being hammered flat, on the ground that the piece of copper is also a statue.

6. Before closing this section, I want to address a question that may have occurred to some readers. Tomorrow, let us suppose, Piece 2 is going to be hammered flat. This will leave a piece of copper we'll call "Piece 3." Of course, I deny the identity of Piece 3 and Piece 2 for the same reason I deny the identity of Piece 2 and Piece 1. But what is the relation between Piece 3 and Piece 1? The answer is that they are one and the same. Piece 1 went out of existence a week ago and will come back into existence tomorrow. Elsewhere (Burke 1980) I have argued, at article length, and for reasons having nothing to do with the desirability of avoiding coincidence, that there need be nothing problematic about intermittent existence in cases, such as that of Piece 1/Piece 3, in which the *components* of the intermittently existing object exist continuously.

7. The fullest statements of this account are found in Wiggins 1980 and Simons 1987. Elements of the account are found in most of the works cited in note 1.

8. Persistence conditions are not properties. Strictly speaking, objects don't "have" persistence conditions. What objects do have is the property of being such as to persist just so long as certain conditions are met. But I will join those who speak of persistence conditions as had or possessed. This way of speaking permits simpler formulations and will not lead us into substantive error.

9. If there are cosatisfiable sortals whose associated persistence conditions are different but not incompatible ('collie' and 'dog', perhaps), then 'the same as' should be replaced by 'compatible with'. For more on this, see the third paragraph of Section IV and notes 17 and 18.

10. See Feldman 1973.

11. More commonly, perhaps, they speak of the identity or reidentification *criteria* associated with sortals. But since I prefer to speak of an object's persistence conditions, rather than of the criteria for reidentifying the object, I will speak, likewise, of the persistence conditions associated with sortals. (For a discussion of identity criteria, and of their association also with singular terms, see Lowe 1989.)

12. For ease of expression, I use '*F*' and '*G*' both as sortal variables and as sortal dummies. This will cause no confusion.

13. I assume that an object's having the persistence conditions it has is explained by its being of a certain sort. (Presumably it must be explained by *something*. And it's hard to imagine what *else* it might be explained by.) The same assumption is evident in the main argument for doctrine (2), Wiggins', which will be discussed later in this section.

14. One runs like this. Whenever sortals associated with different persistence conditions have coextensive instantiations, an object satisfying one of the sortals and having the persistence conditions associated with that sortal *coincides* with an object satisfying the other sortal and having the persistence conditions associated

with that sortal. Now if each of the objects satisfies *both* sortals, then the coinciding objects are of the same sort, which surely is unacceptable. So neither object satisfies the sortal whose associated persistence conditions it fails to have. That is, neither object is a counterexample to doctrine (2). But it is only in such cases (cases in which sortals with different associated persistence conditions are coextensively instantiated) that there is any apparent threat to doctrine (2). So we may conclude that doctrine (2) is true.

Another argument for the doctrine, one we can disregard for the same reason, goes something like this: It is common for an object with one set of persistence conditions to coincide with an object with another set of persistence conditions. Therefore, it is important for us to have convenient means of referring unambiguously to each of two such objects. What we need, and what our language can therefore be expected to supply, is a class of (relatively short) terms each of which applies to all and only those objects that have in common some particular set of persistence conditions. Since it is clear that non-sortal terms (such as 'red object') do not fill the bill, the class must be that of (relatively short) sortals. This sort of argument may be implicit in Doepke 1987, 37–38.

15. 1. For every object, there is a term (even if only a long one) that answers the *what is it* question for that object. [premise]
2. Only sortals answer the *what is it* question; and only a term *satisfied* by an object can answer the *what is it* question for that object. [premise]
3. Every object satisfies a sortal that answers the *what is it* question for that object. [from 1 & 2]
4. Cosatisfiable sortals have the same associated persistence conditions. [doctrine (3)]
5. If all of the sortals satisfied by an object have the same associated persistence conditions, then if any of those sortals answers the *what is it* question for that object, so do the others. [premise]
6. If any of the sortals satisfied by an object answers the *what is it* question for that object, so do the others. [from 4 & 5]
7. Each of the sortals satisfied by an object answers the *what is it* question for that object. [from 3 & 6]

IP2 Every sortal answers, for any object that satisfies it, the *what is it* question. [from 7]

16. Actually, there is one other argument for IP2. It will be more convenient to consider and criticize this argument in Section IV.

17. One sortal restricts a second just in case it is necessarily true that anything that satisfies the first satisfies the second. As customarily defined, a substance sortal is a sortal the satisfaction of which is essential to anything that satisfies it. My account will require a somewhat different definition: A substance sortal is a sortal such that there are or could be things to which it is essential that they satisfy that sortal.

18. The associated persistence conditions would differ only in their levels of generality. If an object has the persistence conditions associated with 'collie' if and only if it will persist just so long as there is an object with which it is spatiotemporally continuous under 'collie', then an object has the persistence conditions associated with 'dog' if and only if it will persist just so long as there is an object with which it

is spatiotemporally continuous under a name for a variety of dog. (There is more about persistence conditions toward the end of this section.)

19. I will make the unfavorable assumption that for every set of two or more objects there is an object, an aggregate, that is composed of all and only the members of that set. If there isn't, it's just that much easier to avoid coincidence. More on aggregates, and how I conceive them, in Section VI.

20. This is the further argument for IP2 mentioned in note 16.

21. Also beyond the scope of the present paper, as will be stressed in Section V, is a defense of the essentialist presuppositions of my account. I am offering an essentialist alternative to the essentialist standard account.

22. Well, not really. It is possible for several pieces of copper to constitute a statue without constituting a single piece of copper. But I do hold that 'copper statue' restricts 'aggregate of copper atoms'.

23. As noted by a referee for *Philosophy and Phenomenological Research*, the advantage of my account with respect to ontological economy is not as great as it might appear. After all, I do recognize all of the *sorts* of objects recognized on the standard account. And over time I recognize almost as *many* objects. (Recall the statue case discussed in Section II. I recognize one object before the sculpting and one object, a different object, afterwards. My opponents recognize one object before the sculpting and two afterwards. But since one of the latter is identified with the former, they recognize over time only the same number of different objects as do I: two. Still, my account does greatly reduce the number of objects existing at any one time. And it slightly reduces the total existing *over* time: In those rare cases that my opponents would describe as cases in which two or more objects are congruent spatially *and temporally*, I recognize over time a total of only one object.

24. This problem is discussed in Burke (1992) and Johnston (1992) [this volume, Chapter 4].

25. If sortals S1 and S2 differ in their associated persistence conditions, but S1 restricts S2, then there is or *could* be at least *one* object with respect to which S1 dominates S2. That much, but only that much, is true simply in consequence of our *definitions*.

26. If it is necessarily *false* that persons are wholly physical, then 'person' and 'human body' aren't cosatisfiable. And the question of which dominates the other doesn't arise. But if it is neither necessarily true nor necessarily false that persons are wholly physical, then my criterion would have to be made more precise before it could yield a clear-cut decision.

27. Wiggins, the leading exponent of the standard account, takes a realist position with regard to sort (1980, 136–38) and is thereby committed to a realist position with regard to essentiality and persistence conditions.

28. To harmonize Shoemaker's example with ours, I have taken the liberty of substituting 'copper' for Shoemaker's 'bronze'.

29. Tyler Burge (1977, 109–10) shows how this account might be extended to mixtures, such as bronze and milk. I would myself prefer to identify the copper with the matter, i.e., the *particles* of matter, of which the statue is composed. Although I think that copper atoms are copper atoms essentially, I think that quantities of copper are not essentially quantities of copper.

30. Note that Wiggins evidently does identify the wood of the tree with the aggregate of its cellulose molecules.

31. If it were insisted that the three propositions provide an implicit *definition* of 'aggregate', this would merely shift the question to whether aggregates, thus defined, *exist.* The proper way to assign a meaning to 'aggregate' will be indicated shortly.

32. For a full articulation of the standard account's conception of aggregates, see Burge 1977.

33. This analysis assumes that Wiggins is right in thinking that there is something of Z's sort where T is. This can be doubted. Recall the analogous doubt over whether there is a "piece of copper" where Statue is.

34. The puzzle of Tib and Tibbles is Peter Geach's adaptation of a medieval *sophisma.* The term 'puss' is Harold Noonan's.

35. Geach (1980b, 215) [this volume, p. 309] maintains that a proper part of a cat may itself be a cat (the *same* cat, albeit not the same lump of feline tissue, as the cat of which it is a part). His argument for this is as follows: A sufficiently large part of a cat clearly *would* be a cat if separated from the rest of the cat; but the separation surely wouldn't *generate* a cat; so the part must *already* be a cat. What is easy to overlook is the possibility of denying the first premise, on the grounds that the separation would cause the part to cease to *exist.* It is eminently plausible to say both that proper parts of cats are non-cats and that non-cats are non-cats *essentially.* If instead one accepts Geach's conclusion that any sufficiently large part of a cat is itself a cat, one is forced either to allow that cats can be identical although discernible (with respect to size, weight, and shape) or else to acquiesce in a monstrous multiplication of cats.

36. Two remarks concerning the locution 'Jane's body'. (1) To speak of "Jane's body" is not thereby to concede the diversity of Jane and her body. At most, it is to concede that their identity is open to question. (2) Perhaps there is a sense of 'body' in which 'Jane's body' refers not to a physical object, but merely to the physical (as opposed to the psychological) *dimension* of Jane. In any such sense of 'body', Jane, although diverse from her body, does not *coincide* with her body. Coincidence requires two physical objects.

37. I am greatly indebted for criticisms and suggestions to John Tilley and James Buxton, to anonymous referees for this journal, to Cindy Stern, who commented on a portion of the paper at the 1992 meeting of the Pacific Division of the American Philosophical Association, to others who made comments at the same meeting, notably Harriet Baber and Greg Ray, and, most especially, to Frederick Doepke.

References

Burge, Tyler. 1977. "A Theory of Aggregates." *Noûs* 11:97–117.

Burke, Michael. 1980. "Cohabitation, Stuff, and Intermittent Existence." *Mind* 89:391–405.

— 1992. "Copper Statues and Pieces of Copper: A Challenge to the Standard Account." *Analysis* 52:12–17.

Carter, William. 1983. "In Defense of Undetached Parts." *Pacific Philosophical Quarterly* 64:126–43.

Cartwright, Richard. 1987. "Scattered Objects." In *Analysis and Metaphysics*, ed. K. Lehrer, 153–71. Dordrecht and Boston: D. Reidel Publishing Co., 1975. Reprinted in *Philosophical Essays*, R. Cartwright, 171–86. Cambridge, Massachusetts: The MIT Press.

Chappell, Vere. 1990. "Locke on the Ontology of Matter, Living Things and Persons." *Philosophical Studies* 60:19–32.

Chisholm, Roderick. 1973. "Parts as Essential to Their Wholes." *The Review of Metaphysics* 26:581–603.

Doepke, Frederick. 1982. "Spatially Coinciding Objects." *Ratio* 24:45–60.

— 1987. "The Structures of Persons and Artifacts." *Ratio* 29:36–52.

Feldman, Fred. 1973. "Sortal Predicates." *Noûs* 7:268–82.

Forbes, Graeme. 1987. "Is There a Problem About Persistence?" *The Aristotelian Society: Supplementary Volume* 61:137–55.

Geach, Peter. 1967. "Identity." *The Review of Metaphysics* 21:3–12.

— 1980. *Reference and Generality*, 3rd ed. Ithaca and London: Cornell University Press.

Gibbard, Allan. 1975. "Contingent Identity." *Journal of Philosophical Logic* 4:187–221.

Heller, Mark. 1990. *The Ontology of Physical Objects: Four-Dimensional Hunks of Matter*. Cambridge: Cambridge University Press.

Hirsch, Eli. 1982. *The Concept of Identity*. New York: Oxford University Press.

Hooker, John. 1978. "Why Essentialism is True." *Southwestern Journal of Philosophy* 9:7–14.

Johnston, Mark. 1992. "Constitution Is Not Identity." *Mind* 101:89–105.

Kripke, Saul. 1971. "Identity and Necessity." In *Identity and Individuation*, ed. M. Munitz, 135–64. New York: New York University Press.

Laycock, Henry. 1972. "Some Questions of Ontology." *The Philosophical Review* 81:3–42.

Lewis, David. 1986. *On the Plurality of Worlds*. Oxford: Basil Blackwell.

Lowe, E. J. 1983. "Instantiation, Identity, and Constitution." *Philosophical Studies* 44:45–59.

— 1989. "What is a Criterion of Identity?" *The Philosphical Quarterly* 39:1–21.

Myro, George. 1985. "Identity and Time." In *Philosophical Grounds of Rationality: Intentions, Categories, Ends*, ed. R. Grandy and R. Warner, 383–409. Oxford: Oxford University Press.

Noonan, Harold. 1985. "The Closest Continuer Theory of Identity." *Inquiry* 28:195–229.

— 1988. "Reply to Lowe on Ships and Structures." *Analysis* 48:221–23.

Pollock, John. 1974. *Knowledge and Justification*. Princeton: Princeton University Press.

Salmon, Nathan. 1981. *Reference and Essence*. Princeton: Princeton University Press.

Schlesigner, George. 1985. "Spatial, Temporal and Cosmic Parts." *The Southern Journal of Philosophy* 23:255–71.

Shoemaker, Sydney and Richard Swinburne. 1984. *Personal Identity*. Oxford: Basil Blackwell.

Shorter, J. M. 1977. "On Coinciding in Space and Time." *Philosophy* 52:399–408.
Sidelle, Alan. 1989. *Necessity, Essence, and Individuation: A Defense of Conventionalism*. Ithaca and London: Cornell University Press.
Simons, Peter. 1987. *Parts: A Study in Ontology*. Oxford: Clarendon Press.
Stalnaker, Robert. 1986. "Counterparts and Identity." In *Midwest Studies in Philosophy XI: Studies in Essentialism*, ed. P. French, T. Uehling, Jr., and H. Wettstein, 121–40. Minneapolis: University of Minnesota Press.
Thomson, Judith. 1983. "Parthood and Identity Across Time." *The Journal of Philosophy* 80:201–220.
Van Inwagen, Peter. 1981. "The Doctrine of Arbitrary Undetached Parts." *Pacific Philosophical Quarterly* 62:123–37.
— 1990. *Material Beings*. Ithaca: Cornell University Press.
Wiggins, David. 1967. *Identity and Spatio-Temporal Continuity*. Oxford: Basil Blackwell.
— 1968. "On Being in the Same Place at the Same Time." *The Philosophical Review* 77:90–95.
— 1980. *Sameness and Substance*. Oxford: Basil Blackwell.
Yablo, Stephen. 1987. "Identity, Essence, and Indiscernibility." *The Journal of Philosophy* 84:293–314.

PART IV

Indeterminacy Solutions

13

Entities Without Identity[1]

Terence Parsons

I want to begin by distinguishing two maxims regarding identity that are currently in favor among many philosophers. They are both commonly articulated by the slogan, "no entity without identity", but they are in fact distinct principles.

> (1) The first is the view that we should not admit into our ontology entities for which we are unable to provide clear "criteria of identity".
> (2) The second is the view that there can be no entity (no value of one's variables) to which the notion of identity fails to apply. In more positive terms, the second view is that the meaningfulness of even discussing things of a certain sort involves quantifying over them and counting them and referring to them, and this is supposed to presuppose that each thing in question either be definitely the same as, or definitely different from, any arbitrarily chosen entity.

Clearly the possibility exists of the second maxim being satisfied—that identity always meaningfully applies in a definite manner to each pair of things under discussion—without the first one being satisfied. For the first one—the one that requires a criterion of identity—asks for a general and *informative* answer to the question "when are x and y the same?". Since we do not know *a priori* for every entity in the universe to which the notion of identity meaningfully applies whether there is some *informative* formulation of when that thing is or is not identical to something, the second maxim might be satisfied without our possessing "criteria of identity". In fact, I doubt whether we have criteria of identity for any interesting sorts of entity at all. But this is an issue that has been much discussed in the literature, and I have nothing particularly new to add on this occasion. Instead, I want to focus on the second maxim, in order to reject it as well. I want to explore the view that there *can* be entities to which identity sometimes fails to apply. I want to sketch a view according to which there is sometimes no answer to the question whether or not x and y are the same, and yet this does not deprive us of important uses of quantification, counting, and referring. (In some cases we are deprived of answers to questions about "how many" things there are; but in these cases we already know that there should be no answers.)

Motivation

The motivation for the view that identity is sometimes indeterminate comes mainly from the existence of a variety of identity puzzles that seem to have no solutions. These are puzzles that engage us with seemingly unanswerable questions, such as:

the ship rebuilt plank by plank = the original ship?
the reconstructed ship = the original ship?
my body = me?
my mind = my brain?
the puddle outside now = the puddle I stepped in yesterday?
the statue = the bronze making up the statue?
the man with the old body and new brain = the original man?
the man with the old brain and new body = the original man?
the property of being a red book = the property of being a book that is red?
the possible fat man in the doorway = the possible bald man in the doorway?

There are three typical reactions to these questions which presume that identity is always determinate:

(1) There is an answer which is unknown; philosophical investigation is needed to uncover the answer. (I will not discuss this reaction in any detail.)
(2) There is no answer because the entities in question are "dubious"; we should not admit them into our ontology.
(3) There is no answer because we are not referring to unique things when we think we are.

Let me illustrate the second and third solutions in connection with a humdrum example. Suppose I am driving down the freeway, and suddenly swerve to avoid a pile of trash. The cleanup crews show up later, and push around a lot of stuff—some of which made up the pile that I swerved around, as well as some other stuff. The next day I drive by a pile of trash.

Is it the same pile as the pile that was there yesterday? In some cases of this sort, the question has no apparent answer.

Some people are inclined to take the purist view that this shows that we should not admit piles of trash into our ontologies. (Solution number 2.) They hold that these are entities that vulgar and unthinking people accept, but philosophers should have higher standards. I find this view unpersuasive. Crudely put, if an object is important enough to swerve your car around it is important enough to put into your ontology. To put it another way, if you swerved around it, that is evidence that you believe in it, and disavowing it in your philosophy is outright insincerity. The pile is there all right, even though we may be uncertain of its longevity and of various questions about its identity.

I find solution number 3 more plausible. This is the view that we speak loosely when we speak of "the pile of trash". There are many piles there, corresponding to all of the natural ways of individuating piles of trash. Some of the piles that you swerved around are by the roadside the next day, and some are not. All of them obey the second maxim about identity.

I cannot show that this view is incorrect, and I will not try. I do think, however, that this solution gets much of its plausibility from the implausibility of solutions 1 and 2, together with the assumption that these are the only alternatives. But there *is* another alternative, and I would like to explore it. In this paper I want to show what it would be like if:

(1) There was one pile of trash that you swerved around. This is the unique referent of 'the pile of trash that you swerved around'.
(2) There was one pile by the roadside the next day. This is the unique referent of 'the pile of trash that was by the roadside the next day'.
(3) There is no answer to the question whether the two piles are the same.

I hope to show that the conjunction of these views does not have the dire consequences alluded to by the proponents of the view that there can be no entity without identity.

Indefiniteness

What is wanted is a theory of indefiniteness, where indefiniteness can be shared by identity as well as by other notions. I take it that it may be neither true nor false (and is thus indefinite) whether Samantha really loves her husband, whether a virus is alive, and whether the pile of trash that you swerved around yesterday is the very pile that is by the roadside today. The view that I am exploring is that these questions lack answers because of a genuine indefiniteness in the world, and not just because of a vagueness in our language. It is difficult to distinguish indeterminateness in the world from vagueness in our language; perhaps in the end it is even impossible to do so. But my starting point is the idea that there is such a difference, and it is indefiniteness in the world—including indefiniteness in the identity relation—that I am hypothesizing.[2]

I assume that the world consists of some objects which definitely have certain properties and which definitely stand in certain relations to each other. I also assume that there will be some characteristics that they neither definitely have nor definitely lack, and there will be relations that they neither definitely stand in nor definitely do not stand in. I am using the word 'definitely' here for emphasis only. A literal way to describe the situation is that an object typically has certain properties, lacks certain others, and neither has nor lacks still others.

As usual, I assume that names of our symbolism name objects, and predicates stand for properties and relations. An atomic sentence is true (false) if the named object definitely has (lacks) the property that the predicate stands for; similarly for relational sentences. I assume that natural results of our theory of the world are:

> 'My chair is physical', symbolized 'Pc', is true.
> 'Virus v is living', symbolized 'Lv', is indeterminate.

Now what about identity? Well, for centuries, Leibniz's account of identity in terms of complete indiscernibility has seemed to hold the key to this notion.[3] The only question is how to explain indiscernibility in a framework in which there is room for indeterminateness. The proposal, roughly expressed, is that:

> a = b iff a and b definitely stand in the same relations to the same objects, and also definitely fail to stand in the same relations to the same objects.

Put more carefully: First, let us say that a is *somewhere defined* just in case there is some n-place relation R and some objects $x_1, \ldots, x_{n-1}$ such that r definitely holds of $x_1, \ldots, {}_{n-1}$,a, or definitely fails to hold of $x_1, \ldots, {}_{n-1}$,a.[4] Then we say that identity is a two-place relation, i, such that:

i *definitely holds* of a,b iff a is somewhere defined, and a and b agree for all properties and relations; i.e. the following holds for every n: For each n-place relation R and objects $x_1, \ldots, {}_{n-1}$, R definitely holds (fails to hold) of $x_1, \ldots, {}_{n-1}$,a iff R definitely holds (fails to hold) of $x_1, \ldots, {}_{n-1}$, b.

i *definitely fails to hold* of a,b iff for some n and some n-place relation R and some objects $x_1, \ldots, x_{n-1}$, R definitely holds of $x_1, \ldots, x_{n-1}$,a and definitely fails to hold of $x_1, \ldots, x_{n-1}$,b or vice versa.[5]

The Piles of Trash

Now let us see how all of this applies to the piles of trash. Let us assume that p is the pile that you swerved around, and that q is the pile by the roadway the next day. Then it seems natural, given our assumptions, to assign the following statuses to the following statements:

p is a pile of trash	TRUE
q is a pile of trash	TRUE
You swerved to avoid p	TRUE
You swerved to avoid q	INDETERMINATE
p is now by the roadside	INDETERMINATE
q is now by the roadside	TRUE

The account of identity and indeterminacy sketched above yields the following as consequences:

p = p	TRUE
q = q	TRUE
p = q	INDETERMINATE

Quantification and Counting

It is often said that if there are cases in which the identity relation is not determinate then this will destroy the coherence of quantification and of counting. There is a grain of truth in this, but only a grain. Indeterminacy in the identity relation typically leads to some cases of indeterminacy in quantification and counting, but only in those cases where that is the intuitively correct answer.

In the face of indeterminacy, it is natural to treat quantification as restricted, giving an account of "Every A is B" rather than "Everything is B".[6]

Here is a natural proposal:

(Every x)[Ax](Bx) is definitely true iff every object that definitely satisfies Ax also definitely satisfies Bx, and every object which definitely dissatisfies Bx also definitely dissatisfies Ax;

(Every x)[Ax](Bx) is definitely false iff some object which definitely satisfies Ax definitely dissatisfies Bx.

(∃x)[Ax](Bx) is definitely true iff some object which definitely satisfies Ax also definitely satisfies Bx;

(∃x)[Ax](Bx) is definitely false iff every object which definitely satisfies Ax definitely dissatisfies Bx and every object which definitely satisfies Bx definitely dissatisfies Ax.

Then the following turn out to be definitely true:

You swerved to avoid a pile of trash; i.e. (∃x)[x is a pile of trash] (you swerved to avoid x).

A pile of trash is by the roadside; i.e. (∃x)[x is a pile of trash](x is by the roadside).

Yet this is indeterminate (assuming that no other piles of trash are in the vicinity):

You swerved to avoid a pile of trash that is by the roadside now: (∃x)[x is a pile of trash & x is by the roadside](you swerved to avoid x).

This illustrates the dreaded infection of quantification by indeterminacy; instead of being incoherent it is just what we expect. We *can* quantify over entities for which identity is sometimes undefined, and in most natural cases we get a perfectly definite truth-value.

Now how about counting? Here is a rough account of the numerical quantifiers:

(∃!nx)(Ax) is definitely true iff there are n objects, each of which definitely satisfies Ax, each of which is definitely distinct from each other, and such that every object that definitely satisfies Ax is definitely identical with one of them.

(∃!nx)(Ax) is definitely false iff (∃!mx)(Ax) is definitely true for $m < n$, or if there are more than n objects, each of which is definitely distinct from each of the others, and each of which definitely satisfies Ax.[7]

For simplicity, assume that there are no piles of trash other than p and q. Then the following will be definitely true:

There is exactly one pile of trash that you swerved to avoid: (∃!1x)(x is a pile of trash & you swerved to avoid x).

Also:

There is exactly one pile of trash by the roadside now: (∃!1x)(x is a pile of trash & x is by the roadside now).

But this will be indeterminate:

There are exactly two piles of trash that have been on or near the freeway.

(It will also be indeterminate if we change "two" to "one".)

Without giving details, it is clear that similar techniques may be extended to definite descriptions; so we may refer uniquely to objects by such means even when identity is sometimes undefined for them.

Arguments Against Indeterminate Identity

It seems to me that the view that I have sketched is quite straightforward and perfectly coherent. However, others have not thought so, and perhaps it is worth spending some time in examining their criticisms. I will discuss two arguments against the notion of indeterminacy of identity, one by Nathan Salmon and one by Gareth Evans.

Salmon's argument proceeds by means of elementary set theory, and it purports to be a *reductio ad absurdum* of the view that identity is sometimes indeterminate. Specifically, he tries to show that the assumption that 'a = b' is indeterminate leads inevitably to the conclusion that 'a = b' is determinately false. The argument goes as follows:

> Suppose there is a pair of entities x and y such that it is . . . indeterminate . . . whether they are one and the very same thing. Then the set {x,y} is definitely not the same set as {x,x}, since it is determinately true that x is one and the very same thing as itself. It follows that x and y must be distinct.[8]

Now this objection makes essential use of sets, and in order to confront it we need to ask ourselves what sets would be like if identity were sometimes indeterminate. Presumably there could still be sets, but they would share in the indeterminacy of their members. In particular, regarding their identity conditions, we would naturally expect that if A and B are sets, then the truth-value status of the claim that A = B should be exactly the same as the status of the claim that A and B have the same members; i.e.:

> A = B iff A and B (definitely) have the same members;
> A ≠ B iff A and B (definitely) do not have exactly the same members;
> It is indeterminate whether A = B iff it is indeterminate whether A and B have exactly the same members.

Applied to Salmon's example where it is indeterminate whether x and y are the same, it follows that it is indeterminate whether {x,y} and {x,x} are the same, since it is clearly indeterminate whether these sets have the same members.[9] Salmon's claim that "{x,y} is quite definitely not the same as {x,x}" is simply unjustified, and the argument fails.

I do not feel comfortable, however, in leaving the issue at this point, for two reasons. First, Salmon claims to have additional reasoning to buttress his argument, and second, there might be other arguments along other lines which would establish the incoherence of set theory in the presence of indeterminacy of identity. I will look at each of these in turn.

Salmon's Backup Reasoning

In his book, Salmon vigorously defends his argument quoted above, though without spelling out the argument in any more detail. He grants that we must carefully avoid fallaciously applying ordinary patterns of reasoning to cases in which there may be indeterminacy, but he denies that such is the case here. This is because we are proceeding from premises that are assumed to be true, not indeterminate, and because we are using reasoning that is safe in such cases. In fact, he sees the crucial step as merely involving an application of Leibniz's Law. For purposes of examining this reasoning we can avoid talk of set theory altogether, and simply focus on the following simple argument. (The point of the argument is to show that the assumption that it is indeterminate whether x = y leads logically to the conclusion that x is definitely not the same as y.)

1. Indeterminate: x = y	Assumption
2. ~(Indeterminate: x = x)	Logical Truth
3. x ≠ y	1,2 Logic of iden.

The issue here is whether step 3 follows from steps 1 and 2. I think that it does not, and there is nothing in Leibniz's Law to persuade us that it does. To see this, we have to clearly distinguish two quite different principles regarding identity, which I will refer to as "Leibniz's Law" and "The Contrapositive of Leibniz's Law". Leibniz's Law I take to be the following:

LEIBNIZ'S LAW:	From: x = y
and:	. . .x. . .
we may infer:	. . .y. . .

That is, from the truth of x = y, and any truth regarding x, we may infer the same truth regarding y. (We must of course treat x and y as variables here, not as place-holders for terms such as definite descriptions, in order to avoid well-known modal and epistemic paradoxes, but nobody is making that mistake here. The "truths" regarding x and y may contain indeterminacy operators.)[10] This law is definitely valid within the framework of indeterminate identity that I am exploring. Indeed, in that framework, from the (definite) truth of x = y we may infer that '. . .x. . .' has exactly the same truth-value status (true, false, or indeterminate) as '. . .y. . .'; the law cited above is for the special case when the truth-value status is "true".

The other principle, which is NOT THE SAME as Leibniz's Law, is this:

CONTRAPOSITIVE OF LEIBNIZ'S LAW:

From: . . .x. . .
and: ~(. . .y. . .)
we may infer: $x \neq y$

It should be clear that THIS is the principle that is operative in the simple argument given above, and it is apparently the principle that lies behind the inference quoted from Salmon above. But in the present framework, this principle is fallacious; the simple argument cited above constitutes a counter-example.[11]

But doesn't the Contrapositive version of Leibniz's Law follow from the regular version? After all, in classical logic, if this argument pattern is valid:

From: A
and: B
infer: C

this one is also valid:

From: ~C
and: B
infer: ~A

And the Contrapositive of Leibniz's Law is related to Leibniz's Law in this manner. However this sort of relationship does not generally hold when indeterminacy is present, and *this* has nothing to do with identity. For example, this is a valid inference pattern:

From: $A \supset B$
and: $B \supset C$
infer: ~ Indeterminate $(A \supset C)$

but the following is fallacious:

From: Indeterminate $(A \supset C)$
and: $B \supset C$
infer: ~ $(A \supset B)$

(This fails when A is true and B and C are indeterminate.)[12] In short, the plausibility of Leibniz's Law given no support whatsoever to the Converse of Leibniz's Law.

The Consistency of Set Theory with Indeterminate Identity

I have tried to indicate that Salmon's argument uses logic that is of dubious validity within a framework in which indeterminacy is possible, and I have suggested that the issue really has nothing to do with set theory. But all that I have actually done is to indicate points in his argument where assumptions are made that are not part of the indeterminate identity view, and that are not justified by recognized principles of logic. I would like to do more. What I want to claim is that no argument of the sort Salmon proposes can succeed. This is because elementary set theory concerned with sets of individuals is consistent with the assumption that there is indeterminacy of identity for individuals.

The most natural version of set theory usually consists of these axiom schemes:

ABSTRACTION: $(x)(x \, \varepsilon \, \{y|P\} \equiv P[x/y])$ (where P is any formula of classical quantification theory constructed using &, ∨, ~, and universal and existential quantifiers, which does not contain x free, and P[x/y] is the result of replacing every free occurrence of y by an occurrence of x).
EXTENSIONALITY: $A = B \equiv (x)(x \, \varepsilon \, A \equiv x \, \varepsilon \, B)$, where 'A' and 'B' are set abstracts as characterized above.

The question of the consistency of this kind of set theory with the indeterminacy of identity can be settled by showing that these axioms may hold even when identity is sometimes indeterminate; and *that* can be established in turn by showing that whenever there is a model for indeterminate identity of the sort described in the first part of this paper, then the model may be extended by the addition of sets, in such a manner that:

$$A = B$$

has the same truth-value status (true/false/neither) as:

$$(x)(x \, \varepsilon \, A \equiv x \, \varepsilon \, B),$$

and, further, that:

$$x \, \varepsilon \, \{y \mid P\}$$

has the same truth-value status as:

$$P\,[x/y].$$

In fact, if we only utilize the notation just introduced, i.e. if no terms other than abstracts are introduced for classes, then we simply have a version of

Quine's virtual set theory, and the consistency result is automatic.[13] If set theory is developed in this way, then it is a consequence that if it is indeterminate that x = y then it is also indeterminate that {x,y} = {x,x}, contrary to Salmon's claim that this must be false. Of course, there is more to set theory than the theory of virtual classes, but I see no obstacle to generalizing this consistency result, and, anyway, the difficulties that Salmon claims to find arise already within the virtual part.

Evans' Argument

Gareth Evans has an argument against what he calls "vague objects"; the argument is relevant here since its thrust is to prove that identities must be either true or false. The argument resembles Salmon's in that it tries to show that the assumption that 'a = b' is indeterminate leads to the conclusion that 'a = b' is false. Instead of introducing sets, it relies on the presence of an indeterminacy operator in the object language, and on property abstraction. Evans supposes that we may introduce into our language an operator 'I' which is such that 'I(S)' is true if 'S' is indeterminate, and otherwise it is false. The argument then goes as follows:

Suppose that it is indeterminate whether a = b. Then:

(1) 'I(a = b)' is true,

though:

(2) 'I(a = a)' is false.

Now consider the property λyI(a = y). By property abstraction, we can infer from (1) and (2) that a lacks this property whereas b has it:

(3) 'λyI(a = y)(b)' is true,

while

(4) 'λyI(a = y)(a)' is false.

But then b definitely has a property that a lacks, and so b is definitely different from a.[14]

The trouble with this type of argument is that it proves too much. The argument can be used to refute the existence of indeterminacy in truth-value of ordinary claims, even under the assumption that identity itself is always determinate. To take a homey illustration, let us suppose that it is indeterminate whether living human bodies are persons. We will prove, using Evans' reasoning, that it is definitely false that all and only living human bodies are persons. Let p be the set of persons, and let b be the set of living human bodies. In addition let m stand for me (the person). Then presumably it is indeterminate whether I am a member of the set of living human bodies, but not indeterminate whether I am a member of the set of persons. So we have:

(1') '$I(m \varepsilon b)$' is true,

whereas:

(2') '$I(m \varepsilon p)$' is false.

By reasoning similar to that above, a consideration of this property:

$\lambda y I(m \varepsilon y)$

yields the following inferences:

(3') '$\lambda y I(m \varepsilon y)(b)$' is true,

while:

(4') '$\lambda y I(m \varepsilon y)(p)$' is false.

But then b and p are definitely different sets, and so we have proved that it is false that all and only living human bodies are persons.

Notice that the argument just given never presumes that identity is ever indeterminate. Further, properly chosen versions of this argument can be used to disprove any claim of indeterminacy, no matter what its form.[15] Evans's argument, then, is not just an argument against "vague objects"; it is an argument against vagueness (indeterminacy) itself.

Evans' argument gets its force from the joint effect of two expansions of the object language: the first is the introduction of an indeterminacy operator, and the second is the assumption that a version of property abstraction holds in the expanded language. I see no objection to the use of an indeterminacy operator; I have, in effect, been using one myself informally in my own discussion of indeterminacy. And I see no objection to the use of property abstraction, when it is suitably restricted. But it is well known that paradoxes result in a variety of ways from the combination of a completely unrestricted property abstraction with a host of expansions of the language beyond classical quantification theory; the Grelling paradox arises if the syntax is suitably unrestricted, and abstraction in epistemic and modal languages must be carefully crafted so as to avoid trouble. In the present case the problem arises from applying a version of property abstraction to a formula containing an indeterminacy operator. If this is prohibited, then Evans' argument fails, and no known difficulties arise from the assumption of indeterminacy.[16] Evans' argument does not force us to give up either the use of an indeterminacy operator or the use of property abstraction that is restricted to classical constructions. It does show us that we cannot extend property abstraction to formulas containing indeterminacy operators. But since this restriction is not special to *identity*, this does not show that indeterminacy of identity is any more problematic than indeterminacy in general.

So What?

The importance of the identity maxims in recent literature has been their role in finding easy objections to philosophical theories. Do we have trouble individuating propositions? Then junk any theory that appeals to them! Likewise for Fregean senses, properties, possible though nonactual objects, etc. Frege, Meinong, and a host of others are seen to have been dabbling in incoherence, and their theories are to be rejected.

Clearly this is too facile to be persuasive. And part of the reason is that difficulties about identity can often be quarantined. For example, it is clearly open to us to accept as definitely true:

> Mary believes several things that John also believes,

or:

> John denied something today that he asserted yesterday.

even if there is no truth of the matter concerning whether the proposition that Sam is a bachelor is the same or different than the proposition that he is an unmarried adult male. And we can hold that Sherlock Holmes and Dr. Watson are definitely distinct nonexistent objects, even if we are uncertain about how many nonexistent fat men there are in a given doorway. Likewise, we can hold that:

> Mary stepped into a puddle

is definitely true, even though we are at a complete loss as to the identity conditions for puddles, and suspect that "same puddle" is often indeterminate. We may even be able to hold that 2 is a different number than 3 even if it is indeterminate whether numbers are identical with certain sets.

A theory may provide us with a great deal of understanding of the world, in spite of its not giving us completely clear answers to identity questions in general. Whether this is so in a given case depends on what the theory says, and cannot be decided in a simple *a priori* fashion, based on simple maxims.

Notes

1. I am indebted to Peter Woodruff, Ralph Kennedy, George Bealer, Nathan Salmon, and Peter van Inwagen for comments on earlier drafts of this paper.

2. One reason I am reluctant to attribute the indeterminacy in question to vagueness is that vagueness seems generally to be a matter of degree. But although it is possible to concoct identity puzzles based on a continuum of examples, there are also puzzles in which there is no matter of degree involved at all. For example, it is hard to see a matter of degree in the question as to whether I am identical with my own body, or whether the statue is identical with the bronze making it up.

3. Actually, the view that identity may be indeterminate does not presuppose that distinct entities are discernible in terms of their properties or relations. But the framework is considerably simplified if this assumption is made, and I do so in this paper.

4. Strictly, this should be expanded to allow a to occur at any given place in the relation, not just the last. Similar remarks apply to the formulas to follow. Also, we assume here and below that a property is a 1-place relation.

5. This account is quite different than those based on popular views which hold identity to be "relative", so that a can be the same F as b but not the same G as b. So-called "relative identity" does not entail indistinguishability, and thus, in my opinion, is misnamed. That is, I see nothing incoherent in the notions that are described under this title, I just find use of the word "identity" in this connection misleading—since there is no connection with identity at all. (Some of the proponents of "relative identity" think that there is no such thing as identity, and use this as a rationale for using the word for something entirely different.)

Note also that in this account "definitely true" should not be thought of as "known to be true". If we were trying to capture the idea of known truth or falsehood, then we should have to allow for the possibility of two objects, a and b, such that

a and b are qualitatively similar in all known respects,

but

it is unknown whether or not a = b.

In the present account, if a and b are similar in all definite respects, then a is definitely identical with b. (The one exception to this is the case in which a and b are both indeterminate in absolutely all respects. The account given here arbitrarily makes it indeterminate then whether a is identical with b.)

6. I say that it is natural to account for the complex form 'All A's are B's' using restricted quantification, but the same effect can be obtained in the usual manner by a combination of a version of unrestricted quantification plus a kind of conditional connective. These will do the trick:

Let '(x)A' be true if 'A' is satisfied by every object, false if it is dissatisfied by some object, and otherwise neither true nor false. Let 'A ⊃ B' be true if 'A' is false or 'B' is true or both are indeterminate, false if 'A' is true and 'B' is false, and otherwise indeterminate.

Then the restricted version of 'Every A is B' in the text is equivalent to '(x)(Ax ⊃ Bx)'.

Regarding the other connectives, I am assuming throughout this paper the following account of negation, conjunction and disjunction:

A negation is true if its negate is false, false if its negate is true, and indeterminate if its negate is indeterminate.

A conjunction is true if both conjuncts are true, false if either is false, and otherwise indeterminate.

A disjunction is true if either disjunct is true, false if both disjuncts are false, and otherwise indeterminate.

7. This is somewhat informally stated; it can be made more precise.

8. N. Salmon, *Reference and Essence*, Princeton University Press, Princeton, 1981, p. 243. I have changed ordered pairs to sets for simplicity.

9. It is indeterminate whether y is a member of {x,x}, and determinate that y is a member of {x,y}. I am assuming that "A and B have the same members" is representable as "(x)(x ε A ≡ x ε B)", where the universal quantifier has the same truth-conditions as sketched above, and where the biconditional P ≡ *Q has the same truth-table as (P* ⊃ Q) & (Q ⊃ P): i.e. it is true when both sides have the same truth-value or both lack truth-value, false when they disagree in truth-value, and indeterminate when one side is indeterminate and the other is truth-valued.

10. I have stated Leibniz's Law as a principle of inference, although it is sometimes given as an axiom schema. I have avoided the schema for two reasons. The first is that the truth of the schema depends in part on the meaning of the conditional connective, which brings issues of language to the forefront. The second is that whether the schema is valid depends on subtleties of its formulation. For example, given the truth-table for '⊃' and '&' used elsewhere in this paper, the following schema is not valid: (x = y & . . . x . . .) ⊃ . . . y . . . (It is indeterminate when x = y is false and . . . y . . . is indeterminate.) The closely related version is also not valid if the language is sufficiently rich: x = y ⊃ (. . . x . . . ⊃ . . . y . . .). This will be indeterminate if x = y is indeterminate and . . . x . . . is true and . . . y . . . is false. (Whether this can actually happen is exactly what is at issue in the argument under discussion.) These sorts of complications are avoided by focussing on the inference principle, which is what is directly relevant anyway.

11. The Contrapositive of Leibniz's Law also seems to be involved in step 3 in the following argument which Salmon has supplied (personal communication) to indicate how his quoted argument should be fleshed out:

1. '=' is neither true nor false of ⟨x,y⟩	Assumption
2. '=' is true of ⟨x,x⟩	Premise
3. ⟨x,y⟩ is distinct from ⟨x,x⟩	1,2 Logic of Iden
4. x is distinct from y	3, set theory
5. '=' is false of ⟨x,y⟩	4, Premise
6. '=' is either true or false of ⟨x,y⟩	1–5, RAA

As I indicate below in the text, I think that 3 does not follow from 1 and 2. Salmon anticipates this objection (since others have directed it to this very argument of his in the past), and so he suggests that this argument could be fleshed out even further by inserting as an extra step the "logical truth".

2′. If ⟨x,y⟩ is identical with ⟨x,x⟩, then if '=' is not true of ⟨x,y⟩ then '=' is not true of ⟨x,x⟩.

He says that step 3 would then follow primarily by *modus tollens*. The details here depend on how the truth-conditions for the conditional are understood. With the truth-table used elsewhere in this paper, step 2′ is not a logical truth at all, since it is indeterminate whenever $x = y$ is indeterminate. (In that case its antecedent is indeterminate and its consequent is false.)

Salmon has replied to this criticism (again, in communication), defending the conditional above on the grounds that it is an instance of a logical schema of English:

If a = b then if Fa then Fb,

where the connective 'if . . . then . . .' is understood "in its ordinary sense in English".

This defense emphasizes the ordinary sense of the English 'if . . . then . . .', and this cannot be ignored. Since there is not agreement on how to treat this connective, I will consider the cases without trying to choose between them. Case I: As Peter Woodruff has pointed out to me, there is a tendency for people to read 'if A then B' as "if 'A' is true then 'B' is true". If the English connective is read in this way, then a good case can be made for regarding Salmon's proposed schema as valid. But then there is an equally good case to be made that *modus tollens* will not be valid for this conditional. (This would then undercut the remainder of Salmon's reasoning.) The point can easily be made without reference to identity. Given the suggested reading of the conditional, this is logically true:

(1) If A ≡ B then (if B is true then A is true).

Now suppose that in fact A is indeterminate and B is true. Then this is true:

(2) ~(if B is true then A is true).

So, by *modus tollens*, this is true:

(3) ~(A ≡ B).

But (3) is indeterminate, not true. So *modus tollens* fails when the conditional is understood in this way.

Case II: Suppose that a conditional (such as that above) with an indeterminate antecedent and a false consequent is not true, but is indeterminate. Then it is not plausible that the conditional cited by Salmon is a logical truth of English. The point can be made by analogy. Salmon's conditional is no more plausible than is this one, not involving identity:

(*) If A ≡ B then if F(A) then F(B).

But then (1) above is a counterexample to (*), when A is indeterminate and B is true.

12. Again using the truth-table for given ⊃ above; but there are many other examples that do not use the conditional at all.

13. See section 1.2 of W. V. Quine, *Set Theory and its Logic*, Harvard U. Press, Cambridge, 1963.

14. Gareth Evans, "Can There Be Vague Objects?" *Analysis* 38 (1978) p. 208.

15. Suppose that 'A' is any indeterminacy, so that 'I(A)' is true. Then let 'B' be any true sentence. Then I({x|Px & A} = {x|Px}) but ~I({x|Px} = {x|Px & B}). So we can show {x|Px & A} ≠ {x|Px & B}. And then, by ordinary set theory, we get that ~(A ≡ B).

16. To be more accurate, it is not only necessary to avoid use of an indeterminacy operator within property abstracts, one must also avoid use of other terminology in terms of which such operators can be defined—such as a determinacy operator plus negation. The restriction that is easiest to state is the same as that imposed on set abstracts in the set abstraction schema discussed in the previous section.

References

Gareth Evans, "Can There Be Vague Objects?" *Analysis* 38 (1978) p. 208.

N. Salmon, *Reference and Essence*, Princeton University Press, Princeton, 1981, p. 243.

W.V. Quine, *Set Theory and its Logic*, Harvard U. Press, Cambridge, 1963.

14

De Re Modality Entails *De Re* Vagueness

Frances Howard-Snyder

I. Introduction

W. V. Quine characterizes the belief in *de re* modality in this way: "Necessity no longer resides in the way in which we talk about something. Now it resides in the things we talk about."[1] An example of the necessity that resided (and still resides) in the way in which we talk about something is the necessity that bachelors be unmarried. This kind of necessity is contrasted with the necessity that I be human, or that water be constituted by H_2O molecules. The first sort of necessity is completely explicable in terms of the meanings of the expressions 'bachelors' and 'unmarried.' The second sort of necessity, its advocates insist, cannot be explained in terms of meanings.

It has recently been suggested that *vagueness* sometimes resides in the things we talk about as well as in the way we talk about them; that is, that there is *de re* vagueness. For example, in "How to Reason About Vague Objects," Peter van Inwagen writes,

> I believe that there can be vague objects, and that there are in fact several ways in which this can happen. [One of them is this:] There could be an occasion (A) on which a speaker refers to an object without making use of any vague general terms; and there could be another such occasion (B); and it could be that it is neither definitely true nor definitely false that the object referred to on occasion A is identical with the object referred to on occasion B.[2]

As my title suggests, I shall argue that if there is *de re* modality, then there is *de re* vagueness. By 'a *de re* modal sentence' I mean the result of prefixing a modal operator to a meaningful sentence that contains either free variables or terms that are used to refer 'directly' to objects—such as demonstrative pronouns or proper names (on certain views of proper names). By 'a *de re* vagueness sentence' I mean a sentence of the form "It is indeterminate whether there is an x such that x is F" where the meaning of 'F' is linguistically determined. Consider some fully determinate predicate like '. . . is composed of four atoms,' or '. . . weighs more than seven grams.' The advocate of *de re* vagueness believes that there are true sentences like, "It is indeterminate whether there is something which is composed of four atoms," or "It is indeterminate whether there is something which weighs more than four grams." Vague identity sentences are also instances of *de re* vagueness sentences if the expressions used to denote the terms of the identity relation are not linguistically vague. For example, "It is indeterminate whether Joe is Tom," is a *de re* vagueness sentence if the names 'Joe' and 'Tom' are not linguistically vague.

II. The Acceptance of *de re* Modal Facts Entails the Rejection of Temporal Parts

To accept *de re* modal facts is in part to believe that there is nothing ill-formed about sentences like "I am necessarily human." Someone who accepts this should also accept that for every directly referring term 'x' and every well-formed predicate 'p,' there is nothing ill-formed about saying that x is necessarily p. It is hard to see how such an operation could produce a meaningful sentence in some cases but not in others. In the view of the advocate of *de re* modality, therefore, 'is necessarily five foot tall,' is a meaningful predicate. It seems to follow that, for every object x, each of these predicates or its contradictory is true of x. Everything should be either necessarily prime or not necessarily prime, either possibly smaller than a breadbox or not possibly smaller than a bread-box, and so on. The underlying principle here—the law of the excluded middle—is one we endorse with regard to other well-formed predicates. (I leave vague predicates aside for the moment.)

Consider the *de re* modal predicate: '. . . possibly dies before age 54.' Call the property expressed by this predicate 'P*.' Descartes died when he was 54. Let's suppose he died when he was exactly 54—at the exact second of the anniversary of his birth. Now by the law of the excluded middle, he either had P* or lacked P*. To say that he lacked it would be to imply that his life was never in the slightest danger at any point before his death, that there was no possibility that he could have died of smallpox as a child, nor that a coal could have been thrown from his stove and caused his robe to catch fire and burn him to death, nor that his coach could have overturned. This is obviously false. So, if we are obliged to say that either Descartes had P* or that he lacked it, it clearly seems better to say that he had it.

Now, it is widely believed[3] that Descartes has temporal parts. Among those parts is an 'improper' temporal part. This is Descartes himself, but let's give it another label, 'D*.' Since Descartes could have lived a shorter time than he did, it follows from Leibniz's Law, that D* has the property of being possibly shorter than it is. But Descartes has other temporal parts. For example, he has a temporal part which starts when he did, but which is exactly 10 years shorter than D* (call it 'D–'). If he had died 10 years earlier than he did, this part would have existed intact. (You have to suppose that this death occurs at exactly the right moment, brought about by God in such a way as to leave no messy edges.)

There are two different things one might be inclined to say about a world, W, in which Descartes dies at 44. Either D* exists in W, and is identical with D–, or it doesn't exist in W.

There is reason to suppose that D* does not exist in W, since temporal extension seems to be of the essence of temporal parts if anything is. In addition, if D* does exist in W, then it is identical with D–. In that case D* would share every property of D–, including the property of being possibly distinct from D* (itself). But, to say that D* has the property of being possibly distinct from D* is obviously absurd.

On the other hand, there is reason to suppose that D* does exist in W, since, *ex hypothesi*, Descartes does exist there and D* is Descartes. So it is obviously false that D* does not exist in W.

Therefore, if we accept temporal parts we must choose between the obviously false and the obviously absurd.

To avoid this sharp pair of horns, we should abandon the assumption that there are temporal parts.[4] We could do this by saying simply that there are none; or by denying that the notion of a temporal part makes any sense at all, refusing to concede that the adjective 'temporal' can meaningfully qualify 'part.'[5] Let's consider the consequences of rejecting temporal parts.

III. If There Are No Temporal Parts, Some Theories of Composition Are False

Without temporal parts, our resources for explaining certain paradoxes are limited. Mark Heller[6] argues that one has to accept one of 'four very unpleasant alternatives' if one rejects temporal parts. These are:

(a) There is no such physical object as my body.
(b) There is no physical object that exactly occupies the space that we would typically say is now exactly occupied by all of my body apart from my left hand.
(c) No physical object can undergo a loss of parts (in the ordinary spatial sense of 'part').
(d) There can be distinct physical objects exactly occupying the same space at the same time.

Heller's argument goes as follows. Suppose we reject all of (a) to (d). If we reject (a) and (b), then we accept that, at the moment, there are two objects here: my body and an object in the space exactly occupied by all of my body except my left hand (call it 'Body-Minus'). If we reject (c), we have no reason to deny that my body can survive the surgical removal of my left hand. Body-Minus survives the operation. If we reject (d), then, since after the operation my body occupies precisely the same space as Body-Minus, there is only one object in that space at that time. That is, my body is identical with Body-Minus after the operation. By the transitivity of identity, it was also identical with my body before the operation. But it was not since they were then of different sizes.[7] The rejection of all of (a) to (d) leads to a contradiction.

Temporal parts permit us to avoid having either to choose one of (a) to (d) or to accept a contradiction. A temporal parts ontology allows us to say that both my body and Body-Minus exist, hence permitting us to avoid (a) and (b). On this view, my body is temporally extended through the times before and after the operation, hence permitting us to avoid (c). Although they occupy the same region after the operation, this is in virtue of their sharing a temporal stage. It doesn't follow that they must share the same temporal stage before the operation.[8,9]

Without the resources of temporal parts, we must accept one of (a) to (d). The easiest to swallow is (b), that is, deny that Body-Minus exists. To accept (a) would be to deny that human bodies exist, which, if materialism is true, is to deny that we exist. To accept (c) is to deny that we last from minute to minute, since we lose parts of our bodies continually. To accept (d) would be to say two different objects could occupy exactly the same space at the same time. For example, Body-Minus and my body could occupy exactly the same Body-Minus shaped region. But Body-Minus weighs 125 lbs. and my body weighs 125 lbs., so together they weigh 250 lbs. But, I assure you, they do *not* weigh 250 lbs.[10] (B) is, therefore, the easiest to swallow. This would be to deny the correctness of certain sorts of ontologies. In particular it would require the rejection of maximally capacious ontologies, by which I mean, ontologies according to which every filled region of space that could contain an object contained one, or according to which the members of every set of particles composed an object. This is because Body-Minus, if it exists, clearly fills a region of space, and it is clearly constituted by a collection of particles.

The rejection of temporal parts, therefore, appears to have the consequence that a maximally capacious ontology is incorrect. In rejecting this ontology we reject the corresponding theory of composition, the one which answers 'always' to the question, "Under what circumstances do particles combine to compose an object?"

Another similarly extreme answer is that particles never combine to compose an object. According to such a theory, the only material objects there are are fundamental particles, that is, objects that have no parts. If this is correct, then there are no camels or other objects that couldn't fit through the eye of a needle. Leibniz and Hume both seem to have had some such view as this.[11] Leibniz used it (together with the belief that material substance would be infinitely divisible) to conclude that there was no material substance at all. Hume used it (together with the view that substance was finitely divisible) to conclude that there were no composite objects, physical or spiritual. This theory entails that our material bodies do not exist. If it is combined with materialism of the form "if we exist, we are material substances" it implies that we don't exist. Because this conclusion is so unpalatable, I shall attempt to find an alternative position.

How about some intermediate answer, an answer which holds that some groups of small objects compose larger objects, and some don't? This would seem to fit with what we ordinarily think about these matters. That is, we think that various cells and various bricks compose our bodies and our houses, but that there is nothing that consists of the southern half of North Dakota, George Bush, the Crown Jewels, and the poster of Virginia Woolf in my study, and only these.

IV. Criteria of Composition Are Vague

But there is reason to think that no plausible intermediate answer will yield a perfectly determinate criterion for composition, a criterion which guarantees that every group of particles at every moment either definitely composes an object or definitely fails to do so.

Someone who was moved to exclude the exotic object made up of George Bush, the jewels, the poster, and the land (but who was not moved to exclude all composite objects) would do so on the grounds that the objects that were alleged to compose it had too little to do with each other. So every non-arbitrary moderate answer will require that the parts of a composite object have 'enough to do with each other.' Suggestions as to how things can have enough to do with each other so as to compose an object include:

- being in contact;
- being stuck together so that it's not easy to separate them;
- being jointly part of some living thing or some functional unit.

But these criteria don't apply absolutely determinately. There are borderline cases of contact, of being firmly enough stuck together, and of common involvement in a functional unit.[12]

David Lewis gives a different argument for more or less the same conclusion. He writes: "To restrict composition in accordance with our intuitions would require a vague restriction."[13] A moderate answer would be an intuitive answer, since the only motivation there would seem to be for having a 'moderate' answer (an answer which excluded some cases and included others) would be a desire for a criterion that selected and excluded cases that we intuitively wanted to select and exclude. But intuitive reasons are vague. Just as we can't see differences between some pairs of shades of red, we can't draw completely fine lines on various continua of candidate relations. We pick relations like 'being in contact' for which there are no determinate criteria, rather than some determinate relation because a determinate relation would be of no use to us. Differences between some groups of particles that entered into a determinate relation and some groups that didn't would be differences that made no difference to us, and, in many cases, differences we could not even perceive.

It therefore looks as if the correct criterion of composition must be indeterminate. But remember that this criterion is supposed to tell us when small objects add up to bigger ones and how many such objects there are at any moment. Since the criterion will inevitably be vague, it will fail to give a determinate answer to the question of whether there are say, 10,000,000,000 or 10,000,000,001 objects in the world.

What is remarkable about that? We don't have any problem conceding that it is indeterminate whether there are 1,000,000 rich people, or that it might be indeterminate whether there are 4 or 5 bald people in this room, or 10 or 11 mountains in a certain range. In these cases, one might reply, there is an explanation for the indeterminacy which is not available in the case of composition. This explanation traces the indeterminacy to the vagueness of certain general terms. The word 'rich' is vague because we haven't assigned it a determinate intension, one which will guarantee that we are able to determine, on the basis of our knowledge of how many dollars x has (and what a dollar will buy, and perhaps what financial commitments x has), whether x is rich. As a consequence, there are some people we can't classify with confidence—we can't give an exact count of the rich.

But if we deny that there are a determinate number of *things* (rather than things of a kind), we can't explain this indeterminacy in terms of our inability to decide whether some objects are correctly described by a particular predicate.

It has been suggested[14] that the indeterminacy as to how many objects there are can be completely explained in linguistic terms, that is, as a product of the linguistic vagueness of '. . . compose an object.' I don't believe that this suggestion will help to diminish the anomalous nature of the vagueness under discussion.

There are two different things it might mean. The first is that we ultimately quantify over particles only. Some groups of these particles collectively have a property expressed by the unanalyzable polyadic predicate, '. . . compose an object.' The word 'object' is ambiguous on this interpretation of the suggestion. In one sense, it simply means 'that which exists'; in another, it is an inseparable part of a predicate describing something that real objects do. But if this is the correct way to understand this suggestion, it amounts to an acceptance of the extreme position I attributed to Hume and Leibniz, i.e., that really there are no composite objects. This can be combined with the view that the members of some sets of non-composite objects are to be *treated*—conventionally and fictionally—as composing larger objects.

The second interpretation of the suggestion is one which treats 'object' as univocal and ' . . . compose an object' as a complex relational predicate which relates groups of particles to the larger objects they compose. According to this suggestion the sentence, C, "Some particles compose an object," is to be rendered as C*, "There are certain particles, and there is a further thing, O, such that those particles compose O." On this interpretation, at least one composite object, i.e., O, must be included within the range of one's quantifiers. But if a sentence with the form of C* is vague, the vagueness cannot be attributed to the vagueness of the relational predicate. To see this, compare C* with a case of a vague sentence whose vagueness *can* be explained in terms of the vagueness of its relational predicate. For example, the relation '. . . is married to . . .' is vague. There may be no fact of the matter as to whether Adam and Eve were married. As a result, there may be no fact of the matter as to whether the sentence, "In the garden of Eden, there was an x, and there was a y, such that x was married to y," is true. The indeterminacy of this is explained by the vagueness of '. . . is married to . . .' In this case, it is indeterminate whether any of the pairs in one's domain of quantification satisfy the predicate, because some pairs clearly fail to satisfy it, and one pair is a borderline case.

The case of '. . . composes . . .' however is very different. What would a borderline case of composition be like? Consider a table composed of a stump (S) and a plank (P). Here {S,P} is a definite case of a set whose members compose something. Now let the relations between S and P be so altered that {S,P} is a borderline case of such a set: it is indefinite whether there is an x such that {S,P} composes x. If the linguistic theory of vagueness is correct, this must be because there is something that is a borderline case of satisfying the predicate "{S,P} compose . . ." Call it 'T.' What are the properties of T? If this is to be analogous to typical cases of linguistic vagueness, T should be a borderline instance of some property. That property, presumably, would have to do with its relations to its parts. But to say this is to assume that *it* (T) exists, that is, that it is determinate that T exists, although it is indeterminate whether T has a certain property. But if T exists, then the relations between S and P must have been sufficient to compose it, *contra hypothesem*.

To see more clearly how the stump/plank case *cannot* be a case of linguistic vagueness, compare it with some paradigmatic case of linguistic vagueness. Consider again the vagueness of the relation '. . . is married to

. . .' Adam and Eve both exist. There is nothing indeterminate about their existence. What is unclear is whether Adam satisfies the predicate '. . . is married to Eve,' and whether Eve satisfies the predicate '. . . is married to Adam.' There is no third thing whose existence depends on their determinately satisfying these predicates. In the case of the stump and the plank, if they were related in such a way as to compose something, there would be a third thing, i.e., T. If they were related in such a way as not to compose something, there would be no third thing. The trouble is that their relations stand somewhere between these two determinate positions. It follows that it is indeterminate whether this third thing exists.

I conclude that we cannot explain away the vagueness of composition in terms of the indefinite satisfaction of a vague predicate by any object or objects. This vagueness, vagueness that attaches to the existential quantifier, vagueness about what there is, vagueness about when an object comes into and goes out of existence, is what I mean by '*de re* vagueness.'

V. Another Argument From the Rejection of Temporal Parts to *de re* Vagueness

There is another, slightly shorter route from the rejection of temporal parts to the adoption of *de re* vagueness. In "How to Reason About Vague Objects," van Inwagen presents a scenario designed to prompt us to believe that there is vague identity.

> Suppose we give a man the pure or 'Kripkean' proper name, 'Alpha,' and that our act of naming is a clear and unproblematic case of the successful conferring of a name. Suppose that later we give a man the Kripkean name 'Omega' (a similar success) . . . Suppose that these two acts of naming are parts of the following longer story. A man receives the name 'Alpha'; he steps into a science-fictional machine—call it 'the Cabinet'—that effects changes in his brain of just such sorts and magnitudes as to create the greatest possible embarrassed hesitation in the making of identity-judgements by someone who holds *your* theory of personal identity: Whatever factor *you* say constitutes the temporal continuity of a person, the Cabinet does its science-fictional best to produce a troublesome borderline case of it. A man, composed, more or less, of the matter that had composed Alpha, steps out of the Cabinet and receives the name 'Omega.'[15]

Van Inwagen argues that this is a case in which the statement, "Alpha is identical with Omega," is neither definitely true nor definitely false, and that this indeterminacy cannot be accounted for by appeal to the vagueness of vague general terms. There are no such terms in the sentence.

Someone might respond to van Inwagen by saying that there are, in fact, vague general terms associated with the sentence. They were used in the introduction of the names 'Alpha' and 'Omega' and those names don't make a meaningful contribution to the sentence unless they are understood in that light.[16] When introducing a name, the suggestion continues, you don't just point and say, 'Fido.' You say or imply, "I dub this dog/man/ship/country 'Fido.' " There can't be a bare pointing. In this case, the general term in question was probably 'person' or 'man.' So, the names 'Alpha' and 'Omega' were introduced as the name of 'that *man*.'

Van Inwagen can respond that the vagueness of 'man' has nothing to do with the indeterminacy of the identity statement. Each naming was the naming of a perfectly clear case of a human being. There are, however, cases of vagueness (linguistic vagueness) where what is indeterminate is not whether x is an F, but whether there is one F or two. 'Puddle,' 'lake,' 'nation,' and 'mountain' all have this feature. That is, part of what is left open about the application of these terms are precise criteria for when it is correct to say we have two puddles, lakes, nations, or mountains, rather than one. But is 'man' like this? And if it is, is that relevant to the case at hand? Neither case of dubbing was the dubbing of something which might have been a man and might have been a pair of men. "Well," the objector might continue, "if there are determinate criteria for where one man ends and the next begins, there should be an answer to the question of when Alpha ceased to exist. If there isn't an answer to this question, that must be because the term 'man' is incompletely defined."

Underlying this suggestion is the assumption that objects have temporal boundaries which are in almost every respect like spatial boundaries, and that there are a number of temporally extended objects in the immediate vicinity of Alpha. Which of these the name 'Alpha' picks out depends on the criteria for carving things up temporally which are associated with the term 'man.' The question of where one *person* ends and another begins is then seen as analogous to the question of where one mountain in a range ends and another begins. The question of whether two people were in The Cabinet between the time Alpha entered and the time Omega left it, is like the question of whether there are one or two lakes in a certain region.

This explanation of the case depends crucially on temporal parts, because it involves the notion of two or more persons or person stages that overlap completely and share all their properties at a time, but that are distinguished by their temporal extent. On the assumption that there aren't any temporal parts, we are left with the conclusion that The Cabinet is an instance of vague identity.

Without temporal parts, there is real vagueness in the world.[17]

VI. Summary of the Foregoing

I have attempted to argue that the advocate of *de re* modality should accept *de re* vagueness. My argument went like this: the intelligibility of *de re* modality requires the acceptance of the law of excluded middle for *de re* modal properties. This entails that either Descartes necessarily existed for exactly 54 years, or that he didn't necessarily exist for exactly 54 years. Of these two options, the latter seems preferable—that he was not necessarily 54 years old. But this brings one into conflict with the view that he had proper temporal parts. The best way out of this, short of abandoning *de re* modality, seems to be to abandon temporal parts. Without temporal parts, one is forced to reject the view that the members of every set of particles compose an object. Given that there are at least some medium-sized objects, we are led to the conclusion that the criteria of existence and identity are vague. So it is sometimes a vague matter how many things there are, and what is identical with what.

The view that there is *de re* vagueness has had a rather cool reception amongst analytic philosophers.[18] One might, of course, begin with that coolness, and run my argument in the contrapositive direction. That is, one could start by insisting with David Lewis that "The only intelligible account of vagueness locates it in our thought and language,"[19] and conclude that there is no *de re* modality.[20]

Notes

1. W.V. Quine, "Three Grades of Modal Involvement," in *The Ways of Paradox and Other Essays* (Cambridge: Harvard University Press, 1966), pp. 156–174.

2. Peter van Inwagen. "How to Reason About Vague Objects," in *Philosophical Topics*, Vol 16, No. 1, Spring 1988, p. 255.

3. Two notable members of this group are Quine, *Word and Object* (Cambridge: MIT Press, 1960), pp. 170–176, and David Lewis, "Survival and Identity," in *Philosophical Papers*, Vol. 1 (Oxford: Oxford University Press, 1983), pp. 55–77.

4. J.A. Burgess suggested as a problem for this argument that it can be generalized to conclude that there are no spatial parts at all. (The sort of considerations that militate against temporal parts also militate against spatial parts.) He argued that we seem then to be faced with a dilemma:

(a) reject composite objects altogether,

(b) hold that macroscopic objects exist but have no parts.

In the following discussion, I address (a) and reject it; and, a qualified version of (b) and accept it. I think this dilemma is a false one. It could be that there are composite objects and that they have no parts the size of D-minus or the size of hands or feet or tongues, but only very small ones like quarks. The paradoxes generated by the larger parts could not be generated by such small parts.

5. This argument is essentially the same as one given by van Inwagen "The Doctrine of Arbitrary Undetached Parts" (Chapter 10 of this volume).

6. Mark Heller, "Temporal Parts of Four Dimensional Objects" (Chapter 17 of this volume).

7. Someone who identifies himself with his body, can replace the term 'my body' throughout the above argument with the terms 'I' or 'me.'

8. For a detailed account of this view, see David Lewis's "Survival and Identity."

9. This may look like an acceptance of (d). To the extent that it is an acceptance of (d), it is not an objectionable interpretation of (d). See note (10) below.

10. Someone who accepts temporal parts as a way of avoiding Heller's paradox does accept something closely analogous to (d). That is, he accepts that two temporally extended objects can at a certain time have exactly the same spatial dimensions. The objection I raise here to (d) would not apply to such a position. I have no complaint against the suggestion that two objects can overlap, that is, have a common part. I only object to the idea that two objects can overlap completely and yet be distinct. If A and B have a common part, and it is the improper part of A, and the improper part of B, then A is B.

11. See Leibniz's letter (No. 19) of 4 March 1687 in *Philosophical Papers and Letters*, ed., L.E. Loemker (Dordrecht: Reidel Publishing Company, 1969), p. 107, and Hume, *A Treatise of Human Nature*, eds., L.A. Selby-Bigge and P.H. Nidditch (Oxford: Oxford University Press, 1978), p. 30.

Hume writes, "'Tis evident, that existence in itself belongs only to unity, and is never applicable to number, but on account of the unities, of which the number is compos'd." On p. 219, he writes, "'Tis confest by the most judicious philosophers, that our ideas of bodies are nothing but collections form'd by the mind of the ideas of the several distinct sensible qualities, of which objects are compos'd. . . . But however these qualities may in themselves be entirely distinct, 'tis certain we commonly regard the compound, which they form, as One thing. . . . The acknowledg'd composition is evidently contrary to this suppos'd simplicity. . . ."

12. Van Inwagen discusses this question in detail in "When Are Objects Parts?" in *Philosophical Perspectives*, Vol. 1, *Metaphysics*, ed., James Tomberlin, (Atascadero, California: Ridgeview Publishing Company, 1987), pp. 21–48.

13. David Lewis, *On the Plurality of Worlds* (Oxford: Basil Blackwell, 1986).

14. By Jonathan Bennett in conversation.

15. In "How to Reason About Vague Objects," p. 256.

16. Van Inwagen explicitly rejects such a suggestion in the part of the passage I left out: "Since Kripkean names are not abbreviations for phrases containing general terms, there is no way in which these names can 'inherit' vagueness from the language of the namers."

17. A different strategy, similar to the one discussed in section (4) might be suggested. That is, to say that '. . . is identical with . . .' is a linguistically vague predicate. This cannot be correct. Suppose it were: '. . . is identical with . . .' would then be a vague one-place predicate like, '. . . is rich,' or a vague two-place predicate like, '. . . is married to. . .'. To say that it is a vague one-place predicate, and that it is satisfied is to say that there is an individual object, call him Jack, of whom it is indefinite whether he is self-identical. To say that it is a vague two-place predicate, and that it is satisfied, is to say that there are two objects, Jack and John, such that it is indefinite whether Jack is identical with John. But this won't work: every object is definitely self-identical, and every object is definitely not identical with any other object. The vagueness of vague identity is indeterminacy as to how many objects there are.

18. Gareth Evans argues that vague identity is incoherent in "Can There be Vague Objects?" in *Analysis*, Vol. 38, 1978, p. 208.

Francis Jeffrey Pelletier, who calls this view, "The Ugly" writes that, "Few writers have advocated—or even explained, except with contempt—such a view." Francis Jeffrey Pelletier, "The Good, the Bad, and the Ugly" *manuscript.*

19. *On the Plurality of Worlds*, p. 212. Lewis has his own account of how to deal with sentences like, "Descartes might have died earlier than he did." He uses the notion of counterpart theory developed in "Counterpart Theory and Quantified Modal Logic" and "Counterparts of Persons and Their Bodies," in *Philosophical Papers*, Vol. 1, pp. 26–46 and 47–54.

20. I am grateful to Daniel Howard-Snyder, Jonathan Bennett, J.A. Burgess, Jan Cover, Paul Hrycaj, and Mark Lance for reading and commenting on an earlier version of this paper. I am especially indebted to Peter van Inwagen for many helpful suggestions and much encouragement.

PART V

Relative Identity and Temporal Parts

15

Reference and Generality (Selections)

Peter T. Geach

30. We must here notice a restriction on the kind of general terms that can ever occur as names. When the same name is used in two acts of naming,† we can always ask whether the same thing is named. It follows that a general term can occur as a name only if it makes sense to prefix the words "the same" to it; by no means all general terms satisfy this condition. And again, only in connection with some terms can the question be asked how many so-and-so's there are. For example, although we have the phrase "the seven seas", nobody could set out to determine how many seas there are; the term "sea" does not determine any division of the water area in the world into seas in the way that the term "letter" (in the typographical sense) does determine a division of the printed matter in the world into letters.

This second ground of distinction between terms was recognized by Frege and by Aquinas. Frege said that only such concepts as 'sharply delimited' what they applied to, so that it was not 'arbitrarily divisible,' could serve as units for counting; to link this up with what I have been saying, we need only observe that for Frege a concept was what language represented by a general term. Frege cagily remarked that in other cases, e.g. "red things", no finite number was determined.[1] But of course the trouble about counting the red things in a room is not that you cannot make an end of counting them, but that you cannot make a beginning; you never know whether you have counted one already, because "the same red thing" supplies no criterion of identity. Aquinas similarly mentions the grammatical fact that, in Latin, substantives have (singular or plural) number on their own account, whereas adjectives have a number determined by the nouns

†Editor's Note: According to Geach, an "act of naming" is the using of a name "outside the context of a sentence simply to call something by name—to acknowledge the presence of the thing". (Section 20, page 52.) It is not the act of conferring a name.

they qualify; I shall follow him in distinguishing general terms as *substantival* and *adjectival.*[2] Grammar is of course only a rough guide here: "sea", for example, could be an adjectival term, although grammatically a substantive.

I had here best interject a note on how I mean this term "criterion of identity". I maintain that it makes no sense to judge whether things are 'the same', or a thing remains 'the same', unless we add or understand some general term—"the same F". That in accordance with which we judge whether identity holds I call a *criterion* of identity: this agrees with the etymology of "criterion". Frege sees clearly that "one" cannot significantly stand as a predicate of objects unless it is (at least understood as) attached to a general term; I am surprised he did not see that the like holds for the closely allied expression "the same". "The same F" does not express a possible way of judging as to identity for all interpretations of "F". I shall call "substantival" a general term for which "the same" does give a criterion of identity. Countability is a sufficient condition for considering a term as substantival; this is so because we (logically) cannot count As unless we know whether the A we are now counting is the same A as we counted before. But it is not necessary, in order that "the same A" shall make sense, for the question "How many As?" to make sense; we can speak of the same gold as being first a statue and then a great number of coins, but "How many golds?" does not make sense; thus "gold" is a substantival term, though we cannot use it for counting.

34. So far, as I said, we have not found any names other than proper names to be used as logical subjects of propositions *regardless of whether the things named are present or absent*; proper names are at any rate the only obvious examples. However, as I shall try to show, it is plausible to suggest that general terms (substantival ones, that is) also admit of such use as logical subjects. Indeed, although the use of proper names in that capacity is much more easily recognized, it is arguable that such use depends on the possibility of general terms' also being logical subjects.

People sometimes speak as if a proper name had meaning just by having a bearer. This is absurd; we certainly do not give a man the meaning of a proper name by presenting him with the object named. In using a proper name we claim the ability (or at least acquaintance, direct or indirect, with somebody else who had the ability) to identify an object; and by giving somebody an object we do not tell him how to identify it. Different proper names of material objects convey different requirements as to identity; the name "Cleopatra's Needle" (which is logically a single word) conveys the requirement of material identity, but neither the name "Thames" nor any proper name of an animal conveys any such thing. For every proper name there is a corresponding use of a common noun preceded by "the same" to express what requirements as to identity the proper name conveys:

"Cleopatra's Needle"—"the same (bit of) stone"; "Jemima"—"the same cat"; "Thames"—"the same river"; "Dr. Jekyll" or "Mr. Hyde"—"the same personality". In all these cases we may say that the proper name conveys a *nominal essence*; thus, "cat" expresses the nominal essence of the thing we call "Jemima", and Jemima's corpse will not be Jemima any more than it will be a cat. (It was for the same reason that I put forward the view that, in a case like "If that is gold I'm a millionaire", "that" must be understood as if it went with a noun like "lump"; otherwise reference would fail for lack of a way to identify *that*.)

I am here deliberately rejecting a well-known thesis of Locke's; but two points for which Locke would have contended must, I think, be granted: first, that the sense of the proper name "Jemima" *need* not include the sense of any predicables like "female" and "tabby" that apply to Jemima but not to all cats (and similarly for proper names of other kinds of things); secondly, that common nouns expressing the nominal essence need not be standing for a kind of substance. The first concession involves rejecting Russell's notorious disguised-description theory of proper names. Russell was obliged of course to admit that, for example, several men may converse intelligently about Bismarck even if the peculiar traits of Bismarck that each has in his mind should differ; this shows that the question which traits the name "Bismarck" recalls is purely psychological and has no bearing on the sense of the name.

The reason for the second concession comes out from one of my examples: the nominal essence of the object called "Thames" is expressed by the common noun "river", and on any view "river" does not stand for a special kind of substance. In the traditional view of substance and accident, it is a mere accident of water that it should flow in a certain watercourse.

I might tell a story involving Jemima and the river Thames without using either of these proper names; I might refer to Jemima as "a cat" and the Thames as "a river" when I first mentioned them, and thereafter speak of "the cat" and "the river"—sc. "the same cat" and "the same river". A hearer unacquainted even by hearsay with Jemima and the Thames, and destined never to make such acquaintance, nor ever to discourse about them again, would lose absolutely nothing by this suppression of the proper names. So if "cat" in this storytelling did not retain the use of a logical subject, how could "Jemima" have such a use? How could we make out that "Jemima" has what it takes to be a logical subject, but "cat" has not?

Although repeated use of a proper name for acts of naming can express an identification, and repeated use of a common noun in this way cannot do so, nevertheless a common noun prefaced by "the same" *can* be used outside the context of a sentence to express an identification. Someone may be trained to say "Jemima" upon seeing Jemima and "cat" upon seeing a cat; someone may also be trained so that he first says "cat" and then says "the same cat" when presented with the same cat as he saw on the first occasion.

Now surely this use of "cat . . . the same cat . . . the same cat . . ." outside the context of a sentence is related to the use of "cat . . . the (same) cat. . . the (same) cat . . ." in telling a story in just the same way as the use of "Jemima" in a series of acts of naming is related to the use of the name in telling the story. And if so, then surely "cat" so used in telling the story is as much a logical subject as "Jemima" is.

If "cat" in such a story is a logical subject, then we need to say what it stands for. It does not stand for Jemima or some other definite cat; my story may have been in fact true (or substantially true) of Jemima, but as told it was not a story about Jemima or about any definite cat, and it need not have been even roughly true of any cat. We cannot say "cat" here stands for an indefinite cat; there is no such animal. In an act of naming, or again in a proposition where it is preceded by a demonstrative, "cat" potentially stands for any cat, and only the concrete application of the utterance to its context ties "cat" down to standing for a given cat then and there present; "cat" in the story is not thus tied down, so we must say that here it refers to any and every cat, equally and impartially. It may rouse our suspicions that though the story is just about a cat, the term "cat" used in it will on this view refer to *every* cat alike. But the suspicion can be dispelled: let us call to mind that, given some complete list of cats, a proposition making a predication "*F*( )", however complex, about a cat must have the same truth-value as would belong to a disjunction "*F*(Jemima) or *F*(Mehitabel) or *F*(Tibbles) . . ." (and so on for all the items of the list); and in this disjunction the names of each and every cat occur symmetrically.

A proper name carrying as part of its sense the criterion of identity expressed by "the same cat" may be called a name *for* a cat; even if "cat" is a name *of* any and every cat, it is not a name *for* any cat. Repeated use of a proper name for a cat requires an intention on the speaker's part to name the same cat each time; repeated use of the name "cat" does not. A proper name is a name *of* a cat if it is not an empty name but does actually name a cat. Each of the names in the list I have just imagined would be a name *of* and *for* a cat. When I speak of a name *of* and *for* an *A* in the sequel, I mean "*A*" to be read as going proxy for some substantial term, and a name *of* and *for* an *A* will be a nonempty proper name whose sense carries the criterion of identity expressed by "the same *A*". (The phrase in quotes, "the same *A*", in the last sentence is of course intended not as mention of that actual expression, but as schematically standing in for quotation of some English phrase in which the letter "*A*" is supplanted by a substantival term; such reading of expressions with schematic letters in them as schematic quotations rather than quoted schemata will often be needed in this work; I rely on the good will and intelligence of readers to see *where*.)

The outward guise of a proper name of course does not show (usually at least) what criterion of identity the name's use carries with it. Many writers on the theory of meaning have been strangely misled by this fact; they have inferred that proper names lack 'connotation', an obscure expression but one that is certainly meant to exclude the proper name's having a sense that includes a criterion of identity. That out of a set of equiform names one may e.g. mean a man, one a dog, one a river or mountain, is another fact mentioned in this connection, and with equal irrelevance; equivocal terms are not confined to the class of proper names, and one might as well argue that "beetle" does not include being an insect as part of its sense because an equiform common noun means a large kind of hammer. (Some have even gone further and denied that proper nouns are words of the language in whose sentences they occur: see section 21.)

The right comment seems to be: What a sign conceals, its use reveals. In vernaculars misunderstanding of proper names is often avoided by adding a suitable common noun in apposition to the proper noun: "Mount Everest", "the river Arrow", "Lake Erie". This device is readily adoptable in formalized languages that contain both proper and common names: if "*a,b,c*, . . ." are letters standing in for proper names and "*A,B,C*, . . ." for common names, then "Ab" could be used to represent a name *for* an *A*, and "*Bc*", a name *for* a *B*. This would obviously be better than e.g. using a new fount of type when proper names for a new kind of object were required—a device that is sometimes employed. But the book contains no formalized proofs; so I shall simply stipulate what the names occurring in it are to be read as names *for*, from one occasion to another.

110. How is "—is the same *A* as—" related to a proper name *for* an *A*? To attack this problem, I shall first set forth a paradox that I developed from a *sophisma* of William of Sherwood.

The fat cat sat on the mat. There was just one cat on the mat. The cat's name was "Tibbles": "Tibbles" is moreover a name *for* a cat.—This simple story leads us into difficulties if we assume that Tibbles is a normal cat. For a normal cat has at least 1,000 hairs. Like many empirical concepts, the concept (*single*) *hair* is fuzzy at the edges; but it is reasonable to assume that we can identify in Tibbles at least 1,000 of his parts each of which definitely is a single hair. I shall refer to these hairs as h_1, h_2, h_3, . . . up to $h_{1,000}$.

Now let c be the largest continuous mass of feline tissue on the mat. Then for any of our 1,000 cat-hairs, say h_n, there is a proper part c_n of c which contains precisely all of c except the hair h_n; and every such part c_n differs in a describable way both from any other such part, say c_m, and from c as a whole. Moreover, fuzzy as the concept *cat* may be, it is clear that not only is c a cat, but also any part c_n is a cat: c_n would clearly be a cat were the hair h_n plucked out, and we cannot reasonably suppose that plucking out a hair *generates* a cat, so c_n must already have been a cat. So contrary to our story, there was not just one cat called "Tibbles" sitting on the mat; there were at least 1,001 sitting there! Of course this would involve a great deal of overlap and sharing of organs among these 1,001 cats, but logic has nothing to say against that; after all, it happens on a small scale between Siamese twins.

All the same, this result *is* absurd. We simply do not speak of cats, or use names of cats, in this way; nor is our ordinary practice open to logical censure. I am indeed far from thinking that ordinary practice never is open to logical censure; but I do not believe our ordinary use of proper names and count nouns is so radically at fault as this conclusion would imply.

Everything falls into place if we realize that the number of cats on the mat is the number of *different cats* on the mat‡ and c_{13}, c_{279}, and c are not three different cats, they are one and the same cat. Though none of these 1,001 lumps of feline tissue is the same lump of feline tissue as another, each *is* the same cat as any other: each of them, then, is a cat, but there is only one cat on the mat, and our original story stands.

Thus each one of the names "c_1, c_2, . . . $c_{1,000}$", or again the name "c", is a name of a cat; but none of these 1,001 names is a name *for* a cat, as "Tibbles" is. By virtue of its sense "Tibbles" is a name, not for one and the same *thing* (in fact, to say that would really be to say nothing at all), but for one and the same *cat*. This name for a cat has reference, and it names the one and only cat on the mat; but just on that account "Tibbles" names, as a shared name, both c itself and any of the smaller masses of feline tissue like c_{12} and c_{279}; for all these are one and the same cat, though not one and the same mass of feline tissue. "Tibbles" is not a name *for* a mass of feline tissue.

So we recover the truth of the simple story we began with. The price to pay is that we must regard "—is the same cat as—" as expressing only a certain equivalence relation, not an absolute identity restricted to cats; but this price, I have elsewhere argued, must be paid anyhow, for there is no such absolute identity as logicians have assumed.

Moreover (slow as I have been to see this) we find ourselves committed to the view of the Polish logician Leśniewski about the category of names: that logic can and must avoid assuming a *syntactical* category of *proper* names. There is a syntactical category of names, but whether a name is a

‡Editor's Note: In an earlier section (Section 109) Geach says that sameness relations govern our counting practices. So, he says

> 'How many cats?' means 'How many different, distinct, cats?'; and 'x and y are different cats' means 'x is a cat and y is a cat and x is not the same cat as y'; and here the one-place predicable '—is a cat' must itself be explained in terms of 'is the same cat as', namely as '—is the same cat as something (or other)'. To borrow a word from Quine, the one-place predicable is a *derelativization* of the two-place predicable, just as "—is a father" is derived by the same logical procedure from "—is father of—". (Geach 1980b, 214; italics in original.)

Thus, in the present example, we are to count only *one* cat because each of the c_n are (in Geach's view) the *same cat,* despite being different lumps of feline tissue.

proper name or a shared name is a matter not of syntax but of semantics; and in any event we must say that what a name's sense restricts it to is not being a name for one and the same *thing*, but rather, for one and the same *A*. As we have seen, a proper name for an *A* may be a shared name of several *B*s, given that each of these *B*s is the same *A* as any of the others.

Let us take another look at an earlier example of ours: proper names for heralds. Let us pretend that "Hilary Handel" is a name *of* and *for* a man, and (with acknowledgment to the late Ian Fleming) that "Sable Basilisk" is a name *of* and *for* a herald. At a given point of time the man Hilary Handel is a herald, in fact he is (the same herald as) the herald Sable Basilisk; conversely, at the same point of time the herald Sable Basilisk is a man, in fact he is (the same man as) the man Hilary Handel. When Hilary Handel is a herald, "Hilary Handel" is a name of a herald; but "the same herald" does not give us the criterion of identity that is built into the sense of "Hilary Handel", so this is not a name *for* a herald. Conversely, "Sable Basilisk" is regularly a name of some man or other, of Hilary Handel, say, at the moment; but because "the same man" does not give us the criterion of identity that is built into the sense of "Sable Basilisk", this is not a name *for* a man. One and the same man, say Hilary Handel, may at different times be (be the same herald as) different heralds: conversely, one and the same herald, say Sable Basilisk, may at different times be (be the same man as) different men. The relation between proper names for heralds and for men, and between the general terms "herald" and "man", is thus quite symmetrical: I could have brought out this symmetry by further elaborating the example in section 91, which did not exploit any logical difference between "man" and "herald". It is of no concern to logic that "man" is a substance term and "herald" is not: this is as little relevant as that God no doubt cares more for men than for heralds.

If we drop the syntactical category distinction between proper and shared names, this rules out a line of thought I followed in earlier editions of this book. I followed Frege in disallowing empty proper names, but I allowed as names empty substantival terms like "dragon". If, as I have argued, a proper name (for an *A*) can be a shared name (of several *B*s, simultaneously or successively), then this line becomes untenable: and so I reject empty names altogether. Where this use of empty common names seems to occur, we need not harshly dismiss discourse as truth-valueless, but may resort to charitable construction as in section 106.

When used as a name, "cat" is a name *of* each cat, impartially and distributively; but it is not a name *for* a cat, except in the cases, discussed in sections 32 and 34, where it stands in grammatical apposition to a demonstrative. (There is a similar case, which I neglected to mention there, when a common noun is being used *pro hac vice* as a proper name of an object of the appropriate kind: in sentences like "Doctor"—or "Nurse"—"will be with you in a minute", "Cook was insolent to Mother today", "Doctor", "Nurse", "Cook", and "Mother" are used as *ad hoc* proper names of a particular doctor, nurse, cook, or mother.) When a name *for* a cat is used twice over, the implication is that we are referring to one and the same cat (apart from accidental homonymy); but there is no such implication when "cat" is used twice over as a name. The connection of "cat" used as a name with "— is the same cat as—" is less direct than the connection a name *for* a cat has: it comes out, for example, in the fact that if there were a finite class of cats, all of them bearing proper names, then "cat" used as a name would be replaceable *salva veritate* by a list of names each corresponding to the criterion of identity given in "the same cat".

I have left to the last one troublesome unsolved problem. If a name "*a*" is a shared name, a predicable "*F*( )" may be true of one thing called "*a*" and false of another: what then is the truth-condition for "*F(a)*"? As we have now seen, this problem arises for what would ordinarily count as proper names, e.g. the proper name "Tibbles" in regard to the predicable "has hair h_{279} as a part". For a regimented language, with a definite and unexpandable vocabulary of primitive predicables, it is not difficult to give recursive truth-conditions such that there is no danger to *consistency* arising over this; but I have thus far found no solution with the *neatness* that ought to characterize logic. So I leave this as a problem for the reader.

Notes

1. Frege, *The Foundations of Arithmetic* (trans. J. L. Austin, Oxford. Blackwell, 1953), p. 66.
2. Aquinas, *Summa Theologica* la. q.39, art.3, c.; ad 1 um; art.5. ad 5 um.

16

Constitutivity and Identity

Hugh S. Chandler

The doctrine that an object is one and the same as the aggregate of its constituents is one element of materialism. I want to clarify this doctrine, and show how it withstands certain objections.[1]

I

How are we to analyze assertions of the form, *a* is made up of *b* and *c*, or of the form, *a* is made up of *b, c,* and *d*, or of the form, *a* is made up of *b, c, d*, and *e*, or . . . etc. etc.?

There are several possibilities. Here is one: constitutivity is treated as *variably polyadic*. Where *a* is made up of *b* and *c*, the relation is considered triadic—holding between *a, b,* and *c*. Where *a* is made up of *b, c*, and *d*, the relation is considered quadradic—holding between *a, b, c*, and *d*. To put the point summarily, the relation is regarded as n + 1-adic, where n is the number of listed constituents. This treatment of constitutivity conflicts with the definitions of relation to be found in some logic books. According to these definitions, every relation has a single fixed additicity.[2]

At least two paths seem open to those who cling to the books. One is the following: It may be held that our problematic "relation" is really no relation at all. It must be analyzed away by means of some real relation. Take *being a part of* as primitive. "*a* is made up of *b* and *c*" means something like "*b* is a part of *a*, and *c* is a part of *a*, and no part of *b* is a part of *c*, and there is no part of *a* such that that part has no parts which are parts of *b* and no parts which are parts of *c*." The analysis of "*a* is made up of *b, c*, and *d*" is slightly more complicated. I call this the *reductive* theory of constitutivity.

The reductive theory is based upon two assumptions: [1] the alleged relation of constitutivity could only be variably polyadic; and [2] no *real* relation is variably polyadic. Both assumptions are questionable. Why, for example, should we accept [1]? And what are the arguments for [2]? In the absence of adequate answers to these questions, I will disregard the reductive theory for the remainder of this paper.

Here is the other path: the constitutivity relation is treated as invariably diadic. We say that if *a* is made up of *b* and *c*, the constitutivity relation holds between *a* and the set whose members are *b* and *c*. Similarly, if *a* is made up of *b, c*, and *d*, the constitutivity relation holds between *a* and the set whose members are *b, c*, and *d*.

It seems to me that we are free to treat constitutivity as a variably polyadic relation, or as a diadic relation holding between an entity and a set. Each procedure has its merits.

II

On the variably polyadic and set interpretations of constitutivity, is a complex entity one and the same as that to which it stands in the constitutivity relation?

The variably polyadic interpretation suggests a negative answer. How can one thing be the same as two, neither of which is the same as the first? A card-board disc is made up of two halves. Obviously the disc is not the same as the first half and not the same as the second. We can say that the disc is the same as the first half and the second, meaning, with the materialist, that the disc is the same as the first half *plus* the second, i.e. that the disc is the same as the *aggregate*, or *sum*, of these halves. But, on the variably polyadic interpretation, it is not (or not *only*) this aggregate which stands in the constitutivity relation to the disc. The halves themselves stand in that relation.

The set interpretation also suggests a negative answer. It is often the case that something, *a*, is (on one level of analysis) made up of two things, *b* and *c*, and (on a different level of analysis) made up of three, *d*, *e*, and *f*. For example, our disc can be thought of as made up of two halves, or of three thirds. The set whose members are *b* and *c* is not the same set as the set whose members are *d, e*, and *f*. But the identity relation is transitive. Hence, if *a* were the same as the set whose members are *b* and *c*, and the same as the set whose members are *d, e*, and *f*, those sets would be the same. This consequent is false. Thus *a* is not the same as the first set, or not the same as the second. We are forced to conclude that an entity is sometimes not the same as the set of its constitutive parts. We are justified in concluding something stronger. Since neither set has a better claim to be the same as *a*, we may hold that neither is, and, more generally, that wherever different levels of analysis into parts are possible, a thing is not the same as the set of its constitutive parts on a given level.

III

Is a complex entity one and the same as the *aggregate* of its constituents? Here are two arguments which purport to prove this impossible.

Argument 1

Suppose that *a* is made up of two things, *b* and *c*, on one level of analysis, and of three things, *d, e,* and *f,* (where none of these are the same as *b* or *c*) on another level.

[1] Aggregate *b* plus *c* is made up of two entities, while aggregate *d* plus *e* plus *f* is not.
[2] Hence, by the indiscernibility of identicals, these aggregates are not one and the same.
[3] Hence *a* is either something distinct from *b* plus *c* or from *d* plus *e* plus *f.*

This, of course, is a modified version of our argument about sets. There is, however, a crucial difference. If a set, S_1, has two members, and a set, S_2, has three, it is absolutely certain that S_1 and S_2 are different sets. On the other hand, I assume that aggregates can be made up of different numbers of entities on different levels of analysis. On this assumption, premiss [1] is false. Aggregate *d* plus *e* plus *f* can be analyzed into two entities, namely *d* plus *e* and *f.*

Argument 2

The second argument is based upon this model:

	t_1	t_2	t_3	t_4
r_1	$[p_1, p_2, p_3]$	$[p_1, p_2, p_4]$	$[p_1, p_5, p_4]$	$[p_6, p_5, p_4]$
r_2	$[p_4, p_5, p_6]$	$[p_3, p_5, p_6]$	$[p_3, p_2, p_6]$	$[p_3, p_2, p_1]$

There are four times, t_1 through t_4, and two regions, r_1 and r_2. The particles, p_1 through p_6, move independently from one region to the other. An "alphe" is a physical object made up of three particles. We assume that the *classification* rules for alphes show that there is one and only one alphe in each region at each time. For example, there is an alphe in r_1 at t_1 made up of p_1, p_2, and p_3, and there is an alphe in r_1 at t_2 made up of p_1, p_2, and p_4, etc. etc. Furthermore, we assume that the *re-identification* rules for alphes show that the *same* alphe is in r_1 at all four times, and that *another* alphe is in r_2 at all four times. Thus there are two alphes in our model. Finally, we assume that aggregates made up of particles are the same aggregate if, and only if, they are made up of the same particles. This is a re-identification rule for aggregates.

The argument is given at t_4.

[1] The alphe now in r_1 has the property of having been in r_1 at t_1.
[2] The aggregate p_4 plus p_5 plus p_6 does not have the property of having been in r_1 at t_1.
[3] Hence, by the indiscernibility of identicals, the alphe now in r_1 cannot be one and the same as p_4 plus p_5 plus p_6.

What do we mean when we say that the alphe in r_1 (at t_4) has the property of having been in r_1 at t_1? We mean, I think, that if the alphe is traced back through time, following the rules for re-identifying alphes, the trail leads to the alphe in r_1 at t_1. A materialist may well claim that premiss [1] is not put with proper precision. It should go like this:

[1b] The alphe now in r_1 has the property of being something which, if traced according to the rules for re-identifying alphes, is traceable to the alphe in r_1 at t_1.

Of course this means that premiss [2] also requires readjustment.

[2b] The aggregate p_4 plus p_5 plus p_6 does not have the property of being something which, if traced according to the rules for re-identifying alphes, is traceable to the alphe in r_1 at t_1.

Does p_4 plus p_5 plus p_6 have this property? It is easy to think it cannot, since, when we trace that aggregate back to t_1, *following the rule for re-identifying aggregates*, the trail leads us, not to r_1, but to r_2. But why can't one and the same thing be traceable to one region, if traced according to one set of rules, and traceable to another region, if traced according to a different set? On the materialist's view, at t_4 the aggregate p_4 plus p_5 plus p_6 *is* something which, if traced according to the rules for re-identifying *alphes*, is traceable to r_1 at t_1, and not to r_2. Hence, I suppose, the materialist rejects [2b].

IV

Let me defend a view hinted at in the discussion of argument 2. The materialist should, I suggest, subscribe to the doctrine that temporal properties are *relative to rules of re-identification*:

It is possible for something, *a*, to have the property of being something which when traced according to certain rules is traceable to an entity having property P at t_n, even though at the same time *a* has the property of being something which when traced according to certain (other) rules is traceable to an entity lacking P at t_n.

Does this doctrine conflict with the fact that identity is transitive? Consider the following argument:

Suppose that the alphe now (at t_4) in r_1 is one and the same as the 3-particle aggregate in r_1 (i.e. p_4 plus p_5 plus p_6).

[1] The 3-particle aggregate now in r_1 is one and the same as the 3-particle aggregate in r_2 at t_1.

[2] Hence, by our supposition and the transitivity of identity, the alphe now in r_1 must be one and the same as the 3-particle aggregate in r_2 at t_1.

[3] But the alphe now in r_1 is one and the same as the alphe in r_1 at t_1.

[4] Hence, by both the transitivity and the symmetry of identity, the 3-particle aggregate in r_2 at t_1 must be one and the same as the alphe in r_1 at t_1.

[5] Hence, by the indiscernibility of identicals, the 3-particle aggregate in r_2 at t_1 cannot have a property which the alphe in r_1 at t_1 lacks.

This argument gives the appearance of showing that the materialist cannot hold that temporal properties are relative to rules of re-identification and admit that identity is transitive. But, I submit, the appearance is deceptive.

The view that temporal properties are relative to rules of re-identification has as a natural correlative the view that there are at least three kinds of identity claim: [a] We refer to an individual of one time in ways that suggest the same re-identification rules (e.g. "this gentleman is the author of *Arundel*". Both "this gentleman" and "the author of *Arundel*" suggest the re-identification rules for *persons*). [b] We refer to an individual of one time in ways that suggest re-identification rules which have the potentiality of leading along divergent paths (e.g. "this man's body is one and the same as the aggregate of particles which presently make up his body"). I call claims of this kind *divergent-form* identity claims. [c] We refer to an individual of two times in ways that suggest the same re-identification rules (e.g. "this man's body is one and the same as the body he had ten years ago"). I call this a *time-crossing* identity claim.

The supposition that the alphe now (at t_4) in r_1 is one and the same as the 3-particle aggregate in r_1 is the supposition of a present divergent-form identity. On the other hand, premiss [1] is a time-crossing identity claim. How does transitivity apply across identities of these two kinds? I take it to apply in such a way as to lead to this conclusion:

[2b] Hence, by our supposition and the transitivity of identity, the alphe now in r_1 must *now* be one and the same as the 3-particle aggregate which was in r_2 at t_1.

Premiss [3] is another time-crossing identity claim for use in a transitivity argument in combination with the hybrid claim in [2b]. The consequence should go as follows:

[4b] Hence, by both the transitivity and the symmetry of identity, the 3-particle aggregate which was in r_2 at t_1 is *now* one and the same as the alphe which was in r_1 at t_1.

This does not say that the 3-particle aggregate which was in r_2 at t_1 was *then* one and the same as the alphe then in r_1. My complaint against [4] is that it could be taken to say precisely this.

Given a divergent-form identity claim of the form "*a* is now one and the same as *b*", the principle of the indiscernibility of identicals tells us that *a* is now indiscernible from *b*. Applied to [4b], the principle yields this result:

[5b] Hence, by the indiscernibility of identicals, the 3-particle aggregate which was in r_2 at t_1 cannot *now* have a property which the alphe which was in r_1 at t_1 *now* lacks.

At t_1 the 3-particle aggregate in r_2 had properties the alphe in r_1 lacked. This is compatible with the claim that the alphe which was in r_1 at t_1 *now* has every property presently possessed by the 3-particle aggregate which was in r_2 at t_1. The materialist is not defeated by his admission that identity is transitive.

Of course the anti-materialist insists that the 3-particle aggregate which was in r_2 at t_1 does now have properties presently lacked by the alphe which was in r_1 at t_1, for example, the property of having been in r_2 at t_1. And, of course, the materialist replies that the temporal property in question has not been described accurately. We are concerned, for example, with the property of being something which, if traced according to the rules for re-identifying aggregates, is traceable to something which was in r_2 at t_1. According to the materialist, *both* the 3-particle aggregate which was in r_2 at t_1 *and* the alphe which was in r_1 at t_1 now have this property. We are back to points made in our discussion of argument [2].

What conclusions can be drawn? Given either the variably polyadic or the set interpretation of constitutivity, a complex entity is not, generally, one and the same as that to which it stands in the constitutivity relation. But it still seems possible to hold that every complex entity is one and the same as the aggregate of its parts. Materialists can defend themselves from the arguments we have examined by holding, among other things, that temporal properties are relative to rules of re-identification. For some, I suppose, this price will seem too high.

Notes

1. While writing this paper I often discussed materialism with Professor Robert Stalnaker: I am very grateful for his help.

2. See, for example, Patrick Suppes' *Introduction to Logic* (Princeton, New Jersey: D. Van Nostrand, Inc., 1957): 210–212.

17

Temporal Parts of Four Dimensional Objects*

Mark Heller

Probably the best objection to there being so-called temporal parts is that no one has adequately made sense of what a temporal part is supposed to be. Such phrases as "temporal part", "temporal phase", and "temporal slice" have been used in ways that suggest such varied purported objects as processes, events, ways things are, sets, and portions of careers or histories. The account which comes closest to making sense of temporal parts is Judith Jarvis Thomson's in 'Parthood and identity across time'.[1] Consider an object O which exists from time t_0 to t_3. On Thomson's account, a temporal part of O, call it P, is an object that comes into existence at some time $t_1 \geqslant t_0$ and goes out of existence at some time $t_2 \leqslant t_3$ and takes up some portion of the space that O takes up for all the time that P exists.[2] Her account has the strength of being reasonably explicit about what she means by "temporal part". Furthermore, as she explains them, temporal parts do, at least on the face of it, seem to be parts. Her account, however, has the weakness of, as Thomson claims,[3] making the existence of temporal parts fairly implausible. I shall offer an account which is at once explicit and supportive.

The basic problem with Thomson's account is that it is developed against the background of an unhelpful presupposition about the nature of physical objects. She thinks of physical objects as being three dimensional and enduring through time. I admit from the outset that this is our normal philosophical way of thinking of physical objects. But it is this way of thinking that makes temporal parts seem implausible. I see nothing in favor of it other than the fact that it is our standard view, and I put very little weight on this advantage. Furthermore, this view leads to having to choose between what I take to be unpleasant alternatives. The alternatives are:

(a) there is no such physical object as my body,
(b) there is no physical object in the space that we would typically say is now exactly occupied by all of me other than my left hand.
(c) no physical object can undergo a loss of parts (in the ordinary sense of "parts"),
(d) there can be distinct physical objects exactly occupying the same space at the same time,
(e) identity is not transitive.

To deny each of these alternatives and to accept three dimensional enduring objects would lead to a contradiction. To show this I present an abbreviated, slightly altered version of an argument of Peter van Inwagen's.[4] If we deny alternative *a*, then there is such an object as my body. Call it Body. If we deny alternative *b*, then there is an object that is all of me other than my left hand. Call that object Body-minus. Now consider some time *t* at which my left hand is cut off. This does not affect Body-minus, so:

(1) the thing that, before *t*, is Body-minus = the thing that, after *t*, is Body-minus.

If we also deny alternative *c*, then my losing my hand does not end my body's existence, so:

(2) the thing that, after *t*, is Body = the thing that, before *t*, is Body.

Further, if we deny *d*, it *seems* to follow that:

(3) the thing that, after *t*, is Body-minus = the thing that, after *t*, is Body.

If we then deny *e*, by transitivity of identity it follows that:

(4) the thing that, before *t*, is Body-minus = the thing that, before *t*, is Body.

But since Body was bigger before *t* than Body-minus was before *t*:

(5) the thing that, before *t*, is Body-minus ≠ the thing that, before *t*, is Body,

and (5) contradicts (4).

In the end, Thomson's preferred way of avoiding this contradiction is to accept *d*.[5] In contrast, van Inwagen avoids the contradiction by accepting *b*.[6] Roderick Chisholm instead accepts *c*.[7] And Peter Geach seems to accept *e*.[8] My way of avoiding the contradiction is to claim that (3) does not follow from the denial of *d* unless we accept the additional thesis that physical objects are three dimensional and endure through time. I will deny this additional thesis. Doing so will allow me to claim that Body and Body-minus are distinct objects that, even after *t*, do not occupy the same space at the same time. It is incumbent upon me, then, to offer a reasonable alternative to the three dimensional view of physical objects.

I propose that a physical object is not an enduring spatial hunk of matter, but is, rather, a spatiotemporal hunk of matter. Instead of thinking of matter as filling up regions of space, we should think of matter as filling up regions of spacetime. A physical object is the material content of a region of spacetime. Just as such an object has spatial extent, it also has temporal extent—it extends along four dimensions, not just three. To see the contrast clearly, consider an object that is created at noon and destroyed at one. If we think of the object as three dimensional and enduring though time, it would be appropriate to say that the object exists at different times; the same object exists at noon and at one. Such an object has boundaries along only three dimensions. The whole object is that hunk of matter which entirely fills up those boundaries. The whole object, therefore, exists at noon and still exists at one. A four dimensional object, on the other hand, has boundaries along an additional dimension. The whole object must fill up all its boundaries and, therefore, does not exist at a single moment. If we accept that physical objects are four dimensional, the appropriate thing to say about the object under consideration is that it takes up more than an instantaneous region of time. It does not exist *at* noon *and* one; rather, it exists *from* noon *until* one. Instead of thinking of an object as existing at various times, we should think of it as existing within regions of time.

In so far as time is just one more dimension, roughly alike in kind to the three spatial dimensions, we should expect that our claims about an object's spatial characteristics have analogues with respect to its temporal characteristics. For instance, just as we might talk about the distance between two points along a line in space, we can also talk about the distance between two points in time. This allows us to understand the notion of temporal boundaries as analogous to that of spatial boundaries. Furthermore, there is an analogy with respect to the part-whole relationship. Just as a spatial part fills up a sub-region of the space occupied by the whole, a temporal part fills up a subregion of the time occupied by the whole. Another important analogy is that, for both spatial and temporal parts, we can, loosely speaking, point at or perceive or name a whole by pointing at, perceiving, or indicating a part. It should be noted that an object's temporal characteristics are not completely analogous to its spatial characteristics. This is because time is not completely alike in kind to the three spatial dimensions. Time, for instance, seems to have a direction. Also, our perception along the temporal dimension is only one directional (memory) and is discontinuous (I can remember what happened on my third birthday without remembering anything that happened between my third and fourth birthdays). Furthermore, temporal units of measurement are not of the same kind as spatial units of measurement. These disanalogies will not affect our present discussion.

One question that arises is whether it is possible to have zero extent along the temporal dimension. I do not have a strong opinion on this issue, although I tend towards the view that zero extent is impossible. What should be noted is that this is no more an issue with respect to the temporal dimension than with any of the spatial dimensions. Could there be any such thing as the surface of a cube? I do not know the answer. Thinking according to our standard three dimensional picture such an object would have zero extent along one of the spatial dimensions and could, therefore, be called a two dimensional object. According to our new four dimensional picture such an object would still have zero extent along one of the spatial dimensions. It could, therefore, be called a three dimensional object, one of the three being the temporal dimension. I shall, for convenience's sake, simply assume that zero extent along the temporal dimension, and along each of the other dimensions, is possible.

Now that we have some understanding of the notion of a four dimensional object, let us turn our attention to the parts of such objects. A four dimensional object is the material content of a filled region of spacetime. A spatiotemporal part of such an object is the material content of a sub-region of the spacetime occupied by the whole. For instance, consider a particular object *O* and the region *R* of spacetime that *O* fills. A spatiotemporal part of *O* is the material content of a sub-region of *R*. A spatiotemporal part, as long as it has greater than zero extent along every dimension, is itself a four dimensional physical object.[9] A spatiotemporal part is not a set or a process or a way something is at a place and time. It, like the object it is part of, is a hunk of matter. If Heller is a physical object, then so is Heller's-left-hand-from-(1:00 p.m., January 3, 1980)-to-(1:01 p.m., January 3, 1980). This spatiotemporal part of me could have, between 1:00 p.m. and 1:01 p.m. on January 3, 1980, been felt, seen, heard, smelled, and, if need be, tasted. It had weight and volume. Thinking of spatiotemporal parts as physical objects corresponds to the way we ordinarily think of parts on our old three dimensional picture. When not being swayed by philosophical considerations we have no doubt that my hand is a physical object. Accepting the account of four dimensional objects presented in this paper, we may continue to hold the general principle that a part of a physical object is itself a physical object.

It should be noted that the fact that any part of *O* is the material content of a sub-region of *R* does not entail that every filled sub-region of *R* contains a part of *O*. I happen to believe that this is true, but it is not a feature

~("any part of O is the material content of a subregion of R" ⇒ DAUP)

of the concept of a spatiotemporal part. One could consistently accept all three of the following:

(i) there are four dimensional objects and spatiotemporal parts of such objects,
(ii) not every filled region of spacetime contains a physical object,
(iii) even for a region of spacetime that does contain a physical object, not every sub-region contains a spatiotemporal part of that object.

I take it that typically someone who accepts all three of these would be accepting (iii) because he accepts (ii). Someone might accept (ii) if he thought that there is good reason to reject scattered objects. Or (ii) might be accepted if independent grounds could be found for some claim like "every object must contain its principle of unity within itself" (whatever that might mean). My goal here is not to supply a means of answering every question of the form "is there a spatiotemporal part here?", but rather to make clear the concept of spatiotemporal parthood.

It is now easy to understand the notion of a temporal part. Any proper part of a four dimensional object is smaller than the whole object along at least one dimension. A proper temporal part is smaller along just one dimension, the temporal dimension. A temporal part of *O* is a spatiotemporal part that is the same spatial size as *O* for as long as that part exists, though it may be a smaller temporal size. Let us suppose that object *O* exactly fills the temporal region from t_0 to t_3. That is, the region of spacetime filled by *O*, namely region *R*, has the temporal boundaries t_0 and t_3. Now consider a certain sub-region of *R* the temporal boundaries of which are $t_1 \geqslant t_0$ and $t_2 \leqslant t_3$ and the spatial boundaries of which are just the spatial boundaries of *R* from t_1 to t_2. Call this sub-region *S*. If the material content of *S* is an object, then it is a temporal part of *O*. In general, using the single letters as variables rather than names, a temporal part of *O* is the material content of a temporal sub-region of *R*. "Temporal sub-region of *R*" means spatiotemporal sub-region that shares all of *R*'s spatial boundaries within that sub-region's temporal boundaries. A temporal part of me which exists from my fifth birthday to my sixth is the same spatial size I am from age five to age six.

One matter of detail that is particularly important for temporal parts specifically and four dimensional objects in general is how to understand such phrases as "_____ exists in region _____" or "_____ exists at time _____". Physical objects are four dimensional hunks of matter. They, therefore, have precise spatiotemporal boundaries. Consider a particular physical object, this piece of paper.[10] Call it Whitey. Whitey has certain spatiotemporal boundaries—there is a region which it exactly occupies. But we also think that it is true to say that Whitey now exists. This way of talking may

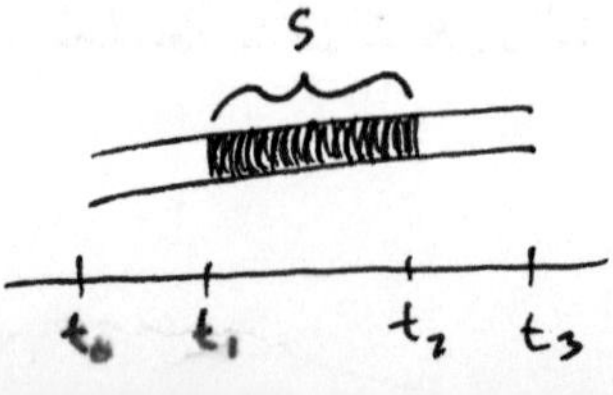

be misleading. If Whitey exists now and existed a minute ago, then it is the same object which exists at both times. But this suggests the old three dimensional picture that we have been denying.

This confusion is easily avoided. When we say that Whitey exists now this should be taken as a loose way of saying that part of Whitey exists now. If we meant strictly that Whitey exists now we would be saying something false. "Whitey" names the whole piece of paper,[11] and that object does not exist now. Strictly speaking, Whitey is temporally too large to exist now. Only a part of Whitey exists now. This, then, is the major difference between the three dimensional and four dimensional pictures. On the three dimensional picture if we said that Whitey exists now and really meant Whitey, the whole piece of paper, we would be saying something true. It is Whitey which exist at different times. On the other hand, on the four dimensional picture Whitey does not, strictly speaking, exist at different times. Whitey's parts exist at different times (different parts at different times), and, in virtue of this fact, we say that Whitey exists at those times.

This can be made clearer by considering a spatial analogy. Put Whitey mostly in a drawer, but leave a small corner sticking out. Now if asked where Whitey is you will answer that it is in the drawer. Strictly speaking, however, your answer would be false. Even on the three dimensional picture, part of Whitey is not in the drawer. But "Whitey" names the whole piece of paper, so if it is not the whole piece in the drawer, then it is not Whitey in the drawer. We say that Whitey is in the drawer because a part of Whitey is in there. Notice also that with some rewording it can be seen that how large a portion of the paper is in the drawer is not crucial. If only a corner of the paper were inside we would be less likely to say that Whitey is in the drawer when asked where Whitey is. But if asked "Does Whitey exist inside that drawer?", I think we would all say "yes". For another case consider Alice's mother screaming at her "Now, Alice, you stay out of that cookie jar!".

Recognizing that we have this loose way of speaking even when using our three dimensional picture, it is not surprising that we also have this loose way of speaking when using our four dimensional picture. Recognizing that such a phrase as "Whitey exists now" is just loose speaking, we see that, strictly speaking, Whitey only exists within the spatiotemporal region which it exactly fills and regions of which that one is a sub-region. To loosely say that Whitey exists now is to strictly say that the present time is within Whitey's temporal boundaries, and thus is equivalent to saying that Whitey has a temporal part that exists now (assuming that there are instantaneous temporal parts).

One nice ramification of these considerations is that an object and a proper part of that object do not, strictly speaking, exist in the same space at the same time. An object is not coincident with any of its proper parts.

Intuitively, the problem with coincident entities is that of overcrowding. There is just not enough room for them. But an object and a part of that object do not compete for room. There is a certain spatiotemporal region exactly occupied by the part; the whole object is not in that region. There is only as much of the object there as will fit—namely, the part. This intuitive understanding of the relationship between part and whole is what I intended to capture with my discussion of our loose way of talking. When we say that Whitey is in the drawer, that is just a loose way of saying that part of Whitey is there. When we say Whitey exists now we are only saying that a part of Whitey exists now. Keeping this in mind allows us to avoid being committed to coincident entities.

Let us consider a spatial case. Even adopting a three dimensional picture, we are not tempted to say that Heller and Heller's left hand are coincident entities. These are not two distinct entities in one place at one time. Strictly speaking, there is only one entity in that hand shaped region of space—my hand. Whatever truth there is in saying that I am in that region can be wholly captured by saying that a part of me is there. The relation between my hand and me is not that of coincidence, but, rather, that of part to whole. Similar points are relevant to cases of spatial overlap. My living room and dining room share a common wall. But this does not entail that there is a wall shaped region of space occupied by both my living room and my dining room. That region is occupied by the wall, and that wall happens to be part of both rooms.

If we adopt the four dimensional view of physical objects, then similar points can be made about the relation between an object and its temporal parts. Heller is not coincident with Heller-during-1983. The only truth there is in saying that I occupy the year long region of time is that I have a part that occupies that region. Strictly speaking, there is only one entity in the relevant spatiotemporal region—my 1983 part. Also, analogous to the case of spatial overlap, there may be cases of temporal overlap. If I were to undergo fission next year, that should not tempt us to say that prior to 1984 there were two objects in the same space at the same time.[12] Rather, we should say that two four dimensional objects overlapped prior to 1984—they shared a common temporal part. Perhaps a less controversial case would be a hunk of gold that is shaped into a ring. The ring then undergoes a gradual replacement of matter until it is entirely composed of silver. Many would be tempted to say that the ring and the hunk of gold were, for a period of time, coincident entities. However adopting the four dimensional view, we can say that the gold and the ring temporally overlap. The gold has a ring shaped temporal part, the ring has a golden temporal part, and the gold's part is identical to the ring's part. The relationship of the part of the one and the part of the other is identity, not coincidence. The relationship between the gold and the ring is that they share a common part, they overlap.[13]

In contrast, trying to make sense of temporal parts without shifting to a four dimensional picture would require a commitment to coincident entities. On Thomson's account, Heller and Heller-now are, in the strictest sense, two distinct entities occupying the same space at the same time.[14] Heller is, at any given time between his birth and his death, complete. Right now I exactly fill all of my three dimensional boundaries. But that supposed temporal part of me called Heller-now also exactly fills those same boundaries. Yet the two entities are distinct because I have a much longer career than Heller-now. Thomson cannot claim that strictly speaking I am temporally too big to be coincident with my instantaneous temporal part, because she avails herself of only three dimensions along which to measure. Along those dimensions I am now exactly the same size as Heller-now.

In fact Thomson's problem of coincident entities is a symptom of a much deeper problem with trying to explain temporal parts without rejecting the old three dimensional picture. Let us return to Whitey, the piece of paper. On the old picture it is, strictly speaking, true that Whitey exists now. It is the same three dimensional object which exists at different times. "Whitey" names the whole piece of paper. So it is true that the whole piece of paper does exist now. So even though Whitey will continue to exist for the next several hours, "Whitey-from-(now + one hour)-to-(now + two hours)" does not pick out a part of Whitey unless that part exists now. But if there were such a temporal part it would not yet have come into existence. So Whitey has no temporal parts other than the one which exists now. Indeed, it does not even have that temporal part, since Whitey (all of it) existed an hour ago, and the temporal part which supposedly exists now did not exist then. If one holds the three dimensional view of physical objects it is perfectly reasonable to think of an ontology including temporal parts as a "crazy metaphysic".[15]

Of course, this is not Thomson's reason for calling it a crazy metaphysic. She does not draw attention to the three dimensional/four dimensional distinction at all. Thomson writes:

> I said this seems to me a crazy metaphysic. It seems to me that its full craziness only comes out when we take the spatial analogy seriously. The metaphysic yields that if I have had exactly one bit of chalk in my hand for the last hour, then there is something in my hand which is white, roughly cylindrical in shape, and dusty, something which also has a weight, something which is chalk, which was not in my hand three minutes ago, and indeed, such that no part of it was in my hand three minutes ago. As I hold the bit of chalk in my hand, new stuff, new chalk keeps constantly coming into existence *ex nihilo*. That strikes me as obviously false.[16]

I suggest that this attack on temporal parts depends on accepting the thesis that physical objects are three dimensional.

Why does Thomson think that temporal parts would come into existence *ex nihilo*? It is obviously not because nothing exists before the temporal part. It is not even because everything that exists before the temporal part continues to exist, for there are prior temporal parts that go out of existence at just the moment that the part in question comes into existence. I suggest that Thomson's claim is founded on the belief that there is no significant material change occurring at the time that the temporal part is supposed to be coming into existence. The piece of chalk does not undergo any alteration. No molecules need be altering their internal structure or their relationships to other molecules. No matter from outside the chalk is added, nor is any matter that was part of the chalk released into the surrounding atmosphere. In short, nothing has occurred that would be enough to bring an object into existence. The temporal part just seems to pop into existence without any sufficient cause.

But this argument ignores one significant change that takes place—the passage of time. It is this change which is responsible for the temporal part's coming into existence. Of course, this passage of time does not provide the whole causal explanation for why the temporal part exists. To give the full explanation we would have to account for why there is matter at that place at that time. It is this passage of time, however, that explains why that matter's being there at that time constitutes a new object's coming into existence. At t_0 the temporal part in question did not exist. At t_1 it did exist. The change which brought this object into existence was just the change in time from t_0 to t_1. Some philosophers—Thomson, for instance—will undoubtably feel that this kind of change is too superficial to bring an object into existence. But this feeling is based on an unwarranted prejudice in favor of the spatial over the temporal. This prejudice, in turn, is founded upon the thesis that physical objects are three dimensional and enduring. Once we surrender this thesis, adopting instead the four dimensional view, I can find no defense for the claim that temporal parts would have to come into existence *ex nihilo*.

To support temporal parts and the four dimensional view of physical objects, recall that earlier in this paper I argued that thinking of objects as three dimensional and enduring would commit us to one of the following five unpleasant alternatives:

(a) there is no such physical object as my body,

(b) there is no physical object in the space that we would typically say is now exactly occupied by all of me other than my left hand,

(c) no physical object can undergo a loss of parts (in the ordinary sense of "parts"),

(d) there can be distinct physical objects exactly occupying the same space at the same time,

(e) identity is not transitive.

We are now in a position to see how viewing objects as four dimensional allows us to avoid all of these alternatives. Once we adopt the four dimensional picture, we can deny all five alternatives without having to be committed to:

(3) the thing that, after *t*, is Body-minus = the thing that, after *t*, is Body.

The objects claimed to be identical in (3) are distinct and do not occupy, except in a loose sense, the same space at the same time.

Body and Body-minus are distinct four dimensional objects, since they have different spatial shapes before *t*. But then, it might be objected, they seem to be distinct but coincident entities—co-occupying a single spatiotemporal region *R* which begins at *t*. The response is that *strictly speaking* neither of them is in *R*. They are both temporally too big. They each take up a spatiotemporal region that is temporally larger than *R*, since their regions begin before *t*. Of course, each has a temporal part that is in *R*, but that does not entail that either Body or Body-minus is in that region. They overlap in *R*, but neither one exactly fills *R*.

Perhaps there may be another way of generating the difficulty. Instead of comparing Body with Body-minus, let us compare that part of Body which does exactly fill *R* with that part of Body-minus which also exactly fills *R*. It might be claimed that here we have an example of two distinct objects in the same space at the same time. But this again would be a mistake, for these temporal parts are not two distinct objects but, rather, one object under two descriptions. Body and Body-minus have a common temporal part, just as my living room and my dining room have a common spatial part.

I have tried to expound a metaphysic for temporal parts that is at least plausible. I have also tried to give one reason why it might be desirable to adopt such a metaphysic. Still, there is much work left to be done. We will have to develop an understanding of change as a relationship between temporal parts of a four dimensional whole. This will have effects on our understanding of causation and, in particular, of an agent's bringing about change. For instance, Paul Bunyan's cutting down a tree should be seen as a relationship between certain of Bunyan's spatiotemporal parts and certain of the tree's spatiotemporal parts. There is also other important work to be done with respect to the question of whether four dimensional objects have their spatiotemporal parts essentially. Still one more relevant task would be to see how issues concerning the relationship between the mental and physical might affect our considerations of four dimensional objects. These are just some of the chores left undone. At least now that we have a better understanding of what four dimensional objects and temporal parts are, we have a solid basis for carrying out these and other future projects.

Notes

* My thanks to Jonathan Bennett, Mark Brown, Jan Cover, Paul Hrycaj. Carl Matheson, Judith Jarvis Thomson, and Peter van Inwagen.

1. Judith Jarvis Thomson, 'Parthood and identity across time' (Chapter 3 of this volume).

2. Thomson would have been better off calling this a spatiotemporal part of *O*, since it may be spatially part of *O* at some of the times at which it exists. She also defines "cross-sectional temporal part", and this could appropriately be called a temporal part.

3. She calls it "a crazy metaphysic" on pp. 34 and 36.

4. Peter van Inwagen, 'The doctrine of arbitrary undetached parts' (Chapter 10 of this volume).

5. Thomson *op. cit.*

6. van Inwagen, *op. cit.*

7. Roderick Chisholm: 'Parts as essential to their wholes', *Review of Metaphysics* 26 (1973) pp. 581–603.

8. Peter Geach: 'Identity', *Review of Metaphysics* 21 (1967–1968), pp. 3–12.

9. I am using "object" to pick out the broadest ontological category. To be is to be an object. To be physical is to be a physical object.

10. Assuming that this piece of paper does have precise boundaries.

11. Notice that my claims here are not presupposing a description theory of names. On a causal theory of names "Whitey" refers to the whole piece of paper if and only if it was the whole piece which was originally baptised when the reference of "Whitey" was fixed.

12. Compare this to David Lewis's discussion in 'Survival and Identity', *The Identity of Persons*, ed. Amelie Oksenberg Rorty (Berkeley: University of California Press, 1976), pp. 17–40.

13. Compare this to John Perry's discussion in 'The same F', *The Philosophical Review* 79 (April 1970), pp 181–200, esp. pp. 198–199.

14. See Thomson, p. 34.

15. See Note 3.

16. Thomson, p. 36.

Appendix
A Formal Statement of the Problem

In this appendix, I provide a more formal statement of the five assumptions described in the introduction to this volume. I also provide a more formal version of the argument that shows that these assumptions are jointly incompatible.

1. The Assumptions

EXISTENCE ASSUMPTION:	$(\exists x)(\exists ps)(\exists t)(x$ is an F & the ps compose x at $t)$
ESSENTIALIST ASSUMPTION:	$(\forall x)(\forall ps)(\forall t)[x$ is an F & the ps compose x at $t \supset (\exists z_1)($the ps compose z_1 at t & $\Box(\forall qs)(\forall t)($the qs compose z_1 at $t \supset z_1$ bears R to the $qs))]$
PACP:	$(\forall x)(\forall ps)(\forall t)[x$ is an F & the ps compose x at $t \supset (\exists z_2)($the ps compose z_2 at t & $\Diamond(\exists qs)(\exists t)$(the qs compose z_2 at t and z_2 does not bear R to the $qs))]$
IDENTITY ASSUMPTION:	$(\forall x)(\forall y)(\forall ps)(\forall t)($the ps compose x at t & the ps compose y at $t \supset x = y)$
NECESSITY ASSUMPTION:	$(\forall x)(\forall y)[x = y \supset \Box((x$ exists $\vee$ y exists$) \supset x = y)]$

2. The Argument

(1) S is an F and the *ps* compose S at *t*. (Instantiation of Existence Assumption)

(2) There is a z_1 such that the *ps* compose z_1 at *t* and, necessarily, for all *qs* and *t*, the *qs* compose z_1 at *t* only if z_1 bears R to the *qs*. (From 1, Essentialist Assumption)

(3) There is a z_2 such that the *ps* compose z_2 at *t* and, possibly, there are *qs* and *t* such that the *qs* compose z_2 at *t* and z_2 does not bear R to the *qs*. (From 1, PACP)

(4) The *ps* compose Z_1 at *t* and, necessarily, for all *qs* and *t*, the *qs* compose Z_1 at *t* only if Z_1 bears R to the *qs*. (Instantiation of 2)

(5) The *ps* compose Z_2 at *t* and, possibly, there are *qs* and *t* such that the *qs* compose Z_2 at *t* and Z_2 does not bear R to the *qs*. (Instantiation of 3)

(6) $Z_1 = Z_2$. (From Identity Assumption, 4, 5)
(7) Possibly, Z_1 exists or Z_2 exists and $Z_1 \neq Z_2$. (From 4, 5)
(8) $Z_1 \neq Z_2$. (From 7, Necessity Assumption)
** Contradiction (6, 8)

Select Bibliography

This bibliography includes a list of works cited in the foregoing essays, as well as a select list of additional sources that may be of use or interest to the reader. Particular editions of historical works are listed only if they are cited in the essays above; otherwise, just the work itself is listed. Essays reprinted in this anthology are not listed here.

Works Cited

Adams, Robert M. 1979. "Primitive Thisness and Primitive Identity." *Journal of Philosophy* 76: 5–26.

Aquinas, Thomas. *Summa Theologica, Pars Prima.*

———. *Commentary on the Sentences.*

Aristotle. *Physics.*

Augustine. *Confessions.*

Ayer, A. J. 1956. *The Problem of Knowledge.* London: Macmillan.

Ayers, M. 1974. "Individuals Without Sortals." *Canadian Journal of Philosophy* 4: 113–48.

Bayle, Pierre. 1734–41. A *General Dictionary: Historical and Critical,* trans. Rev. J. P. Bernard, Rev. Thomas Birch, John Lockeman, et al. London: Bettenham.

———. 1965. *Historical and Critical Dictionary: Selections,* ed. R. H. Popkin. Indianapolis: Bobbs-Merrill.

Black, Max. 1952. "The Identity of Indiscernibles." *Mind* 61: 153–64. (Reprinted in Loux 1976.)

Bressan, Aldo. 1972. *A General Interpreted Modal Calculus.* New Haven, CT: Yale University Press.

Brody, Baruch. 1972. "Locke on the Identity of Persons." *American Philosophical Quarterly* 9: 327–34.

Burge, Tyler. 1977. "A Theory of Aggregates." *Noûs* 11: 97–117.

Burke, Michael. 1980. "Cohabitation, Stuff and Intermittent Existence." *Mind* 89: 391–405.

———. 1992. "Copper Statues and Pieces of Copper: A Challenge to the Standard Account." *Analysis* 52: 12–17.

———. 1994. "Dion and Theon: An Essentialist Solution to an Ancient Puzzle." *Journal of Philosophy* 91: 129–39.

Butler, Joseph. 1839. *The Whole Works of Joseph Butler, LL.D.,* ed. Samuel Halifax. London: Tegg.

Care, Norman, and Robert Grimm. 1969. *Perception and Personal Identity.* Cleveland: Case-Western Reserve Press.

Carnap, Rudolf. 1947. *Meaning and Necessity: A Study in Semantics and Modal Logic*. Chicago: University of Chicago Press.

Carter, W. R. 1982. "On Contingent Identity and Temporal Worms." *Philosophical Studies* 41: 213–30.

———. 1983. "In Defense of Undetached Parts." *Pacific Philosophical Quarterly* 64: 126–43.

Cartwright, Helen Morris. 1965. "Heraclitus and the Bath Water." *Philosophical Review* 74: 466–85.

———. 1970. "Quantities." *Philosophical Review* 79: 25–42.

Cartwright, Richard. 1975. "Scattered Objects." In *Analysis and Metaphysics* (pp. 153–71), ed. K. Lehrer. Dordrecht: Reidel. (Reprinted in Cartwright 1987a.)

———. 1987. *Philosophical Essays*. Cambridge, MA: MIT Press.

Chappell, Vere. 1990. "Locke on the Ontology of Matter, Living Things, and Persons." *Philosophical Studies* 60: 19–32.

Charlton, W. 1970. *Aristotle's Physics, I, II*. Oxford: Clarendon.

Chisholm, Roderick. 1966. *Theory of Knowledge*. Upper Saddle River, NJ: Prentice-Hall.

———. 1973. "Parts as Essential to Their Wholes." *Review of Metaphysics* 26: 581–603.

———. 1976. *Person and Object*. La Salle, IL: Open Court Publishing Company.

Descartes, René. 1960. *Meditations on First Philosophy*, trans. L. Lafleur. Indianapolis: Library of Liberal Arts.

Doepke, Frederick. 1987. "The Structures of Persons and Artifacts." *Ratio* 29: 36–52.

Dummett, Michael. 1959. "Truth." *Proceedings of the Aristotelian Society* 59: 141–62.

Evans, Gareth. 1978. "Can There Be Vague Objects?" *Analysis* 38: 208.

Feldman, Fred. 1968. "Geach and Relativised Identity." *Review of Metaphysics* 22: 547–55.

———. 1973. "Sortal Predicates." *Noûs* 7: 268–82.

Forbes, Graeme. 1987. "Is There a Problem about Persistence?" *Proceedings of the Aristotelian Society, Suppl.* 61: 137–55.

Frege, Gottlob. 1953. *Foundations of Arithmetic*. German text with *en face* translations by J. L. Austin, 2d ed. Oxford: Blackwell.

———. 1966. "On Sense and Reference," trans. Max Black. In *Translations from the Philosophical Writings of Gottlob Frege* (pp. 55-78), ed. P. T. Geach and M. Black. Oxford: Blackwell.

Geach, P. T. 1962. *Reference and Generality*. Ithaca, NY: Cornell University Press.

———. 1965. "Some Problems about Time." *Proceedings of the British Academy* 51: 320–36. (Reprinted in Geach 1980a.)

———. 1967. "Identity." *Review of Metaphysics* 21: 3–12. (Reprinted in Geach 1980a.)

———. 1969a. "A Reply." *Review of Metaphysics* 22: 556–59. (Reprinted in Geach 1980a.)

———. 1969b. *God and the Soul*. London: Routledge & Kegan Paul.

———. 1980a. *Logic Matters*. Berkeley: University of California Press.

———. 1980b. *Reference and Generality*. 3d ed. Ithaca, NY: Cornell University Press.

Gibbard, Allan. 1976. "Natural Property Rights." *Noûs* 10: 77–88.

Goodman, Nelson. 1977. *The Structure of Appearance*, 3d ed. Dordrecht: Reidel.

Grice, H. P. 1969. "Vacuous Names." In *Words and Objections* (pp. 118–45), ed. D. Davidson and J. Hintikka. Dordrecht: Reidel.

Griffin, Nicholas. 1977. *Relative Identity*. Oxford: Clarendon.

Gupta, Anil. 1980. *The Logic of Common Nouns*. New Haven, CT: Yale University Press.

Haack, Susan. 1978. *Philosophy of Logics*. New York: Cambridge University Press.

Heller, Mark. 1990. *The Ontology of Physical Objects: Four-Dimensional Hunks of Matter*. Cambridge: Cambridge University Press.

Hirsch, Eli. 1982. *The Concept of Identity*. Oxford: Oxford University Press.

Hobbes, Thomas. 1839. *The English Works of Thomas Hobbes*. Vol. 1, *Concerning Body*, ed. William Molesworth. London: Bohn.

Hooker, John. 1978. "Why Essentialism Is True." *Southwestern Journal of Philosophy* 9: 7–14.

Hume, David. 1969. *A Treatise of Human Nature*, ed. Ernest Mossner. Middlesex: Penguin Books.

———. 1978. *A Treatise of Human Nature*, ed. L. A. Selby-Bigge, 2d ed. Oxford: Clarendon.

Johnston, M. 1987. "Is There a Problem about Persistence?" *Proceedings of the Aristotelian Society, Suppl.* 61: 107–35.

Jones, Barrington. 1974. "Aristotle's Introduction of Matter." *Philosophical Review* 83: 474–500.

Kant, Immanuel. 1965. *Critique of Pure Reason*, trans. Norman Kemp-Smith. New York: St. Martin's.

Kaplan, David. 1975. "How to Russell a Frege-Church." *Journal of Philosophy* 72: 716–25. (Reprinted in Loux 1979.)

———. 1978. "Transworld Heir-Lines." In Loux 1979, 88–109.

Kripke, Saul. 1963. "Semantical Considerations on Modal Logic." *Acta Philosophica Fennica* 16: 83–94.

———. 1971. "Identity and Necessity." In Munitz 1971, 135–164. (Reprinted in Schwartz 1977.)

———. 1980. *Naming and Necessity*. Cambridge, MA: Harvard University Press.

Laycock, Harold. 1972. "Some Questions of Ontology." *Philosophical Review* 81: 3–42.

Leibniz, G. W. 1969. *Philosophical Papers and Letters*, ed. L. E. Loemker. Dordrecht: Reidel.

———. 1981. *New Essays on Human Understanding*, trans. and ed. Peter Remnant and Jonathan Bennett. Cambridge: Cambridge University Press.

———. 1973. *Discourse on Metaphysics*, trans. George Montgomery, 2d ed. La Salle, IL: Open Court.

Leonard, Henry S., and Nelson Goodman. 1940. "The Calculus of Individuals and Its Uses." *Journal of Symbolic Logic* 5: 45–55.

Lewis, David. 1968. "Counterpart Theory and Quantified Modal Logic." *Journal of Philosophy* 65: 113–26. (Reprinted in Loux 1979 and, with added postscripts, in Lewis 1983.)

———. 1971. "Counterparts of Persons and Their Bodies." *Journal of Philosophy* 68: 203–11. (Reprinted in Lewis 1983.)

———. 1973. *Counterfactuals*. Oxford: Blackwell.

———. 1976. "Survival and Identity." In Rorty 1976, 17–40. (Reprinted with added postscripts in Lewis 1983.)

———. 1979a. "Attitudes *De Dicto* and *De Se*." *Philosophical Review* 88: 513–43. (Reprinted with added postscripts in Lewis 1983.)

———. 1979b. "Scorekeeping in a Language Game." *Journal of Philosophical Logic* 8: 339–59. (Reprinted in Lewis 1983.)

———. 1983. *Philosophical Papers*. Vol. 1. New York: Oxford University Press.

———. 1986. *On the Plurality of Worlds*. New York: Blackwell.

Lewis, David, and Stephanie Lewis. 1970. "Holes." *Australasian Journal of Philosophy* 48: 206–12. (Reprinted in Lewis 1983.)

Locke, John. 1894. *An Essay Concerning Human Understanding*, ed. Alexander C. Fraser. New York: Dover.

———. 1975. *An Essay Concerning Human Understanding*, ed. P. H. Nidditch. Oxford: Clarendon.

Loux, Michael J. 1979. *The Possible and the Actual*. Ithaca, NY: Cornell University Press.

Lowe, E. J. 1983. "Instantiation, Identity, and Constitution." *Philosophical Studies* 44: 45–59.

———. 1989. "What Is a Criterion of Identity?" *Philosophical Quarterly* 39: 1–21.

Marsh, Robert, ed. 1956. *Logic and Knowledge*. New York: Macmillan.

Matthews, Gareth. 1982. "Accidental Unities." In *Language and Logos* (pp. 251–62), ed. M. Schofield and M. Nussbaum. Cambridge: Cambridge University Press.

———. 1992. "On Knowing How to Take Aristotle's Kooky Objects Seriously." Paper presented at the Pacific Division meeting of the American Philosophical Association, Portland, OR.

Mondadori, Fabrizio. 1983. "Counterpartese, Counterpartese*, Counterpartese$_D$." *Histoire, Epistémologie, Langage* 5: 69–94.

Munitz, Milton, ed. 1971. *Identity and Individuation*. New York: New York University Press.

Nahm, Milton. 1934. *Selections from Early Greek Philosophy*. New York: Crofts.

Nock, O. S. 1967. *History of the Great Western Railway*. Vol. 3. Shepperton, Surrey: Allan.

Noonan, Harold. 1976. "Wiggins on Identity." *Mind* 85: 559–75.

———. 1985a. "Wiggins, Artefact Identity and 'Best Candidate' Theories." *Analysis* 45: 4–8.

———. 1985b. "The Closest Continuer Theory of Identity." *Inquiry* 28: 195–229.

———. 1988. "Reply to Lowe on Ships and Structures." *Analysis* 48: 221–23.

Parsons, Terence. 1969. "Essentialism and Quantified Modal Logic." *Philosophical Review* 78: 35–52.

Perry, John. 1970. "The Same F." *Philosophical Review* 79: 181–200.

Plantinga, Alvin. 1974. *The Nature of Necessity*. New York: Clarendon.

———. 1985. "Self-Profile." In *Alvin Plantinga* (pp. 3–100), ed. J. Tomberlin and P. van Inwagen. Dordrecht: Reidel.

———. 1987. "Two Concepts of Modality." In *Philosophical Perspectives*. Vol. 1. *Metaphysics* (pp.189–232), ed. J. Tomberlin. Atascadero, CA: Ridgeview.

Plato. *Phaedo*.

Plutarch. *Life of Theseus*.

Pollock, John. 1974. *Knowledge and Justification*. Princeton, NJ: Princeton University Press.

Quine, W. V. 1950. "Identity, Ostension, and Hypostasis." (Reprinted in Quine 1963, pp. 65–79.)

———. 1960. *Word and Object*. Cambridge, MA: MIT Press.

———. 1961. "Reference and Modality." In Quine 1980, 139–59.

———. 1963. *Set Theory and Its Logic*. Cambridge, MA: Harvard University Press.

———. 1964. Review of P. T. Geach's *Reference and Generality*. *Philosophical Review* 73: 100–4.

———. 1966. "Three Grades of Modal Involvement." In *The Ways of Paradox and Other Essays* (pp. 156–74). Cambridge, MA: Harvard University Press.

———. 1969. *Ontological Relativity and Other Essays*. New York: Columbia University Press.

———. 1980. *From a Logical Point of View*, 2d ed. Cambridge, MA: Harvard University Press.

Quinton, Anthony. 1962. "The Soul." *Journal of Philosophy* 59: 393–409.

———. 1973. *The Nature of Things*. London: Routledge & Kegan Paul.

Rea, Michael. 1995a. "The Problem of Material Constitution." *Philosophical Review* 104: 525–52.

———. 1995b. "An Aristotelian Solution to the Problem of Material Constitution." Paper presented at the Eastern Division Meeting of the American Philosophical Association, New York City.

Reid, Thomas. 1854. *On the Intellectual Powers of Man*. In *The Works of Thomas Reid, D.D*, ed. Sir William Hamilton. Edinburgh: MacMillan & Stewart.

Robinson, Denis. 1982a. *The Metaphysics of Material Constitution*. Ph. D. Dissertation, Monash University.

———. 1982b. "Re-Identifying Matter." *Philosophical Review* 81: 317–41.

Russell, Bertrand. 1905. "On Denoting." In Marsh (ed.) 1956, 41–56.

———. 1924. *The Philosophy of Logical Atomism*. In Marsh (ed.) 1956, 177–282.

Ryle, Gilbert. 1951. "Categories." In *Logic and Language* (pp. 281–98), ed. Antony Flew. Oxford: Blackwell.

Salmon, N. 1981. *Reference and Essence*. Princeton, NJ: Princeton, University Press.

Sanford, David H. 1975. "Borderline Logic." *American Philosophical Quarterly* 12: 29–39.

Schlesinger, George. 1985. "Spatial, Temporal and Cosmic Parts." *Southern Journal of Philosophy* 23: 255–71.

Sedley, David. 1982. "The Stoic Criterion of Identity." *Phronesis* 27: 255–75.

Sherwood, William. 1968. *William of Sherwood's Treatise on Syncategorematic Words*. Translated with an introduction by Norman Kretzmann. Minneapolis: University of Minnesota Press.

Shoemaker, Sydney. 1963. *Self-Knowledge and Self-Identity*. Ithaca, NY: Cornell University Press.

Shoemaker, Sydney, and Richard Swinburne. 1984. *Personal Identity*. Oxford: Blackwell.

Shorter, J. M. 1977. "On Coinciding in Space and Time." *Philosophy* 52: 399–408.

Sidelle, Alan. 1989. *Necessity, Essence, and Individuation: A Defense of Conventionalism*. Ithaca, NY: Cornell University Press.

Simons, Peter. 1985. "Coincidence of Things of a Kind." *Mind* 94: 70–75.

———. 1987. *Parts: A Study in Ontology*. Oxford: Clarendon.

Sosa, Ernest. 1984. "Mind-Body Interaction and Supervenient Causation." *Midwest Studies in Philosophy.* Vol. 9. *Causation and Causal Theories* (pp. 271–82), ed. P. French, T. Uehling, and H. Wettstein. Minneapolis: University of Minnesota Press, 271–82.

Stalnaker, Robert. 1968. "A Theory of Conditionals." In *Studies in Logical Theory* (pp. 98-112), ed. Nicholas Rescher. Oxford: Blackwell.

———. 1986. "Counterparts and Identity." In French Uehling, and Wettstein, eds., 1986, 121–40.

Stalnaker, Robert, and Richmond Thomason. 1970. "A Semantic Analysis of Conditional Logic." *Theoria* 36: 23–42.

Strawson, P. F. 1970. "Chisholm on Identity through Time." In *Language, Belief, and Metaphysics* (pp. 183–6), ed. H. E. Kiefer and M. K. Munitz. Albany: State University of New York Press.

Suppes, Patrick. 1957. *Introduction to Logic.* Princeton, NJ: Van Nostrand.

Taylor, Richard. 1973. *With Heart and Mind.* New York: St. Martin's Press.

Thomason, Richmond, and Robert Stalnaker. 1968. "Modality and Reference." *Noûs* 2: 359–72.

Thomson, Judith. 1977. *Acts and Other Events.* Ithaca, NY: Cornell University Press.

Unger, Peter. 1979a. "There Are No Ordinary Things." *Synthese* 41: 117–54.

———. 1979b. "Why There Are No People." In *Midwest Studies in Philosophy.* Vol. 4. *Studies in Metaphysics* (pp. 177–222), ed. P. French, T. Uehling, and H. Wettstein. Minneapolis: University of Minnesota Press.

———. 1980a. "Skepticism and Nihilism." *Noûs* 14: 517–45.

———. 1980b. "The Problem of the Many." In *Midwest Studies in Philosophy.* Vol. 5. *Studies in Epistemology* (pp. 411–68), ed. P. French, T. Uehling, and H. Wettstein. Minneapolis: University of Minnesota Press.

———. 1990. *Identity, Consciousness, and Value.* New York: Oxford University Press.

van Inwagen, Peter. 1980a. "Philosophers and the Words 'Human Body.'" In van Inwagen 1980b, 283–99.

———. 1980b. *Time and Cause: Essays Presented to Richard Taylor.* Dordrecht: Reidel.

———. 1985. "Plantinga on Trans-World Idenity." In *Alvin Plantinga* (pp. 101–20), ed. J. Tomberlin and P. van Inwagen. Dordrecht: D. Reidel.

———. 1987. "When Are Objects Parts?" In *Philosophical Perspectives.* Vol. 1. *Metaphysics* (pp. 21–48), ed. J. Tomberlin. Atascadero, CA: Ridgeview.

———. 1988. "How to Reason about Vague Objects." *Philosophical Topics* 16: 255–84.

———. 1990. *Material Beings.* Ithaca, NY: Cornell University Press.

Vesey, Godfrey. 1974. *Personal Identity.* London: Macmillan.

Wheeler, Samuel C. 1967. "Reference and Vagueness." *Synthese* 30: 367–79.

Wiggins, David. 1963. "Individuation of Places and Things." *Proceedings of the Aristotelian Society, Suppl.* 37: 177–202.

———. 1967. *Identity and Spatio-Temporal Continuity.* Oxford: Blackwell.

———. 1968. "On Being in the Same Place at the Same Time." *Philosophical Review* 77: 90–5

———. 1980. *Sameness and Substance.* Cambridge, MA: Harvard University Press.

Williams, Bernard. 1973. *Problems of the Self.* Cambridge: Cambridge University Press.

Williams, D. C. 1966. "The Elements of Being." In *Principles of Empirical Realism*, ed. A. Ruja. Springfield, IL: Charles Thomas.
———. 1986. "Universals and Existents." *Australasian Journal of Philosophy* 64: 1–14.
Xenophon. *Memorabilia.*
Yablo, Stephen. 1987. "Identity, Essence, and Indiscernibility." *Journal of Philosophy* 84: 293–314.

Additional Sources

Aristotle. *Categories.*
———. *Topics.*
———. *On Generation and Corruption.*
———. *Metaphysics.*
Armstrong, David. 1980. "Identity through Time." In van Inwagen 1980b, 67–78.
Bennett, Jonathan. 1988. *Events and Their Names*. Indianapolis: Hackett.
Blackson, Thomas. 1992. "The Stuff of Conventionalism." *Philosophical Studies* 68: 65–81.
Brennan, Andrew. 1988. *Conditions of Identity*. New York: Oxford University Press.
Broad, C. D. 1927. *Scientific Thought*. New York: Harcourt Brace.
Brody, Baruch. 1980. *Identity and Essence*. Princeton, NJ: Princeton University Press.
Carnap, R. 1967. *The Logical Structure of the World/Pseudoproblems in Philosophy*, trans. R. George. Berkeley, CA: University of California Press.
Cartwright, Helen Morris. 1993. "On Two Arguments for the Indeterminacy of Personal Identity." *Synthese* 95: 241–73.
Cartwright, Richard. "On the Logical Problem of the Trinity." In Cartwright 1987, 187–200.
Chisholm, Roderick. 1979. "Objects and Persons: Revisions and Replies." In Sosa 1979, 317–88.
Code, Alan. "Aristotle's Response to Quine's Objections to Modal Logic." *Journal of Philosophical Logic* 5: 159–86.
Cowley, F. 1971. "The Identity of a Person and His Body." *Journal of Philosophy* 68: 678–83.
Dauer, Francis. 1973. "How Not to Reidentify the Parthenon." *Analysis* 33: 63–4.
Davis, Lawrence. 1973. "Smart on Conditions of Identity." *Analysis* 33: 109–10.
Della Rocca, Michael. 1996. "Essentialists and Essentialism." *Journal of Philosophy* 93: 186–202.
Denkel, Arda. 1995a. "Artifacts and Constituents." *Philosophy and Phenomenological Research* 54: 311–22.
———. 1995b. "Theon's Tale: Does a Cambridge Change Result in a Substantial Change?" *Analysis* 55: 166–70.
French, Peter, Theodore Uehling, and H. Wettstein, eds. 1986. *Midwest Studies in Philosophy*. Vol. 21. *Studies in Essentialism*. Minneapolis: University of Minnesota Press
Gallois, André. 1990. "Occasional Identity." *Philosophical Studies* 58: 203–24.
Garrett, B. J. 1985. "Noonan, 'Best Candidate' Theories and the Ship of Theseus." *Analysis* 45: 212–15.

Geach, P. T. 1973. "Ontological Relativity and Relative Identity." In Munitz 1973, 287–302.

Haslanger, Sally. 1989a. "Endurance and Temporary Intrinsics." *Analysis* 49: 119–25.

———. 1989b. "Persistence, Change, and Explanation." *Philosophical Studies* 56: 1–28.

———. 1994. "Humean Supervenience and Enduring Things." *Australasian Journal of Philosophy* 72: 339–59.

Heller, Mark. 1993. "Varieties of Four-Dimensionalism." *Australasian Journal of Philosophy* 71: 47–59.

Henry, D. P. 1972. *Medieval Logic and Metaphysics*. London: Hutchinson University Library.

Hestevolt, H. Scott. 1981. "Conjoining." *Philosophy and Phenomenological Research* 41: 371–83.

Hughes, Christopher. 1986. "Is a Thing Just the Sum of Its Parts?" *Proceedings of the Aristotelian Society,* n. s. 86: 213–33.

———. 1994. "The Essentiality of Origin and the Individuation of Events." *Philosophical Quarterly* 44: 26–44.

Johnston, M. 1989. "Fission and the Facts." In *Philosophical Perspectives*. Vol. 3. *Philosophy of Mind and Action Theory* (pp. 369–97), ed. J. Tomberlin. Atascadero, CA: Ridgeview.

Karmo, Toomas. 1977. "Disturbances." *Analysis* 37: 147–48.

Kim, Jaegwon. 1966. "On the Psycho-Physical Identity Theory." *American Philosophical Quarterly* 3: 227–35.

Lewis, David. 1986a. *Philosophical Papers*. Vol. 2. New York: Oxford University Press.

———. 1991. *Parts of Classes*. New York: Blackwell.

Lewis, Frank. 1991. *Substance and Predication in Aristotle*. New York: Cambridge University Press.

Long, A. A., and D. N. Sedley, eds. 1987. *The Hellenistic Philosophers*. Vol 1. Cambridge: Cambridge University Press.

Loux, Michael J., ed. 1976. *Universals and Particulars*. Notre Dame, IN: University of Notre Dame Press.

———. 1991. *Primary Ousia*. Ithaca, NY: Cornell University Press.

Lowe, E. J. 1983a. "On the Identity of Artifacts." *Journal of Philosophy* 80: 220–32.

———. 1989b. *Kinds of Being: A Study of Individuation, Identity, and the Logic of Sortal Terms*. Oxford: Blackwell.

———. 1995. "Coinciding Objects: In Defense of the Standard Account." *Analysis* 55: 171–78.

Mackie, Penelope. 1993. "Ordinary Language and Metaphysical Commitment." *Analysis* 53: 243–51.

Merricks, T. 1994. "Endurance and Indiscernibility." *Journal of Philosophy* 91: 165–84.

———. 1995. "On the Incompatibility of Enduring and Perduring Entities." *Mind* 104: 523–31.

———. 1996. "Against the Doctrine of Microphysical Supervenience." Paper presented at the Pacific Division Meeting of the American Philosophical Association, Seattle WA.

———. Forthcoming. "Fission and Personal Identity over Time." *Philosophical Studies*.

Moravcsik, J. 1976. "The Discernibility of Identicals." *Journal of Philosophy* 73: 587–98.

Munitz, Milton K, ed. 1973. *Logic and Ontology*. New York: New York University Press.

Noonan, Harold. 1989. *Personal Identity*. New York: Routledge.

———. 1991. "Indeterminate Identity, Contingent Identity, and Abelardian Predicates." *Pacific Philosophical Quarterly* 41: 183–93.

———. 1993. "Constitution Is Identity." *Mind* 102: 133–45.

Noonan, Harold, ed. 1993a. *Personal Identity*. Brookfield, VT: Dartmouth.

———. 1993b. *Identity*. Brookfield, VT: Dartmouth.

Nozick, Robert. 1981. *Philosophical Explanations*. Cambridge, MA: Harvard University Press.

Parfit, Derek. 1971. "Personal Identity." *Philosophical Review* 80: 3–27.

———. 1984. *Reasons and Persons*. New York: Clarendon.

Pellettier, Francis J. 1979. *Mass Terms: Some Philosophical Problems*. Dordrecht: Reidel.

Plantinga, Alvin. 1975. "On Mereological Essentialism." *Review of Metaphysics* 28: 468–76.

———. 1976. "Actualism and Possible Worlds." *Theoria* 42: 139–60. (Reprinted in Loux 1979.)

Plato. *Theaetetus*.

———. *Parmenides*.

Poundstone, William. 1988. *Labyrinths of Reason*. New York: Anchor Books, Doubleday.

Prior, A. N. 1968. "Time, Existence, and Identity." In *Papers on Time and Tense* (pp. 78–87), ed. A. N. Prior. Oxford: Clarendon.

Putnam, Hilary. 1981. "Why There Isn't a Ready-Made World." In Putnam 1983, 205–28.

———. 1983. *Realism and Reason*. New York: Cambridge University Press.

Reid, Thomas. 1983. *Inquiry and Other Essays*, ed. R. Beanblossom and K. Lehrer. Indianapolis: Hackett.

Robinson, Denis. 1985. "Can Amoebae Divide without Multiplying?" *Australasian Journal of Philosophy* 63: 299–319.

———. 1989. "Matter, Motion, and Humean Supervenience." *Australasian Journal of Philosophy* 67: 394–409.

Rorty, Amelie O., ed. 1976. *The Identities of Persons*. Berkeley: University of California Press.

Sainsbury, R. M. 1995. *Paradoxes*. 2d ed., New York: Cambridge University Press.

Scaltsas, Theodore. 1980. "The Ship of Theseus." *Analysis* 40: 152–57.

———. 1981. "Identity, Origin, and Spatio-temporal Continuity." *Philosophy* 56: 395–402.

Scaltsas, Theodore, David Charles, and Mary Louise Gill, eds. 1994. *Unity, Identity, and Explanation in Aristotle's Metaphysics*. Oxford: Clarendon.

Schwartz, Stephen. 1977. *Naming, Necessity, and Natural Kinds*. Ithaca, NY: Cornell University Press.

Shoemaker, Sydney. 1984. *Identity, Cause, and Mind.* Cambridge: Cambridge University Press.

Smart, Brian. 1972. "How to Reidentify the Ship of Theseus." *Analysis* 32: 145–48.

———. 1974. "The Ship of Theseus, the Parthenon, and Disassembled Objects." *Analysis* 34: 24–7.

———. 1975. "The Statues and a Problem of Identity." *Ratio* 17: 229–36.

Smart, J. J. C. 1972. "Space-Time and Individuals." In *Logic and Art: Essays in Honor of Nelson Goodman* (pp. 3–20), ed. Richard Rudner and Israel Scheffler. New York: Macmillan.

Smith, Barry, ed. 1982. *Parts and Moments: Studies in Logic and Formal Ontology.* Munich: Philosophia.

Sosa, Ernest, ed. 1979. *Essays on the Philosophy of Roderick M. Chisholm.* Amsterdam: Rodopi.

Strawson, P. F. 1990. *Individuals.* New York: Routledge.

Tomberlin, James, ed. 1987. *Philosophical Perspectives.* Vol. 1. *Metaphysics.* Atascadero, CA: Ridgeview.

van Cleve, James. 1986. "Mereological Essentialism, Mereological Conjunctivism, and Identity Through Time." In French, Uehling, and Wettstein, eds. 1986, 141–56.

———. 1991. "Entity, Identity, and Actuality: A Critical Review." *Philosophical Papers* 20: 37–50.

van Fraassen, Bas. 1995. "'World' Is Not a Count Noun." *Noûs* 29: 139–57.

van Inwagen, Peter. 1988. "And Yet They Are Not Three Gods But One God." In *Philosophy and the Christian Faith* (pp. 241–78), ed. Thomas V. Morris. Notre Dame, IN: University of Notre Dame Press.

———. 1990. "Four-Dimensional Objects." *Noûs* 24: 245–56.

———. 1994. "Composition as Identity." In *Philosophical Perspectives.* Vol. 8; *Logic and Language*, ed. James Tomberlin. Atascadero, CA: Ridgeview.

———. Forthcoming. "Materialism and the Psychological-Continuity Account of Personal Identity." To appear in a forthcoming volume of *Philosophical Perspectives*, ed. James Tomberlin. Atascadero, CA: Ridgeview.

Wheeler, Samuel C. 1979. "On That Which is Not." *Synthese* 41: 155–73.

White, Nicholas. 1986. "Identity, Modal Individuation, and Matter in Aristotle." In *Midwest Studies in Philosophy.* Vol. 11. *Studies in Essentialism* (pp. 475–94), ed. P. French, T. Uehling, and H. Wettstein. Minneapolis: University of Minnesota Press.

Whitehead, A. N. 1929. *Process and Reality.* New York: MacMillan.

Wittgenstein, L. 1992. *Tractatus Logico-Philosophicus*, trans. D. F. Pears and B. F. McGuinness. Atlantic Highlands, NJ: Humanities Press International.

Zemach, Eddy. "In Defence of Relative Identity." *Philosohpical Studies* 26: 207–18.

Zimmerman, Dean. 1995. "Theories of Masses and Problems of Constitution." *Philosophical Review* 104: 53–110.

———. 1996. "Could Extended Objects Be Made Out of Simple Parts?" *Philosophy and Phenomenological Research* 56: 1–29.

Index

About the Contributors

MICHAEL B. BURKE is associate professor of philosophy at Indiana University–Purdue University, Indianapolis.

HUGH S. CHANDLER is associate professor of philosphy at the University of Illinois at Urbana-Champaign.

RODERICK M. CHISHOLM is emeritus professor of philosophy and Andrew W. Mellon Professor of Humanities at Brown University.

FREDERICK C. DOEPKE is professor of philosophy at the Metropolitan State College of Denver.

PETER T. GEACH is emeritus professor of logic at the University of Leeds.

ALLAN GIBBARD is Richard B. Brandt Distinguished University Professor of Philosophy at the University of Michigan, Ann Arbor.

MARK HELLER is associate professor of philosophy at Southern Methodist University.

FRANCES HOWARD-SNYDER is assistant professor of philosophy at Western Washington University.

PETER VAN INWAGEN is John Cardinal O'Hara Professor of Philosophy at the University of Notre Dame.

MARK JOHNSTON is professor of philosophy at Princeton University.

DAVID LEWIS is Stuart Professor of Philosophy at Princeton University.

GEORGE MYRO was associate professor of philosophy at the University of California at Berkeley.

TERENCE PARSONS is professor of philosophy at the University of California, Irvine.

ERNEST SOSA is professor of philosophy and Romeo Elton Professor of Natural Theology at Brown University.

JUDITH JARVIS Thomson is Lawrence S. Rockefeller Professor of Philosophy at the Massachusetts Institute of Technology.

PETER UNGER is professor of philosophy at New York University.

DAVID WIGGINS is professor of philosophy at New College, Oxford University, and a fellow of the British Academy.